ALAN ROGERS SELE

EUROPE

over 400 of the best campsites across Europe

alan rogers

full page listings
comprehensive writeups
useful travel information

Compiled by: Alan Rogers Travel Ltd

Cover photo: Glen of Aherlow Caravan and Camping Park IR940 (page 293)

Editorial & Production
Editor: Robin Fearn – enquiries@alanrogers.com
Editorial Assistant: Florrie Wood
Production & Cartography: Robert Baker
Visual Design: Ben Tully

Advertising Agencies
France: ICCS International Tourism Promotions - info@iccsfrance.com
Spain: Servicios Turisticos Heinze Latzke S.A. - info@servitur-heinze.com
Portugal: Roteiro Lda - info@roteiro-campista.pt
UK: Space Marketing - davidh@spacemarketing.co.uk
Switzerland: Spatz Camping & Tourist Service AG - nicole.jugenheimer@scts.ch
Austria, Germany, Italy Croatia & Slovenia: IGL Werbedienst GmbH - k.perner@igl.at
Other Countries: trafficking@alanrogers.com

Alan Rogers Travel
Chief Operating Officer: Chris Newey
Finance Manager: Alison Harris
IT Manager: Roland Greenstreet

Special thanks to our Campsite Assessors
John & Margaret Corrall
Pete Lowen & Ann Cazenave
Martin & Cheryle Cawley
Mike & Anita Winks
Mike Annan
Ken Elborn
Paul Johnson

Published by: Alan Rogers Travel Ltd,
Spelmonden Old Oast, Goudhurst, Kent TN17 1HE
www.alanrogers.com

56th edition - February 2024
ISBN 978-1-909057-97-5

Printed in Great Britain by S&G

Stay in touch alanrogers.com/signup
Contact us alanrogers.com/contact

 facebook.com/alanrogerstravel

 x.com/alanrogers (formerly known as Twitter)

 instagram.com/alanrogerstravel

Contents & map

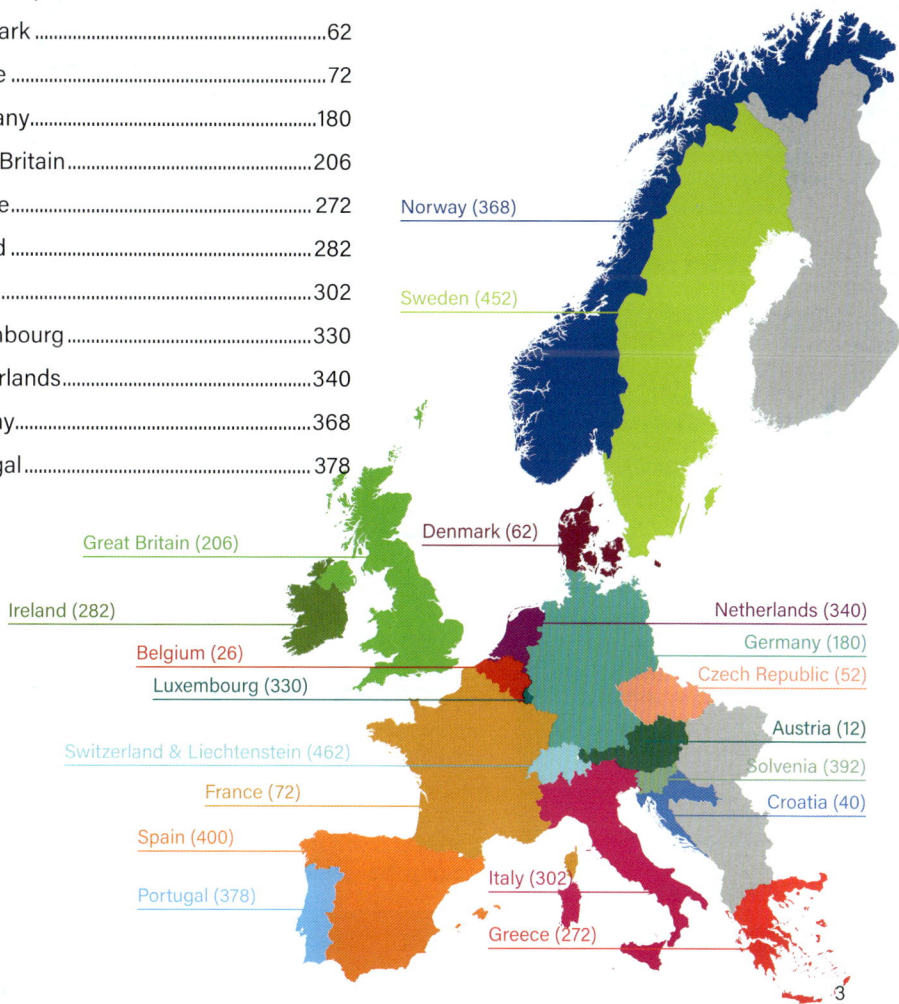

Norway (368)

Sweden (452)

Denmark (62)

Great Britain (206)

Netherlands (340)

Germany (180)

Ireland (282)

Czech Republic (52)

Belgium (26)

Luxembourg (330)

Austria (12)

Solvenia (392)

Switzerland & Liechtenstein (462)

Croatia (40)

France (72)

Spain (400)

Portugal (378)

Italy (302)

Greece (272)

Our top travel tips

Foreign travel advice

The UK Foreign & Commonwealth Office provides advice about travelling abroad, safety and security, entry requirements and travel warnings, as well as the latest information regarding travel within the European Union. Visit **gov.travel** or check your local government travel website.

Top tip GB stickers are no longer valid. You now need a UK sticker if your number plate doesn't include a UK identifier. See page 11.

Driving on the continent

Driving overseas can be daunting for both experienced tourers and newcomers because of the road's differing laws and regulations. Whilst the EU has meant that some rules are uniform across the continent, others remain specific to certain countries.

Avoid unnecessary stress and read more at **ar.camp/driving-tips**

Accessibilty

We believe that travel should be accessible to everyone. But for some, it can be challenging.

Each country in this guide is rated against our accessibility criteria and given a score out of five.

To read and download our free mini-guide to accessible travel, visit **ar.camp/open-to-all**

Winter driving

Travelling during the winter has benefits, but it also brings additional challenges. We suggest doing a little extra planning before your trip, as driving rules are often different during this period. For information and advice, visit **ar.camp/winter-driving**

Sustainability

Camping is one of the most eco-friendly ways to holiday. Just remember; dispose of waste properly, leave what you find, respect wildlife, be considerate of others. Learn more at **ar.camp/be-green**

Euro Standards

Since 1992, new cars have been subject to strict EU regulations which aim to improve air quality. Every vehicle produced since then has to meet a certain Euro emissions standard. Currently, the Euro standard runs from 1-6, with 7 likely to be added in 2025.

Registered from	Emission standard
Dec 1992	Euro 1
Jan 1997	Euro 2
Jan 2001	Euro 3
Jan 2006	Euro 4
Jan 2011	Euro 5
Sep 2015	Euro 6

All Low Emission Zone schemes in the EU and UK use this standard to calculate what you pay to enter a LEZ or whether your vehicle is banned altogether, so it's worth knowing what standard your vehicle is.

For further information and frequently asked questions regarding emission standards, visit **ar.camp/euro-standard**

Welcome to the 56th edition

Alan Rogers Guides were first published in 1968. Since Alan Rogers published the first campsite guide that bore his name, the nature of European campsites has changed immeasurably.

Back then, many campsites, though well established, were still works in progress, having been converted from farms and orchards in the post-war years. Of course, there were fewer to choose from than today and the quality levels varied hugely.

Since the first edition of the Alan Rogers guide, the quality of most campsites has evolved in leaps and bounds. In terms of today's facilities, infrastructure, technology and accommodation types, there is very little comparison with what was on offer half a century ago.

At Alan Rogers we have developed longstanding relationships with many campsites. We have worked with different generations of campsite owners and shared the trials and tribulations along the way with many of them. Typically, campsite owners are a hardy breed, passionate about their campsite, and keen to show it and their region off to every visitor.

The Alan Rogers guides have always aimed to celebrate the variety, recognise the quality and salute the unique. So read on and find the perfect campsite for your next holiday, whatever type of campsite that may be.

1968

Alan Rogers launched his first guide. It contained over 50 "really good sites" personally recommended by Alan.

1970s

1975 Our first guide to camping in Britain is published

1980s

1985 Our first guide to French campsites is published.

1986 After 18 years of development, Alan Rogers retires. The company is purchased by Clive and Lois Edwards.

1990s

1998 Our first guide to Rented Accommodation in France is published.

2000s

2001 Mark Hammerton buys the business from Clive and Lois.

2003 Dutch language guides are first published.

2010s

2013 The company is acquired by the Caravan and Motorhome Club.

2019 Venturing further than ever before, Worldwide Caravan and Motorhome Holidays are launched.

2020s

2024 Welcome to our 56th year!

Our founder, ▶
Alan Rogers

Our first guide,
published in 1968.
It featured 50 'really
good' sites and cost
▼ four shillings.

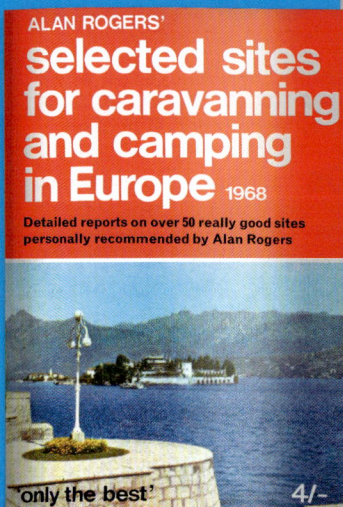

ALAN ROGERS'
**selected sites
for caravanning
and camping
in Europe** 1968

Detailed reports on over 50 really good sites
personally recommended by Alan Rogers

'only the best'   4/-

1918   Alan Rogers is born in Warwickshire.

1939   Rogers works as a wireless telegrapher for the RAF during World War Two.

1948   After the war, Rogers devoted much of his leisure time to his twin passions of rallying and caravanning. He spent long periods over the summer with his wife Ruth, exploring newly-founded continental campsites and collecting information about them.

1968   Alan's first official guide to camping goes on sale. Work on compiling information and reviews began a year earlier.

1986   Rogers retires. He continues assessing campsites until the mid 1990s.

2001   Aged 81, Alan passes away. His legacy lives on through the annual guides that still bear his name.

Alan Rogers: in search of 'only the best'

There are many thousands of campsites across Europe of varying quality: this guide contains impartially written reports on over 400, including many of the very finest, in 19 countries. Are there more? Yes, of course, and in countries not included in this book. Online at alanrogers.com, you'll find details of many more - over 8,000 campsites.

Put simply, a guide like this can never be exhaustive. We have had to make difficult editorial decisions to provide you with a selection of the best, rather than information on all – in short, a more selective approach.

We are mindful that people want different things from their choice of campsite, so we try to include a range of campsite 'styles' to cater for a wide variety of preferences.

Those with more specific interests, such as sporting facilities, cultural events or historical attractions, are also catered for. Whether part of a chain or privately owned, the size of the site should make no difference in terms of quality. The key is that it should be 'fit for purpose' in order to shine and stand out.

If a campsite can identify and understand what kind of campsite it sets out to be and who it wants to attract, it can enhance its kerb appeal by developing with that in mind.

By way of example, a lakeside campsite with credentials as a serious windsurfing centre should probably offer equipment for hire, secure storage for customers' own kit, courses and tuition, meteorological feeds, and more.

A campsite in the heart of the Loire Valley might offer guided excursions to local châteaux, weekly tastings of regional wine and cheese, suggested walking or cycling itineraries to local châteaux with entry discounts, and so on.

Whatever style of campsite you're seeking, we hope you'll find some inspiration here.

Alan Rogers believes strongly that there is no point in camping uncomfortably when, with a little planning, you can do so in quite reasonable comfort.

*He considers too that the greatest degree of comfort is obtained by using organised camping sites and, more especially, by using **only the best** of these sites. Alan Rogers' Selected Sites for Caravanning and Camping in Europe 1968 enables you to do just this.*

▲ Taken from our very first guide, Alan coins the 'only the best' term.
Alan Rogers, 1968

Read our first edition guide at **ar.camp/1968** or scan the QR code

Campsite Name

A description of the site in which we try to give an idea of its general features – its size, situation, strengths and weaknesses. This section should provide a picture of the site itself with reference to the provided facilities and if they impact its appearance or character.

We include details on approximate pitch numbers, electricity (with amperage), hardstandings etc., in this section as pitch design, planning and terracing affect the site's overall appearance. Similarly, we include a reference to pitches used for caravan holiday homes, chalets, and the like.

Lists more specific information on the site's facilities and amenities and when they are open (if not for the whole season).

At a glance

Alan Rogers Reference
Every campsite listed on our website has a reference number. This allows you to search for a site quickly.

Accommodations

Pitches

GPS

Postcode

what3words
what3words is a quick and simple way to find, share and save exact locations using three random words.

Contact
Email
Telephone
Website

Opening (touring pitches)
From and to or all year

🏅 **Alan Rogers Awards**
Years won

Key features

Below we list 'Key Features'. These are features that we believe are important or make the site unique.

🐾 **Pets Accepted**

♿ **Disabled Facilities**

🏊 **Swimming Pool**

🚲 **Bike Hire**

🎣 **Fishing**

Find out more

Campsite URL and QR code
Try scanning with your smartphone

How to best use this guide

The layout of this edition is similar to our previous 'new-style' Europe guides but different from our pre-2018 editions. We still aim to provide comprehensive information, written in plain English in an easy to use format, but a few words of explanation regarding the content may be helpful.

Toilet blocks Typically, toilet blocks will be equipped with WCs, washbasins with hot and cold water and hot shower cubicles. They will have all the necessary shelves, hooks, plugs and mirrors. There will be a chemical toilet disposal point, and the campsite will provide water and waste-water drainage points and bin areas.

Shop Basic or fully supplied, and any date restrictions.

Bar, restaurant, takeaway facilities and entertainment We try to note any seasonal open dates.

Swimming pools These might vary from a simple, conventional swimming pool to an elaborate complex with multiple pools and waterslides. Opening dates and levels of supervision are provided where we have been notified. There is a regulation whereby Bermuda shorts may not be worn in swimming pools (for health and hygiene reasons). It is worth ensuring that you take 'proper' swimming trunks with you.

Leisure facilities For example, playing fields, bicycle hire, organised activities and entertainment.

Dogs If dogs are not accepted, or restrictions apply, we state it here. If planning to take a dog or other pet, we always recommend you check in advance.

Opening dates Campsites can and sometimes do alter these dates throughout the year, often for good reasons. If you intend to visit shortly after a published opening date or shortly before the closing date, it is wise to check the site will be open at the time required. Similarly, some sites operate a restricted service during the low season, only opening some of their facilities (e.g. swimming pools) during the main season. It is always wise to check.

Sometimes, campsite amenities may be dependent on there being enough customers on-site to justify their opening. Some campsites may not be fully ready by their stated opening dates. They also tend to close down some facilities at the end of the season and generally wind things down.

We usually give an overview of the pitches, including an approximate quantity. This figure may vary year on year, so it is rarely absolute.

> **HANDY TIP**
>
> For swift access to the campsite, simply append the Alan Rogers Reference to the end of the URL, such as https://ar.camp/**AU0020**

Useful information

The Schengen Area

The Schengen Area is comprised of 26 European countries that have relaxed internal border controls, allowing for free movement. Not all countries in the European Union are part of this agreement, so it's worth checking before you embark on your journey.

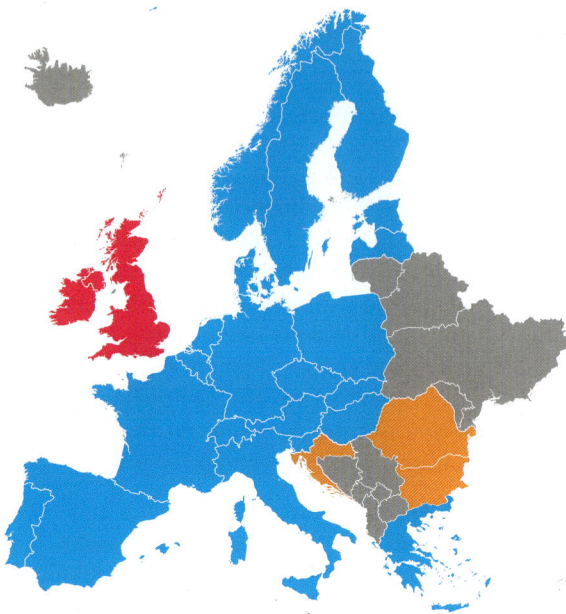

- ■ Schengen Member States
- ■ Not yet Schengen Member States
- ■ UK & Ireland Common Travel Area (CTA)

Member States Austria; Belgium; Czech Republic; Denmark; Estonia; Finland; France; Germany; Greece; Hungary; Iceland (non-EU); Italy; Latvia; Liechtenstein (non-EU); Lithuania; Luxembourg; Norway (non-EU); Poland; Portugal; Slovakia; Slovenia; Spain; Sweden; Switzerland (non-EU).

Monaco, San Marino and Vatican City all operate open borders but are not part of the Schengen Area.

The Republic of Ireland is not a member of the Area.

ETIAS & EES

To strengthen its external borders, the European Union has launched a new Entry-Exit System (EES) and the European Travel Information and Authorisation System (ETIAS). These systems will affect UK and non-EU travellers entering the EU.

What's the difference between the EES and the ETIAS? The EES will register visa-free and visa-required travellers entering the EU by collecting facial images and fingerprints, replacing the need to stamp passports manually. The ETIAS is a travel authorisation and new entry requirement for all countries that do not require a visa for short stays in the EU. The scheme is similar to those used in the USA and Australia.

What do I need to do? You will need to apply for an ETIAS travel authorisation well in advance of your holiday. A fee of €7 is charged, and your authorisation to travel within the EU is valid for three years or until your passport expires, whichever is sooner. Upon expiry, you will need to renew your travel authorisation.

Do I need a UK car sticker?

If you plan to drive in Europe, you must display a UK sticker if your vehicle doesn't already have a UK identifier. GB car stickers are no longer valid. See below to find out if you need a sticker.

YES	NO	YES	YES	YES	YES	YES	NO
GB	**UK**	**ENG**	**SCO**	**CYM**			**UK**
GB with Euro symbol	UK with Union Flag	National Flag of England	National Flag of Scotland	National Flag of Wales	No Identifiers (standard)	No Identifiers (EV)	Post Sept 2021 (UK Badge)

Sustainability & Driving Safety

Staying sustainable when on holiday and driving safely aren't usually two things we'd group together, but in an effort to simplify how we display information, we've introduced a traffic light system covering recycling abroad, Low Emission Zones, and the use of dashcams and speed camera detection features found on sat navs and mobile devices.

Recycling abroad

Recycling is part of our everyday life - that shouldn't change when we're abroad. Look out for the recycling symbol ♻ or ask where the nearest recycling bins are at your campsite reception.

- ♻ **Green** Well-established and widespread
- ♻ **Amber** A little hit and miss, check locally
- ♻ **Red** Complex or poorly observed

Low Emission Zones

Most major cities across Europe have implemented Low Emission Zones (LEZ) so it's good to know before you go.

- **LEZ** **Green** Low Emission Zones in place
- **LEZ** **Red** No Low Emission Zones in place

Dashcams & Speed Camera Detectors

In some European countries, the use of dashcams and sat navs that warn of static and mobile speed cameras is restricted. Regulations vary from country to country, so always check before travelling. Find out more at **ar.camp/road-aware**

- **Green** Legal
- **Amber** Advised against
- **Red** Illegal

> **LEAVE NO TRACE** Leave your pitch how you found it. What you leave behind can impact nature, no matter how small. And while it might not be realistic to go waste-free, it's important to be mindful of leaving as little a trace as possible during your stay.

Capital Vienna
Currency Euro (€)
Language German
Time Zone CET (GMT+1)
Telephone Code +43
Emergency Number 112
Tourist Website austria.info/uk

Shops Larger stores are open 8am to 8pm weekdays, smaller shops open later and close earlier. Many close early on Sat and stay closed on Sun. Bakeries open Sun morning.

Money ATMs are widespread, accessible 24hrs a day and have multilingual instructions. Daily withdrawal limits should be expected. Major cards are accepted at transport hubs, supermarkets and some restaurants; expect to pay cash elsewhere.

Travelling with children Activities are usually organised for children over the summer period. Many lakes have supervised beach areas. Many museums in Vienna are free for under 18s. Restaurants often have children's menus or will prepare smaller portions.

Public Holidays 1 Jan New Year's Day; 6 Jan Epiphany; Mar/Apr Easter Monday; 1 May Labour Day; May Ascension; May/Jun Whit Monday; Jun Corpus Christi; 15 Aug Assumption; 26 Oct National Day; 1 Nov All Saints; 8 Dec Conception; 25 Dec Christmas Day; 26 Dec Boxing Day

LEZ

Accessible Travel Score
Generally well catered for in cities and larger towns, especially Vienna. Most, but not all, attractions and public services offer assistance.

Driving in Austria All vehicles must pay a toll to use motorways. You must display a sticker on your windscreen to show you have paid. All vehicles above 3.5t max permitted laden weight must use a GO Box. It is legal to overtake a tram (at slow speed), providing passengers are not endangered. At traffic lights, a green flashing light means the green phase is ending, and drivers should prepare to stop. There are currently no Low Emission Zones in place affecting cars. The use of dashcams and speed camera detectors is legal.

Austria

View all campsites in Austria
ar.camp/austria

See campsite map page 472

Climate Moderately hot summers, cold winters and snow in the mountains.

☀ **Avg. summer temp**
21°C

🌧 **Wettest month**
July

Austria is primarily known for two contrasting attractions: the capital Vienna with its cathedral, wine bars and musical events, and the skiing and hiking resorts of the Alps. It is an ideal place to visit year-round for the Easter markets, winter sports, the many cultural and historical attractions, and the breathtaking scenery.

The charming Tirol region in the west is easily accessible and popular with tourists who flock to its ski resorts in winter. It is transformed into a verdant landscape of picturesque valleys dotted with wildflowers, a paradise for walkers in the summer.

Situated in the centre is the Lake District and Salzburg, the city of Mozart, with its wealth of gardens, churches and palaces. Vienna's iconic Ferris wheel is a must for taking in the beautiful parks and architecture from a height of 200ft.

The neighbouring provinces of Lower Austria, Burgenland and Styria, land of vineyards, mountains and farmland, are off the tourist routes but provide good walking territory. Further south, Carinthia enjoys a mild, sunny climate dominated by crystal-clear lakes and soaring mountains. There are numerous monasteries and churches, and the cities of Villach and Klagenfurt, known for its old square and attractive Renaissance buildings.

Scan QR code to browse more campsites on our website

📍 **Braz, Vorarlberg**

Alan Rogers Ref: AU0020
Accommodations: 14
Pitches: 94
GPS: 47.14256, 9.92589
Post Code: A-6751

what3words:
clocking.outtake.longs

Contact:
info@landhauswalch.at
Tel: +43 555 228 102
www.landhauswalch.at

Open Dates:
All year - Excl. Nov.

Walch's Camping & Landhaus

Walch's Camping & Landhaus is found in the Vorarlberg region of Western Austria. The site has 94 marked-out pitches, mostly without shade. The reception building houses a small shop, laundry, toilet facilities and ski/boot room, while the upper floor has a small wellness centre, comprising of a Finnish style sauna and solarium which looks out onto the mountain ranges. You can also find a children's playground on-site during the summer months.

The campsite is rightly proud that up to 80% of their energy is generated through geothermal activity. Conveniently connected to the Sonnenkopf ski area, Walch's Camping & Landhaus provides a gateway to winter sports enthusiasts.

Excellent, accessible facilities. Fishing nearby. Easy access to ski slopes. Ski hire available. Children's playground and indoor playroom. Wellness centre with Sauna, steam bath and solarium. Breakfast is available (seasonal). Fresh bread is available. Small shop. Gas available. Laundry with washer/dryer. Boot/Ski room. BBQs allowed. WiFi throughout.

Key Features

🗓 Book Online

🐾 Pets allowed

♿ Accessible Facilities

🛝 Childrens Play Area

Find Out More
Visit **ar.camp/au0020**
or scan the QR code.

Natters, Tirol

Ferienparadies Natterer See

Alan Rogers Ref: AU0060
Accommodations: 50
Pitches: 200
GPS: 47.23755, 11.34201
Post Code: A-6161

what3words:
devoid.complaining.landline

Contact:
info@natterersee.com
Tel: +43 512 546 732
www.natterersee.com

Open Dates:
All year.

Alan Rogers Awards Won
2022

In a quiet location arranged around two lakes and set amidst beautiful alpine scenery, this site, founded in 1930, is renowned as one of Austria's top sites. Over the last few years, many improvements have been carried out, and pride of place goes to the innovative, award-winning, multifunctional building at the entrance to the site. This contains all the sanitary facilities expected of a top site, including a special section for children, private bathrooms to rent, and a dog bath.

The reception, shop and café/bar/bistro are on the ground floor, and a panoramic lounge and cinema are on the upper floor. Almost all of the 200 generous pitches are for tourers. They are terraced, set on gravel/grass, and all have electricity; most have water and drainage. Most offer a splendid view of the mountains.

Two modern sanitary blocks with underfloor heating, private cabins, and facilities for children & accessible sanitary facilities. Laundry facilities. Motorhome services. Fridge box hire. Restaurant, Pizzeria and takeaway (open Easter-September). Mini market. Playgrounds. Children's activity programme and child minding (seasonal). Sports field. Archery. Outdoor gym. Cinema. Mountain bike hire. Bathing lake. Aquapark. Canoes & pedaloes (charged). Daily entertainment programme (seasonal). WiFi (charged). Glamping and accommodations. Bus service to Innsbruck.

Key Features

- Book Online
- All Year
- Pets allowed
- Accessible Facilities
- Childrens Play Area
- Bar on Site
- Bicycle Hire on Site
- Fishing on Site

Find Out More
Visit **ar.camp/au0060**
or scan the QR code.

📍 Fieberbrunn, Tirol

Alan Rogers Ref: AU0110
Accommodations: 4
Pitches: 240
GPS: 47.46837, 12.55474
Post Code: A-6391

what3words:
roosters.roped.intrudes

Contact:
office@tirol-camp.at
Tel: +43 535 456 666
www.tirol-camp.at/en

Open Dates:
Mid May - Early Nov. and Start
Dec. - Late April.

Tirol Camp

This is one of many Tirol campsites that cater equally for summer and winter (here seemingly more for winter, when a reservation is essential). Tirol Camp is in a quiet and attractive mountain situation on sloping ground and has 240 touring pitches, all on wide flat terraces, plus 26 deluxe pitches with their own bathroom at the pitch. Marked out mainly by the electricity boxes or low hedges, they are 80-100 sq.m. and all have 10A electricity, gas, water/drainage, TV and telephone connections.

There is a fitness and wellness centre (free to campers) with an indoor/outdoor pool complex, sauna, steam room, solarium and aromatherapy massage. The site is very close to a ski lift centre and a ski and snowboard school for winter stays. In addition, horse-drawn sledge rides, floodlit tobogganing runs and langlauf skiing are available.

The upgraded toilet block in the main building is excellent, with some washbasins in cabins and some private bathrooms on payment. A modern heated block at the top end of the site has spacious showers and washbasins in cabins. Accessible sanitary facilities, Washing machines, dryers and drying room. Motorhome services. Shop and snacks. Restaurant (closed Oct, Nov and May). Separate general room. Outdoor swimming pool (12 x 8m). Indoor pool and wellness centre. Sauna. Fitness centre. Outdoor chess. Playground. Entertainment and activity programmes (July/Aug). Internet point. WiFi (charged).

Key Features

🐾 Pets allowed

♿ Accessible Facilities

🏊 Indoor Pool on Site

🛝 Childrens Play Area

🍸 Bar on Site

Find Out More
Visit **ar.camp/au0110**
or scan the QR code.

St Martin bei Lofer, Salzburg

Camping Grubhof

Alan Rogers Ref: AU0265
Accommodations: 10
Pitches: 200
GPS: 47.57427, 12.70602
Post Code: A-5092

what3words:
siblings.year.forestry

Contact:
home@grubhof.com
Tel: +43 658 882 370
www.grubhof.com

Open Dates:
All year.

Alan Rogers Awards Won
2023, 2019, 2016

Camping Grubhof is a beautifully laid out, level and spacious site set in the former riding and hunting park of the 14th-century Schloss Grubhof. The 200 touring pitches have been carefully divided into separate areas for different types of visitors – dog owners, young people, families and groups, and a quiet area. All the generous XXL pitches (at least 180 sq.m) provide electricity (16A), water and drainage (also in winter), many along the bank of the Saalach River.

Although new, the central building has been built in traditional Tirolean style using, in part, materials hundreds of years old reclaimed from old farmhouses. The result is most attractive. On the ground floor, you will find the reception, a cosy café/bar, a restaurant and a small shop, and on the first floor, a deluxe sauna, a beauty and wellness suite, two apartments and a relaxation room.

Three attractive, modern sanitary units constructed of concrete, wood and glass provide excellent facilities. XXL-family bathrooms (free for guests on XXL-pitches, to rent in winter). Washing machine, dryer and drying gallery. Gym upstairs (€10 membership per pitch/week). Recreation and conference room and a small library. Saunas, steam bath and massage. Ski and canoe storage room. Motorhome services. Luxury dog shower. Shop, restaurant and bar. Adventure-style playground. Youth room. Playroom. Watersports. Cabins to rent. Hotel and B&B accommodation. Free WiFi hotspots, on pitches against fee.

Key Features

- Book Online
- All Year
- Pets allowed
- Accessible Facilities
- Childrens Play Area
- Bar on Site
- Skiing on Site
- Bicycle Hire on Site

Find Out More
Visit ar.camp/au0265
or scan the QR code.

📍 **Bruck an der Glocknerstraße, Salzburg**

Alan Rogers Ref: AU0180
Accommodations: 40
Pitches: 300
GPS: 47.28372, 12.81695
Post Code: A-5671

what3words:
elevates.versatility.automation

Contact:
info@sportcamp.at
Tel: +43 654 573 030
www.sportcamp.at

Open Dates:
All year.

**Alan Rogers
Awards Won**
2018, 2015

Sportcamp Woferlgut

Sportcamp Woferlgut, a family-run site, is one of the best in Austria. It lies in the village of Bruck at the northern end of the Großglocknerstrasse mountain road in the Hohe Tauern National Park, near the Zeller See. The level grass pitches are marked out by shrubs, and each has 16A metered electricity, water, drainage, cable TV socket and a gas point.

The site's own lake is popular for swimming and sunbathing and has an adventure timber ropeway and playground. A free entertainment programme for kids of all ages is provided during the peak periods. The first-class toilet and shower facilities, as well as a wellness centre and 5 pools, has everything you need for a relaxing stay in the Austrian mountains.

Three modern sanitary blocks have excellent facilities, including private cabins and underfloor heating. Washing machines and dryers. Accessible facilities. Family bathrooms for hire (some with bathtubs). Motorhome services. Shop, bar, restaurant and takeaway. Heated outdoor pool and children's pool as well as a swimming lake with rope garden. TV rooms and lounge with a library. Gym with a bathing house and adventure centre with sauna. Three playgrounds, indoor playroom and children's cinema. Fun train. Tennis and horses' meadow for Pony rides. Bicycle hire. Watersports and lake swimming. Crazy golf course. WiFi over site (charged).

Key Features

📅 Book Online

📆 All Year

🐾 Pets allowed

♿ Accessible Facilities

🏊 Indoor Pool on Site

🛝 Childrens Play Area

🍸 Bar on Site

⛷ Skiing on Site

Find Out More
Visit ar.camp/au0180
or scan the QR code.

📍 **St Wolfgang, Upper Austria**

Camping Ried

Camping Ried is a small, attractive site at the edge of Lake Wolfgangsee. A walk along a quiet street next to the lake will take you to the beautiful St.Wolfganger promenade and the centre of St.Wolfgang, approx. 10 minutes. The site has 40 grass pitches surrounded by many trees for shadow. From the terraces, you have beautiful views over the lake and mountains from most pitches.

Adjacent to the site is a sailing school with the opportunity for tube riding and boat hire. You could also try the recently opened Austrian-style Spa with a sauna area and several indoor and outdoor pools, which are only 800 meters away. 10% reduction for site guests. In the immediate surroundings are some good restaurants. Apartments are available to hire.

Heated toilet block with showers, wash basins, and WCs. Laundry with washing machine, tumble dryer, and ironing facilities. Motorhome service point. Terrace cafe with homemade specialities. Small restaurant with snacks, drinks, and ice cream. Shop. Table tennis, Table football, and Games room. WiFi charged. Pets allowed (dog lead required).

Alan Rogers Ref: AU0346
Accommodations: 4
Pitches: 40
GPS: 47.74275, 13.43353
Post Code: A-5360

what3words:
handprints.gazes.snail

Contact:
camping-ried@aon.at
Tel: +43 664 736 00 854
seeterrassecamping-reid.at

Open Dates:
Early April - Mid October.

Key Features

🐾 Pets allowed

🎏 Childrens Play Area

🍸 Bar on Site

🚲 Bicycle Hire on Site

🎣 Fishing on Site

⛵ Sailing on Site

Find Out More
Visit **ar.camp/au0346**
or scan the QR code.

Hermagor, Carinthia

Alan Rogers Ref: AU0440
Accommodations: 29
Pitches: 272
GPS: 46.63141, 13.39598
Post Code: A-9620

what3words:
versatility.noticeably.equips

Contact:
hermagor@europarcs.com
Tel: +43 434 28 22 051
www.schluga.com

Open Dates:
All year.

Ferienpark Hermagor

Formerly known as Schluga Camping, Ferienpark EuroParcs Hermagor is situated in a flat valley with views of the surrounding mountains. The touring pitches are 100-120 sq.m; many with water, drainage, and satellite TV connections. Electricity connections are available throughout (16A). Mainly on grass-covered gravel on either side of tarmac surfaced access roads, they are divided by shrubs and hedges.

The site is open all year, to include the winter sports season, and has a well kept, tidy appearance, although it may be busy in high season. English is spoken. There is an impressive wellness centre with saunas, spas and relaxation areas.

Four sanitary blocks (a splendid new one, plus one modern and two good older ones) are heated in cold weather. Most washbasins in cabins and good showers. Family washrooms to rent. Baby rooms and suites with accessible facilities. Washing machines and dryers. Drying rooms and ski rooms. Motorhome services. Well-stocked shop (Seasonal). Bar/restaurant with terrace (closed Nov). Heated indoor (all year) and outdoor (May-Oct) swimming pools. Natural swimming pond (500 sq.m). Playground. New kindergarten and youth games room. Bicycle hire. Sauna. Solarium. Steam bath. Fitness centre. TV room. Internet point. Kindergarten programme for small children. Playing field. Dog walking area. WiFi throughout (charged).

Key Features

- Book Online
- All Year
- Pets allowed
- Accessible Facilities
- Indoor Pool on Site
- Childrens Play Area
- Bar on Site
- Bicycle Hire on Site

Find Out More
Visit ar.camp/au0440
or scan the QR code.

Ossiach, Carinthia

Camping Ossiacher See

Terrassen Camping Ossiacher See is a gently terraced site, protected by rising hills with lovely views across the lake to the mountains beyond. Trees, flowers, hedges and bushes abound, adding atmosphere to this neat and tidy site. The 429 level pitches, all with electricity, are in rows on the level grass terraces separated by hard roads and some divided by hedges. A separate area (40-50 pitches) is provided for campers with dogs. Good English is spoken.

The site does become full in high season, and although there is sufficient room on the pitches, it may give the initial impression of being overcrowded. The thick growth of reeds at the water's edge all around the lake means that access is limited to two small clearings within the site.

Five well maintained sanitary blocks are heated in cool weather, some with washbasins in cabins. Ten family washrooms (charged), baby rooms and accessible facilities. Laundry facilities. Motorhome services. Restaurant (Seasonal). Well-stocked supermarket. ATM. High-season entertainment programme. Beach volleyball. Trampoline. Playgrounds, games rooms and disco courtyard. Water-skiing and windsurfing schools and boats for hire. Tennis. Bicycle and moped hire. Fishing. Riding. WiFi.

Alan Rogers Ref: AU0460
Accommodations: 35
Pitches: 429
GPS: 46.66371, 13.97480
Post Code: A-9570

what3words:
satellite.potential.omnivore

Contact:
martinz@camping.at
Tel: +43 424 82 757
www.terrassen.camping.at

Open Dates:
Start May - Start October.

Key Features

- Book Online
- Pets allowed
- Accessible Facilities
- Childrens Play Area
- Bar on Site
- Bicycle Hire on Site
- Fishing on Site
- Riding on Site

Find Out More
Visit ar.camp/au0460
or scan the QR code.

📍 Feldkirchen, Lower Austria

Alan Rogers Ref: AU0379
Accommodations: 9
Pitches: 56
GPS: 46.70456, 14.14556
Post Code: A-9560

what3words:
colognes.pelts.spacious

Contact:
office@seewirt-spiess.com
Tel: +43 427 72 637
www.seewirt-spiess.com

Open Dates:
Start May - End September.

Maltschacher Seewirt

The small-scale Camping Maltschacher Seewirt is located in the south of Austria, in the state of Carinthia, with direct access and views of the lake. During high season, the campsite provides plenty of entertainment for the whole family with chilled campfire evenings with the entertainment team or sports tournaments such as volleyball, badminton and football.

The hotel on-site offers fresh breakfasts and a menu of good-value regional dinner dishes, which can be consumed on the restaurant terrace or packed up to take away to a scenic spot of your choice should you wish. A large beach by the lake is also open to the public so that it can get busy during peak season. With only 50 touring pitches on site, this is the perfect camping location to stay in Austria. The hotel orders fresh bread daily, and the shop is a 2-minute walk from the campsite.

Accessible sanitary facilities, Bar, Restaurant, Shop (Small), Laundry facilities, Washing up area with Dishwashing by EasyBe, Volleyball, badminton and football pitch, Children's playground, Lake swimming, Entertainment (High season), Pets allowed, WiFi.

Key Features

🐾 Pets allowed

♿ Accessible Facilities

🛝 Childrens Play Area

🍸 Bar on Site

🐟 Fishing on Site

Find Out More
Visit **ar.camp/au0379**
or scan the QR code.

📍 **Mühlen, Steiermark**

Camping Am Badesee

Set in a beautiful open alpine valley alongside an unspoilt rural lake in the southern part of the Steiermark region and on the slopes of Mount Zirbitz, this family-run site will provide you with a warm welcome and a relaxing holiday. The 60 good-sized pitches are well spaced on open grassy terraces, and with only about 25 long-stay units, mostly in a separate area, there is plenty of room for touring units. 50 of which have electricity hook-up points.

From the reception, you can order bread, milk, eggs and basic provisions. A small café/snack bar with a terrace which overlooks the lake serves regional dishes made with local produce. The lake can be used for swimming, fishing, canoeing, and paddle boats.

A modern heated sanitary unit provides spacious hot showers, some washbasins in cubicles, and child-size showers and washbasins. Hairdressing and shaving areas. The laundry room also has a baby bath and changing facility. No accessible facilities. Communal barbecue. Playground. Pets' Corner. Trampoline. Lake for swimming, fishing and boating. Bicycle hire.

Alan Rogers Ref: AU0520
Pitches: 60
GPS: 47.03740, 14.48760
Post Code: A-8822

what3words:
paged.weakest.slingshot

Contact:
office@camping-am-badesee.at
Tel: +43 358 62 418
www.camping-am-badesee.at

Open Dates:
Late April - End September.

Key Features

🐾 Pets allowed

🧗 Childrens Play Area

🍸 Bar on Site

🐟 Fishing on Site

Find Out More
Visit **ar.camp/au0520**
or scan the QR code.

Au an der Donau, Upper Austria

Alan Rogers Ref: AU0332
Accommodations: 9
Pitches: 45
GPS: 48.22778, 14.57912
Post Code: A-4332

what3words:
spare.hatch.gemstone

Contact:
info@camping-audonau.at
Tel: +43 726 253 090
www.camping-audonau.at

Open Dates:
Start April - End September.

Camping Au an der Donau

You can be sure of a friendly welcome in English at this attractive site on the Danube cycle route. Reception, bar, restaurant and flowered terrace are located on the dam top from where there are views of the Danube and surrounding countryside – an ideal place to try out the local drink, cider, and home-smoked trout. The 45 touring pitches are in a protected area behind the dam, all with 13A electricity. A separate area accommodates 30 tents; each area has its own well-maintained sanitary facility. The pitches are grassy and separated by hedges.

This is a small, well-organised site where a lot of thought and work has been put in by the two owners. Although the camping area is comfortable and attractive with landscaping, flowers and a small lake, most visitors will spend their time either enjoying the views from the restaurant terrace or touring the region.

Two modern sanitary units with hot water, free controllable showers and accessible sanitary facilities. Laundry room with washing machine and dryer. Motorhome services. Small bar (Seasonal). Restaurant (Seasonal) serving local specialities (breakfast and fresh bread available). Playground. Regular entertainment on the site's stage. Access to Danube beach and small motorboat to hire. Bicycle hire. Table tennis, Barbecue and campfire areas. Tourist information in reception. Free WiFi over site.

Key Features

- Book Online
- Pets allowed
- Accessible Facilities
- Childrens Play Area
- Bar on Site
- Bicycle Hire on Site
- Fishing on Site

Find Out More
Visit **ar.camp/au0332**
or scan the QR code.

📍 **Wien-Ost, Vienna**

Camping Wien Neue Donau

This is a very good site from which to visit Vienna. It is easily accessible from the Autobahn system, and the city centre is quickly reached from the site by the efficient Vienna U-Bahn system, via line U2. Some train tickets can be purchased at reception. There is some traffic and train noise, as found on most city sites. There are 200 level touring pitches with electricity, a further 12 with water and drainage, and a separate area for tents. The site is large, and people come and go regularly. The site is close to the Donauinsel, a popular recreation area.

At the campsite itself, there is a children's playground, volleyball court and table tennis. In high season, the site's mini shop and the café-restaurant are open in the morning and evening. The Neue Donau (New Danube), a 20 km. The long artificial side arm of the Danube provides swimming, sports and play areas, while the Danube bicycle trail runs past the site. This is a useful location for an overnight stop or a short break to visit Vienna and the Danube.

Modern toilet facilities are clean and well maintained with free showers. Accessible sanitary facilities. Washing machines and dryers. Motorhome services. Campers' kitchen with cooking facilities, fridges, freezers and TV. Shop. Small restaurant (July/Aug). Play area. Barbecue areas. Bicycle hire and free guided bicycle tours. Table tennis, WiFi (free).

Alan Rogers Ref: AU0302
Accommodations: 2
Pitches: 200
GPS: 48.20848, 16.44733
Post Code: A-1220

what3words:
boot.walnuts.punt

Contact:
neuedonau@campingwien.at
Tel: +43 120 24 010
www.campingwien.at

Open Dates:
Easter - Mid September.

Key Features

🐾 Pets allowed

♿ Accessible Facilities

🚼 Childrens Play Area

🍸 Bar on Site

🚲 Bicycle Hire on Site

Find Out More
Visit **ar.camp/au0302**
or scan the QR code.

Capital Brussels
Currency Euro (€)
Language French, Flemish and German
Time Zone CET (GMT+1)
Telephone Code +32
Emergency Number 112
Tourist Website visitbelgium.com

Shops Most shops are open 10am to 6pm weekdays or until 7pm/8pm on Sat. Some shops open on Sun and close on Mon morning but check before visiting. Some close for an hour at lunchtime.

Money ATMs are widespread, accessible 24hrs a day and have multilingual instructions. Major cards are widely accepted, although some shops may only accept cash.

Travelling with Children Many cities have museums and other attractions that run activity days for children. Entrance fees for many attractions are reduced for those under 12.

Public Holidays 1 Jan New Year's Day; Mar/Apr Easter Monday; 1 May Labour Day; May Ascension; May/Jun Whit Monday; 21 Jul National Day; 15 Aug Assumption; 1 Nov All Saints; 11 Nov Armistice Day; 25 Dec Christmas Day

Accessible Travel Score
Most public areas and services are suitable for wheelchair users and less able individuals. Transport is well-equipped.

Driving in Belgium Motorways are toll-free for all vehicles except those over 3.5t. Drink-driving and using your mobile whilst driving are illegal. Trams always have priority. If you are stationary, you should switch off the engine. Blue Zone parking areas exist in most major cities. Parking discs can be obtained from police stations, garages and some shops. Discs should only be used inside Blue Zone areas if the parking meter is out of use. Low Emission Zones exist in all major cities, and vehicle registration is required for entry. The use of dashcams and speed camera detectors is legal.

Belgium

View all campsites in Belgium
ar.camp/belgium

See campsite map page 473

Climate Temperate, similar to Britain. Cool, damp winters and mild summers.	☀️ **Avg. summer temp** 19°C	🌧️ **Wettest month** December

A small country divided into three regions, Flanders in the north, Wallonia in the south and Brussels the capital. Belgium is rich in scenic countryside, culture and history, notably the great forest of Ardennes, the historical cities of Bruges and Ghent, and the western coastline with its long sandy beaches.

Brussels is at the very heart of Europe. It is a must-see destination with its heady mix of shops, bars, exhibitions and festivals – a multicultural and multilingual city that is a focal point of art, fashion and culture.

In the French-speaking region of Wallonia lies the mountainous Ardennes, home to picturesque villages rich in tradition and folklore. It is a favourite of nature lovers and walkers who enjoy exploring its many castles and forts. The safe, sandy beaches on the west coast run for forty miles. The cosmopolitan resort of Ostend, with its yacht basin and harbour, offers year-round attractions, including a carnival weekend and a Christmas market, and the myriad seafood restaurants will suit every taste. Bruges is Europe's best-preserved medieval city, crisscrossed by willow-lined canals, where tiny cobbled streets open onto pretty squares. After visiting the many museums and art galleries, why not sample some of the delicious chocolate for which the city is famous.

Scan QR code to browse more campsites on our website

📍 **West Flanders, Flanders**

Alan Rogers Ref: BE0544
Accommodations: 251
Pitches: 40
GPS: 51.15423, 2.75922
Post Code: B-8434

what3words:
combed.branched.enthusiast

Contact:
info@racbcamping.be
Tel: +32 58 24 10 77
www.racbcamping.be

Open Dates:
All year.

R.A.C.B. Camp

Owned by the Royal Automobile Club of Belgium, this site is situated within the village of Westende, and a 15-minute walk will bring you to the seafront promenade. Several shops and restaurants are within easy reach. Only around 40 touring pitches are dotted among the 300 pitches occupied by seasonal units. All are level and have 10A electricity, but little shade.

A 6-hole golf course is immediately adjacent, and the club restaurant with its pleasant terrace is open daily throughout the year. The site is approximately 600 metres from the sea, with direct access to walking and cycling routes. Outside July, August, and Belgian Bank Holidays, the facilities are limited to those at the adjacent golf club.

Only one heated sanitary block is open outside the high season. Shop, bar and snack bar (high season and B.Hs). Restaurant at the neighbouring golf course. Games room. Adventure playground. Entertainment (July/Aug). Table tennis, Tennis court and multisport pitch, WiFi, Pets allowed.

Key Features

📅 All Year

🐾 Pets allowed

♿ Accessible Facilities

⛱ Seaside Beach Nearby

🛝 Childrens Play Area

🍸 Bar on Site

⛳ Golf on Site

Find Out More
Visit **ar.camp/be0544**
or scan the QR code.

East Flanders, Flanders

Camping Groeneveld

Camping Groeneveld is a quiet, clean, traditional site in a small village within easy reach of Gent. It has a friendly atmosphere and is also open over a long season. Although this site has 98 pitches, there are a fair number of seasonal units, leaving around 50 large touring pitches with 10A electricity. Hedges and borders divide the grassy area, access roads are gravel, and there is an area for tents. Family entertainment and activities organised in high season include themed dinners, musical evenings, barbecues, pétanque matches, etc.

The village of Bachte-Maria-Leerne has a butcher, general store, café and bar, chemist, two restaurants, baker, plus a newsagent, tabac and ATM. The site has produced a location map of these for guests. The city of Gent is just 15 km. north of the site and 5 km. to the south is the pleasant town of Deinze.

Two fully updated toilet blocks provide British-style WCs, washbasins and free hot showers. Accessible facilities. Motorhome services. Washing machine. Freezer (free). Traditional Flemish-style bar (Seasonal & W/ends) with a comprehensive range of speciality and local beers. Small coarse fishing lake. Floodlit pétanque court. Adventure play area. Internet (at reception) and free WiFi. Bicycles on loan from reception (free). Max. 2 dogs.

Alan Rogers Ref: BE0600
Accommodations: 48
Pitches: 50
GPS: 51.00509, 3.57229
Post Code: B-9800

what3words:
orchestra.pylons.engage

Contact:
info@campinggroeneveld.be
Tel: +32 494 05 79 81
www.campinggroeneveld.be

Open Dates:
Start April - End September.

Key Features

🐾 Pets allowed

♿ Accessible Facilities

🛝 Childrens Play Area

🍸 Bar on Site

🚲 Bicycle Hire on Site

🐟 Fishing on Site

Find Out More
Visit **ar.camp/be0600**
or scan the QR code.

📍 **Antwerp, Flanders**

Camping Het Veen

Floreal Het Veen can be found 20km—North of Antwerp in a woodland area with many activities to keep the whole family entertained whilst staying here. There are around 305 marked pitches (approximately 75 for touring units) on level grass, most with shade and 10A electricity (long leads in some places) and six hardstandings.

Amenities include an indoor sports hall (hourly charge), while you can find a multisport pitch outside. There are also three playgrounds for children, an above-ground swimming pool and an entertainment program run in the main season for children and adults; this includes sports tournaments, bingo and card games. For those who don't want to cook whilst they are away, the campsite has an onsite restaurant where you can sample local dishes or enjoy a snack and hot drink.

Three spacious toilet blocks include a few washbasins in cubicles (only two are close to the touring pitches). Accessible sanitary facilities. Laundry facilities. Motorhome services. Shop. Restaurant, bar, café and takeaway (Seasonal & W/ends). Outdoor swimming pool, water spray park, Multisport pitch. Table tennis, Badminton. Boules. Playgrounds and children's entertainment (seasonal) Fishing. Canoeing. Bicycle hire. WiFi (free). Wooden chalets to rent. Max 1 Dog allowed (on a lead). BBQs permitted.

Alan Rogers Ref: BE0650
Accommodations: 230
Pitches: 75
GPS: 51.30513, 4.58622
Post Code: B-2960

what3words:
gales.crept.venomous

Contact:
info@campinghetrietveen.nl
Tel: +32 36 36 13 27
www.florealgroup.be/nl/
camping/camping-het-veen

Open Dates:
All year.

Key Features

📅 Book Online

📅 All Year

🐾 Pets allowed

♿ Accessible Facilities

🏊 Outdoor Pool on Site

🛝 Childrens Play Area

🍸 Bar on Site

🚲 Bicycle Hire on Site

Find Out More
Visit ar.camp/be0650
or scan the QR code.

Antwerp, Flanders

Camping De Lilse Bergen

This attractive, quietly located holiday site has 494 shady pitches, of which 206 (all with 10A Europlug electricity) are for touring units. The site has a Mediterranean feel and is set on sandy soil among pine trees and rhododendrons and arranged around a large lake.

The site's main attractions are the swimming lakes, separate areas for adults, and a water sports zone where kayaking and windsurfing are available; there is also a diving platform and a giant slide located in the deeper regions of the lake. And a children's swimming lake with comprehensive climbing fame and play area. For those who want to relax, there is a sandy beach by the lake with plenty of picnic areas. A restaurant and snack bar are open throughout the high season, overlooking the lake.

Three of the six heated toilet blocks are modern. Some washbasins in cubicles and good hot showers (on payment). Well-equipped baby rooms. Accessible sanitary facilities. Laundry. Barrier keys can be charged up with units for operating showers, washing machines, etc. First aid post. Motorhome services. Takeaway (Seasonal). Bar and well-stocked shop Seasonal). Tennis. Minigolf. Boules. Climbing wall. Playground, trampolines and skateboard ramp. Pedalos, kayaks and bicycles for hire. Entertainment in high season, Children's electric cars and pedal kart tracks (fee payable). Mobile home rental. Free WiFi over site.

Alan Rogers Ref: BE0655
Accommodations: 20
Pitches: 494
GPS: 51.28908, 4.85508
Post Code: B-2275

what3words:
winkle.storms.cleaner

Contact:
info@lilsebergen.be
Tel: +32 14 55 79 01
www.delilsebergen.be

Open Dates:
All year.

Key Features

📅 Book Online

📅 All Year

🐾 Pets allowed

♿ Accessible Facilities

🧒 Childrens Play Area

🍸 Bar on Site

🚲 Bicycle Hire on Site

Find Out More
Visit ar.camp/be0655
or scan the QR code.

📍 **Lalaing, Wallonia**

Alan Rogers Ref: BE0535
Pitches: 90
GPS: 50.58382, 4.19328
Post Code: B-7191

what3words:
festoons.defied.crackers

Contact:
info@ladime.be
Tel: + 32 478 96 78 92
www.ladime.be

Open Dates:
Start April - End October.

La Dîme Camping

The campsite is in a quiet rural area, surrounded by trees and only 40 kilometres from Brussels. La Dîme Camping has 90 pitches on fairly level grass, of which around eight are hard-standing pitches. All pitches have 10A or 16A electricity. Pitches are a minimum area of 100 m² for motorhomes and caravans. This site is perfect for those who want to get away from it all and enjoy a relaxing holiday. The facilities on site are limited, but there is a small outdoor swimming pool, children's play area and fishing pond.

Other amenities, including restaurants, are available around 3km away in the town. In Ecaussinnes, you can visit Chateau Fort d'Ecaussinnes-laying, Tunnel des Amoooureux and The Sloping Lock of Ronquières. The campsite is an excellent base for walking or cycling, including a pleasant, flat route along the canal. The access road is narrow, and some larger motorhomes may struggle. This campsite can be very busy during the peak season, with little or no space for caravans and motorhomes looking for an overnight stay.

Dated but clean, sanitary block with coin-operated showers, Bar, Children's Playground, Billiards, Small outdoor swimming pool, Table tennis, Boules, Fishing on-site, Pets allowed, WiFi.

Key Features

🐾 Pets allowed

♿ Accessible Facilities

🏊 Outdoor Pool on Site

🛝 Childrens Play Area

🍸 Bar on Site

🐟 Fishing on Site

Find Out More
Visit **ar.camp/be0535**
or scan the QR code.

Limburg, Flanders

Camping Heidestrand

Heidestrand is a large family site of 30 hectares with a broad range of facilities. The site can be found north of Hasselt in the Flemish province of Limburg. There are over 600 seasonal pitches here and around 80 touring pitches, all with electricity and water. In the middle of the park, you will find a large shallow swimming lake with a sandy beach, perfect for those who want to build sand castles, take a cooling dip or enjoy a good book on the beach. This pond has been nominated as the best natural pond in Limburg.

If the lake isn't enough, the outdoor water activities don't stop there. The site also boasts an excellent outdoor swimming pool with a separate paddling pool, water slides and diving pool. There is another pond well stocked with a wide variety of fish for those avid anglers to enjoy.

Two toilet blocks have free showers and accessible sanitary facilities but may be stretched in peak season. Laundry in one block (some distance from the touring field). Swimming pool complex with slides. Supermarket. Bar and restaurant. Snack bar. Disco. Sports fields. Play area. Leisure pavilion for children. Entertainment for children. Dance evenings. Boat hire. Fishing ponds. WiFi in reception (charged). Pets allowed.

Alan Rogers Ref: BE0787
Accommodations: 627
Pitches: 83
GPS: 50.98668, 5.31342
Post Code: B-3520

what3words:
haunted.risks.balancer

Contact:
receptie@heidestrand.be
Tel: +32 11 52 01 90
www.heidestrand.be

Open Dates:
Early April - Start October.

Key Features

- Pets allowed
- Outdoor Pool on Site
- Childrens Play Area
- Bar on Site
- Bicycle Hire on Site
- Fishing on Site

Find Out More
Visit ar.camp/be0787
or scan the QR code.

📍 **Liège, Wallonia**

Camping les Murets

On the bank of the Ourthe River, Les Murets is a peaceful, traditional family campsite in the countryside south of Liège. There are 80 grass touring pitches, separated mainly by hedges and with mature trees giving plenty of shade and an open field for campers. A few pitches are seasonal, but there are no mobile homes or chalets and only one caravan to rent. The River Ourthe, as well as being ideal for swimming and fishing, is a haven for nature lovers, with kingfishers and otters among its residents.

The area offers plenty of walking, cycling, climbing, and diving opportunities, and the campsite makes special provision for hikers. The campsite provides fresh wood-fired pizza to take away and enjoy on their terrace daily during high season and sells Belgian beers and ice cream, too! Across the river is the attractive little village of Esneux with a few shops, restaurants and bars and a weekly market. Historical Liège has, it is claimed, the largest pedestrianised shopping area in Europe and is easily reached by road or rail.

Modernised sanitary block with free showers (not accessible.) A small, well-stocked bar with a terrace. Takeaway (seasonal). Evening entertainment weekly during high season, Campfire and communal BBQ facilities, Playground. WiFi. Fishing and swimming in River Ourthe. Pets allowed.

Alan Rogers Ref: BE0709
Accommodations: 1
Pitches: 80
GPS: 50.53983, 5.56956
Post Code: B-4130

what3words:
papers.animate.colleague

Contact:
camping.lesmurets@gmail.com
Tel: +32 479 34 59 25
www.lesmurets.be

Open Dates:
Early April - Early October.

Key Features

🐾 Pets allowed

🏛 Childrens Play Area

🍸 Bar on Site

🐟 Fishing on Site

Find Out More
Visit ar.camp/be0709
or scan the QR code.

Luxembourg, Wallonia

Camping le Val de l'Aisne

From a nearby hill, Château de Blier overlooks Camping le Val de l'Aisne, a large site attractively laid out around a 1.5-hectare lake in the Belgian Ardennes. The site has around 450 pitches, with 110 for touring units, on level ground and with 16A electricity. Tarmac roads circle the site, providing easy access. Trees provide some shade, although the site is fairly open, allowing views of the surrounding hills and the château.

Activities play a large part on this site, ranging from quiet fishing competitions in the lake to organised excursions, which include quad bike tours in the surrounding hills. To the left of the entrance, a building houses the reception and the bar/restaurant.

Three toilet blocks provide showers (paid key required) and mainly open washbasins. Accessible sanitary facilities, Baby room. Washing machines and dryers. Motorhome services. Bar/restaurant and snack bar with takeaway. Bread can be ordered in reception. Tennis courts, Table tennis, Football pitch, Fishing, swimming, kayaks (for hire). Mountain bike hire. Play area. Entertainment programme (summer). An activities team arrange adventure activities, including paintball and canyoning (High season). WiFi (free). Pets allowed.

Alan Rogers Ref: BE0725
Accommodations: 280
Pitches: 110
GPS: 50.28150, 5.55050
Post Code: B-6997

what3words:
ingests.tenfold.raindrop

Contact:
info@levaldelaisne.be
Tel: +32 86 47 00 67
www.levaldelaisne.be

Open Dates:
All year.

Key Features

All Year

Pets allowed

Childrens Play Area

Bar on Site

Bicycle Hire on Site

Fishing on Site

Find Out More
Visit ar.camp/be0725
or scan the QR code.

35

📍 **Luxembourg, Wallonia**

Camping le Festival

Alan Rogers Ref: BE0733
Accommodations: 290
Pitches: 75
GPS: 50.22469, 5.52603
Post Code: B-6987

what3words:
carnivorous.forge.tweezer

Contact:
camping.festival@florealgroup.be
Tel: +32 84 47 73 71
florealgroup.be/nl/camping/domein-le-festival

Open Dates:
All year.

Floreal le Festival is attractively located in the wide wooded valley of the River Ourthe and is open all year. There are 365 pitches of a good size, and hedges surround each. Seventy-five are for tourers, and all have electrical connections. The touring area is closest to the river and is more open. On-site amenities include a restaurant with a terrace offering traditional cuisine from March to October. This is where the evening entertainment is held for the whole family to enjoy this inclusive bingo and live shows.

For those that enjoy staying active whilst on holiday there are a couple of sports facilities with a football field, table tennis and volleyball. For those more adventurous, there are plenty of making and paddle-boarding opportunities on the river. The region is also ideal for walking and mountain biking, and the site's managers are more than happy to help you plan your excursions.

Three traditional toilet blocks have washbasins (open style and in cabins), free showers, baby bath and accessible sanitary facilities. Washing machines and dryers. Restaurant and bar, Small shop for basics. Takeaway meals. Play area. Volleyball. Table tennis, Football. Games room, Entertainment programme during high season. Fishing. Mobile homes for rent. Free WiFi. Pets allowed.

Key Features

📅 All Year

🐾 Pets allowed

♿ Accessible Facilities

🛝 Childrens Play Area

🍸 Bar on Site

🐟 Fishing on Site

Find Out More
Visit ar.camp/be0733
or scan the QR code.

📍 Luxembourg, Wallonia

Camping Lohan

This pleasant, typically Flemish site is situated alongside the River Ourthe and is a pretty base for exploring the Belgian Ardennes. The campsite has around 120 level grassy touring pitches, is numbered, and has 10A electricity (long leads required). This site is also very popular with locals and has around 100 permanent pitches. There are many activities to keep you occupied whilst staying at this site; during the summer, there are themed dinners and live shows held at the on-site restaurant. Here, you can try regional dishes or have a lighter snack at the Le Chalet snack bar.

There is also plenty of entertainment for children, including bouncy castles, clowns, creative crafts and various games. The campsite also has two ponds perfect for those who enjoy a spot of fishing. Fishing competitions are held here during the summer. The River Ourthe runs straight alongside the site, where you can swim, kayak and paddleboard during warmer weather. There is also a small boat launch here.

Three toilet blocks are evenly spaced around the site, with preset showers (token), baby bath and accessible sanitary facilities. Washing machines. Small shop. Bar, restaurant and takeaway. TV room. Play area. Relaxed Entertainment (July/Aug). Bouncy castle, Creative crafts, Fishing. Kayaking, River swimming, WiFi, Pets allowed. Accommodation is available.

Alan Rogers Ref: BE0826
Accommodations: 100
Pitches: 120
GPS: 50.18083, 5.60639
Post Code: B-6980

what3words:
scarred.love.swirling

Contact:
reservation@campinglohan.be
Tel: +32 84 41 15 45
www.campinglohan.be

Open Dates:
Start April - Start October.

Key Features

🐾 Pets allowed

♿ Accessible Facilities

🛝 Childrens Play Area

🍸 Bar on Site

🐟 Fishing on Site

Find Out More
Visit ar.camp/be0826
or scan the QR code.

📍 **Luxembourg, Wallonia**

Alan Rogers Ref: BE0710
Accommodations: 85
Pitches: 218
GPS: 49.58015, 5.54773
Post Code: B-6760

what3words:
gales.crept.venomous

Contact:
info@collinederabais.be
Tel: +32 63 42 21 77
www.collinederabais.be

Open Dates:
All year.

Camping Colline de Rabais

Floreal Camping Colline de Rabais is a large site on a hilltop looking out over the surrounding wooded countryside. The Dutch owners offer a warm welcome and slowly improve the site while maintaining its relaxed atmosphere. There are around 220 touring pitches, all supplied with 16A electricity (some long leads needed), 46 mobile homes and bungalows to rent and a few tour operator tents. Various activities are organised throughout the summer months. An entertainment team keeps the children entertained during the day with games and creative crafts. In the evening, there are live shows and bingo.

The adjacent forest is open to walkers and cyclists alike – you can keep going without seeing another person. The French border is only 10 km. to the south if you fancy a taste of France, whilst the Duchy of Luxembourg is about 30 km. to the east, and its capital city is less than an hour's drive away.

3 sanitary blocks, baby room, en-suite room with accessible facilities. Cleaning and maintenance can be variable; not all blocks are open in low season. Washing machines and dryers. Shop (seasonal). Bar/restaurant and takeaway (Apr-Oct). Small outdoor swimming pool (seasonal) with wood decking for sunbathing. Children's play area, Table tennis, football pitch, entertainment, Entertainment programme, Bicycle hire. Free WiFi over part of the site.

Key Features

📅 Book Online

📅 All Year

🐾 Pets allowed

♿ Accessible Facilities

🏊 Outdoor Pool on Site

🛝 Childrens Play Area

🍸 Bar on Site

🚲 Bicycle Hire on Site

Find Out More
Visit ar.camp/be0710
or scan the QR code.

Namur, Wallonia

Alan Rogers Ref: BE0860
Accommodations: 23
Pitches: 17
GPS: 50.12569, 5.18668
Post Code: B-5580

what3words:
pralines.frozen.butternut

Contact:
han.tourisme@skynet.be
Tel: +32 84 37 72 80
www.campingshansurlesse.be

Open Dates:
Start April - Early November.

Camping le Pirot

Le Pirot is an attractive, simple site on an island in the River Lesse, on the edge of the pleasant village of Han. Because of the access, it is more suitable for small caravans, motorhomes and tents. Bars, restaurants and shops are within walking distance located in the village. There are just 40 pitches on site, 17 of which are for touring with electric hook-up connections, and two areas are available for tents.

There are views across both branches of the river. A tourist tram takes visitors from the village to the famous caves of Han-sur-Lesse, and the tourist office offers bicycle hire and has information about cycling and walking routes and a wide variety of attractions in the area. Nearby, Parc de Chevetogne has lakes with canoeing, forest activities, themed gardens, an aquarium, riding, a swimming pool, restaurants, minigolf, a children's farm and play areas, and organises occasional concerts.

Recently modernised sanitary facilities, including washbasins in cabins with hot and cold water and controllable showers. There are no accessible facilities, chemical disposal, or on-site motorhome services. Communal barbecue area (no barbecues on pitches). Pets allowed.

Key Features

🐾 Pets allowed

🛝 Childrens Play Area

🐟 Fishing on Site

Find Out More
Visit **ar.camp/be0860**
or scan the QR code.

Capital Zagreb
Currency Euro (€)
Language Croatian
Time Zone CET (GMT+1)
Telephone Code +385
Emergency Number 112
Tourist Website croatia.hr

Shops 8am to 8pm weekdays, until 2pm or 3pm on Sat, closed on Sun. Some shops shorten their hours or shut down in the summer months.

Money ATMs are widespread, accessible 24hrs a day, and some have multilingual instructions. Smaller restaurants and shops often only accept cash. Major cards are widely accepted, Amex less so.

Travelling with Children Beaches are safe. Many museums and historical attractions run activity trails. Child fees are applicable for those under 9 years of age. Eating out is relaxed, and many restaurants will offer a children's menu.

Public Holidays 1 Jan New Year's Day; 6 Jan Epiphany; Mar/Apr Easter Monday; 1 May Labour Day; 30 May Statehood Day; May/Jun Corpus Christi; 22 Jun Anti-Fascist Struggle Day; 5 Aug Victory Day; 15 Aug Assumption; 1 Nov All Saints; 18 Nov Remembrance Day; 25 Dec Christmas Day; 26 Dec Boxing Day

Accessible Travel Score

Largely unequipped for less able travellers but improving. Public transport in larger cities is generally good.

Driving in Croatia Tolls are present on some roads. Roads along the coast can become congested in summer, and queues are possible at border crossings. Children under 12 cannot sit in the front of a vehicle. Parking is illegal on or near a bend, intersection, brow of a hill or bus/tram or taxi stop. Drink-driving and using your mobile whilst driving are illegal. There are no Low Emission Zones in place. The use of dashcams and speed camera detectors is legal.

Croatia

View all campsites in Croatia
ar.camp/croatia

See campsite map page 474

Climate Warm, dry summers and wet, long winters. Warmer along the coast.	☀️ **Avg. summer temp** 22°C	🌧️ **Wettest month** June

Croatia has developed into a lively and friendly tourist destination while retaining its coastal ports' unspoilt beauty and character, traditional towns and tiny islands with their secluded coves. Its rich history is reflected in its Baroque architecture, traditional festivals and two UNESCO World Heritage sites.

The most developed tourist regions in Croatia include the peninsula of Istria, where you will find the preserved Roman amphitheatre in Pula, the beautiful town of Rovinj with cobbled streets and wooded hills, and the resort of Umag, with a busy marina, charming old town and an international tennis centre. The coast is dotted with islands, making it a mecca for watersports enthusiasts, and there is an abundance of campsites in the area.

Further south, in the province of Dalmatia, Split is Croatia's second-largest city and lies on the Adriatic coast. It is home to the impressive Diocletian's Palace and a starting point for ferry trips to the islands of Brac, Hvar, Vis and Korcula, with their lively fishing villages and pristine beaches. The old walled city of Dubrovnik is 150 km. south. A favourite of George Bernard Shaw, who described it as 'the pearl of the Adriatic', it has a lively summer festival, numerous historical sights and a newly restored cable car to the top of Mount Srd.

Scan QR code to browse more campsites on our website

📍 **Samobor, Central**

Alan Rogers Ref: CR6610
Pitches: 10
GPS: 45.81061, 15.73891
Post Code: HR-10430

what3words:
revival.forced.levels

Contact:
postmoderna@zg.t-com.hr
Tel: +385 992 262 515
www.campsamobor.com

Open Dates:
Start May - End October.

Camp Vugec Plac

Camp Vugec Plac is located at the edge of the medieval town of Samobor, just 15km from the capital, Zagreb. This small site is a hidden gem with only ten touring pitches available, all with electric hook-up points. You will indeed have a quiet, relaxing stay when camping here. You have all the basic necessities to enjoy your holiday, along with a small outdoor swimming pool and a covered outdoor terrace where you can purchase cold refreshments.

It is an ideal starting point for numerous walking excursions in the Samobor Mountains and the Žumberačka gora Park, known for its rolling hills and the numerous vineyards that cover them. After a full day exploring the surrounding area, guests can try the local produce the region offers, which includes many wines from the surrounding vineyards, including the traditional flavoured wine called Bermet. Those with a sweet tooth should not miss tasting kremšnita, the most famous Samobor dessert.

Small sanitary block with two shower cubicles and toilets, chemical disposal point, outdoor covered communal BBQ area and terrace, outdoor swimming pool, and pets allowed. Free WiFi. TV.

Key Features

🐾 Pets allowed

〰 Outdoor Pool on Site

Find Out More
Visit **ar.camp/cr6610**
or scan the QR code.

📍 **Velika, Central**

Campsite Duboka

Alan Rogers Ref: CR6620
Pitches: 200
GPS: 45.47520, 17.65762
Post Code: HR-34330

what3words:
revival.forced.levels

Contact:
turizam@pp-papuk.hr
Tel: +385 913 352 209
campsite-duboka.business.site

Open Dates:
Start April - Start November.

Campsite Duboka is located on the edge of the Nature Park Papuk, in Velika. It is the first modern-style campsite in the eastern part of Croatia, located in the natural oasis of the Dubočanka Creek valley. The site can accommodate up to 200 campers. However, only 11 touring pitches are available with access to electricity and water. One part of the campsite is also set up to accommodate tent guests. You will also find a small communal kitchen that guests can use to cook and prepare food. Particular attention is paid to environmental conservation, alternative energy sources, wastewater treatment and waste management, while the campsite mainly uses natural materials.

The campsite surroundings offer many recreational possibilities, such as hiking, climbing and cycling. You can hire bicycles at the park to explore the trails straight from the site. Thanks to its position, the campsite is an ideal starting point for visiting the Papuk Mountain, included on the UNESCO World Geoparks list, and enjoying many gastronomic specialities typical for this part of Slovenia. For those who would like a challenging morning or afternoon, there is a newly built tree-top adventure course with Aerial walkways and zip lines in the park.

One sanitary block with accessible facilities, children's play area, Shop and bar nearby, Bicycle hire in the park, Tree top adventure course, Communal kitchen, Pets allowed. WiFi.

Key Features

🐾 Pets allowed

♿ Accessible Facilities

🛝 Childrens Play Area

Find Out More
Visit **ar.camp/cr6620**
or scan the QR code.

📍 Savudrija, Istria

Alan Rogers Ref: CR6721
Pitches: 32
GPS: 45.49061, 13.49258
Post Code: HR-52475

what3words:
purchaser.shops.orients

Contact:
info@camp-lighthouse.hr
Tel: +385 52 866 943
www.camp-lighthouse.hr

Open Dates:
All year.

Camp Lighthouse

Camp Lighthouse is situated next to the old lighthouse in Savudrija, close to the Croatian border with Slovenia. It is a small, relaxing site with 32 spacious pitches, all with water and electricity hook-up points available. The campsite is 50 metres from the sea, giving each pitch spectacular views of the surrounding area, and on clear sunny days, you may see Italy on the horizon.

The facilities on site are of a high standard, with a laundry room and dishwashers available. During the winter, the sanitary block is heated, providing guests with complete comfort while staying here. There is also staff support available 24/7 all year round. The site is ideal for exploring medieval hilltop towns and picturesque coastal towns of Northwestern Istria. Savudrija has a rocky coastline with hidden pebble beaches, pleasant sea temperatures and constant winds ideal for windsurfing, scuba diving and adrenaline sports. One side of the cape has calmer waters. For cyclists, there are signed bike trails to discover hidden gems of Istria.

Modern toilet block (chargeable). Washer-dryer. Laundry. EasyBe dishwasher. Service station. CamperClean station. Pets allowed. Free WiFi.

Key Features

📅 All Year

🐾 Pets allowed

⛱️ Seaside Beach Nearby

🐟 Fishing on Site

Find Out More
Visit **ar.camp/cr6721**
or scan the QR code.

Rovinj, Istria

Camping Val Saline

Alan Rogers Ref: CR6741
Accommodations: 60
Pitches: 366
GPS: 45.11495, 13.62855
Post Code: HR-52210

what3words:
reopening.nice.improperly

Contact:
camp@valsaline.hr
Tel: +385 052 804 850
www.campvalsaline.hr

Open Dates:
Late April- End September.

Camping Val Saline is located seven kilometres northwest of Rovinj on a bay close to the Lim Fjord. It is a 12-hectare site, flat or partly terraced, and most of the 366 touring pitches are close to the waterfront, although those further away also have good sea views. Pitches are good-sized (90-140 sq.m), all have 10-16A electricity and around half have water connections.

The site's own 700 m. long pebble beach slopes gently down to the crystal clear water, and there is a jetty for mooring small boats. Val Saline lies adjacent to its sister site, the Valalta Naturist Camp (CR6731.) You are spoilt for choice with the onsite facilities here, with many swimming opportunities. The site has a seawater-fed pool from the nearby bay, an outdoor swimming pool, and a small children's splash park.

Modern sanitary blocks with hot showers, private cubicles, and facilities for children accessible sanitary facilities. Washing machines. Motorhome services. Shop and bar (Seasonal). Internet café. Restaurant and takeaway (Seasonal). Outdoor swimming pool (Seasonal). Outdoor fitness. Wellness area with sauna and whirlpool. At reception, you can rent SUP, kayak and pedal boats. Playgrounds. 5-a-side football pitch with artificial turf, table tennis, Tennis, use at extra charge, Badminton, Bouls, multipurpose court, Mini-golf, beach volleyball, Entertainment programme (July/Aug). Children's club, Live music, inflatable aqua park. Bicycle hire. Currency exchange. Dogs are not accepted. WiFi. EV charging points.

Key Features

♿ Accessible Facilities

⛱ Seaside Beach on Site

🏊 Outdoor Pool on Site

🛝 Childrens Play Area

🍸 Bar on Site

🚲 Bicycle Hire on Site

🐟 Fishing on Site

⛵ Sailing on Site

Find Out More
Visit ar.camp/cr6741
or scan the QR code.

Premantura, Istria

Alan Rogers Ref: CR6737
Accommodations: 210
Pitches: 710
GPS: 44.79780, 13.91366
Post Code: HR-52100

what3words:
sarongs.fortress.allocating

Contact:
arenastupice@arenacampsites.com
Tel: +385 052 575 111
www.arenacampsites.com

Open Dates:
Mid April - Early October.

Arena Camping Stupice

This quiet site, which offers superb views over the sea to the nearby islands, is situated in a delightful strip of coast on the Istrian peninsula near the small village of Premantura. Most of the site is covered with undulating, dense pinewood, providing ample shade with a carpet of pine needles. There are nearly 1,000 pitches, with around half dedicated to touring in three different sizes, mostly slightly sloping and some with sea views. A narrow pebble beach and flat rocks separate the sea from the site, providing a perfect place to relax and enjoy the view.

Sections of the sea are netted off from motorsports, making them safe for swimming. There is a boat launch with a marina and sporting activities. For those who enjoy a sunny position, a small circular rocky spit of land approximately 500 m. in diameter extends from the site. Surrounded by water and enjoying excellent views, there is room for about 60 pitches, with no shade or facilities on the spit.

The six toilet blocks, although old, are immaculately clean. Toilets are a mixture of styles. Showers and free hot water. Washing machines. Good supermarket. Kiosk and several good small bars and grills. Minigolf. Modern playground. Multi-sports field, Tennis court(s), Beach volleyball, Stand-up Paddleboards, Kayak. Activities for children. Some live entertainment at the restaurant in high season. Rock and pebble beach. Marina, boat launching, jetty and scuba diving. Bicycle and beach buggy hire. Aquapark. Free WiFi over 80% of the site.

Key Features

- Book Online
- Pets allowed
- Accessible Facilities
- Seaside Beach on Site
- Childrens Play Area
- Bar on Site
- Bicycle Hire on Site
- Fishing on Site

Find Out More
Visit ar.camp/cr6737
or scan the QR code.

📍 Stara Baska, Kvarner

Alan Rogers Ref: CR6922
Accommodations: 42
Pitches: 300
GPS: 44.96632, 14.67407
Post Code: HR-51521

what3words:
blatantly.specialists.clone

Contact:
camping@valamar.com
Tel: +385 052 465 010
www.camping-adriatic.com/
skrila-camp-krk

Open Dates:
Mid April - Mid October.

Škrila Sunny Camping

Škrila Sunny Camping is located in a secluded and quiet spot close to Stara Baška in the southern part of the island of Krk. Škrila is ideal for guests who appreciate a more modest pace of life away from crowded tourist resorts. There are around 300 pitches with electric hook-up points on well-tended terraces, giving you fantastic views of the Kvarner islands and magnificent sunsets. Amenities include an à la carte restaurant and an attractive beach bar. Try local fish and meat specialities, pasta dishes and pizzas in the restaurant. The beach bar with a terrace is found next to the main beach. Here, you can have a cocktail or smoothie and enjoy the sea view. There is also a well-stocked shop if you want to prepare your meals back at your pitch.

On-site activities include kayaks and stand-up paddle boards to rent during summer. There are also jet skis available to hire. There are four coves on this 700-long stretch of beach, one especially for walking your dog, one for naturists and the other 2 for families to enjoy. You will also find beach volleyball on one of the family beaches. Don't miss out on diving to interesting underwater sites nearby or walk along the marked trails near the campsite.

Two refurbished sanitary blocks with accessible facilities, Restaurant, Bar, Snack bar, Takeaway food, Shop, 700m Seaside beach on site for families, naturists and pets, Kayaking, SUPs, Diving, Jet ski hire, Beach volleyball, Free WiFi at reception, Pets allowed.

Key Features

📅 Book Online

Naturist

🐾 Pets allowed

♿ Accessible Facilities

⚓ Seaside Beach on Site

🍸 Bar on Site

🐟 Fishing on Site

Find Out More
Visit **ar.camp/cr6922**
or scan the QR code.

📍 **Mali Losinj, Kvarner**

Camp Čikat

Camp Čikat is in picturesque Čikat Bay, surrounded by a thick pine forest and near Mali Lošinj, the largest town of all the Croatian islands. This beautiful site has been carefully planned using natural materials, colourful shrubs and flowers and enjoys direct access to the sea. It offers around 700 pitches for touring, all with 10A or 16A electricity and water. These are either set on terraces at the front of the site with excellent sea views or to the rear under the shade of mature trees.

On-site amenities include a quality restaurant, a bar overlooking the sea and an outdoor swimming pool with water slides. During high season, there are many activities for the whole family, with an entertainment programme and kids club with everything from sports tournaments to live music to aqua zumba. There is also a well-stocked supermarket. There is ample space for sunbathing on the rocks or paved terraces at the water's edge.

Seven excellent sanitary blocks with washbasins in cabins and free showers. Facilities for babies and children. Accessible sanitary facilities. Family bathrooms to rent. Laundry facilities. Motorhome service point. Supermarket. Bar. Restaurant. Play area. Outdoor swimming pool with slides. Bicycle hire. Massage (high season). Entertainment and activity programme. Mobile homes, chalets and tents to rent. Direct sea access. Outdoor water sports centre 500 metres from the site. No charcoal barbecues. WiFi over site.

Alan Rogers Ref: CR6754
Accommodations: 508
Pitches: 706
GPS: 44.53596, 14.45090
Post Code: HR-51550

what3words:
farmhouse.kittens.foxhole

Contact:
info@camp-cikat.com
Tel: +385 051 232 125
www.camp-cikat.com

Open Dates:
All year.

Key Features

📅 All Year

🐾 Pets allowed

♿ Accessible Facilities

⛱ Seaside Beach on Site

🌊 Outdoor Pool on Site

🛝 Childrens Play Area

🍸 Bar on Site

🚲 Bicycle Hire on Site

Find Out More
Visit ar.camp/cr6754
or scan the QR code.

Zadar, Dalmatia

Camping Falkensteiner

Camping Falkensteiner is close to the historic town of Zadar with its old fortress, many shops, bars and restaurants. The site has about 370 pitches, with around 270 for touring units and all with 10A electricity. All pitches are level, on gravel, and there are views of the Adriatic from some. Expect to pay a premium for a pitch closer to the sea.

The site is part of a hotel complex, and guests may use the hotel's amenities, including tennis courts, a giant water slide and a minigolf course. The site has a pebble beach on the lagoon. The sea is shallow here, which provides safe swimming from the beach or from a jetty, which can also be used to moor small boats.

Seven modern, fully equipped sanitary blocks with hot showers and a family unit to rent. Facilities for children and accessible sanitary facilities. Washing and drying machine. Motorhome services. Newsagent. Supermarket. Outdoor swimming pool with slides, Restaurant. Playground. Tennis courts, Minigolf, Entertainment programme, Water sports centre, Gym, Spa, Fishing. Pebble beach. Bicycle hire. Boat launching. WiFi (charged). Pets allowed.

Alan Rogers Ref: CR6783
Accommodations: 93
Pitches: 267
GPS: 44.13510, 15.21605
Post Code: HR-23000

what3words:
workshops.barefoot.detection

Contact:
campingzadar@reservations.falkensteiner.com
Tel: +385 023 332 074
www.falkensteiner.com

Open Dates:
All year.

Key Features

All Year

Pets allowed

Accessible Facilities

Seaside Beach on Site

Outdoor Pool on Site

Childrens Play Area

Bar on Site

Bicycle Hire on Site

Find Out More
Visit ar.camp/cr6783
or scan the QR code.

📍 **Split, Dalmatia**

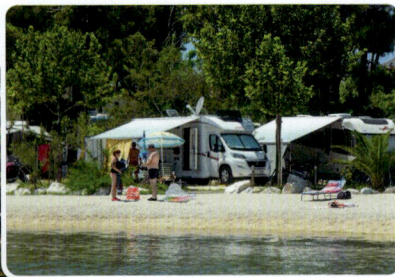

Alan Rogers Ref: CR6855
Accommodations: 53
Pitches: 272
GPS: 43.50333, 16.52750
Post Code: HR-21311

what3words:
registry.conned.facing

Contact:
camping.split@gmail.com
Tel: +385 021 325 426
www.campingsplit.com

Open Dates:
All year.

Camping Stobrec Split

Camping Stobrec is ideally located for those visiting Croatia and travelling down the coastal road or visiting the old town of Split - a must! The site has 272 touring pitches on a small peninsula, all with 10/16A electricity and some with water connections. Around 40 of these are in a separate area reserved for tents.

The site benefits from the mature trees, which give shade and privacy to most pitches, which are level. Some of the pitches have views over the sandy beach and across the bay. Set on top of rocks at the point of the peninsula is a large, comfortable restaurant with several terraces and wonderful views — an ideal place for a quiet drink or evening meal before taking a walk on the beach.

Three sanitary blocks include free hot water, controllable showers accessed by wristbands, and some washbasins in cabins. Accessible sanitary facilities. Laundry facilities. Motorhome services. Three outdoor swimming pools, Wellness area with sauna, gym and whirlpool. Dog Wash facilities and fenced-off dog beach. Beach bars and a restaurant. Supermarket at the entrance. Play area. Multisports pitch, Table tennis, Children's club and entertainment programme (high season). Bicycle hire. Fishing. Kayaking, Stand-up paddle boards, Small boat launch, Internet access and WiFi throughout (free).

Key Features

📅 Book Online

📅 All Year

🐾 Pets allowed

♿ Accessible Facilities

⛱ Seaside Beach on Site

🌊 Outdoor Pool on Site

🛝 Childrens Play Area

🍸 Bar on Site

Find Out More
Visit **ar.camp/cr6855**
or scan the QR code.

Orašac, Dalmatia

Alan Rogers Ref: CR6700
Accommodations: 35
Pitches: 45
GPS: 42.69967, 18.00540
Post Code: HR-20234

what3words:
bewildered.undergraduate.
griddled

Contact:
bozo@orasac.com
Tel: +385 20 891 169
www.orasac.com

Open Dates:
Start April - Start November.

Camp Pod Maslinom

Camp Pod Masilinom is a small terraced campsite located in the small village of Orasac,11km from the well-known tourist destination of Dubrovnik. You will find 80 pitches, 45 for touring(10A), nestled between 100-year-old olive trees, hence the campsite's name. This site is perfect for those looking to get away to experience true Croatian camping life, with great views of the sea surrounding it. There aren't many facilities on site, but you have all the necessities for a quiet, relaxing holiday.

A short walk through the campsite leads to two small pebbled beaches and a small dock for mooring boats. These sheltered coves are perfect for taking a relaxing swim after a day of exploring Dubrovnik. The site owners here are very helpful and welcoming and speak multiple languages. They can also organise boat trips for you to the Elaphites islands, including Koločep, Lopud and Šipan.

Good quality and well-maintained sanitary facilities. Accessible sanitary facilities. Chemical disposal point. Seasonal excursions program. Small children's playground. Fridge and safes for hire. Laundry with washing machines. Gas and electric BBQs are permitted. Dogs allowed.

Key Features

🐾 Pets allowed

♿ Accessible Facilities

⚓ Seaside Beach on Site

🐟 Fishing on Site

Find Out More
Visit **ar.camp/cr6700**
or scan the QR code.

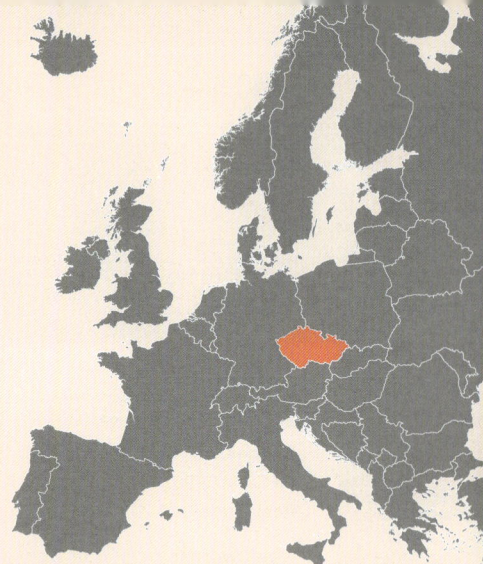

Capital Prague
Currency Czech Koruna (CZK)
Language Czech
Time Zone CET (GMT+1)
Telephone Code +420
Emergency Number 112
Tourist Website visitczechrepublic.com

Shops Hours can vary, but generally, shops are open 9am to 6pm weekdays, 9am to 1pm Sat and closed Sun. Shopping centres operate extended hours.

Money ATMs are widespread, accessible 24hrs a day and have multilingual instructions. Cash is still the most popular payment option but major cards are widely accepted, Amex not so much. Some chain stores accept payment in euros but will give change in CZK.

Travelling with Children Prague has been rated the most kid-friendly city in Europe. Most restaurants will cater for children. Historical attractions are geared towards kids. Child rates apply up to the age of 18.

Public Holidays 1 Jan New Year's Day; Mar/Apr Good Friday; Mar/Apr Easter Monday; 1 May May Day; 8 May Liberation Day; 5 Jul St Cyril & St Methodius Day; 6 Jul Jan Hus Day; 28 Sep Statehood Day; 28 Oct Independence Day; 17 Nov Freedom & Democracy Day; 24 Dec Christmas Eve; 25 Dec Christmas Day; 26 Dec Boxing Day

Accessible Travel Score

Behind when it comes to accessibility. Older buildings, including museums, are not well equipped. Transport in cities is improving.

Driving in Czech Republic The road network is well-signposted throughout the country. To use motorways, you will need a vignette which can be purchased at border points, post offices and some petrol stations. Drink-driving and using your mobile whilst driving are illegal. Dipped headlights should be used at all times. Winter tyres are compulsory between November and April. Give way to trams and buses. There are no Low Emission Zones in place. The use of dashcams and speed camera detectors is legal.

Czech Republic

View all campsites in Czech Republic
ar.camp/czech-republic

See campsite map page 472

Climate Summers are warm and dry and winters are cold, sometimes snowy.

☀

Avg. summer temp
18°C

🌧

Wettest month
June

Once known as Bohemia, the Czech Republic is a land of fascinating castles, romantic lakes and valleys, picturesque medieval squares, and famous spas. It is divided into two main regions, Bohemia to the west and Moravia in the east.

Although small, the Czech Republic has a wealth of attractive places to explore. The historic city of Prague is the hub of tourist activity and a treasure trove of museums, historic architecture, art galleries and theatres, and the annual 17-day beer festival!

The beautiful region of Bohemia, known for its Giant Mountains, is popular for hiking, skiing and other sports. West Bohemia is home to three renowned spas: Karlovy Vary, Mariánské Lázne and Františkovy Lázne, which have developed around the hundreds of mineral springs which rise in this area and offer a wide variety of restorative treatments.

Brno is the capital of Moravia in the east, lying midway between Prague, Vienna and Budapest. Visitors will admire its beautiful architecture, notably Mies van der Rohe's Villa Tugendhat. North of Brno is the Moravian Karst. The underground Punkya River has carved out a network of caves, some open to the public and connecting with boat trips along the river.

Scan QR code to browse more campsites on our website

📍 Šluknov, North Bohemia

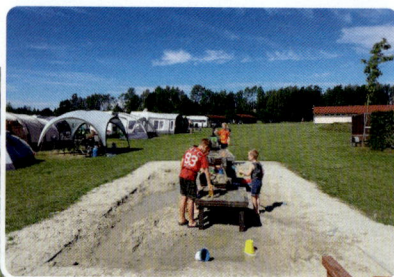

Alan Rogers Ref: CZ4680
Accommodations: 12
Pitches: 148
GPS: 51.00228, 14.46680
Post Code: CZ-40777

what3words:
lyricist.clammed.impossibly

Contact:
info@campingregenboog.com
Tel: +420 607 513 973
www.campingregenboog.nl

Open Dates:
Mid May - End September.

Camping de Regenboog

Camping de Regenboog enjoys a beautiful location in the north of the Czech Republic and is only 5 km from the border of Germany. The campsite sits on 13 hectares, so the pitches are incredibly spacious. They also have log cabins for rent, which sleep up to 6 people.

Adjacent to the campsite, there is a recreation lake for swimming and boating, and you can walk or cycle in the nature reserve 'Bohemian Switzerland', as it is perfect for sports enthusiasts and nature lovers. Fresh bread is available from the bakery situated 50 metres from the site, and the supermarket is only 400 metres away. For dinner, there are a few local restaurants nearby, and the prices are very reasonable. The campsite organises excursions to the nearby Skoda factory and museum.

The sanitary facilities are well-maintained (coin-operated). Large recreational lake for swimming and boating, Table tennis. Beach volleyball court. Football field. Campfire. Recreation/Youth room. Children's playground. Bowls. Archery (Weekly). Horse riding nearby. Sheep pasture, where children can help to feed the sheep. Recreation programme for all ages (High season), Campfire evenings, barbecues and Sunday gatherings (High season) this is in Dutch, with a translation available on request. Free WiFi.

Key Features

📅 Book Online

🧗 Childrens Play Area

🚲 Bicycle Hire on Site

🐟 Fishing on Site

⛵ Sailing on Site

Find Out More
Visit **ar.camp/cz4680**
or scan the QR code.

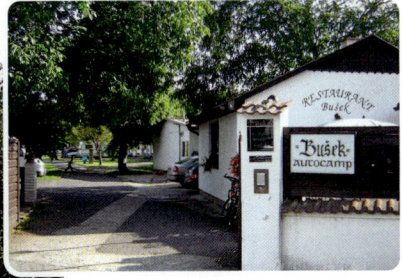

Camping Busek Praha

Alan Rogers Ref: CZ4845
Accommodations: 56
Pitches: 24
GPS: 50.16472, 14.48558
Post Code: CZ-18200

what3words:
zoned.employer.steams

Contact:
campbusek@gmail.com
Tel: +420 283 910 254
www.campbusek.cz

Open Dates:
All year.

No trip to the Czech Republic would be complete without a visit to the capital, Prague. At this site, you can do just that without getting tangled up with the city traffic. Just about 8 km. from the centre, there is an excellent bus link from the site to the new metro station at Ládví, which is a part of the new integrated transport system.

The site is part of a small motel complex and provides just 24 level and unnumbered pitches, all with 10A electricity. It is on the edge of a small, rural village, which offers peace and quiet at the end of a long day's sightseeing. In 40 minutes, you can be in the heart of Prague, free to enjoy everything this vibrant city has to offer. Some road noise can be heard.

Older-style sanitary block with clean toilets, hot showers and washbasins. Washing machine. Kitchen and dishwashing facilities. Small restaurant with breakfast service (High season). WIFI (on request). Swimming pool nearby. Pets allowed.

Key Features

All Year

Pets allowed

Bar on Site

Find Out More
Visit **ar.camp/cz4845**
or scan the QR code.

📍 **Prague, Central Bohemia**

Alan Rogers Ref: CZ4840
Accommodations: 7
Pitches: 120
GPS: 49.95145, 14.47517
Post Code: CZ-25241

what3words:
pitchers.scanning.cobbles

Contact:
info@campingoase.cz
Tel: +420 241 932 044
www.campingoase.cz

Open Dates:
Start May - Start September.

Camping Oase Praha

Camping Oase Praha is an exceptional site, only five kilometres from Prague, with easy access between the site and the city. You can take the bus (from outside the site) or drive to the underground stop (ten minutes). The site has 120 pitches, all around 100 sq.m, with 6/12A electricity and 55 with water and drainage, on level, well-kept fields.

The site is very well maintained and has just about everything one would expect, including an outdoor pool and an indoor pool with a separate paddling pool, a restaurant and a bar. Children can amuse themselves with trampolines, a playground, an indoor play area, volleyball and a football field.

An outstanding toilet block includes washbasins, controllable showers and child-sized toilets. Accessible sanitary facilities. Family showers. Laundry facilities. Campers' kitchen with hob, fridge freezer and dishwasher. Motorhome services. Shop (essentials only). Bar and restaurant. Outdoor pool and separate paddling pool with slide (High season), heated indoor pool (All season). Jacuzzi with sauna and massage (Seasonal). Adventure-style playgrounds and covered mini club. Trampolines. Football. Minigolf. TV and video. Board games. CCTV cameras. Barbecues are permitted. Internet point and WiFi (charged).

Key Features

🗓 Book Online

🐾 Pets allowed

♿ Accessible Facilities

🏊 Indoor Pool on Site

🛝 Childrens Play Area

Find Out More
Visit **ar.camp/cz4840**
or scan the QR code.

Vychodocesky, North Bohemia

Alan Rogers Ref: CZ4860
Accommodations: 60
Pitches: 70
GPS: 50.11582, 16.21683
Post Code: CZ-51741

what3words:
barge.watchtower.pauses

Contact:
lodkyorlice@seznam.cz
Tel: +420 737 406 741
www.autokemporlice.cz

Open Dates:
End March - Mid October.

Autocamping Orlice

Autocamping Orlice is located on the bank of the Orlice River, near a modern swimming pool and tennis courts near the edge of the town. Surrounded by tall trees, the grass pitches are generous, although not marked or numbered, and are located on each side of a concrete grid road that runs the length of this rectangular site. There is room for 70 units, half with electric points (16A) and shade in parts. There is a hotel alongside the campsite with 60 cabins also available to rent on-site.

On-site facilities include a restaurant with a garden with plenty of outdoor seating areas; here, you can enjoy breakfast and a quick snack during the day with a large selection of refreshing drinks available. During high season, social events are held here. Part of the restaurant also has a children's corner. Outside, you will find a children's playground with swings, a sandpit and a slide. There is also a trampoline available. Next to this, there is a communal BBQ and bonfire area.

The central sanitary block includes hot water in washbasins, sinks and good showers (payment) – it is of a good standard for the Czech Republic. Limited food supplies are available in a bar/lounge during July/Aug. Café/bar (Seasonal) Bicycle hire. WiFi.

Key Features

- Pets allowed
- Childrens Play Area
- Bar on Site
- Fishing on Site

Find Out More
Visit **ar.camp/cz4860**
or scan the QR code.

📍 **Severocesky, North Moravia**

Alan Rogers Ref: CZ4686
Accommodations: 52
Pitches: 100
GPS: 49.41296, 16.80847
Post Code: CZ-79862

what3words:
apart.mortgage.zing

Contact:
info@baldovec.cz
Tel: +420 606 744 265
www.baldovec.cz

Open Dates:
Late February - End December.

Camping Baldovec

Camping Baldovec is in the Moravian Karst region, a few kilometres from the Macocha Gorge, Europe's largest sinkhole. It lies in the Bílá Vody valley, surrounded by deep forests and unspoiled nature. There are 100 good-sized pitches on slightly sloping grass or hard ground. Some areas have low terracing. In July and August, touring pitches must be reserved in advance.

The site offers a restaurant with an outdoor terrace, offering a wide range of food, and evening entertainment is held here during the high season. There is also a wellness centre with artificial salt caves, a water world and a massage room. A wide range of sporting activities is available on site, including a ropes course and a 23-meter climbing tower, Archery, Paintballing, and Multisport courts where team games can be held. Escape rooms are also available to hire, and marked cycling and hiking trails direct from the site.

Heated sanitary facilities. Washing machine and dryer. Snack bar, fresh bread (high season). Restaurant (all season). Small swimming pool and sunbathing area (High season). Games room. Children's play area. Wellness centre. Climbing tower. Rope course. Tarzan Jump. Paintball. Archery. Tennis. Football. Volleyball. Slingshot. Multisports centre (floodlit). WiFi throughout (free). Accommodation to rent.

Key Features

🐾 Pets allowed

♿ Accessible Facilities

🏊 Outdoor Pool on Site

🛝 Childrens Play Area

🍸 Bar on Site

🚲 Bicycle Hire on Site

Find Out More
Visit **ar.camp/cz4686**
or scan the QR code.

📍 Jihomoravsky, South Moravia

Alan Rogers Ref: CZ4895
Pitches: 55
GPS: 49.27657, 16.45263
Post Code: CZ-66471

what3words:
condiments.onside.storyteller

Contact:
camping.hana@seznam.cz
Tel: +420 607 905 801
www.campinghana.com

Open Dates:
Late April - End September.

Camping Hana

Camping Hana is a small, family-run campsite in the village of Veverská Bityska in South Moravia. It is situated on a triangle of land bounded by the River Svratka and the old millrace. The campground has 55 touring pitches, all with electric hook-up points available. There is a well-stocked buffet/café about 100 meters from the campground entrance where refreshments can be purchased. Hana Musilova runs the site to very high standards, speaks excellent English and Dutch and provides lots of local information.

Brno, the capital of Moravia and the Czech Republic's second-largest city, is a short boat or bus ride away. The village of Veverska Bityska has shops, restaurants, bars, an ATM, and a reasonable, small supermarket. On-site amenities include a sanitary block with warm showers, a communal kitchen with a cooker, a fridge, washing machines, and driers. A small shop on site also sells maps, postcards, stamps, and tram and bus tickets.

The modernised sanitary block provides ample and clean toilets, hot showers (token, 1st free per person, thenpaid), washbasins and baby changing. Washing machine and dryer. Kitchen and dishwashing facilities. Small shop with essential supplies. Table tennis, Bicycle hire. Free WiFi throughout. Charcoal and gas BBQs are allowed.

Key Features

🐾 Pets allowed

♿ Accessible Facilities

🧗 Childrens Play Area

🚲 Bicycle Hire on Site

🐟 Fishing on Site

Find Out More
Visit **ar.camp/cz4895**
or scan the QR code.

📍 **Jihocesky, South Bohemia**

Alan Rogers Ref: CZ4715
Pitches: 160
GPS: 48.76102, 14.02793
Post Code: CZ-38226

what3words:
lilt.backside.knowhow

Contact:
info@caravancamping-hp.cz
Tel: +420 380 738 231
www.caravancamping-hp.cz

Open Dates:
Start May - Late October.

Camping Horni Plana

Caravan Camping Horni Plana is a large campsite located directly on the shore of Lake Lipno in the picturesque town of Horni Plana in southern Bohemia. It is the largest campsite on the lake and offers a variety of amenities for campers of all ages. There are 160 unmarked pitches for touring, all with good shade and some situated directly on the lake. They are slightly sloping, and the sand and gravel access roads can get muddy in wet weather.

On-site amenities include a restaurant serving various Czech and international dishes, two tennis courts, and a large children's playground with swings and slides. There is also mini golf on-site for all ages to enjoy. The site is located directly on Lake Lipno; you can expect various water sports and activities here, including paddle boat rental and a beach volleyball court. There is plenty of space for the anglers staying here, and you can purchase a license directly from the campsite reception. Several other water sports can be enjoyed, including kayaking, canoeing, and windsurfing.

Modern toilet facilities with British-style toilets, open washbasins and controllable hot showers (payment). Accessible sanitary facilities. Washing machine. Kiosk for basics, serving as a bar in the evening. Restaurant. WiFi (free).

Key Features

♿ Accessible Facilities

🍸 Bar on Site

🐟 Fishing on Site

⛵ Sailing on Site

Find Out More
Visit **ar.camp/cz4715**
or scan the QR code.

📍 Zapadocesky, West Bohemia

Camping Stanowitz

The town of Mariánské Lázne (Marienbad - 2.5km) is an old-style health resort in the heart of Western Bohemia, a region full of historical and natural beauty. The town became popular as a spa resort between 1870 and the 1920s, with around 100 mineral springs. However, this is not the only reason to stay at Camp Stanowitz.

This cosy, family-size campsite has only 30 pitches, all with 10A electricity, in a slightly sloping, unmarked apple and plum orchard (look out for falling fruit in the Autumn). Drainage is good. The owner makes a real effort to show off his beautiful country to interested visitors and probably has more brochures than the average tourist office. Attached to the site is a pension (bed and breakfast) and a small restaurant with a terrace, which offers a limited menu but receives positive reports from visitors.

Modern, heated toilet block with free hot showers. Washing machine. Restaurant/bar. Riding. Internet. Free WiFi. BBQs permitted. Max 2 Dogs allowed. No children's entertainment program.

Alan Rogers Ref: CZ4655
Accommodations: 3
Pitches: 30
GPS: 49.94419, 12.72797
Post Code: CZ-35301

what3words:
transparency.heightened.blearily

Contact:
info@stanowitz.cz
Tel: +420 354 624 673
www.stanowitz.com

Open Dates:
Start April - End October.

Key Features

🐾 Pets allowed

🍸 Bar on Site

Find Out More
Visit **ar.camp/cz4655**
or scan the QR code.

Capital Copenhagen
Currency Danish Krone (kr)
Language Danish
Time Zone CET (GMT+1)
Telephone Code +45
Emergency Number 112
Tourist Website visitdenmark.com

Shops 10am to 6pm weekdays, until 4pm on Sat. Larger stores may be open Sun. Supermarkets open from 8am to 9pm. Bakeries (incl in-store supermarket bakeries) sometimes open earlier.

Money ATMs are widespread and are accessible 24hrs a day, some have multilingual instructions. All cards accepted widely incl Amex and Diner's Club. Denmark is a primarily cashless society.

Travelling with Children Very child-friendly, with many attractions from theme parks and zoos to family-friendly beaches. Entry to most museums is free. Many campsites have special programs for children during peak season.

Public Holidays 1 Jan New Year's Day; Mar/Apr Maundy Thursday; Mar/Apr Good Friday; Mar/Apr Easter Sunday; Mar/Apr Easter Monday; Apr/May Prayer Day; May Ascension; May/Jun Whit Sunday; May/Jun Whit Monday; 25 Dec Christmas Day; 26 Dec Boxing Day

Accessible Travel Score

Generally considered among the most accessible countries in Europe. Buildings are well-equipped, outdoor spaces are level and nearly all transport is accessible.

Driving in Denmark Driving is much easier than at home as roads are much quieter. Denmark has no tolls except the Oresund Bridge that links the country with Sweden. Dipped headlights are compulsory at all times. There are no emergency phones on motorways, so make sure you have a mobile phone. Drink-driving and using your mobile whilst driving are illegal. Low Emission Zones exist in all major cities, affecting diesel cars registered before 2011. The use of dashcams and speed camera detectors is legal.

Denmark

View all campsites in Denmark
ar.camp/denmark

See campsite map page 475

Climate Generally mild although changeable throughout the year.	☀️ **Avg. summer temp** 18°C	🌧️ **Wettest month** August

Denmark offers a diverse landscape, all within a relatively short distance. The countryside is green and varied with flat plains, rolling hills, fertile farmland, many lakes and fjords, wild moors and long beaches, interspersed with pretty villages and towns.

It is the easiest of the Scandinavian countries to visit, and distances are short, so it is easy to combine the faster pace of the city with the tranquillity of the countryside and the beaches. It comprises the peninsula of Jutland, the larger islands of Zeeland and Funen, and hundreds of smaller islands, many uninhabited.

Zeeland is home to the climate-friendly capital city, Copenhagen, with its relaxing waterside cafés, vibrant nightlife, Michelin-star restaurants and the stunning Frederiksborg castle.

Funen is Denmark's second-largest island, linked to Zeeland by the Great Belt Bridge.

Known as the Garden of Denmark, its gentle landscape is dotted with orchards and pretty thatched, half-timbered houses. It also has plenty of safe, sandy beaches. Jutland's flat terrain makes it ideal for cycling, and its long beaches are popular with windsurfers.

Scan QR code to browse more campsites on our website

📍 **Ribe, Jutland**

Alan Rogers Ref: DK2018
Accommodations: 5
Pitches: 300
GPS: 55.61973, 8.11892
Post Code: DK-6840

what3words:
corridors.corrective.extinction

Contact:
info@vejersstrandcamping.dk
Tel: +45 75 27 70 50
www.vejersstrandcamping.dk

Open Dates:
Mid March - Late October.

Vejers Strand Camping

Vejers Strand Camping is a camping ground located in the town of Vejers Strand in western Denmark. It is situated directly on the North Sea coast, with stunning dunes and beach views. At this unique destination, you can choose your pitch, with each being fully equipped with electricity and a water supply and able to accommodate tents, campervans, and motorhomes of various sizes.

You'll find a grocery store on-site, offering a selection of necessities for daily meals and freshly baked bread. You can also get ice cream at the campsite's ice cream shop or enjoy a delicious pizza from the grill bar to take to the beach or have back at your pitch. Other on-site facilities include a shared picnic area, a communal kitchen and a children's playground featuring a bouncy cushion, slide, swing, and climbing frame; for those who wish to explore the North Sea, a private footpath leads to it just 100 meters away.

Modern and well-maintained sanitary facilities with showers and toilets and accessible facilities, Laundry facilities, Chemical toilet disposal point, Communal kitchen, Bar, Restaurant, Shop, Children's playground, TV, BBQs allowed, Pets allowed, dog showers, WiFi Free.

Key Features

🐾 Pets allowed

♿ Accessible Facilities

⛱ Seaside Beach on Site

🛝 Childrens Play Area

🍸 Bar on Site

🐟 Fishing on Site

⛵ Sailing on Site

Find Out More
Visit ar.camp/dk2018
or scan the QR code.

📍 Ringkøbing, Jutland

Nissum Fjord Camping

Alan Rogers Ref: DK2422
Accommodations: 60
Pitches: 200
GPS: 56.31928, 8.14989
Post Code: DK-6990

what3words:
toned.scorecards.arrive

Contact:
kontakt@nissumfjordcamping.dk
Tel: +45 97 49 60 11
www.nissumfjordcamping.dk

Open Dates:
All year.

Nissum Fjord Camping is an all-year site in the village of Fjand, situated between Nissum Fjord and the Husby Klitpantage. Its location on Cycle Route 1 makes this site ideal for cycling enthusiasts. It also allows easy access to the North Sea beaches. The site comprises various fields with 270 spacious pitches, of which 200 are for touring units with 16/13 amp hook-up points. These are separated by rose bushes, offering plenty of privacy, providing shelter from the westerly winds and producing some shade.

There are also 30 mobile homes, bungalows, log cabins, etc., available to hire. The pitches at the campsite are generously sized, so you'll have plenty of space for alfresco dining. You can buy supplies for your picnics or barbecues in Ulfborg, a small town about 5 kilometres from the campsite. On-site amenities include a small shop with a fresh bread delivery service. There's also a café just by the site entrance for coffee and snacks. An outdoor swimming pool is on-site, with plenty of sun loungers to relax on. There's also a children's playground on site.

Accessible sanitary facilities, Restaurant, Bar, Shop, Children's playground, fully-equipped kitchen fitted with range tops, an oven, and a microwave. Bicycle hire, Entertainment during high season, Outdoor swimming pool, Communal firepit, Multisport pitch, boules alley, Sea fishing, TV, Dogs allowed, WiFi.

Key Features

📅 All Year

🐾 Pets allowed

♿ Accessible Facilities

⛱ Seaside Beach Nearby

🧗 Childrens Play Area

🍸 Bar on Site

🚲 Bicycle Hire on Site

Find Out More
Visit ar.camp/dk2422
or scan the QR code.

📍 **Nordjylland, Jutland**

Alan Rogers Ref: DK2130
Accommodations: 40
Pitches: 100
GPS: 56.63588, 9.78131
Post Code: DK-9500

what3words:
soups.tingly.lamest

Contact:
info@hobrocitycamping.dk
Tel: +45 98 52 32 88
www.hobrocamping.dk

Open Dates:
All year.

Hobro Camping Gattenborg

Hobro Camping Gattenborg is located in Hobro, Denmark, in a natural setting with views over Vesterfjord and Mariagerfjord. This neat and well-tended municipal site is imaginatively landscaped and has around 140 pitches on terraces arranged around a bowl-shaped central activity area. Most pitches (100 for touring units) have electricity (10A) and many trees and shrubs. Footpaths connect the various terraces and activity areas.

There are 30 seasonal units and ten cabins. The reception building, with a small shop and tourist information, has a covered picnic terrace behind it and houses a large TV lounge. The small, heated outdoor swimming pool with a small water slide, sauna and jacuzzi is free to campers and open in high season, weather permitting. Extra facilities include two children's playgrounds with swings, slides, a bouncy cushion, a climbing wall and a sandpit. There are also billiards, giant chess and an unusual woodland moon-buggy (go-kart) track.

The main heated sanitary building includes washbasins in cubicles and hot showers (on payment). Two family bathrooms. Accessible sanitary facilities. Baby room. Kitchen with hobs, sinks and free herbs. Washing machine and dryer. The tiny unit in the centre of the site has two unisex WCs and washbasins (cold water only) and a small kitchen. Motorhome services. Shop (order bread before 9pm). Swimming pool (high season). Play areas. TV lounge with board games and library. Bicycle hire. Limited WiFi available.

Key Features

🐾 Pets allowed

♿ Accessible Facilities

⛱ Seaside Beach Nearby

🏊 Outdoor Pool on Site

🛝 Childrens Play Area

🚲 Bicycle Hire on Site

Find Out More
Visit ar.camp/dk2130
or scan the QR code.

Århus, Jutland

Skanderborg Sø Camping

Alan Rogers Ref: DK2051
Accommodations: 3
Pitches: 160
GPS: 56.02098, 9.89064
Post Code: DK-8660

what3words:
argues.anticipated.wobbles

Contact:
info@campingskanderborg.dk
Tel: +45 86 51 13 11
www.campingskanderborg.dk

Open Dates:
Late April - Early September.

Skanderborg Lake (Sø) Camping is a cosy site where varied ground creates a beautiful setting for a relaxing stay. It is a former orchard where several of the old fruit trees and many other trees and shrubs provide good shelter and shade. The site is divided into sections, with planting creating secluded pitches and nooks. It is built on sandy soil, so the ground is never soft or muddy. The site has 160 touring pitches, most with electric hook-up points. There are also cabins for 2-5 persons available to hire. There are no seasonal units; therefore, all the pitches are available for touring units.

The site is 8 hectares, about 1/3 of which has no designated pitches but well-groomed ground with plenty of space for play and activities. The site has a private beach about 300 m away, which can be accessed along a small path through the forest; there are plenty of activities for the whole family to enjoy, including swimming, fishing, and kayaking.

Four toilet blocks provide showers, washbasins and WCs. Accessible sanitary facilities. Laundry with washing machine and dryer. Baby changing room. Drying room. Dogs are welcome. Free WiFi (partial site.) Children's play area. Bread to order. Gas sales. Motorhome service point. Restaurant 3 km. Boat and kayak hire, Miniature golf. Table tennis.

Key Features

- Pets allowed
- Accessible Facilities
- Childrens Play Area
- Fishing on Site

Find Out More
Visit **ar.camp/dk2051**
or scan the QR code.

📍 **Fyn, Islands**

Alan Rogers Ref: DK2202
Accommodations: 70
Pitches: 125
GPS: 55.43990, 9.82389
Post Code: DK-5580

what3words:
loudness.recaps.consult

Contact:
info@camping-ferie.dk
Tel: +45 64 42 17 63
www.camping-ferie.dk

Open Dates:
Start April - Mid September.

Ronæs Strand Camping

Ronæs Strand Camping is a terraced campsite at the end of Gamborg Fjord on the island of Funen. It is a popular destination for families, couples, and groups, offering various accommodation options and activities to suit all needs. Ronæs Strand has 185 pitches, with 125 for touring units, all with 7/10A electricity. From some areas, there are beautiful views of the Gamborg Fjord. The marked and level pitches, a few with hardstanding, are in long rows on well-kept grass with gravel access lanes. A variety of mature trees and bushes separates these lanes. Six fully serviced pitches have electricity, water, and wastewater.

The campsite has a sandy beach directly on-site, making it the perfect place to relax and enjoy the Danish summer. Guests can swim, sunbathe, build sandcastles, or walk along the shore. There is also a small jetty where guests can rent kayaks, paddleboards, and other water sports equipment. Water skiing or sailing is possible directly from the site in good weather.

Key Features

🐾 Pets allowed

♿ Accessible Facilities

⛱ Seaside Beach on Site

🛝 Childrens Play Area

🍸 Bar on Site

🚲 Bicycle Hire on Site

🎣 Fishing on Site

Two modern toilet blocks with washbasins in cabins, controllable hot showers (on payment), toilets and showers for children and accessible sanitary facilities. Baby room. Two laundries. Campers' kitchen. Motorhome services. Car wash. Shop (high season). Takeaway (High season). Football field. Fishing. Watersports, pedaloes and boat launching. Barbecue area. Extensive games room. Playground. Bicycle hire. English is spoken. WiFi throughout.

Find Out More
Visit ar.camp/dk2202
or scan the QR code.

Fyn, Islands

Camp Hverringe

Camp Hverringe (Bøgebjerg Strand) is one of the excellent TopCamp sites in Denmark and has a great location on the waters of the Storebælt and Romsø Sund. This makes it an ideal base for all kinds of watersports (the site rents out motor boats) or for a relaxing holiday on the beach in what is said to be one of the sunniest and driest parts of Denmark. This well-maintained campsite has 375 pitches, some with marvellous views over the sea and to Romsø Island. Around 340 level pitches for touring units, all with 10/16A electricity, are on well-kept grassy lawns separated by hedges and shrubs.

The water park is one of the main attractions at Camp Hverringe, with something for everyone to enjoy. There are three swimming pools, slides, and a water playground for all ages. The children's playground is another popular spot for children, with various equipment to keep them entertained, including trampolines, bouncy castles, swings, slides, and more.

One refurbished toilet block has washbasins (open style and in cabins) and controllable hot showers (card-operated). Spacious family rooms. Private sanitary facilities and jacuzzi to rent. Accessible sanitary facilities. Fully equipped laundry. Campers' kitchen. Motorhome services. Car wash. Shop. Bar. Takeaway. Outdoor pool (10x10m) with paddling pool. Adventure playground. Playing field. Mini golf, Petting zoo, Film nights. Games and TV rooms. Full entertainment programme in high season. Fishing. Water sports. Motorboat and fishing equipment hire. WiFi over part of the site (charged).

Alan Rogers Ref: DK2207
Accommodations: 29
Pitches: 346
GPS: 55.50902, 10.71184
Post Code: DK-5380

what3words:
contacting.naturals.replaces

Contact:
info@camphverringe.dk
Tel: +45 65 34 10 52
www.camphverringe.dk

Open Dates:
End March - Late October.

Key Features

- Pets allowed
- Accessible Facilities
- Seaside Beach on Site
- Outdoor Pool on Site
- Childrens Play Area
- Bar on Site
- Bicycle Hire on Site
- Fishing on Site

Find Out More
Visit ar.camp/dk2207
or scan the QR code.

Sjælland, Islands

Alan Rogers Ref: DK2267
Accommodations: 16
Pitches: 200
GPS: 54.77172, 11.49321
Post Code: DK-4930

what3words:
stuttering.punt.intact

Contact:
info@maribo-camping.dk
Tel: +45 54 78 00 71
www.maribo-camping.dk

Open Dates:
All year.

Maribo So Camping

Maribo Lake (Sø) Camping is located on the island of Lolland, Denmark. It is situated in a forest and by the Søndersø Lake, a popular spot for swimming, fishing, and boating. You will find 216 grass pitches on site, of which 200 are for touring units with 16-amp hook-up points available. There are also 11 log cabins or bungalows available to hire. Several facilities are on-site for the whole family, including an outdoor swimming pool and mini golf course. For food options, there is an on-site restaurant, bar, and shop with all the necessities needed to cook a delicious meal back at your pitch.

The campsite is located directly on the Nature Park Maribosøerne, a protected nature park in which the medieval town of Maribo was built. The rich animal and plant life makes the nature park an obvious excursion destination. The campsite offers canoe, kayak, dinghy rentals, water bikes, and SUP boards.

The heated toilet block has showers, washbasins and WCs. Accessible facility. Family and Baby room. Dishwashing area. Laundry with washing machine and dryer. Motorhome service point. Chemical toilet point. Restaurant, Bar, Kitchen and Microwave. Free WiFi. Shop. Bread to order. Freezer for ice packs. TV/living room. Children's playground. Games room. Table tennis. Dogs and BBQs are allowed. Communal BBQ area. Defibrillator. Bike hire. Lake swimming.

Key Features

- Pets allowed
- Accessible Facilities
- Childrens Play Area
- Bar on Site
- Bicycle Hire on Site
- Fishing on Site

Find Out More
Visit **ar.camp/dk2267**
or scan the QR code.

Charlottenlund Fort

Alan Rogers Ref: DK2265
Pitches: 75
GPS: 55.74480, 12.58538
Post Code: DK-2920

what3words:
hems.ribs.glares

Contact:
info@campingcopenhagen.dk
Tel: +45 39 62 36 88
www.campingcopenhagen.dk

Open Dates:
Early March - Late October.

Camping Charlottenlund Fort is a small campsite located on the grounds of the disused Charlottenlund Fort, about 8 km north of the centre of Copenhagen. There are 75 pitches on grass, all with 10A electricity. The limitation on the space available means that pitches are relatively close together, but many are quite deep. The site is very popular and is usually packed every night, so a reservation is necessary.

The campsite is located right on the beach, with stunning views of the Øresund Sound. There is a high-quality restaurant in the fort (under separate management) with excellent sea views. The campsite also has several other facilities, including a children's playground, a barbecue area, and a small shop where you can buy basic groceries and camping supplies.

Sanitary facilities located in the old armoury are newly rebuilt, well maintained and heated. Free showers. Kitchen facilities include gas hobs and a dining area. Laundry. Motorhome services. Small café in reception. Restaurant with terrace and views. Bicycle hire. Free WiFi over site. Beach.

Key Features

- Pets allowed
- Accessible Facilities
- Seaside Beach on Site
- Bar on Site
- Bicycle Hire on Site
- Fishing on Site

Find Out More
Visit **ar.camp/dk2265**
or scan the QR code.

Capital Paris
Currency Euro (€)
Language French
Time Zone CET (GMT+1)
Telephone Code +33
Emergency Number 112
Tourist Website france.fr

Shops Hours vary throughout the year, often opening for shorter hours during low and shoulder seasons. In high season shops are open 10am to noon and 2pm-7pm weekdays and Sat. Longer hours, including Sun for shops in tourist zones.

Money ATMs are widespread, accessible 24hrs a day and have multilingual instructions. Major cards are widely accepted, but cash is still popular in smaller stores and rural areas.

Travelling with Children One of the most child-friendly countries in Europe, France has a good mix of cultural sights, historical monuments and other attractions. Most museums and galleries are free for under 18s.

Public Holidays 1 Jan New Year's Day; Mar/Apr Easter Monday; 1 May Labour Day; 8 May Victory Day; May Ascension; May/Jun Whit Sunday; May/Jun Whit Monday; 14 Jul Bastille Day; 15 Aug Assumption; 1 Nov All Saints; 11 Nov Armistice Day; 25 Dec Christmas Day

Accessible Travel Score

Efforts to improve are being made but the Paris metro is unusable for wheelchair users and many historic buildings are yet to be adapted.

Driving in France The road network comprises Autoroutes, N, D, and local C roads. Drink-driving and using your mobile whilst driving are illegal. Low Emission Zones exist in all major cities, and Zero Emission Zones also cover Paris. If you plan to drive through any major cities, you will need a Crit'Air sticker - there are different stickers depending on the age of your vehicle (EVs are currently not exempt). The use of dashcams is legal, but speed camera detectors are not, so make sure to disable this feature on sat navs and mobile devices before entering the country.

France

View all campsites in France
ar.camp/france

See campsite map pages 476–478

Climate Warmer in the east/ south, wetter in the north/ west, snow in the mountains.	☀ **Avg. summer temp** 18°C (N), 25°C (S)	🌧 **Wettest month** Jul (N), Oct (S)

From the hot sunny climate of the Mediterranean to the more northerly and cooler regions of Normandy and Brittany, with the Châteaux of the Loire and the lush valleys of the Dordogne, and the mountain ranges of the Alps, France offers holidaymakers a huge choice of destinations to suit all tastes.

France boasts every type of landscape, from the wooded valleys of the Dordogne to the volcanic uplands of the Massif Central, the rocky coast of Brittany to the lavender-covered hills of Provence and snow-capped peaks of the Alps. The diversity of these regions is reflected in the local customs, cuisine, architecture and dialect.

France has a rich cultural heritage with a wealth of festivals, churches, châteaux, museums and historical monuments to visit. Many rural villages hold festivals to celebrate the local saints. You can also find museums devoted to the rural arts and crafts of the regions. The varied landscape and climate ensure many opportunities for outdoor pursuits, from hiking and cycling, wind- and sand-surfing on the coast and rock climbing and skiing in the mountains. And no trip to France is complete without sampling the fantastic local food and wine.

Scan QR code to browse more campsites on our website

Morbihan, Brittany

Alan Rogers Ref: FR56100
Accommodations: 14
Pitches: 66
GPS: 47.69515, -2.34913
Post Code: F-56220

what3words:
prodding.aspiring.inroad

Contact:
camping@gredesvents.fr
Tel: +33 2 97 43 37 52
campingaugredesvents.com

Open Dates:
End March - End September.

Camping Au Gré des Vents

Sites et Paysages Au Gré des Vents is a quiet family site in wooded countryside, 600 m. from the town. Philippe and Benedicte Lambert purchased this neat, tidy and organised site in 2001. There are 85 pitches (66 for tourers, 43 with 6/10A electricity) of reasonable size (80-150 sq.m) on neat grass on two levels. With limited electrical hook-ups, the upper level is flat, and pitches are divided by young shrubs. The lower level is partly sloping with mature trees, shade and electricity on all pitches.

The reception and bar are at the site's entrance, just beyond the security gate. Other on-site facilities include a covered swimming pool, a children's playground with a trampoline, table tennis, a football pitch, and a basketball court. During the summer months, activities are organised for the whole family. There is also live music in July and August. Various catering trucks also stop at the site in the evenings during summer.

The modern heated sanitary block is kept very clean and includes large, comfortable showers, cabins with washbasins and British-style WCs. Accessible facilities. Baby room. Laundry facilities with washing lines. Motorhome services. Bread delivered each morning. Bar. Takeaway. Indoor heated swimming pool (Seasonal). Tennis. Football area. Two play areas. WiFi (charged).

Key Features

- Book Online
- Pets allowed
- Accessible Facilities
- Seaside Beach Nearby
- Indoor Pool on Site
- Childrens Play Area
- Bar on Site

Find Out More
Visit ar.camp/fr56100
or scan the QR code.

Morbihan, Brittany

Alan Rogers Ref: FR56390
Accommodations: 42
Pitches: 150
GPS: 47.61135, -3.02880
Post Code: F-56340

what3words:
piazzas.targets.carnival

Contact:
info@lelac-carnac.com
Tel: +33 2 97 55 78 78
www.lelac-carnac.com

Open Dates:
Start April - End October.

Camping Carnac Le Lac

Overlooking the lake and situated between the Morbihan Gulf and the Quiberon peninsula, this site is only 3 km. from the port of La Trinité-sur-Mer while the famous megaliths are even closer. The site is well maintained, with flowering landscaped gardens and mature trees and shrubs, giving plenty of shade and some privacy. The 150 pitches are of various sizes, many providing superb views of the lake; there is good access for larger units.

The owner aims to appeal to young families and couples looking for a quiet holiday in an idyllic setting. The lake is ideal for canoeing, and one- and two-person canoes are available to rent on-site. Canoeing courses are also on offer in peak season.

Two sanitary blocks, including baby baths and laundry units, are kept clean and well-maintained. Accessible Facilities. Small shop (all season) with limited takeaway (High season). Heated swimming pool (Seasonal). Play area with trampolines. Games room with electronic games and table football. TV room. Kids club, Fishing. Bicycle hire. Mini farm, Cycling and canoe activities are arranged regularly. Kayaks, surfboards and cars for hire. WiFi (free).

Key Features

🗓 Book Online

🐾 Pets allowed

⛱ Seaside Beach Nearby

🏊 Outdoor Pool on Site

🛝 Childrens Play Area

🚲 Bicycle Hire on Site

🐟 Fishing on Site

Find Out More
Visit ar.camp/fr56390
or scan the QR code.

📍 **Finistère, Brittany**

Alan Rogers Ref: FR29050
Accommodations: 70
Pitches: 199
GPS: 47.97685, -4.11102
Post Code: F-29000

what3words:
revision.swelling.snitch

Contact:
contact@lanniron.com
Tel: +33 2 98 90 62 02
www.camping-lanniron.com

Open Dates:
Late March - Mid November.

L'Orangerie de Lanniron

Camping L'Orangerie de Lanniron is a beautiful and peaceful family site set in ten acres of a 17th-century, 38-hectare country estate on the banks of the Odet River, formerly the home of the Bishops of Quimper.

The site has 199 grassy pitches (156 for touring units) of three types varying in size, services and price. They are on flat ground, laid out in rows alongside access roads, with shrubs and bushes providing separation. All have electricity, and 88 have three services. The original outbuildings have been attractively converted around a walled courtyard.

Excellent heated block in the courtyard and a second modern block serving the top areas of the site. Accessible facilities. Washing machines and dryers. Motorhome services. Shop & Bar (Seasonal). Gas supplies. Restaurant and takeaway (open daily). Swimming and paddling pool. Aquapark with waterfall, Balnéo, spa, jacuzzi, fountains and water slides. Small play area. Tennis. Minigolf. Golf course (9 holes), driving range, two putting greens, training bunker and pitching area (packages available). Fishing. Archery. Bicycle hire. Reading, games and billiards rooms. TV/video room. Karaoke. Outdoor activities. Pony rides and tree climbing (High season). Mini farm, Trampolines, Orienteering, Treasure hunts, bouncy castle, Internet access and WiFi throughout (charged).

Key Features

📅 Book Online

🐾 Pets allowed

♿ Accessible Facilities

⛱ Seaside Beach Nearby

🏊 Outdoor Pool on Site

🛝 Childrens Play Area

🍸 Bar on Site

🚲 Bicycle Hire on Site

Find Out More
Visit ar.camp/fr29050
or scan the QR code.

Finistère, Brittany

Camping Les Mouettes

Yelloh! Village Camping Les Mouettes is a sheltered site on the edge of an attractive bay, with access to the sea at the front of the site. In a wooded setting with many attractive trees and shrubs, the 474 pitches include 68 for touring units, all with electricity, water and drainage. The remainder are taken by tour operators and by 406 mobile homes and chalets to rent.

At the centre of the 'village' are shops, a bar, a restaurant, an entertainment stage, sports facilities, an impressive heated pool complex with swimming, paddling and water slide pools, plus a 'Tropical river', jacuzzi and sauna. There is also an excellent indoor swimming pool.

A clean sanitary block with controllable showers and washbasins in cabins. There are showers with washbasins and delightful rooms for children and babies. Accessible Facilities. Laundry. Shop (limited hours outside the main season). Takeaway. Bar with TV. Restaurant/pizzeria/grill. Heated pool complex indoor (All season) and outdoor. Beauty salon. Games rooms (a special one for under 5s). Play area. Multisports ground. Minigolf. Bicycle hire. Entertainment all season. Large units should phone first. Free WiFi throughout.

Alan Rogers Ref: FR29000
Accommodations: 406
Pitches: 68
GPS: 48.65807, -3.92833
Post Code: F-29660

what3words:
magician.composed.bunking

Contact:
contact@les-mouettes.com
Tel: +33 2 98 67 02 46
www.yellohvillage.co.uk/
camping/les_mouettes

Open Dates:
Early April - Early September.

Key Features

- Pets allowed
- Accessible Facilities
- Seaside Beach Nearby
- Indoor Pool on Site
- Childrens Play Area
- Bar on Site
- Bicycle Hire on Site
- Riding on Site

Find Out More
Visit ar.camp/fr29000
or scan the QR code.

📍 **Côtes d`Armor, Brittany**

Alan Rogers Ref: FR22500
Accommodations: 200
Pitches: 355
GPS: 48.60670, -2.49674
Post Code: F-22430

what3words:
illuminate.damsel.bolsters

Contact:
camping@saintpabu.com
Tel: +33 2 96 72 24 65
www.saintpabu.com

Open Dates:
Early April - Late September.

Camping Saint Pabu Plage

Camping Saint Pabu Plage is a lovely site on a wide sandy beach 4 km from the centre of Erquy. It has direct access to the beach and a beautiful panoramic sea view. If you're travelling with a tent, caravan, van or camper van, you'll enjoy lush, hedged pitches with electricity and water. Most pitches are located on the lower, flat part of the campsite. Pitches are not shaded and can accommodate a maximum of 4 people. On-site amenities include a bar, a restaurant, and a well-stocked shop.

Erquy is 4 km. distant and has an attractive fishing port and a wealth of good seafood restaurants and shops. The town boasts ten fine beaches. Some wonderful cliff-top walks extend to the peninsula of Cap Fréhel to the north.

The clean and well-maintained sanitary block is equipped with individual shower cabins, sink areas and WC areas (toilet paper is provided!). The campsite also has "duo cabins" with a shower and separate sink. You will also find showers for returning from the beach (one part for women, one part for men), hand washbasins with soap dispensers, hand dryers and hair dryers. The site also has a snack bar-restaurant (on-site or to take away), a grocery store, a laundry area, fridge rental, and a baby kit (travel bed with mattress, chair high, bathtub). Pets are not accepted.

Key Features

📅 Book Online

🏖 Seaside Beach on Site

🛝 Childrens Play Area

🍸 Bar on Site

🚲 Bicycle Hire on Site

🐟 Fishing on Site

Find Out More
Visit ar.camp/fr22500
or scan the QR code.

Camping SAINT PABU PLAGE

Erquy - Côtes d'Armor - Bretagne

Located on the SEASIDE with an EXCEPTIONAL SEA VIEW and DIRECT ACCESS TO THE BEACH for pleasant moments of relaxation, swimming and water sports.

Free loan included in your stay:
ELECTRIC BIKE, normal bike, KAYAK, paddle, SURF, bodyboard, snorkeling outfit, wetsuit, BEACH CHAIR, barbecue, beach games, outdoor games, board games, landing nets... And much more !

Camping Saint Pabu Plage
Plage de Saint Pabu 22430 Erquy
www.saintpabu.com. camping@saintpabu.com
+33(0)2 96 72 24 65

📍 Ille-et-Vilaine, Brittany

Alan Rogers Ref: FR35080
Accommodations: 18
Pitches: 203
GPS: 48.38205, -1.83475
Post Code: F-35190

what3words:
probe.gasp.tomcat

Contact:
domainedulogis@wanadoo.fr
Tel: +33 2 99 45 25 45
www.domainedulogis.com

Open Dates:
End March - Start October.

📍 **Alan Rogers Awards Won**
2023, 2016, 2015

Domaine du Logis

Camping le Domaine du Logis is an attractive rural site with enthusiastic owners, set in the grounds of an old château. The site's upgraded modern facilities are housed in traditional converted barns and farm buildings, which are well-maintained and equipped. There are 203 pitches, 67 of which are for touring units. The grass pitches are level, of a generous size and divided by mature hedges and trees. All have 10A electricity connections, water and drainage.

This site would appeal to most age groups, with plenty to offer the active, including a fitness room with a good range of modern equipment and a sauna for those who prefer to relax or perhaps enjoy a quiet day's fishing by the lake. A water playground for children is on site.

One comfortable toilet block with washbasins and showers. Accessible Toilet and shower. Laundry facilities. Bar with Sky TV. Restaurant and takeaway (High season). Outdoor swimming pool and whirlpool (Seasonal). Fitness and games rooms. Sauna. BMX circuit. Bicycle hire. Lake fishing. Unfenced play areas. Club for children (High season). WiFi throughout (free).

Key Features

📅 Book Online

🐾 Pets allowed

♿ Accessible Facilities

🏊 Outdoor Pool on Site

🛝 Childrens Play Area

🍸 Bar on Site

🚲 Bicycle Hire on Site

Find Out More
Visit **ar.camp/fr35080**
or scan the QR code.

Manche, Normandy

Alan Rogers Ref: FR50030
Accommodations: 60
Pitches: 134
GPS: 48.79778, -1.52498
Post Code: F-50380

what3words:
arrogant.swerves.unfocused

Contact:
bonjour@lez-eaux.com
Tel: +33 2 33 51 66 09
www.lez-eaux.com

Open Dates:
Start April - Mid September.

Château de Lez Eaux

Set in the grounds of a château, Castel Camping le Château de Lez Eaux lies in a rural situation just off the main route south, under two hours from Cherbourg. Of the 134 touring pitches, all with electricity (10A, Europlug) and 90 with water and drainage. Most of the pitches are good-sized, partly separated by trees and shrubs on flat or slightly sloping, grassy ground overlooking Normandy farmland and a small fishing lake.

The campsite offers several kinds of camping accommodations and pitches depending on your desires and needs - from treehouses to mobile homes with jacuzzis and chalets to camping pitches for tents, caravans, and mobile homes. Activities include a tropical-themed indoor water park with water slides and a children's aqua splash fun area. There is a paddling pool, swimming pool, games area, bouncy castles, fishing lake, tennis court and bike rental.

Three sanitary blocks (1 heated) are equipped with showers, private washing cubicles, baby facilities and accessible facilities. Washing machines and dryers. Shop. Bar. Takeaway. Fresh bakery in the morning. Covered water park (pool, slides, paddling pool) 1 outdoor pool. Games areas and bouncy castles. Fishing lake. Football. Volleyball grounds. TV room and games room. Bicycle hire. Tennis court hire. Kids club during the summer. Summer activities: 2 weekly concerts, local market, daily aqua aerobics in the indoor pool.

Key Features

- Book Online
- Pets allowed
- Accessible Facilities
- Seaside Beach Nearby
- Indoor Pool on Site
- Childrens Play Area
- Bar on Site
- Bicycle Hire on Site

Find Out More
Visit **ar.camp/fr50030**
or scan the QR code.

📍 **Manche, Normandy**

Alan Rogers Ref: FR50060
Accommodations: 50
Pitches: 120
GPS: 49.49452, -1.84246
Post Code: F-50340

what3words:
calmly.opal.arranges

Contact:
info@legrandlarge.com
Tel: +33 2 33 52 40 75
www.legrandlarge.com

Open Dates:
Mid April - Mid September.

Camping le Grand Large

Le Grand Large is a well-established, quality family site with direct access to a long sandy beach within 20 km. drive of Cherbourg. It is a neat site with about 120 touring pitches divided and separated by hedging, giving an orderly, well-laid-out, attractive appearance. Almost all have electricity (10A Europlug), water and drainage. There are 50 mobile homes to rent in three separate areas.

The reception area is at the entrance (with a security barrier), and the forecourt is decorated with flower beds. To the rear of the site and laid out in the sandhills is an excellent play area. Not surprisingly, the sandy beach is a big attraction. The length of units is restricted to eight metres to prevent any problems accessing pitches.

Two well-maintained toilet blocks. The main one is modern and includes washbasins in cubicles and some family rooms. Some showers and WCs have access to the outside of the building. Accessible facilities, Baby bathroom. Laundry area. Motorhome services. Shop for basics. Bar (all season). Snacks (July/Aug). Heated swimming and paddling pools (indoor all season, outdoor - seasonal). Play area. Football, Tennis. Pool table, Boules. Fishing. TV room. Some entertainment (July/Aug). WiFi over site (charged).

Key Features

📅 Book Online

🐾 Pets allowed

♿ Accessible Facilities

⛱ Seaside Beach on Site

🌊 Indoor Pool on Site

🎏 Childrens Play Area

🍸 Bar on Site

🐟 Fishing on Site

Find Out More
Visit ar.camp/fr50060
or scan the QR code.

Calvados, Normandy

Sous Les Etoiles

You will receive a warm welcome at this small family-run site in quiet and picturesque countryside. Grouped around a converted farmstead, the 50 touring pitches (all with 6A electricity) are laid out in a manicured lawn garden, set in small groups separated by shrubs and flower borders. The reception is in the old farmhouse where plenty of tourist information is available. A bar and snug have been tastefully created in an outbuilding, and hot bar snacks are served here.

The site is well located for those travelling to or from the ferry ports, but most stay longer to explore the area. There are many possible destinations for days out, including the D-Day beaches, the Cotentin peninsula and the towns of Saint Lô and Caen. Even Mont Saint-Michel is within easy reach.

Sanitary facilities include free hot showers with accessible facilities. Washing machine. Motorhome service point. Bar/snug with hot snacks and takeaway. Small playground. Indoor games room. Pétanque. Ice cream. Bread and Croissants to order. Caravan storage. WiFi throughout.

Alan Rogers Ref: FR14080
Pitches: 50
GPS: 49.00953, -0.85732
Post Code: F-14350

what3words:
yours.lovably.pioneered

Contact:
info@sous-les-etoiles.camp
Tel: +33 6 37 87 99 53
www.sous-les-etoiles.camp

Open Dates:
Start February - End November

Key Features

📅 Book Online

🐾 Pets allowed

♿ Accessible Facilities

🛝 Childrens Play Area

🍸 Bar on Site

Find Out More
Visit **ar.camp/fr14080**
or scan the QR code.

📍 **Calvados, Normandy**

La Côte de Nacre

Alan Rogers Ref: FR14010
Accommodations: 357
Pitches: 132
GPS: 49.32600, -0.39052
Post Code: F-14750

what3words:
leaders.manage.bendable

Contact:
vacances@sandaya.fr
Tel: +33 4 11 32 90 00
www.sandaya.co.uk

Open Dates:
Early April - Early September.

La Côte de Nacre is a large, popular commercial site with many facilities of high standards. It is an ideal holiday location for families. Two-thirds are given over to mobile homes (approx 357), and some tour operators are on the site. The 132 touring pitches are reasonable in size and condition, with 10A electricity, water and drainage. There is some hedging, a few trees and pleasant, well-cared-for flowerbeds.

The state-of-the-art, heated pool complex includes open and covered (sliding roof) areas, slides, whirlpools and water jets, and on a hot day, becomes the focal point of the campsite. The small seaside town of Saint Aubin-sur-Mer with its delightful old town buildings is ten minutes away, and the lovely promenade, perfect for brisk walks and a stop for coffee or beer, is only a few minutes further.

The toilet block provides toilets and showers, washbasins in cubicles, and a large room for toddlers and babies. Accessible sanitary facilities. Dishwashing and laundry room. Motorhome services. Grocery with fresh bread baked on site. Bar, restaurant and takeaway. Pool complex. Hammam, sauna and body treatments (charged). Play area for young children with bouncy castle and climbing frames. Multisports court. Synthetic skating rink. Library. Games room. Bicycle hire. Children's clubs and mini-discos. Entertainment includes bingo, karaoke and discos. WiFi. Mobile homes to rent.

Key Features

📅 Book Online

🐾 Pets allowed

♿ Accessible Facilities

⛱ Seaside Beach Nearby

〰 Indoor Pool on Site

🛝 Childrens Play Area

🍸 Bar on Site

🚲 Bicycle Hire on Site

Find Out More
Visit ar.camp/fr14010
or scan the QR code.

Calvados, Normandy

Alan Rogers Ref: FR14160
Accommodations: 20
Pitches: 32
GPS: 49.30937, -0.01963
Post Code: F-14640

what3words:
affiliates.boggled.uptake

Contact:
camping-bellevue@wanadoo.fr
Tel: +33 2 31 87 05 21
www.camping-bellevue.com

Open Dates:
Start April - End October.

Camping Bellevue

Bellevue is located just west of Villers-sur-Mer with its sandy beach and nine and a half kilometres west of fashionable Deauville. It is ideally situated for cross-channel ferry ports and visiting the D-Day landing beaches.

It is a reasonably large site with 257 pitches in total, but including 195 privately owned mobile homes and 30 units to rent, only 32 pitches are left for tourers, 31 of which have electricity (6A). Many of these are on sloping ground, individual and relatively small with restricted access, so they are suitable only for smaller units. Double-axle caravans will have difficulty and can only access pitches adjacent to the road. Five slightly sloping pitches behind reception are used mainly by motorhomes (levelling blocks required).

Two sanitary units provide unisex facilities, all in individual cubicles, with some wide-door cubicles suitable for use as accessible facilities. Baby room. Laundry room with washing machine and dryer. Swimming pool complex (heated, seasonal). Bar (High season). Takeaway van (July/Aug). Shop for basics. Bread can be ordered daily. Boules. Video games machines. Pool table. Playground. Gym, Organised activities in peak season. WiFi (charged).

Key Features

- Pets allowed
- Accessible Facilities
- Seaside Beach Nearby
- Indoor Pool on Site
- Childrens Play Area
- Bar on Site

Find Out More
Visit ar.camp/fr14160
or scan the QR code.

📍 **Calvados, Normandy**

Alan Rogers Ref: FR14090
Accommodations: 12
Pitches: 132
GPS: 49.22525, 0.30438
Post Code: F-14130

what3words:
dentists.piazzas.amber

Contact:
contact@campinglebrevedent.com
Tel: +33 2 31 64 72 88
www.campinglebrevedent.com

Open Dates:
End April - Mid September.

🏅 **Alan Rogers Awards Won**
2017

Camping Le Brévedent

Castel Camping Le Brévedent is a well-established, traditional site with 132 pitches (105 for touring units, 31 used by tour operators) set in the grounds of an elegant, 18th-century hunting pavilion. Pitches are around the fishing lake in the lower gardens (level) or the old orchard (gently sloping). All have 10A electricity.

It is an excellent holiday destination within easy reach of the Channel ports, and its peaceful, friendly environment makes it ideal for mature campers or families with younger children (note: the lake is unfenced). The reception provides a good selection of tourist information, and English is spoken.

Three toilet blocks include washbasins in cubicles and accessible facilities, refurbished with spacious en-suite cubicles (shower, washbasin and baby bath). Laundry facilities. Kitchen for mothers with babies. Motorhome services. Shop (baker delivers each morning). Bar in château open evenings. Restaurant (Seasonal). Takeaway (Seasonal). Café (July/Aug). Clubroom. TV and library. Heated swimming and paddling pools (Seasonal, unsupervised). Playgrounds. Minigolf. Boules. Games room. Fishing. Canoeing. Bicycle and buggy hire. Organised excursions. Musical evenings and children's club (July/Aug). WiFi (free in café). Dogs are not accepted.

Key Features

- 📅 Book Online
- ♿ Accessible Facilities
- ⛱ Seaside Beach Nearby
- 🏊 Outdoor Pool on Site
- 🛝 Childrens Play Area
- 🍸 Bar on Site
- 🚴 Bicycle Hire on Site
- 🎣 Fishing on Site

Find Out More
Visit ar.camp/fr14090
or scan the QR code.

Seine-Maritime, Normandy

Alan Rogers Ref: FR76160
Accommodations: 21
Pitches: 135
GPS: 49.69878, 0.27560
Post Code: F-76790

what3words:
merchant.instead.soundtracks

Contact:
camping@aiguillecreuse.com
Tel: +33 2 35 29 52 10
campingaiguillecreuse.com

Open Dates:
Early April - Mid September.

l'Aiguille Creuse

L'Aiguille Creuse, conveniently close to Le Havre, is named after a rock, alleged to be hollow, near Etretat. The site is set back from the Côte d'Albâtre in the village of Les Loges, between Etretat and the fishing port of Fécamp. There are 135 good-sized grassy pitches, slightly sloping in parts and divided by neat hedges. Of these, 78 are for touring, all with 10A electricity and 14 with water and drainage.

The village is within easy walking distance, and buses run from here to Fécamp, Etretat and Le Havre. An alternative and more adventurous way of getting to Etretat is by booking a rail buggy and pedalling yourselves down the hill – you are then brought back up to the village by road in a 'petit train'.

Two modern toilet blocks (one heated, the other open in July/Aug) with unisex toilets (no seats), controllable showers, washbasins in cubicles, baby changing and accessible facilities. Laundry. Motorhome services. Modern bar (with 30 mins. free WiFi daily). Takeaway (High season). Heated pool with a retractable roof. Children's playground. Entertainment and kids club, tennis court, Table tennis, Bicycle hire, WiFi (charged). Card-operated barrier.

Key Features

- Book Online
- Pets allowed
- Accessible Facilities
- Seaside Beach Nearby
- Indoor Pool on Site
- Childrens Play Area
- Bar on Site
- Bicycle Hire on Site

Find Out More
Visit **ar.camp/fr76160**
or scan the QR code.

📍 Eure, Normandy

Alan Rogers Ref: FR27070
Accommodations: 7
Pitches: 115
GPS: 49.23564, 1.40005
Post Code: F-27700

what3words:
virtue.debater.jammers

Contact:
contact@camping-troisrois.com
Tel: +33 2 32 54 23 79
www.camping-troisrois.com

Open Dates:
Mid March - Mid November.

l'Ile des Trois Rois

One hour from Paris, on the banks of the Seine and overlooked by the impressive remains of Château Gaillard (Richard Coeur de Lion), this attractive and spacious ten-hectare site will appeal to couples and young families. The site offers mobile units to rent and touring pitches in separate areas. These are either riverside or in a large central triangle, all very close to the Seine; all pitches are divided by low hedging, and some offer a degree of shade.

Facilities are excellent and clean; as you leave the reception, you see a modern swimming pool and bar/restaurant complex, forming the centre for the site activities. (The only drawback is that this area is the only tap to serve the whole site with drinking water, although, on level ground, it can be quite a walk from the far end of the site).

Four small, heated toilet blocks have showers and washbasins in cubicles. One has accessible facilities, and another has a laundry facility. Motorhome services. Heated swimming and paddling pools (Seasonal). Bar, restaurant and takeaway (High season). Fenced play area. Adult open-air exercise area. Evening entertainment (High season). Bicycles and barbecues for hire. Satellite TV. Internet access. WiFi throughout (charged).

Key Features

- Book Online
- Pets allowed
- Accessible Facilities
- Outdoor Pool on Site
- Childrens Play Area
- Bar on Site
- Bicycle Hire on Site
- Fishing on Site

Find Out More
Visit **ar.camp/fr27070**
or scan the QR code.

Somme, Picardy

Camping Le Champ Neuf

Alan Rogers Ref: FR80020
Accommodations: 118
Pitches: 197
GPS: 50.26895, 1.60263
Post Code: F-80120

what3words:
atop.guzzle.attribute

Contact:
contact@camping-lechampneuf.com
Tel: +33 3 22 25 07 94
camping-lechampneuf.com

Open Dates:
Start April - End October.

Le Champ Neuf is located in Saint Quentin-en-Tourmont on the Bay of the Somme. It is a quiet site, 900 m. from the ornithological reserve of Marquenterre, the favourite stop for thousands of migratory birds; birdwatchers will appreciate the dawn chorus and varied species. This eight-hectare site has 197 pitches, 79 for touring, on level grass with 6/10A electricity.

The site has many leisure facilities to enjoy while holidaying here; there is a sizeable indoor swimming pool with water slides, a lazy river, waterfalls and a water park for the younger children. There are many sporting activities to get involved with, from a multiport pitch to tennis and archery. During the high season, an extensive array of entertainment is available, with a kids' club, karaoke evenings, live music, and pony rides, to name a few.

Four unisex toilet blocks have showers, washbasins in cubicles, family cubicles and accessible facilities. Laundry facilities. Motorhome services. Bar, snack bar and entertainment area. Play area. TV. Games room. Covered, heated pool complex including slides (Seasonal), jacuzzi and children's pool. Fitness room. Sauna. Multisport court. Table tennis. Kids' club, WiFi over site (free). Gas barbecues are not accepted.

Key Features

- Book Online
- Pets allowed
- Accessible Facilities
- Seaside Beach Nearby
- Indoor Pool on Site
- Childrens Play Area
- Bar on Site
- Bicycle Hire on Site

Find Out More
Visit **ar.camp/fr80020**
or scan the QR code.

📍 **Somme, Picardy**

Château des Tilleuls

The Château des Tilleuls is a charming campsite located in the heart of the Baie de Somme, two hours from Paris, near Abbeville and the beaches of Saint Valéry sur Somme and Le Crotoy. The site has 50 grassy touring pitches shaded and separated by hedges for privacy with 10amp hook-up points. There are also a couple of pitches with private sanitary facilities.

During high season, many activities keep the whole family entertained; with live shows, bouncy castles, tournaments, and many sports, it will be hard to have a dull holiday here. For those who would instead relax while on-site, you will find an outdoor heated swimming pool. Discover the riches of the Bay of Somme, ranked among the most beautiful bays in the world and the 10th major site in France.

The three toilet blocks, one heated, have showers, washbasins and WCs. Accessible facilities. Laundry with washing machine and dryer. Restaurant. Snack bar, Takeaway food. Shop. Bread delivered daily. Heated Outdoor swimming pool. Children's pool. Children's playground. Multisport ground. Tennis court. Beach volleyball. Boules. Table tennis. Weights room. Billiards. Table football. Electronic games. Mini golf. Inflatable structures (July and August). Entertainment. Live shows (High season). Bicycle rental. Pets allowed. Mini farm.

Alan Rogers Ref: FR80280
Accommodations: 186
Pitches: 50
GPS: 50.14136, 1.76233
Post Code: F-80102

what3words:
residences.viable.meriting

Contact:
contact@chateaudestilleuls.com
Tel: +33 3 22 24 07 75
www.chateaudestilleuls.com

Open Dates:
Early March - End October.

Key Features

📅 Book Online

🐾 Pets allowed

🏊 Outdoor Pool on Site

🛝 Childrens Play Area

🍸 Bar on Site

🚲 Bicycle Hire on Site

Find Out More
Visit **ar.camp/fr80280**
or scan the QR code.

Pas-de-Calais, Nord/Pas-de-Calais

Alan Rogers Ref: FR62010
Accommodations: 60
Pitches: 200
GPS: 50.86632, 1.85698
Post Code: F-62340

what3words:
sundress.restrictions.aliens

Contact:
castels@bien-assise.com
Tel: +33 3 21 35 20 77
camping-la-bien-assise.com

Open Dates:
Start April - End September.

Alan Rogers Awards Won
2023

Camping La Bien Assise

Les Castels Camping de La Bien-Assise is a mature and well-developed campsite on the grounds of a country house dating back to the 1500s. There are around 200 grassy pitches here, including 4 with hardstanding; pitches are large, between 90m2 & 190m2 level and divided by well-manicured hedges. All have 10 amp E.H.U., but you have a choice of pitch upgrades: Simple, Drainage, or Premium. They're connected by surfaced and gravel roads and are of a good size (up to 300 sq.m), with well-maintained shrubs and hedging dividing most of the pitches.

This site is part of the independent Les Casteles group, and you are always assured a very high standard at all of the sites within this group. Chateau de la Bien-Assise is no exception. Being close to Calais, the Channel Tunnel exit and Boulogne make this a good stopping point en route, but La Bien-Assise is well worth a longer stay to explore the beautiful Opal Coast.

Three well-equipped toilet blocks provide many washbasins in cubicles, showers and baby rooms. Accessible facilities, Laundry facilities. The main block is in four sections, two unisex. Two motorhome service points. Shop. Restaurant. Bar/grill and takeaway (all from mid-April). TV room. Pool complex (Mid-April - Mid-Sept) with toboggan, covered paddling pool and outdoor pool. Play areas. Minigolf. Tennis. Bicycle hire. WiFi (charged, but free with a drink in the bar).

Key Features

- Book Online
- Pets allowed
- Accessible Facilities
- Seaside Beach Nearby
- Indoor Pool on Site
- Childrens Play Area
- Bar on Site
- Bicycle Hire on Site

Find Out More
Visit **ar.camp/fr62010**
or scan the QR code.

📍 Pas-de-Calais, Nord/Pas-de-Calais

Alan Rogers Ref: FR62170
Accommodations: 2
Pitches: 14
GPS: 50.80852, 2.05553
Post Code: F-62890

what3words:
beverages.relight.pack

Contact:
contact@hotel-camping-bal.fr
Tel: +33 3 21 35 65 90
www.hotel-camping-bal.fr

Open Dates:
Start April - End October.

Camping Bal

Camping Bal is a natural site on 4.5-hectare grounds and adjacent to Hotel Bal. The site is within easy reach of the A26 (7 km). This is an excellent overnight stop and very convenient for Calais. There are 14 pitches with hardstanding for touring units, 12 in one area separated by grass. A few additional grass pitches are scattered around the site. Electricity is available. Visitors may dine in the attractive restaurant and bar at the adjacent hotel, where free WiFi is provided.

The local village is within walking distance and offers a bakery, pharmacy and more. There are lovely views across the wooded valley from the top of the site: the site and the adjacent hotel offer very good value for overnight stops.

In low season, there are minimal facilities for the touring pitches (a single toilet, shower and washbasin). The main sanitary block is open for July/Aug. Accessible facilities, Small play area. Tennis court. Boules. Games room (July/Aug). Hotel bar and restaurant (from 18.00 all year). WiFi in the hotel (free).

Key Features

🗓️ Book Online

🐾 Pets allowed

♿ Accessible Facilities

⛱️ Seaside Beach Nearby

🛝 Childrens Play Area

🍸 Bar on Site

Find Out More
Visit **ar.camp/fr62170**
or scan the QR code.

📍 **Nord, Nord/Pas-de-Calais**

Du Mont Des Bruyeres

Family-friendly Camping Le Mont Des Bruyères sits pretty much in the very centre of the Scarpe-Escaut Regional Natural Park, which should also tell you something about the excellent surroundings of this site. Green scenery has plenty of options for walks, bike rides, horse riding and watersports. It is still easy to get to amenities like shops and restaurants a couple of kilometres away in the centre of Saint-Amand-Les-Eaux.

The campsite has 49 touring pitches with plenty of shade from the trees when it gets warm. The fully serviced pitches here have water and electricity points and access to a launderette and 24-hour bathrooms. You can find a heated swimming pool, an on-site playground, and an outdoor fitness area. There are options for food with a café/takeaway, drinks from the bar or meals made from the grocery shop and bread point. Evening entertainment runs in summer, including friendly, themed meals.

Accessible facilities, Fresh bread available, Groceries: limited selection, Restaurant, Bar, Entertainment (high season), Outdoor swimming pool, Children's play area, Table tennis table, Multi-sports field, Jeu de boules alley, Giant chess, Games room, WiFi, Pets allowed.

Alan Rogers Ref: FR59090
Accommodations: 18
Pitches: 49
GPS: 50.43537, 3.46303
Post Code: F-59230

what3words:
conspire.keychain.populations

Contact:
aurore.mancon@orange.fr
Tel: +33 3 27 48 56 87
campingmontdesbruyeres.com

Open Dates:
Mid March - End October.

Key Features

📅 Book Online

🐾 Pets allowed

♿ Accessible Facilities

🏊 Outdoor Pool on Site

🛝 Childrens Play Area

🍸 Bar on Site

Find Out More
Visit **ar.camp/fr59090**
or scan the QR code.

📍 **Aisne, Picardy**

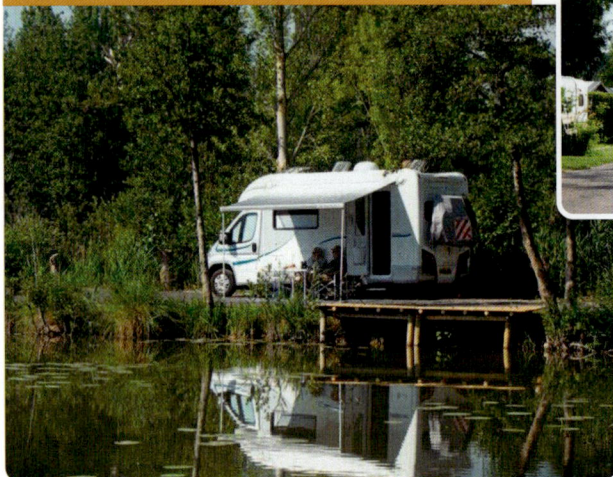

Vivier aux Carpes

Vivier aux Carpes is a small, quiet site close to the A26, two hours from Calais, so it is an ideal overnight stop on your journey into Europe or an afternoon departure from Calais. This is also a great sport to extend your stay if you wish to relax and explore Picardy. Access to this site is easy as it is situated in the village with local shops and facilities. This neat, purpose-designed site is imaginatively set around an attractive 7ha fishing lake ideal for avid anglers.

The 67 well-spaced pitches are at least 100 sq.m, mainly on flat grass with dividing hedges. The 40 touring pitches all have 10A electricity, and there are particular pitches on gravel for motorhomes. The facilities on-site include a bar and restaurant in high season with outdoor table's in a courtyard area next to a modern heated covered outdoor swimming pool. The site also offers excellent facilities, including a modern laundry/ironing room; a large indoor games room with various activities is above the laundry room.

The clean, modern toilet block has spacious shower cubicles (push-button controls) and a couple of washbasins in cabins. Toilet facilities may be under pressure at busy times. Separate, heated, accessible sanitary suite. Laundry facilities. Basic motorhome services. Open-air snack bar and takeaway (July/Aug). Outdoor swimming pool, Large games room. Large play area with an acrobatic structure and football area. Pétanque. Fishing (Fee payable). Gates open from 07.00-22.00. Rallies welcome. WiFi over site (charged). Cycling and walking tours from the site.

Alan Rogers Ref: FR02000
Accommodations: 4
Pitches: 67
GPS: 49.78197, 3.21315
Post Code: F-02790

what3words:
restrictions.eyeholes.daily

Contact:
contact@camping-picardie.com
Tel: +33 3 23 60 50 10
www.camping-picardie.com

Open Dates:
Late March - Late October.

Key Features

📅 Book Online

🐾 Pets allowed

♿ Accessible Facilities

🏊 Outdoor Pool on Site

🛝 Childrens Play Area

🍸 Bar on Site

🐟 Fishing on Site

Find Out More
Visit **ar.camp/fr02000**
or scan the QR code.

Aisne, Picardy

Alan Rogers Ref: FR02060
Accommodations: 18
Pitches: 62
GPS: 49.43200, 3.97040
Post Code: F-02190

what3words:
dark.unveiling.cower

Contact:
campingguignicourt@orange.fr
Tel: +33 3 23 79 74 58
www.camping-aisne-picardie.fr

Open Dates:
Start April - End October.

Camping Au bord de l'Aisne

Enthusiastic owners took over this former municipal site in 2011 and have transformed it into a delightful location for an overnight stop or a more extended stay. Bookings are accepted all year round via email.

It has 100 pitches, of which 80 are available for touring units, with 10 occupied by chalets to rent and eight by seasonal units. Pitches are generally large and level, separated by young bushes, and all have 10A electrical connections available. Those along the riverbank have delightful views of the Aisne River, though access is via a coded gate in the secure fence. The town is quite attractive and is worthy of an evening stroll.

The sanitary block is fully equipped with sensor-controlled showers (one on each 'side' with en-suite washbasin), washbasins in cubicles and hairdryers. En-suite accessible facilities for visitors (with controllable showers). Baby bath on ladies' side. Laundry room. Fresh croissants, pain au chocolat & bread delivered daily (must be ordered the day before.) Bar serving snacks and takeaways. Covered heated swimming and paddling pools, which are accessible. Play area (2-4 yrs.) Swings. Trampoline. Boules. Fishing. Note: all facilities, including reception, bar, swimming pool and both toilet blocks, are on an upper level, with ramps or steps leading down to the pitches on the lower level. Chalets to rent.

Key Features

- Book Online
- Pets allowed
- Accessible Facilities
- Outdoor Pool on Site
- Childrens Play Area
- Bar on Site
- Bicycle Hire on Site
- Fishing on Site

Find Out More
Visit **ar.camp/fr02060**
or scan the QR code.

📍 **Seine-et-Marne, Paris/Ile de France**

Alan Rogers Ref: FR77030
Accommodations: 15
Pitches: 154
GPS: 48.91378, 2.73451
Post Code: F-77450

what3words:
token.softest.sorry

Contact:
welcome@camping-jablines.com
Tel: +33 1 60 26 09 37
www.camping-jablines.com

Open Dates:
Late March - End October.

International de Jablines

International de Jablines is a modern site in a prime location for active families. The leisure facilities of the adjacent Espace Loisirs are a big draw, with large lakes offering many water sports and activities like tree climbing, riding, children's playground, sports fields and more. The 400 metres of fine sandy beaches are open every day in July and August and on the weekends in May and June - the Grand Lac is said to have the largest beach in the Ile-de-France. But for some, the proximity to Disneyland Paris (6 km and there's a shuttle at certain times) and Paris (30 km) seals the deal.

The site has 154 pitches, of which 139 are for touring units. Most are of a good size (100-120 sq.m), often slightly sloping, with gravel hardstanding and grass, accessed by tarmac roads and marked by young trees. All have 10A electrical connections; 60 are fully serviced. There are about a dozen wooden chalets to rent.

Two toilet blocks, heated in cool weather, include pushbutton showers and some washbasins in cubicles. Accessible facilities. Laundry facilities. Motorhome services (charged). Shop (All season). Sailing, waterskiing, windsurfing, kayaking, pedalos. Mini golf. Tennis. Table tennis. Football. Play area. Boules. WiFi throughout (free). Ticket sales for Disneyland and Parc Astérix. Mobile homes to rent.

Key Features

🐾 Pets allowed

♿ Accessible Facilities

🛝 Childrens Play Area

Find Out More
Visit ar.camp/fr77030
or scan the QR code.

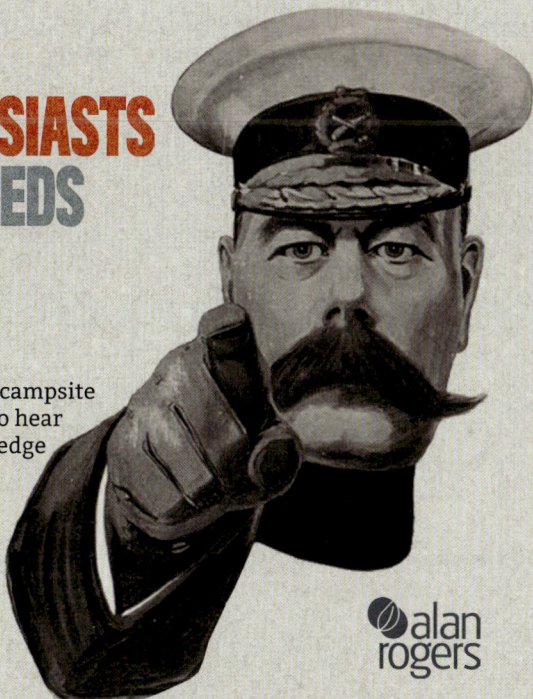

📍 **Ardennes, Champagne-Ardenne**

Alan Rogers Ref: FR08040
Accommodations: 15
Pitches: 98
GPS: 49.42640, 4.94010
Post Code: F-08240

what3words:
whimpering.dossier.
administered

Contact:
contact@camping-
lasamaritaine.fr
Tel: +33 3 24 30 08 88
www.camping-lasamaritaine.fr

Open Dates:
Mid April - Mid September.

Camping la Samaritaine

This delightful site, a member of the Flower group, is situated in the heart of the Ardennes between Reims and Luxembourg. It is peacefully located just outside the village beside a stream, and the rolling countryside is delightful, perfect for family bike rides and exploring on foot. A feature is a large lake, popular with anglers but with a designated beach area for swimming. Not far from the lake is a playground and a boules pitch, while some play equipment (adult supervision only) is at the lake. Lake swimming is supervised only at certain times (2 m. deep, with a paddling area up to 1.2 m).

This is a charming, well-run site with an attractively floral entrance, plenty of bushes, and small trees separating the pitches. The 98 numbered touring pitches all have electricity (10A) and are on level grass off hard access roads. They vary in size up to 130 sq.m. and 55 have water and drainage.

Sanitary blocks provide private cabins, family room and accessible facilities. Laundry facilities. Motorhome services. Bread is delivered daily. Essentials are kept in reception. Snack bar/takeaway (seasonal). Large recreation room with TV, games and books. Play area. Boules. Accompanied walks and entertainment programme (high season). Bicycle hire. WiFi throughout (free).

Key Features

🗓 Book Online

🐾 Pets allowed

♿ Accessible Facilities

🛝 Childrens Play Area

🚲 Bicycle Hire on Site

Find Out More
Visit **ar.camp/fr08040**
or scan the QR code.

📍 **Aube, Champagne-Ardenne**

Camping Le Lac d'Orient

Camping Le Lac d'Orient can be found at the centre of the large Forêt d'Orient natural park and is just 100 m. from the Lac d'Orient, which is ideal for water sports. Previously a small municipal site, it has been rebuilt and expanded. It offers a modern restaurant, bar, takeaway, a heated indoor pool, and outdoor swimming pools with slides, all in one complex with the reception and the shop.

Le Lac d'Orient offers various entertainment programs for all ages, including water aerobics, volleyball and pétanque competitions. In the evenings, occasionally, there is live music, dance evenings and karaoke. There is also a children's club run during the summer with creative crafts, treasure hunts and games. In addition to the activities available, there is also a multisport pitch, fitness equipment and table tennis.

One purpose-built toilet block and one refurbished, both of a high standard. Accessible sanitary facilities. Laundry facilities. Restaurant, bar and takeaway (Seasonal). Shop (all season). Heated indoor pool (as site) and outdoor swimming pools with slides (Seasonal). Paddling pool with small slides. Play area. Multisport court. Kid club, Table tennis, Entertainment, Max. one dog. WiFi (free for 30 mins every 6 hours).

Alan Rogers Ref: FR10020
Accommodations: 68
Pitches: 200
GPS: 48.26331, 4.34666
Post Code: F-10140

what3words:
belonged.spurn.nappies

Contact:
info@camping-lacdorient.com
Tel: +33 3 25 40 61 85
www.camping-lacdorient.com

Open Dates:
Mid April - Late September.

Key Features

📅 Book Online

🐾 Pets allowed

♿ Accessible Facilities

🏊 Indoor Pool on Site

🛝 Childrens Play Area

🍸 Bar on Site

Find Out More
Visit ar.camp/fr10020
or scan the QR code.

📍 **Haute-Marne, Champagne-Ardenne**

La Forge de Sainte Mar

This attractive campsite in a secluded valley is accessed through a narrow arched gateway. It was created in 1995 by carefully conserving original forge buildings and the surrounding land. The River Rongeant meanders through the site, widening into a small fishing lake. A picturesque bridge links the site's upper part to the reception area.

Grass pitches, 160 for touring units, are of varying sizes on terraces, amongst trees or in more open spaces. Electricity (10A, Europlug) and water are available, and 120 pitches are fully serviced. Eight premium pitches have a cabin with a shower, toilet, sink, and refrigerator. There are also 52 mobile homes (some with jacuzzi) and cottages refurbished. Larger units should take care when manoeuvring.

Two sanitary blocks provide all facilities, including those for children and accessible facilities. Family shower room. Additional facilities at reception and pool complex. Laundry facilities. Shop, restaurant and bar with terrace (view over the lake). A heated indoor pool and one for children (Seasonal). Play areas. Bicycle hire. Fishing (charged). Games room. Organised games for children and entertainment (July/Aug). WiFi (free of charge).

Alan Rogers Ref: FR52020
Accommodations: 52
Pitches: 160
GPS: 48.40644, 5.27109
Post Code: F-52230

what3words:
daydream.jilted.colleague

Contact:
info@laforgedesaintemarie.com
Tel: +33 5 82 06 01 30
laforgedesaintemarie.com

Open Dates:
Start April - Start October.

Key Features

📅 Book Online

🐾 Pets allowed

♿ Accessible Facilities

🏊 Indoor Pool on Site

🛝 Childrens Play Area

🍸 Bar on Site

🚲 Bicycle Hire on Site

🐟 Fishing on Site

Find Out More
Visit **ar.camp/fr52020**
or scan the QR code.

Meuse, Lorraine

Camping les Breuils

Les Breuils is a well-established and potentially attractive site beside a small fishing lake close to Verdun and the Citadel. It provides 162 flat pitches of varying sizes on two levels (144 for touring units), many with shade. Separated by trees or hedges, they are beside the lake and 120 offer 6A electricity connections (long leads will be necessary for many pitches).

The French owner is very welcoming and will give you any information about the surrounding area. By reception, you will find the restaurant with a terrace offering a small but satisfying menu. A small shop also offers necessities and a daily bread service. There is a children's playground, multisport pitch, and table tennis.

Two sanitary blocks are a mixture of old and new, including washbasins in cabins for ladies. Laundry facilities. Accessible Facilities. Motorhome services. Shop. Guide books on sale at reception (Seasonal). Restaurant (Seasonal), bar (seasonal). Shop (small).Swimming pool (200 sq.m) and children's pool (Seasonal). Fenced gravel play area. Multisport complex. Table tennis, Bicycle hire. WiFi.

Alan Rogers Ref: FR55010
Accommodations: 23
Pitches: 162
GPS: 49.15404, 5.36573
Post Code: F-55100

what3words:
flaming.shapes.altogether

Contact:
camping.lesbreuils@orange.fr
Tel: +33 3 29 86 15 31
www.camping-lesbreuils.com

Open Dates:
Start March - End September.

Key Features

- Book Online
- Pets allowed
- Accessible Facilities
- Outdoor Pool on Site
- Childrens Play Area
- Bar on Site
- Bicycle Hire on Site
- Fishing on Site

Find Out More
Visit ar.camp/fr55010
or scan the QR code.

101

📍 **Meurthe-et-Moselle, Lorraine**

Alan Rogers Ref: FR54060
Accommodations: 26
Pitches: 198
GPS: 48.74734, 6.05715
Post Code: F-54460

what3words:
matters.hone.merchant

Contact:
contact@
lesbouclesdelamoselle.com
Tel: +33 3 83 24 43 78
lesbouclesdelamoselle.com

Open Dates:
Late April - End September.

Camping la Moselle

On the banks of the Moselle River, at the foot of the medieval village of Liverdun, this grassy site offers 198 level pitches, 187 for touring, all with electricity (6A/10A). A variety of trees, planted in rows, provide shade and give the appearance of an orchard. A gate leads out onto the quiet road running along the grassy, tree-lined river bank, which offers opportunities for walking, cycling, fishing and various boating activities.

The hilltop village of Liverdun (with a tourism office) is within walking distance and provides a few snacks/restaurants and a baker. This site is mainly used as a stopover, although the swimming pool and opportunities for fishing, cycling and walking may attract visitors for longer.

Two modern & clean sanitary blocks include a family/baby room and accessible facilities. Washing machine. Small shop for essentials. Bar, snack bar and bread to order. Outdoor heated swimming pool (High season). Tennis. Fishing. Tourist information. Area for ball games. Pétanque. Volleyball. Bicycle hire. Charcoal barbecues are accepted. WiFi (Free).

Key Features

📅 Book Online

🐾 Pets allowed

♿ Accessible Facilities

〰️ Outdoor Pool on Site

🛝 Childrens Play Area

🍸 Bar on Site

🚲 Bicycle Hire on Site

🐟 Fishing on Site

Find Out More
Visit **ar.camp/fr54060**
or scan the QR code.

Bas-Rhin, Alsace

Alan Rogers Ref: FR67140
Accommodations: 33
Pitches: 145
GPS: 48.73109, 7.35529
Post Code: F-67700

what3words:
look.presume.reader

Contact:
camping@vacances-seasonova.com
Tel: +33 3 88 91 35 65
www.vacances-seasonova.com

Open Dates:
Late March - Late October.

Les Portes d'Alsace

Seasonova Les Portes d'Alsace is a charming site on the southern edge of Saverne. It has a relaxed and quiet feel thanks to its grassy open spaces and mature trees, which shade the large pitches. There are 145 pitches, 129 being touring pitches with electric hook-up points. The site is adjacent to a riding school, with some pitches overlooking the outdoor schooling area. The facilities are immaculate and include a pool, play area and bicycle hire - there are some excellent cycling routes. A takeaway van visits three times a week, and activities are organised for children in high season.

This is a lovely setting at the foot of the Vosges mountains, with superb access to the heart of nature and Alsace's picturesque scenery, yet with handy access to local facilities. Saverne is a lovely town just a short walk away, and the magnificent 18th century Rohan Castle, with its museum and arts centre, is a must-see, just a couple of kilometres away. Families will enjoy Océanide, the town's water park, and those looking to venture further afield can easily reach elegant Strasbourg by train.

Bar. Barbecues allowed (charcoal, gas, electric). Café. Accessible facilities. Late arrivals area without electric hook-up. Motorhome service point. Shop. Swimming pool. Children's playground. Entertainment (high season). Takeaway. TV room. WiFi (charged).

Key Features

- Book Online
- Pets allowed
- Accessible Facilities
- Outdoor Pool on Site
- Childrens Play Area
- Bar on Site
- Bicycle Hire on Site
- Riding on Site

Find Out More
Visit ar.camp/fr67140
or scan the QR code.

📍 **Bas-Rhin, Alsace**

Alan Rogers Ref: FR67060
Accommodations: 48
Pitches: 195
GPS: 48.57551, 7.71506
Post Code: F-67200

what3words:
camped.hounded.kettles

Contact:
info@camping-strasbourg.com
Tel: +33 3 88 30 19 96
www.camping-strasbourg.com

Open Dates:
All year.

Camping de Strasbourg

Camping Indigo Strasbourg is a beautifully designed and built city site in south-west Strasbourg. There are plenty of pitches to choose from during the low season here, but reservations are advised during the Christmas markets and high season as the site becomes full. There are 195 pitches, 115 for touring with electricity connections (6-9A, Europlug). A lodge is centrally located within the campsite, which houses the campsite's main services, including the modern restaurant and bar, the games room and the communal relaxing lounge area.

Here, you will also find local information and the on-site shop. Other services include a children's playground, Bicycle rental and a heated outdoor swimming pool. A bus stop is 200 m. from the site, and the city tram runs into town. The city centre is only 30 minutes' walk. This site is an ideal base from which to explore the city.

Refurbished heated sanitary blocks with facilities for families and accessible sanitary facilities. Washing machines and dryer. Motorhome services. Bar, restaurant and takeaway (All high season). Outdoor heated swimming pool (Seasonal). Bicycle hire. Free WiFi on part of the site. Wood and canvas tents and Romany-style caravans are available to rent. Pool table, table football. Pets allowed.

Key Features

📅 Book Online

📅 All Year

🐾 Pets allowed

♿ Accessible Facilities

♨️ Outdoor Pool on Site

🛝 Childrens Play Area

🍸 Bar on Site

🚲 Bicycle Hire on Site

Find Out More
Visit **ar.camp/fr67060**
or scan the QR code.

Haut-Rhin, Alsace

Alan Rogers Ref: FR68110
Accommodations: 30
Pitches: 163
GPS: 48.07962, 7.38652
Post Code: F-68180

what3words:
sounds.retrain.hurt

Contact:
info@campingdelill.fr
Tel: +33 3 89 41 15 94
www.campingdelill.fr/en

Open Dates:
Early March - Late December.

Camping de l'Ill Colmar

Stretching alongside the l'Ill River in urban Colmar, this site has 163 unseparated pitches, 120 for touring, arranged on terraces. Due to possible flooding on the lowest terrace during the winter months, this part of the site is closed seasonally. Despite some noise from the A35 motorway, this is a pleasant, well-maintained setting with some shade from mature trees.

All pitches have 10A electricity connections (Europlug; some pitches require long leads). The reception is comfortable and welcoming, and English is spoken. This pleasant, friendly site has been renovated and has plenty to entertain the whole family whilst staying here. There is an outdoor swimming pool, children's playground, and a small shop which sells essentials and fresh bread and pastries every morning. The campsite also has a restaurant and bar with a terrace which looks out over the river. Rental accommodation includes wood and canvas tents and wooden lodges. A supplement is payable for twin-axle caravans.

One modern heated sanitary block next to the main building and two older blocks (one closed in low season). Washbasins in cubicles, hot showers and accessible facilities. Washing machine and dryer. Motorhome services. Bread to order at reception. Bar (All season). Restaurant and takeaway (May-Sept). New heated pool and paddling pool. Play area. Outdoor chess. Table tennis, TV room. Boules. Fishing. Bicycle hire. Barbecue hire. WiFi (free in the TV lounge).

Key Features

- Book Online
- Pets allowed
- Accessible Facilities
- Childrens Play Area
- Bar on Site
- Bicycle Hire on Site
- Fishing on Site

Find Out More
Visit ar.camp/fr68110
or scan the QR code.

📍 **Loire-Atlantique, Pays de la Loire**

Alan Rogers Ref: FR44050
Accommodations: 89
Pitches: 110
GPS: 47.08450, -2.03667
Post Code: F-44760

what3words:
horizontally.braved.envies

Contact:
info@chadotel.com
Tel: +33 2 40 82 76 95
www.chadotel.com

Open Dates:
Early April - Late September.

Camping Les Ecureuils

Close to the sea and the centre of the little village of La Bernerie, Camping Chadotel Les Ecureuils is a pleasant and spacious family-run site. The site has 110 touring pitches, all with 10A electricity close by and 19 with their water tap and drain. There are also 89 mobile homes and chalets for rent and a further 50 privately owned. There are many options on-site to keep everyone active while staying here. You will find an outdoor swimming pool complex with slides, a children's pool and a jacuzzi. There are many sports opportunities too with a multisport pitch, table tennis and pétanque area.

An animation team keeps everyone busy during high season with games, kids clubs and evening entertainment. The site is located just 350m from a sandy beach. Swimming is restricted to high tide as the sea goes out a long way and can be pretty dangerous. During low tide, a lagoon remains, perfect for young children.

Two toilet blocks have been renovated to an excellent standard, with controllable showers and washbasins in cubicles. En-suite accessible units. Baby rooms. Motorhome services. Bar with terrace, also selling bread, plus a snack bar and takeaway (July/Aug). Pool complex with heated leisure, swimming and paddling pools, water slides, and a flume (Seasonal). Renovated playground with trampolines. Kids club, Entertainment, EV Charging points, Tennis/multisports court. Communal barbecue area. WiFi over site (charged; free in bar).

Key Features

- Book Online
- Pets allowed
- Accessible Facilities
- Seaside Beach Nearby
- Indoor Pool on Site
- Childrens Play Area
- Bar on Site
- Bicycle Hire on Site

Find Out More
Visit ar.camp/fr44050
or scan the QR code.

📍 **Loire-Atlantique, Pays de la Loire**

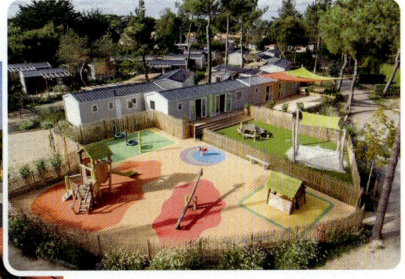

Camping Le Fief

Sunêlia Le Fief is in a wonderful setting just 900 metres from a vast sandy beach and the gently shelving waters of southern Brittany's Jade Coast, yet close to handy local amenities. The beautiful seaside resort of Saint-Brevin-Les-Pins is on the doorstep, making this an excellent choice for a family beach holiday with young children or lively teenagers. Le Fief is a well-established site, long a favourite for its magnificent aquapark with outdoor and covered swimming pools, paddling pools, slides, river rapids, fountains, jets and more. There's plenty of space for sun lounging, and the bar/restaurant terrace overlooks the whole complex. It's all very well thought through and run.

The site has 99 pitches for touring units, all of a good size (around 100 m sq) with 8A electricity, partly shaded, and with lush, well-established vegetation. There are also 227 mobile homes and chalets to rent and 39 privately owned units. An impressive Taos mobile home village includes a well-organised "Sunny Club" for children.

Accessible facilities, Bar, restaurant, takeaway. Shop. Pool complex with slides and various pools (Seasonal). Covered pool (All season). Wellness centre/spa. Play area. Padel tennis. Pétanque. Archery. Games room. Organised entertainment & children's activities (April/June weekends, High season daily). Bike hire. WiFi (Payable).

Alan Rogers Ref: FR44190
Accommodations: 227
Pitches: 99
GPS: 47.23486, -2.16757
Post Code: F-44250

what3words:
gazed.files.graceful

Contact:
camping@lefief.com
Tel: +33 2 40 27 23 86
www.camping-le-fief.com

Open Dates:
Early April - Late September.

Key Features

📅 Book Online

🐾 Pets allowed

♿ Accessible Facilities

🏖 Seaside Beach Nearby

🏊 Indoor Pool on Site

🛝 Childrens Play Area

🍸 Bar on Site

🚲 Bicycle Hire on Site

Find Out More
Visit **ar.camp/fr44190**
or scan the QR code.

📍 **Loire-Atlantique, Pays de la Loire**

Le Moulin de l'Eclis

Camping Sandaya Le Moulin de l'Eclis is an attractive, rural site with direct access to the picturesque Pont-Mahé beach. There are 183 pitches, of which around half are available for tourers, most with 10A electricity. Most pitches are of a generous size on grass and are divided by small trees and shrubs. Many tall pine trees provide good shade, and sunnier pitches can be found in the newer higher area of the campsite. This is an amicable and typically French site. A mixture of wooden chalets and traditional brick buildings house the facilities of a good standard.

Guests can access a large swimming pool complex with slides and a children's pool. The solar-heated pool with retractable cover is ideal when the weather is cooler at the start and end of the season. You can also use the on-site spa area with sauna and jacuzzi.

Three bright, modern, heated toilet blocks include some washbasins in cabins and large preset showers with dividers. A new block has family cabins and facilities for children. Good accessible facilities. Laundry facilities. A small shop sells fresh bread (Seasonal). Butcher's van calls in high season. Bar with snacks and takeaway (July/Aug). Covered solar-heated pool and paddling pool. Spa with sauna and jacuzzi, Play area. Entertainment, Kids club, Water sports. Free WiFi over part of the site.

Alan Rogers Ref: FR44330
Accommodations: 114
Pitches: 183
GPS: 47.44548, -2.45161
Post Code: F-44410

what3words:
memory.connect.wooed

Contact:
moulindeleclis@sandaya.fr
Tel: +33 2 40 01 76 69
www.sandaya.fr/nos-campings/moulin-de-l-eclis

Open Dates:
Early April - Late September.

Key Features

🗓 Book Online

🐾 Pets allowed

♿ Accessible Facilities

⛱ Seaside Beach on Site

〰 Indoor Pool on Site

🛝 Childrens Play Area

🍸 Bar on Site

🚲 Bicycle Hire on Site

Find Out More
Visit ar.camp/fr44330
or scan the QR code.

📍 **Loire-Atlantique, Pays de la Loire**

Camping le Deffay

A family-managed site, Camping le Deffay is a refreshing departure from the usual formula in that it is not over-organised or supervised and has no tour operator units. The 170 good-sized, fairly level pitches (103 for touring) have pleasant lake views. They are either on open grass, on shallow terraces divided by hedges, or informally arranged in a central, slightly sloping wooded area. All have 10A electricity. The site's landscaping is designed to blend harmoniously with the natural surroundings, and a large, well-stocked lake is available for fishing or kayaking.

The bar, restaurant, and covered pool are located within the old courtyard area of the smaller château, which dates from before 1400. The large, unfenced lake, which is well-stocked for fishermen and even has free pedalos for children, is a significant attraction of the site.

The main toilet block is well maintained, if a little dated, and is well equipped, including washbasins in cabins, Accessible facilities, and a baby bathroom. Laundry facilities. Shop. Bar and small restaurant with takeaway. Heated swimming pool with sliding cover and paddling pool (all season). Play area. TV. Entertainment in season, including mini club. Fishing and pedaloes on the lake. Torches useful. WiFi throughout (charged).

Alan Rogers Ref: FR44090
Accommodations: 58
Pitches: 170
GPS: 47.44106, -2.15981
Post Code: F-44160

what3words:
successes.plights.home

Contact:
info@camping-le-deffay.com
Tel: +33 2 40 88 00 57
www.camping-le-deffay.com

Open Dates:
Start May - End September.

Key Features

- Book Online
- Pets allowed
- Accessible Facilities
- Seaside Beach Nearby
- Indoor Pool on Site
- Childrens Play Area
- Bar on Site
- Bicycle Hire on Site

Find Out More
Visit ar.camp/fr44090
or scan the QR code.

📍 **Sarthe, Pays de la Loire**

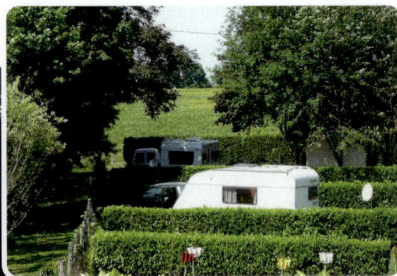

Alan Rogers Ref: FR72210
Accommodations: 23
Pitches: 50
GPS: 48.18917, -0.14120
Post Code: F-72140

what3words:
parodied.justice.numbing

Contact:
campinglestournesols@
orange.fr
Tel: +33 2 43 20 12 69
campinglestournesols.com

Open Dates:
Start May - End September.

Camping les Tournesols

Le Grez, Sarthe is home to Les Tournesols, a relatively small campsite with 50 touring pitches set under trees for well-needed shade. Everyone needs space to enjoy the great outdoors and a little relaxation; this campsite certainly offers this. This rural campsite is set in the Park Natural Régional Normandie-Maine, about 30km from Le Mans and 1km from Sille-le-Guillaume. There are two shower blocks, the newest featuring accessible facilities. There's also a snack bar and takeaway, with the town nearby offering a wider choice of bars.

Plenty of facilities are on-site, including an outdoor swimming pool, volleyball, boules, crazy golf, and an indoor activity area. You can also hire bicycles to explore the surrounding area. In high season, there is entertainment for the whole family to enjoy, from themed food nights to discos.

Sanitary block with accessible facilities in the same building, Bar, Snack bar, shop (Small) Takeaway (High season), Outdoor swimming pool, Children's playground, Entertainment (high season), Table tennis, Jeu de boules alley, crazy golf, WiFi, Pets allowed.

Key Features

📅 Book Online

🐾 Pets allowed

♿ Accessible Facilities

🏊 Outdoor Pool on Site

🛝 Childrens Play Area

🍸 Bar on Site

🚲 Bicycle Hire on Site

Find Out More
Visit ar.camp/fr72210
or scan the QR code.

Sarthe, Pays de la Loire

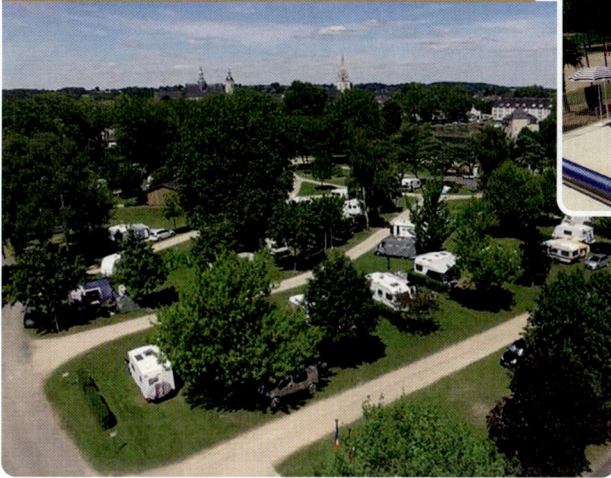

Camping la Route d'Or

This is a very busy site as La Flèche lies at the junction of the Le Mans-Angers and Laval-Saumur roads. Set in quiet, park-like surroundings on the south bank of the River Loir (not to be confused with the River Loire, a few miles to the south), the site is a pleasant stroll from the town centre, with plenty of shops and restaurants. There are 177 touring pitches marked out on flat grass, many in excess of 100 sq.m. and some with dividing hedges.

A further 17 pitches offer mobile homes to rent. Some are in the open park; others are shaded by tall trees. Electricity (10A) is available in all areas (long leads are frequently needed). There are 35 shady pitches with water and drainage and one overnight hardstand suitable for larger units or American RVs – phone in advance. The facilities on site are well maintained, and there are many activities to keep everyone occupied whilst staying here.

Two heated sanitary blocks, one older block with rather cramped showers, and British and squat-style WCs. The central block is more modern and includes a second unit with accessible facilities. An additional separate block with laundry can be heated in cool weather (available for use by other campers in winter). Motorhome services. Bakery service each morning. Swimming pool and paddling pool. Tennis. Boules. Play area. Pedalos and canoes for hire on the river. Bicycle hire (routes in English from reception). WiFi throughout (free). Twin axle caravans are not accepted.

Alan Rogers Ref: FR72010
Accommodations: 17
Pitches: 177
GPS: 47.69514, -0.07927
Post Code: F-72200

what3words:
handwriting.routines.quarrel

Contact:
info@camping-laroutedor.com
Tel: +33 2 43 94 55 90
www.camping-lafleche.com

Open Dates:
Mid March - Start November.

Key Features

- Book Online
- Pets allowed
- Accessible Facilities
- Outdoor Pool on Site
- Childrens Play Area
- Bicycle Hire on Site
- Fishing on Site

Find Out More
Visit ar.camp/fr72010
or scan the QR code.

📍 **Maine-et-Loire, Pays de la Loire**

Alan Rogers Ref: FR49040
Accommodations: 52
Pitches: 110
GPS: 47.36110, -0.43530
Post Code: F-49320

what3words:
streak.changer.inflecting

Contact:
info@campingetang.com
Tel: +33 2 41 91 70 61
www.campingetang.com

Open Dates:
End April - Start September.

⊙ **Alan Rogers Awards Won**
2023

Camping de l'Etang

At Camping de l'Etang, many of the 110 large, level touring pitches have pleasant views across the countryside. Separated and numbered, some have a little shade, and all have electricity (16A) with water and drainage nearby; 24 are fully serviced. A small bridge crosses the River Aubance, which runs through the site (well-fenced), and there are two lakes where free fishing can be enjoyed.

The site has a vineyard, and the wine produced can be purchased on the campsite. The adjacent Parc de Loisirs is a paradise for young children with many activities (discounts for campers). These include boating, pedaloes, pony rides, miniature trains, a water slide, a bouncy castle and swings. A Sites et Paysages campsite.

Three well-maintained toilet blocks provide all the usual facilities. Laundry facilities. Baby room. Accessible facilities. Motorhome services. The farmhouse houses the reception, a shop (all season) and takeaway snacks (seasonal) when the bar is closed. A bar/restaurant serves crêpes, salads, etc. (evenings July/Aug). Swimming pool (heated and covered) and paddling pool. Fishing. Play area. Bicycle hire. Wide variety of evening entertainment for families in high season. WiFi throughout (charged).

Key Features

📅 Book Online

🐾 Pets allowed

♿ Accessible Facilities

🏊 Indoor Pool on Site

🛝 Childrens Play Area

🍸 Bar on Site

🚲 Bicycle Hire on Site

🐟 Fishing on Site

Find Out More
Visit **ar.camp/fr49040**
or scan the QR code.

📍 **Maine-et-Loire, Pays de la Loire**

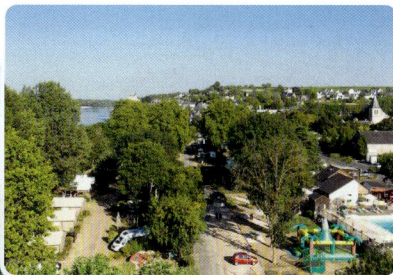

Camping l'Isle Verte

This friendly, natural site, with pitches overlooking the Loire River, is just 200 m. from the nearest shop, bar and restaurant in Montsoreau, making it an ideal base to explore the western Loire area. Low hedges separate most of the 114-shaded, level and good-sized touring pitches, but grass tends to be relatively sparse during dry spells. All have 16A electricity.

The campsite has a pleasant restaurant and bar offering various local dishes and quick takeaway food. The restaurant has a terrace partially covered during the summer and is a great area to enjoy summer evenings. You will also find a communal BBQ area to cook for yourself. The campsite offers wine tastings and a weekly market with local producers in July and August. Once a week, they also have a popular Guinguette evening where you can enjoy a traditional local meal, all while listening to live music. Opposite the bar and restaurant, you will find the heated outdoor swimming pool. In high season, an entertainment team also organises fun activities for kids to enjoy.

A modern, well-maintained building provides all necessary facilities, including accessible facilities. Baby room. Laundry facilities. Motorhome services. Bar and restaurant (Seasonal). Heated swimming and paddling pools (Seasonal). Small play area. Bouncy castle. Trampoline. Tennis. Boules. Fishing. Organised family activities. Live music in the summer, Boat launching. WiFi (charged).

Alan Rogers Ref: FR49090
Accommodations: 27
Pitches: 114
GPS: 47.21820, 0.05265
Post Code: F-49730

what3words:
seesaws.hark.softball

Contact:
contact@campingisleverte.com
Tel: +33 2 41 51 76 60
www.campingisleverte.com

Open Dates:
Early April - Early October.

◎ **Alan Rogers Awards Won**
2023

Key Features

🗓 Book Online

🐾 Pets allowed

♿ Accessible Facilities

🏊 Outdoor Pool on Site

🛝 Childrens Play Area

🍸 Bar on Site

🐟 Fishing on Site

Find Out More
Visit **ar.camp/fr49090**
or scan the QR code.

📍 Indre-et-Loire, Val de Loire

Alan Rogers Ref: FR37115
Accommodations: 15
Pitches: 128
GPS: 47.53926, 0.88480
Post Code: F-37110

what3words:
bling.lighthouses.helps

Contact:
orangeriedebeauregard@gmail.com
Tel: +33 9 51 40 51 43
orangeriedebeauregard.com

Open Dates:
Start June - Start September.

📍 **Alan Rogers Awards Won**
2023

Orangerie de Beauregard

You will find Castel Camping L'Orangerie de Beauregard set in an area of outstanding natural beauty in the heart of a property totalling 53 hectares of privately owned woodland and fields on the edge of the beautiful village 'fleuri' of Villedômer in the Loire valley. There are 128 touring pitches, most with electricity and water and 15 fixed accommodations comprising camping barrels, fully furnished glamping tents and wooden cabins, especially for cyclists. They also offer three gites for rent.

Many outdoor pursuits are available, from horse riding and cycling to walking and canoeing on the nearby Loire and Cher rivers. The pool is set in a stunning location in front of the Orangerie, and there are numerous game areas for children both indoors and out. A restaurant and a coffee shop sell home-cooked food, a mini-market with local produce and a Bar in the Orangerie.

Two sanitary blocks are equipped with showers, private washing cubicles, facilities for babies, and accessible facilities. Washing machines and dryers. Well-stocked shop. Bar, restaurant and coffee shop. Heated outdoor pool. All weather multisport pitch. Boules pitch. Indoor and outdoor table tennis tables. TV room. Indoor games hall. Children's outdoor playground. Bicycle hire, pony rides on site, and canoe trips nearby. During the high season, children's activities are supervised. Free WiFi in the communal areas.

Key Features

📅 Book Online

🐾 Pets allowed

♿ Accessible Facilities

🛝 Childrens Play Area

🍸 Bar on Site

🚲 Bicycle Hire on Site

⭕ Riding on Site

Find Out More
Visit ar.camp/fr37115
or scan the QR code.

Indre-et-Loire, Val de Loire

Camping le Moulin Fort

Camping le Moulin Fort is a tranquil riverside site with British owners John and Sarah Scarratt. The 130 pitches are enhanced by trees and shrubs, offering plenty of shade, and 115 pitches have electricity (6A). From the snack bar terrace adjacent to the restored mill building, a timber walkway over the mill race leads to the unheated swimming pool and paddling pools.

Although the river is unfenced, the site is ideal for couples and families with young children. There is occasional noise from trains passing on the river's opposite bank. Visitors will find information boards throughout the campsite about local nature (birds, fish, trees and shrubs) and the mill's history. The owners are keen to encourage recycling on the site.

Two toilet blocks with all the usual amenities are of a good standard and include washbasins in cubicles, baby baths and accessible facilities. Washing machines and dryer. Motorhome services. Shop (Seasonal). Bar, restaurant and takeaway (All seasonal, closed Wed. low season). Swimming pool (Seasonal). Excellent play area. Minigolf. Pétanque. Games room and TV. Library. Fishing. Bicycle hire. In high season, regular family entertainment includes wine tasting, quiz evenings, activities for children, light-hearted games, tournaments and live music events. Table tennis, Pool table, Outdoor fitness equipment. WiFi in the bar area (Charged).

Alan Rogers Ref: FR37030
Accommodations: 5
Pitches: 130
GPS: 47.32735, 1.08936
Post Code: F-37150

what3words:
lobbing.outnumber.averts

Contact:
contact@lemoulinfort.com
Tel: +33 2 47 23 86 22
www.lemoulinfort.com

Open Dates:
Late May - Late September.

Alan Rogers Awards Won
2017

Key Features

- Book Online
- Pets allowed
- Accessible Facilities
- Outdoor Pool on Site
- Childrens Play Area
- Bar on Site
- Bicycle Hire on Site
- Fishing on Site

Find Out More
Visit **ar.camp/fr37030**
or scan the QR code.

📍 **Eure-et-Loir, Val de Loire**

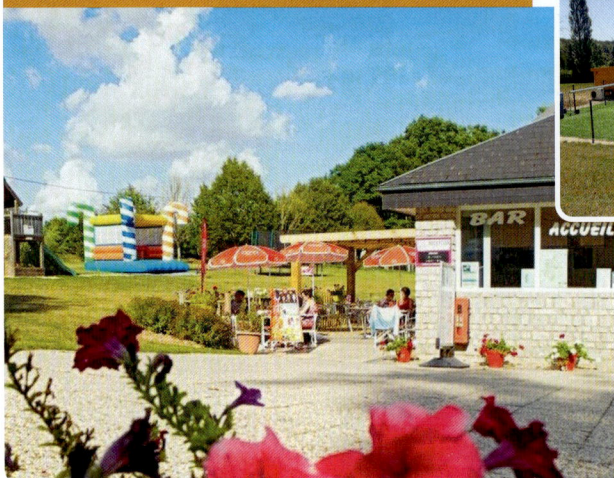

Camping le Bois Fleuri

The elegant city of Chartres is best known for its sublime cathedral, widely considered the finest Gothic cathedral in France and included on the UNESCO list of World Heritage sites. Le Bois Fleuri is a small, wooded site, 20 km. from Chartres, open for an extended season. There are 78 pitches in addition to 18 mobile homes to rent. Pitches range from 'Nature' (without electricity) to 'Grand Comfort' (large pitches with 10A electricity). The adjacent park has an attractive community swimming pool and various other amenities.

On-site, there is bicycle hire and a playground for children, Inflatable structures (depending on the weather), Swings, a slide, a football field, a Badminton court, Table tennis, Trampolines, a Sandpit pétanque court and a Ninja and Zipline course. Recently added to the campsite is an uncovered heated outdoor swimming pool and a mini golf course.

The sanitary block is fully tiled, with some washbasins in cabins and accessible facilities. Motorhome services. Small bar, takeaway (All season) and shop (July/Aug). Bread to order. The covered picnic area has a gas stove, table, and chairs. Play area and sandpit. Trampoline. Bouncy castle. TV room. Jacuzzi, Outdoor swimming pool, Mini golf, Bicycle hire. WiFi (free in the bar).

Alan Rogers Ref: FR28100
Accommodations: 18
Pitches: 78
GPS: 48.28611, 1.22742
Post Code: F-28120

what3words:
tastefully.outright.runes

Contact:
contact@camping-chartres.com
Tel: +33 2 37 24 03 04
www.camping-chartres.com

Open Dates:
Late April - End September.

Key Features

📅 Book Online

🐾 Pets allowed

♿ Accessible Facilities

🏊 Outdoor Pool on Site

🧗 Childrens Play Area

🍸 Bar on Site

🚲 Bicycle Hire on Site

🎣 Fishing on Site

Find Out More
Visit ar.camp/fr28100
or scan the QR code.

Loiret, Val de Loire

Alan Rogers Ref: FR45030
Accommodations: 26
Pitches: 200
GPS: 47.68229, 2.62315
Post Code: F-45500

what3words:
objectivity.boards.ingests

Contact:
info@camping-gien.com
Tel: +33 2 38 67 12 50
www.camping-gien.com

Open Dates:
Mid March - End October.

Camping de Gien

Sites et Paysages Camping Touristique de Gien is an open, attractive, well-cared-for site on the bank of the Loire with views of the town of Gien and its château. It has a long river frontage, which includes a good expanse of sandy beach. On the banks of the Loire, as you cross the bridge from Gien, turn right, and the site is just a short distance on the right; access is easy. There are 200 good-sized, level, grassy pitches, with 150 for touring. Mature trees shade some, and many have good views over the river. All have 10A electricity.

The bar and restaurant, with a pleasant outdoor area, are open to the public and meals are reasonably priced. Soirées with different themes are held weekly in July and August. This site is very close to Gien, and you can walk into the town where you have good rail links to Paris and Orleans; the site may be able to offer you a lift to the station or arrange a taxi. Or, of course, you could spend some time exploring this quintessential French market town and the surrounding area of the Loire.

Two unisex toilet blocks, one heated, are pretty basic but clean and have washbasins in cabins, controllable showers, accessible facilities, and a laundry. The bar and restaurant (Seasonal) are both open to the public. Swimming pool (with removable roof) and paddling pools (High season). Play area and grassed games area. Outdoor exercise equipment. Minigolf. Bicycle and pedal cart hire. Canoe hire. Fishing. Large sandy beach. Some organised activities (July/Aug). WiFi over site (Charged).

Key Features

- Book Online
- Pets allowed
- Accessible Facilities
- Indoor Pool on Site
- Childrens Play Area
- Bar on Site
- Bicycle Hire on Site
- Fishing on Site

Find Out More
Visit **ar.camp/fr45030**
or scan the QR code.

📍 La Barre-de-Monts, Vendée

Alan Rogers Ref: FR85840
Accommodations: 287
Pitches: 800
GPS: 46.88580, -2.14770
Post Code: F-85550

what3words:
unwavering.binging.reflectors

Contact:
vacances@sandaya.fr
Tel: +33 2 51 68 51 89
sandaya.co.uk/our-campsites/
la-grande-cote

Open Dates:
Mid May - Late September.

Camping La Grande Côte

A site that lives up to its name, Camping Sandaya La Grande Côte, is extensive with 800 pitches, of which 293 are numbered touring pitches in rows spread over undulating dunes with sparse grass under pine, all with 10A electricity and over 287 chalets and mobile homes to rent.

The site is served by eight relatively modern and fairly well-maintained toilet blocks. Some of the terraced pitches at the rear of the site have views of the impressive bridge onto the Ile de Noirmoutier, and there is direct access to a sandy beach via a gate. Some road noise is to be expected from the nearby bridge. Also on site is an outdoor heated swimming pool. In July and August, the site offers clubs for children of all ages, whilst adults can enjoy themed tapas, karaoke, cabaret, and aqua gym.

Eight toilet blocks, all of a similar design, include some washbasins in cubicles, seatless toilets, a baby bath, and a good accessible unit. Laundry room. Outdoor heated swimming pools, including one for children (Seasonal). Shop for bread and basics, bar and takeaway (High season). Playgrounds and bouncy castle. Games room. TV room. Entertainment and clubs for children (July/Aug). Multisports court. Boules. Minigolf. Bicycle hire. No charcoal barbecues (Communal areas provided). Supplement for twin-axle caravans. WiFi (Charged).

Key Features

🗓 Book Online

🐾 Pets allowed

♿ Accessible Facilities

⛱ Seaside Beach on Site

🏊 Outdoor Pool on Site

🛝 Childrens Play Area

🍸 Bar on Site

🚲 Bicycle Hire on Site

Find Out More
Visit **ar.camp/fr85840**
or scan the QR code.

Chauché, Vendée

Domaine de l'Oiselière

Domaine de l'Oiseliere is ideal for camping and campervan holidays and jsut 35 minutes from the Grand Parc du Puy du Fou. This is a small site with just 45 large pitches to choose from, 30 of which are for touring and are 200m2 and separated by hedges. There is a choice of full sun or shaded pitches with cover provided by oak trees. For families travelling in a caravan, large plots enable you to extend your awning easily. The site is a pedestrian zone; vehicles can drive to and from the pitches upon arrival and before departure. Otherwise, campers must use the adjacent parking area.

The campsite has a heated swimming pool and a paddling pool for the little ones. Children will enjoy the more than 3,000 m² play area, offering slides, swings and tunnels. Older children can test the giant zip line and the climbing net in the small woods, while the younger ones can visit the sheep on the mini-farm.

There is a single heated toilet block with showers, washbasins and WCs. Accessible sanitary facilities, Laundry with washing machines and dryers. Family bathroom. Dishwashing area. Children's play area. Motorhome aire. Zipline and climbing net. Outdoor swimming pool. Library. Animal farm. Lawned area. Hammock. Restaurant. Bar. Small shop. Access to a water point close to each pitch. Access to 10amp electrical hook-up point (European plugs). WiFi (Charged). The site does not accept twin-axle caravans. The earliest arrival time is 2 pm. Departure is before noon.

Alan Rogers Ref: FR85535
Accommodations: 35
Pitches: 45
GPS: 46.84099, -1.30087
Post Code: F-85140

what3words:
promptly.position.trembling

Contact:
contact@loiseliere.com
Tel: +33 2 51 41 38 74
www.loiseliere.com

Open Dates:
All year.

Key Features

📅 Book Online

📅 All Year

🐾 Pets allowed

♿ Accessible Facilities

🏊 Outdoor Pool on Site

🛝 Childrens Play Area

🍸 Bar on Site

🚴 Bicycle Hire on Site

Find Out More
Visit **ar.camp/fr85535**
or scan the QR code.

📍 **Saint Julien-des-Landes, Vendée**

Camping La Garangeoire

Castel Camping La Garangeoire is a stunning campsite situated some 15 km inland, near the village of Saint Julien-des-Landes. Set in 200 hectares of parkland surrounding the small château of la Garangeoire, of which there is an outstanding view as you approach through the gates. With a spacious, relaxed atmosphere, the main camping areas are on either side of the old road, edged with mature trees.

The 357 pitches (154 for touring), all named rather than numbered, are individually hedged, some with shade. They are well-spaced and are especially large (most 150-200 sq.m); 87 have electricity (16A, Europlug), 45 have water and drainage, and 4 have private WC/shower facilities.

Ample, first-class sanitary toilet facilities. All have washbasins in cabins and showers. Facilities for babies & accessible facilities. Laundry facilities. Motorhome services. Chemical toilet point. Shop, a full restaurant and takeaway with bars & terrace. Outdoor swimming lagoon and beach. The pool complex has a heated, covered pool, water slides, fountains, and a children's pool. Spa & well-being centre. Safe hire. Vending machine for still and sparkling water. Play field with play equipment. Football pitch. Games room. Dog shower. Tennis courts (charged July/Aug). Multisports court. Bicycle hire. Minigolf. Seasonal Archery and Riding. Fishing and Boating. Bouncy castle. Trampolines. Children's club. Only gas barbecues are allowed. Shuttle bus to the beach. WiFi on part of the site (free). Car hire. Evening entertainment (High season)

Alan Rogers Ref: FR85040
Accommodations: 58
Pitches: 154
GPS: 46.66365, -1.71340
Post Code: F-85150

what3words:
witty.calmed.rapids

Contact:
info@garangeoire.com
Tel: +33 2 51 46 65 39
camping-la-garangeoire.com

Open Dates:
Early May - Mid September.

◎ **Alan Rogers Awards Won**
2023

Key Features

📅 Book Online

🐾 Pets allowed

♿ Accessible Facilities

⛱ Seaside Beach Nearby

🏊 Outdoor Pool on Site

🛝 Childrens Play Area

🍸 Bar on Site

🚲 Bicycle Hire on Site

Find Out More
Visit **ar.camp/fr85040**
or scan the QR code.

📍 **La Tranche-sur-Mer, Vendée**

Camping La Belle Henriette

Camping La Belle Henriette has an impressive pool complex, a heated outdoor pool with a slide and paddling pool, and an indoor pool with a jacuzzi. The fine sandy beach is accessible 400m away by a magnificent wooden footbridge that spans the Belle Henriette Nature Reserve. The 33 touring pitches, all with 10A electricity (Europlug), are level and grassy; bushes hedge many, and a large variety of trees provide shade in places. Eighty-seven accommodation units are available to rent.

La Belle Henriette campsite is in an exceptional natural setting with miles of walking or cycling available. A free shuttle bus will take you to the city centre and the markets, going back and forth every hour from 10 a.m. to midnight.

The sanitary block provides washbasins and showers in cubicles with children's facilities, Washing machines and dryers. Restaurant (High season), Pizzeria Bar / Snack bar (High season), Kids club (High season), Outdoor children's play area, Table tennis, Multisport pitch, Entertainment (High season), WiFi, Petanque. Bicycle hire, Pets allowed.

Alan Rogers Ref: FR85021
Accommodations: 87
Pitches: 33
GPS: 46.34993, -1.37093
Post Code: F-85360

what3words:
///contracted.commitments.argues

Contact:
reservation@grouperomanee.com
Tel: +33 5 79 87 02 59
campingbellehenriette.com

Open Dates:
Early April - Late September.

Key Features

🐾 Pets allowed

⛱ Seaside Beach Nearby

🏊 Indoor Pool on Site

🛝 Childrens Play Area

🍸 Bar on Site

🚴 Bicycle Hire on Site

Find Out More
Visit **ar.camp/fr85021**
or scan the QR code.

📍 **Charente-Maritime, Poitou-Charentes**

Camping Séquoia Parc

Alan Rogers Ref: FR17140
Accommodations: 536
Pitches: 154
GPS: 45.81095, -1.06109
Post Code: F-17320

what3words:
expendable.trooping.waged

Contact:
vacances@sandaya.fr
Tel: +33 5 46 85 55 55
www.sandaya.fr

Open Dates:
Early April - Late September.

🎖 **Alan Rogers Awards Won**
2023, 2022, 2018

The overall winner of the Caravan and Motorhome Club Campsite of the Year Awards in 2023, Séquoia Parc, is just 7 km from the beach (Marennes-Plage). This is a high-quality family campsite in the heart of the Charente-Maritime region, set on the grounds of La Josephtrie, a castle with beautifully restored outbuildings and a courtyard area with a bar and restaurant.

The pitches are between 120 and 140m² with 6/10A electricity connections, separated by shrubs providing plenty of privacy. The site has mobile homes, chalets and fully equipped tents for up to 7 people. This is a popular site, and reservations are necessary for high season.

Three spotless toilet blocks include units with washbasins and showers. Accessible Facilities. Large laundry. Motorhome services. Supermarket with fresh bread. Restaurant/bar. Takeaway with wood oven pizzas. 2000 m² swimming pool complex with water slides, lazy river and large paddling pool. Wellness & Fitness Centre with indoor swimming pool, sauna, hammam and Jacuzzi. Massage rooms, spa treatments & fitness area with cardio & weight training equipment. Playgrounds. Multisports pitch. Tennis. Games & TV rooms. Bicycle & pedal-go-kart hire. Entertainment/excursions in high season. Free children's club for children from 4-12 years. Animal farm. Equestrian centre (seasonal). New playgrounds with zipline. WiFi zones (charged).

Key Features

📅 Book Online

🐾 Pets allowed

♿ Accessible Facilities

⛱ Seaside Beach Nearby

🏊 Indoor Pool on Site

🎠 Childrens Play Area

🍸 Bar on Site

🚲 Bicycle Hire on Site

Find Out More
Visit **ar.camp/fr17140**
or scan the QR code.

Camping Îl De Ré

Camping at Seasonova Île de Ré, you are right by the beach when staying on this scenic site, just 200 metres from the sands of La Plage du Groc Jonc. Start your island day with a French breakfast using the handy croissant and pain au chocolat ordering service at reception before heading out to explore. Perhaps opt for a day on-site, lazing around the grounds and enjoying a spot of yoga. There is a bar to lounge around at, too – or you could bag up your supplies to take to the beach.

The local town Les Portes-en-Ré is less than half a kilometre away; a trip to the daily market in Freedom Square will add oysters to your alfresco haul, too. A food takeaway van visits the site twice a week. The site has 108 pitches, all with electric hook-ups. Also, there are 21 units to rent.

The toilet block provides showers, washbasins & WCs. Accessible facilities. Laundry. Drying room. Chemical toilet point. Shop. Wi-Fi charged. Bar. Takeaway. Beach nearby. Motorhome service point. Tourist information office adjacent. Children's play area. Late-night arrivals area. Dogs allowed. Cycle hire. Three kids' clubs on the nearby beach. Twin axle vehicles are not permitted on site. No arrivals before 16.00. Small supermarket adjacent.

Alan Rogers Ref: FR17880
Accommodations: 21
Pitches: 108
GPS: 46.24841, -1.49283
Post Code: F-17880

what3words:
unedited.beware.twiddle

Contact:
camping.seasonova.iledere@gmail.com
Tel: +33 5 46 29 51 04
www.vacances-seasonova.com

Open Dates:
Early April - End October.

Alan Rogers Awards Won
2023

Key Features

- Book Online
- Pets allowed
- Accessible Facilities
- Seaside Beach Nearby
- Childrens Play Area
- Bar on Site
- Bicycle Hire on Site

Find Out More
Visit **ar.camp/fr17880**
or scan the QR code.

📍 **Vienne, Poitou-Charentes**

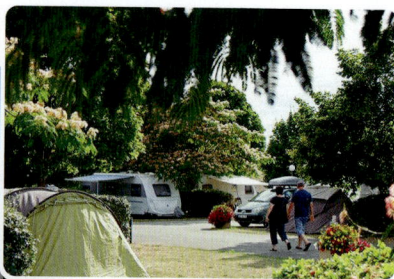

Alan Rogers Ref: FR86040
Accommodations: 16
Pitches: 123
GPS: 46.66447, 0.39456
Post Code: F-86130

what3words:
avenge.endears.airstrip

Contact:
camping-le-futuriste@
wanadoo.fr
Tel: +33 5 49 52 47 52
www.camping-le-futuriste.fr

Open Dates:
All year.

Camping le Futuriste

Le Futuriste is a neat, modern site, open all year and very close to Futuroscope. Its location is also very convenient for the A10 and N10 motorway network. There is a total of 123 individual, level, grassy pitches of a generous size, divided by flowering hedges, 74 with 6A electricity and 55 with water. There are also six chalets and ten mobile homes to rent.

The large pitches mostly have the benefit of shade from trees. All are accessed via tarmac roads. This site has lovely panoramic views, and the popular attraction of Futuroscope can be seen across the valley. Large units are accepted by prior arrangement.

Excellent, clean, sanitary facilities in two heated blocks. Good accessible facilities. Laundry facilities. Shop (Seasonal, bread to order). Bar/restaurant snack bar and takeaway (July/Aug). Heated pool with slide and paddling pool (July/Aug). Covered pool (Seasonal). Games room. Boules. Multisports area. Table tennis, Lake fishing. Daily activities in high season. Youth groups are not accepted. Only gas and electric barbecues are allowed. WiFi throughout (charged). Pets allowed.

Key Features

📅 Book Online

📅 All Year

🐾 Pets allowed

♿ Accessible Facilities

🧗 Childrens Play Area

🍸 Bar on Site

🐟 Fishing on Site

Find Out More
Visit ar.camp/fr86040
or scan the QR code.

Charente, Poitou-Charentes

Les Gorges du Chambon

Les Gorges du Chambon is a wonderful site with 28 hectares of protected natural environment in the rolling Perigord Vert countryside. Of the 132 pitches, the 92 for touring are incredibly generous in size (150 sq.m), some level, others on a gentle slope, and they enjoy a mixture of sunshine and shade.

This spacious site offers fine walks through the woodlands and around the grounds. Flora and fauna are as nature intended. Here, you can feel at peace and enjoy precious moments of quiet. Much work has been done with the ecology association. The songs of the birds can be heard against the backdrop of water flowing gently down a small river on one side of the campsite. A wide variety of birds can be seen around the site.

Traditional-style sanitary blocks include accessible facilities. Washing machine, dryer. Shop stocks regional produce and groceries. Bar, restaurant (All season). Takeaway (all season). Modern swimming pool (All season, heated with slides), children's pool. Large play area. Games room, TV and library with English books. Pony riding and Yoga (July/Aug). Table Tennis. Minigolf. Volleyball. Multisports pitch. Bicycle hire. Beach, Fishing in the river. Canoe hire nearby. Organised activities (July/Aug), children's club, and youth disco. WiFi (Charged).

Alan Rogers Ref: FR16020
Accommodations: 37
Pitches: 132
GPS: 45.65980, 0.55767
Post Code: F-16220

what3words:
adored.packers.drool

Contact:
gorges-chambon@koawa.com
Tel: +33 5 45 70 71 70
www.camping-gorges-chambon.fr

Open Dates:
Mid April - Mid September.

Key Features

- Book Online
- Pets allowed
- Accessible Facilities
- Outdoor Pool on Site
- Childrens Play Area
- Bar on Site
- Bicycle Hire on Site
- Fishing on Site

Find Out More
Visit **ar.camp/fr16020**
or scan the QR code.

📍 Yonne, Burgundy

Alan Rogers Ref: FR89110
Accommodations: 17
Pitches: 115
GPS: 47.51683, 3.47916
Post Code: F-89480

what3words:
quieter.fizzles.soreness

Contact:
info@campingauboisjoli.com
Tel: +33 3 86 81 70 48
www.campingauboisjoli.com

Open Dates:
Start April - Start October.

Camping Au Bois Joli

Sites et Paysages Au Bois Joli is located near Andryes, in Burgundy's heart, nestled in over 4.5 hectares of forest and meadow. The campsite has 115 pitches with electrical hook-up points available. All are shaded with mature trees and are separated by hedges, giving privacy to neighbours. The site also has 17 rental accommodations available to hire.

This campsite is ideal for families with young children, one of the sanitary buildings is equipped with smaller toilets and sinks where children can brush their teeth. The campsite has several play areas. The main play area has a zip line, trampoline, slide and a swing. An animation team runs a children's club four times a week with plenty of activities for kids to get stuck into. Not forgetting the adults, there are themed evenings held twice a week during high season at the campsite bar and restaurant. The restaurant offers a variety of options to eat in or take away. You will discover different dishes every day, as well as r regional dishes adapted according to the weather.

Family Sanitary facilities, Restaurant, Bar, Small shop, Takeaway pizza, Communal BBQ area, Heated outdoor swimming pool, children's pool, Children's Playground, Entertainment programme (High season), Kids Club (High season), Table tennis, Multi-sports pitch, Dog allowed. WiFi.

Key Features

🗓 Book Online

🐾 Pets allowed

♨ Outdoor Pool on Site

🛝 Childrens Play Area

🍸 Bar on Site

Find Out More
Visit **ar.camp/fr89110**
or scan the QR code.

Nièvre, Burgundy

Camping le Manoir de Bezolle

Alan Rogers Ref: FR58030
Accommodations: 23
Pitches: 74
GPS: 47.05732, 3.81547
Post Code: F-58110

what3words:
deep.tracers.transitional

Contact:
campingmanoirdebezolle@orange.fr
Tel: +33 3 86 84 42 55
campingmanoirdebezolle.com

Open Dates:
Start April - End September.

From the terraces of Le Manoir de Bezolle, you can admire the peaceful hills of the Morvan Natural Park, which give all their charm to Burgundy, ideally positioned at the crossroads of 4 large cities, Dijon, Auxerre, Bourges, Macon, and only 3 hours from Paris. This superb, landscaped site will be the ideal starting point to discover what the Morvan and Burgundy offer.

The campsite offers two large outdoor swimming pools, which are surprisingly large considering the size of this campsite, so there is plenty of room for a swim when the site is at capacity. There is also a small children's swimming pool. A grassed sunbathing area surrounds the pools. In addition to the swimming pool, other on-site activities include table tennis, mini golf, a children's playground and an animal farm. There is also a restaurant on site which offers a selection of local dishes and, during high season, sometimes holds a paella evening and live music.

Three toilet blocks provide Showers, Washbasins and WCs. Accessible facilities. Baby room. Dishwashing area. Laundry with washing machine and tumble dryer. Motorhome service point. 2 outdoor swimming pools. Children's pool. Table tennis. Boules. Children's play area. Trampoline. Mini golf. Badminton. Billiards. Table football. Walking and cycling trails. Fishing pond. Children's Farm. Restaurant. Bar. Bread to order. Supermarket 11 km. Shop. WiFi free. Pets allowed.

Key Features

- Book Online
- Pets allowed
- Accessible Facilities
- Outdoor Pool on Site
- Childrens Play Area
- Bar on Site
- Fishing on Site

Find Out More
Visit **ar.camp/fr58030**
or scan the QR code.

127

📍 **Saône-et-Loire, Burgundy**

Du Pont de Bourgogne

Camping du Pont de Bourgogne is a well-presented and cared-for site, useful for an overnight or extended stay to explore the local area. It is close to the A6 autoroute, and the attractive market town of Châlon-sur-Saône is within 2 km. The site is over 3.3ha with 100 mainly level pitches (90 sq.m), all with 10A Europlug, most on grass, but 30 have a gravel surface. Pitches are large, well spaced out, separated by beech hedging, and a variety of mature trees provide shade. Many pitches overlook the river, an excellent spot to watch the passing boats, and a cycle route runs alongside. Access is easy for large outfits.

The sanitary facilities are clean and modern and cater for the entire family. There are also ten mobile homes to rent on-site. The bar, restaurant and terrace are close to the entrance and overlook the river. Across the river is a large municipal swimming pool, and a golf club and sailing club are within 1 km. Takeaway meals are available from the bar all season, but the restaurant is open only in July and August.

Three sanitary blocks, two of which are superb modern buildings, are kept very clean and have high-quality fittings, including a children's bathroom, an accessible bathroom and a family shower. Motorhome services. Laundry facilities. There is no shop, but essentials are kept in the bar (bread to order). Modern bar/restaurant (July/Aug). Simple play area. Bicycle hire arranged. WiFi (free in the bar). Chalets for rent, one adapted for those with reduced mobility.

Alan Rogers Ref: FR71140
Accommodations: 10
Pitches: 100
GPS: 46.78448, 4.87295
Post Code: F-71380

what3words:
parks.clerics.motion

Contact:
campingchalon71@wanadoo.fr
Tel: +33 3 85 48 26 86
www.camping-chalon.com

Open Dates:
Start April - End September.

Key Features

📅 Book Online

🐾 Pets allowed

♿ Accessible Facilities

🚼 Childrens Play Area

🍸 Bar on Site

🚲 Bicycle Hire on Site

🐟 Fishing on Site

Find Out More
Visit **ar.camp/fr71140**
or scan the QR code.

Saône-et-Loire, Burgundy

Château de l'Epervière

Castel Camping Château de l'Epervière is a popular high-quality site peacefully situated on the wooded grounds of a 16th-century château close to the A6 and near the village of Gigny-sur-Saône. It is a beautiful site surrounded by the vineyards of Southern Burgundy. Access to the site is good, and English is spoken at reception. Upon arrival, you will be impressed by the building and its surroundings, and as you drive down by the fishing lake over a long bridge to your pitch, you see the extent of the Chateau's grounds.

There are 160 pitches arranged over two areas separated by a small fishing lake. All have 10A electricity, some are on hard standing, and 96 are fully serviced. Pitches are large and well-spaced, some with shade, others open; specify your requirements when checking in. There are modern facilities around the site, but the pool, shop, cycle hire, and restaurant and wine-tasting events are all within the confines of the Chateau.

Two well-equipped, spotless toilet blocks with all necessary facilities, including those for babies and accessible facilities. Washing machine/dryer. Motorhome services. Restaurant with a good menu, takeaway, and basic shop (all seasonal). Cellar with wine tasting. Converted barn with bar, large TV. Outdoor swimming pool and paddling pool with slides (Heated seasonally) partly enclosed by old stone walls. Smaller indoor heated pool (All season). Children's play area, multi-sports pitch, mini farm, fishing lake, wine tasting evenings and cycle hire. Free WiFi in the bar area.

Alan Rogers Ref: FR71070
Accommodations: 3
Pitches: 160
GPS: 46.65485, 4.94463
Post Code: F-71240

what3words:
guarding.recited.hooves

Contact:
info@domaine-eperviere.com
Tel: +33 3 85 94 16 90
www.domaine-eperviere.com

Open Dates:
Start April - End September.

Key Features

- Book Online
- Pets allowed
- Accessible Facilities
- Indoor Pool on Site
- Childrens Play Area
- Bar on Site
- Bicycle Hire on Site
- Fishing on Site

Find Out More
Visit ar.camp/fr71070
or scan the QR code.

📍 Jura, Franche-Comté

Alan Rogers Ref: FR39010
Accommodations: 30
Pitches: 218
GPS: 47.00284, 5.66300
Post Code: F-39380

what3words:
limped.scratching.vegetables

Contact:
plageblanche@huttopia.com
Tel: +33 3 84 37 69 63
www.europe.huttopia.com/en/
site/la-plage-blanche

Open Dates:
Late April - Late September.

La Plage Blanche

Huttopia La Plage Blanche is located in the Jura, by the rippling waters of the River Loue. This spacious eight-hectare site has 218 pitches (171 for touring, 40 on the riverbank). All are large, grassy and level with 10A electricity (Europlugs).

This is an excellent site for family holidays with its children's activities and themed evenings in the bar/restaurant (DJ or live music) in high season. Other activities include kayaking, canoeing, fishing, fly fishing and woodland walks in the campsite's woods. Several distinctive safari-style tents are available to rent. At low water levels the river provides an ideal setting for children to swim and play safely in the gently flowing, shallow water.

Three sanitary blocks include showers, washbasins in cabins, facilities for babies, and accessible facilities. Launderette. Motorhome service area. Shop with basics. Bar/snack bar/pizzeria with terrace. Takeaway. Heated swimming and paddling pools (All season). Adults-only spa with a small pool, jacuzzi and sauna. Play area. Entertainment and activities for children and families. TV room. Library. Volleyball. Boules. River fishing and fishing lake. Woodland walks. Canoeing. WiFi (Free).

Key Features

📅 Book Online

🐾 Pets allowed

♿ Accessible Facilities

🏊 Outdoor Pool on Site

🛝 Childrens Play Area

🍸 Bar on Site

🐟 Fishing on Site

Find Out More
Visit **ar.camp/fr39010**
or scan the QR code.

Doubs, Franche-Comté

Alan Rogers Ref: FR25090
Accommodations: 13
Pitches: 61
GPS: 46.95974, 6.13289
Post Code: F-25270

what3words:
devout.amazing.couched

Contact:
camping@camping-dela-foret.com
Tel: +33 3 81 89 53 46
www.camping-dela-foret.com

Open Dates:
End April- Mid September.

Camping de la Forêt

In the heart of the Jura Mountains and one of the most extensive fir forests in Europe, between Doubs and Loue, you will be charmed by this campsite in Franche-Comté. Camping de la Forêt is in a unique rural setting on the forest's edge. The campsite has 61 marked touring pitches with electric hook-up points available; these are surrounded by mature trees offering plenty of shade during the summer months.

On-site facilities include a children's playground and an outdoor swimming pool at the front of the site to maintain an atmosphere of peace and nature. The campsite also has a large sports field perfect for football, volleyball and badminton. There are also table tennis tables, table football and a loan of board games at the campsite. During the summer, the campsite restaurants offer various meals throughout the day. A fresh bread and pastry service is also available every morning.

One Heated sanitary block with children's facilities, Laundry facilities, Bar, Restaurant (Limited), snack bar, Shop (Small), Sports field, Table tennis, Outdoor swimming pool, Boules, WiFi, Pets allowed, Entertainment (High season)

Key Features

- Book Online
- Pets allowed
- Outdoor Pool on Site
- Childrens Play Area
- Bar on Site

Find Out More
Visit **ar.camp/fr25090**
or scan the QR code.

📍 **Jura, Franche-Comté**

Alan Rogers Ref: FR39280
Accommodations: 35
Pitches: 188
GPS: 46.74676, 5.89904
Post Code: F-39300

what3words:
profited.aptness.halved

Contact:
contact@camping-boyse.com
Tel: +33 3 84 52 00 32
www.camping-boyse.com

Open Dates:
Start April- Mid September.

Camping de Boÿse

Access to this site is excellent, and a little English is spoken. The site is large and spacious, set on the river Ain's banks, where a small beach and swimming, boating, and fishing can be enjoyed. There are 35 cabins and chalets for rent and 188 spacious pitches, with 115 having EHU, and tents are very welcome. Facilities are modern and clean, and an open-air heated swimming pool is on-site. You are only a 5-minute walk from a supermarket and 90 meters from the city centre.

Plenty of activities at the campsite include A multi-sports field, Children's playground, tennis and volleyball. Petanque lovers will enjoy weekly competitions with other campers, and there are also Ping pong tables and mini golf where you can hire equipment at the campsite's reception. Around the campsite, you can go canoeing, canyoning, hiking, and fishing on an adventure course in Salins-les-Bains or test yourself on the via Ferrata.

Accessible sanitary facilities, Restaurant, Bar, Snack Bar, Pizzeria, Takeaway meals, Outdoor swimming pool, Entertainment, Children's playground, Games room, crazy golf, Table tennis, Multisport field, Jeu de boules alley, Fishing, TV, Pets allowed, WiFi.

Key Features

📅 Book Online

🐾 Pets allowed

♿ Accessible Facilities

🏊 Outdoor Pool on Site

🛝 Childrens Play Area

🍸 Bar on Site

🐟 Fishing on Site

Find Out More
Visit ar.camp/fr39280
or scan the QR code.

Jura, Franche-Comté

Alan Rogers Ref: FR39140
Accommodations: 73
Pitches: 156
GPS: 46.58715, 5.69541
Post Code: F-39130

what3words:
coursed.tame.reached

Contact:
contact@camping-pecheurs.com
Tel: +33 3 84 48 31 33
www.camping-pecheurs.com

Open Dates:
Early May - Mid September.

Camping des Pêcheurs

Des Pecheurs has the advantage of being in the town and within walking distance of all its services. It is also a fairly level site and is more suited to motorhomes than other sites in the area. The mobile home and seasonal pitch areas are on the upper terrace; the touring area is on the lower. There are 156 touring pitches, and most have 6A electricity hook-ups (Europlug, long leads may be required). A riverside site, it is popular with fishermen and those looking to take a freshwater swim or explore the area via the water using a kayak.

Other on-site facilities include an outdoor swimming pool and a small children's pool with a fountain. There are plenty of activities to keep the children active as they can make use of the multisport court, children's playground and table tennis. A children's club with creative crafts and activities during the high season also exists. There is some entertainment for adults, such as live music occasionally held by the pool area in the evenings.

Two unisex sanitary blocks have some shower and washbasin units and accessible facilities. Private sanitary facilities are available on premium pitches, Washing machines and dryers. Sink for fish preparation outside. Bar and takeaway (High season). Outdoor covered swimming pool, Children's pool, Boules. Fishing. Small play area. Multisport ground, Table tennis, Children's club (5-12 yrs, High season). Entertainment, EV charging points, and WiFi (Charged).

Key Features

- Book Online
- Accessible Facilities
- Outdoor Pool on Site
- Childrens Play Area
- Bar on Site
- Fishing on Site

Find Out More
Visit ar.camp/fr39140
or scan the QR code.

📍 **Haute-Vienne, Limousin**

Alan Rogers Ref: FR87090
Accommodations: 22
Pitches: 107
GPS: 45.63502, 1.16058
Post Code: F-87800

what3words:
mutant.veered.subdivision

Contact:
campinglairdulac@
flowercampings.com
Tel: +33 5 55 58 79 18
www.campinglairdulac.com

Open Dates:
Start June - Mid October.

Camping l'Air du Lac

Saint Hilaire-les-Places is a pretty village famous for its floral displays. It can be found at 28 km. South of Limoges, best known for its fine porcelain and Gothic cathedral, is an ideal base for exploring the Limousin region. The site forms part of a 31-hectare recreation area and has 107 pitches, of which 84 are reserved for tourers, all of which are of good size and have electric hook-up points available. Most are separated by hedges, allowing privacy, and mature trees give much-needed shade during summer. Other pitches are occupied by mobile homes and chalets (available to rent)

The campsite has direct access to a large lake with a water slide and a diving platform from which you can jump from various heights. The lake also offers multiple activities, such as windsurfing, kayaking, and pedal boating. Other on-site activities include mini golf, a children's playground, beach volleyball, and an indoor games room. The campsite's lakeside restaurant offers various dishes if all the day activities work up an appetite. A daily bread service can also be picked up from the campsite shop.

Two toilet blocks are clean and have open-style washbasins, preset showers and facilities for children and accessible facilities. Washing machines and dryer. Small shop in reception. Lakeside bar and snack bar (May-Sept). Play area. Minigolf. Games room. Fishing. WiFi (charged).

Key Features

📅 Book Online

🐾 Pets allowed

♿ Accessible Facilities

🛝 Childrens Play Area

🍸 Bar on Site

🎣 Fishing on Site

Find Out More
Visit ar.camp/fr87090
or scan the QR code.

Haute-Vienne, Limousin

Alan Rogers Ref: FR87020
Accommodations: 2
Pitches: 78
GPS: 45.93299, 1.29006
Post Code: F-87270

what3words:
soundest.remix.delivered

Contact:
contact@leychoisier.com
Tel: +33 5 55 39 93 43
www.leychoisier.com

Open Dates:
Mid April - Mid September.

Le Château de Leychoisier

You will receive a warm welcome at the beautiful, family-run site Castel Camping le Château de Leychoisier. It offers peace in superb surroundings. It is ideally situated for short or long stays, only 2 km. from the A20 and 10 km. north of Limoges.

The large, slightly sloping and grassy pitches are in a parkland setting with many magnificent mature trees offering varying shade. The 78 touring pitches have 10A electricity, and many have a tap. The small heated swimming pool with sunbathing area is accessed through the reception and bar, and the restaurant serves high-quality, freshly prepared meals.

The sanitary block is very clean, with separate accessible facilities. Some washbasins in cabins. Family bathroom. Washing machine and dryer. Basic grocery provisions (Bread can be ordered daily). Restaurant, bar, TV room, small heated swimming pool with sunbathing area (All season). Lake. Fishing. Play area. Tennis and boules courts. Torch useful. WiFi (Charged).

Key Features

- Book Online
- Pets allowed
- Accessible Facilities
- Outdoor Pool on Site
- Childrens Play Area
- Bar on Site
- Fishing on Site

Find Out More
Visit **ar.camp/fr87020**
or scan the QR code.

📍 **Creuse, Limousin**

Le Château de Poinsouze

Le Château de Poinsouze is a well-established site arranged on an open, gently sloping, grassy park with views over a small lake and château. It is an attractive, well-maintained, high-quality site in the unspoilt Limousin region.

The 113 very large (120m²-300m²) grassy touring pitches, some with lake frontage, all have electricity (6-20A Europlug), water and drainage, and 57 have sewerage connections. The site has a friendly, family atmosphere with many organised activities in the main season, including a children's club. There are marked walks around the park and woods. All facilities are open all season.

High-quality sanitary units include accessible facilities located centrally on-site. Facilities for babies. Washing machines and dryers. Motorhome services. Shop for basics. Takeaway. Bar and restaurant. Swimming pool, slide, children's pool and new water play area with fountains. Fenced playground. Entertainment, Kids club, Pétanque. Bicycle hire. Free fishing in the lake, boats and lifejackets can be hired. Sports facilities. Table tennis, Petting farm, Accommodation to rent (Pets not accepted). WiFi over site (Charged). No dogs in high season (Early July to Late August).

Alan Rogers Ref: FR23010
Accommodations: 31
Pitches: 113
GPS: 46.37243, 2.20268
Post Code: F-23600

what3words:
mozzarella.databases.crikey

Contact:
campingpoinsouze@gmail.com
Tel: +33 5 55 65 02 21
camping-de-poinsouze.com

Open Dates:
Early May - Early September.

Key Features

- Book Online
- Pets allowed
- Accessible Facilities
- Outdoor Pool on Site
- Childrens Play Area
- Bar on Site
- Bicycle Hire on Site
- Fishing on Site

Find Out More
Visit **ar.camp/fr23010**
or scan the QR code.

Corrèze, Limousin

Beaulieu sur Dordogne

Huttopia Beaulieu sur Dordogne is an enjoyable and well-equipped site on a beautiful small island in the River Dordogne, only two minutes from the centre of the medieval town of Beaulieu-sur-Dordogne, with its ancient streets, old churches, and many shops and restaurants. This seven-hectare site has 185 shady grass pitches and 144 available for touring, all with 10A electricity. These are spread across the site over mowed lawns and under tall trees, providing shade during the hot summer weather.

The campsite's swimming pool is large and has a small children's pool with play equipment. There are also loungers and umbrellas to relax under and for those who want to watch their children while they enjoy the water. During the season, there are plenty of activities for young and old alike. There is a climbing wall for those who wish to face their fear of heights, and plenty of activities and creative crafts are held throughout the day. The campsite also provides a restaurant and bar which offers various food options and overlooks the swimming pool.

Three modern, clean toilet blocks. Accessible facilities, Baby room. Laundry room. Motorhome services. Small shop for basics with local produce and bread to order. Heated pool (May-Sept), poolside bar, snacks. Boules. Canoe hire can be arranged. Fishing. Children's entertainment (3-12 yrs) 4 days per week. Evening soirées (2 evenings per week in July/Aug). WiFi.

Alan Rogers Ref: FR19130
Accommodations: 42
Pitches: 185
GPS: 44.97971, 1.84015
Post Code: F-19120

what3words:
finite.genre.midgets

Contact:
beaulieu@huttopia.com
Tel: +33 5 55 91 02 65
europe.huttopia.com/site/camping-beaulieu-sur-dordogne

Open Dates:
Late April - Late September.

Alan Rogers Awards Won
2023

Key Features

- Book Online
- Pets allowed
- Accessible Facilities
- Outdoor Pool on Site
- Childrens Play Area
- Bar on Site
- Bicycle Hire on Site
- Fishing on Site

Find Out More
Visit ar.camp/fr19130
or scan the QR code.

📍 **Puy-de-Dôme, Auvergne**

Alan Rogers Ref: FR63050
Accommodations: 260
Pitches: 450
GPS: 45.56251, 2.93852
Post Code: F-63790

what3words:
handier.expectancy.clauses

Contact:
vacances@sandaya.fr
Tel: +33 4 73 88 64 29
www.sandaya.co.uk/our-campsites/la-ribeyre

Open Dates:
Early May- Late September.

Camping La Ribeyre

At the heart of the Auvergne, only 35 km to the South of Clermont-Ferrand and 12 km from Besse St. Anastaise, much care has been put into the spacious Sandaya la Ribeyre campsite. This unique 5-star campsite offers around 450 level, grassy pitches, of which around 200 are for tourers, and 108 have electricity (6/10A). Electricity, water and drainage are available on some pitches. They also offer a wide range of mobile homes for rent.

A superb large indoor/outdoor water park includes slides, toboggan and lazy river. A small artificial lake at one end of the campsite provides facilities for water sports. It is an excellent base for touring, being only 1 km. from Murol, dominated by its ancient château, 6 km. from Saint Nectaire and about 20 km. from Le Mont Dore and Puy-de-Sancy, the highest peak in the area.

Five sanitary blocks have showers, private washing cubicles and baby facilities. Accessible facilities, Washing machines and dryers. Bar. Snack bar. Large indoor/outdoor water park (heated July/Aug). TV. Games room. Tennis. Sports facilities, Fishing. Lake swimming and canoeing. Many organised activities in high season. Children's club (6 to 12 years) is free in high season. WiFi (charged).

Key Features

🗓 Book Online

🐾 Pets allowed

♿ Accessible Facilities

♨ Indoor Pool on Site

🛝 Childrens Play Area

🍸 Bar on Site

🚲 Bicycle Hire on Site

Find Out More
Visit ar.camp/fr63050
or scan the QR code.

Haute-Loire, Auvergne

Camping de Vaubarlet

Expect a warm welcome at Sites et Paysages de Vaubarlet, a peaceful and spacious family-run site. Located in a beautiful riverside setting, it has 131 marked, level, grassy pitches, with those around the perimeter having shade (young trees and shrubs separate the large pitches). The family has made great efforts to ensure all guests benefit equally from its facilities.

There are 92 pitches, all with 16A electricity for touring units. The remaining places are occupied by site-owned tents and mobile homes, including two fully equipped for those with reduced mobility. Excellent, accessible facilities for guests, including an electric buggy, hoist to assist entry into the pool and well-equipped sanitary facilities.

Very good, clean toilet blocks include a baby room. There are two family bathrooms that double as accessible facilities. Washing machine, dryer. Small shop, bread. Bar, restaurant and takeaway (mid-May - mid-Sept). Attractive swimming pool, children's pool. Separate solarium. Boules. Extensive riverside grass games area. Playground. Activities in season include campfire, music evenings, and children's canoe lessons. Kids club, Trout fishing. Birdwatching. WiFi (free).

Alan Rogers Ref: FR43030
Accommodations: 30
Pitches: 92
GPS: 45.21630, 4.21240
Post Code: F-43600

what3words:
postage.settlers.effaced

Contact:
campingdevaubarlet@gmail.com
Tel: +33 4 71 66 64 95
www.vaubarlet.com

Open Dates:
Start May - End September.

Key Features

📅 Book Online

🐾 Pets allowed

♿ Accessible Facilities

🌊 Outdoor Pool on Site

🛝 Childrens Play Area

🍸 Bar on Site

🐟 Fishing on Site

Find Out More
Visit **ar.camp/fr43030**
or scan the QR code.

📍 **Rhône, Rhône Alpes**

Alan Rogers Ref: FR69010
Accommodations: 74
Pitches: 159
GPS: 45.81974, 4.76120
Post Code: F-69570

what3words:
impulse.clocks.forecast

Contact:
lyon@camping-indigo.com
Tel: +33 4 78 35 64 55
www.camping-lyon.com

Open Dates:
All year.

Camping de Lyon

This is a short stay, city site just off the A6 autoroute and within easy reach of Lyon centre. Kept busy with overnight trade, the reception and the café (in July and August) is open until quite late. There are 159 separate numbered plots, all with 6/10A electricity, and 140 of these also provide water and waste water drainage. Those for caravans and motorhomes are mostly on hardstandings on a slight slope, while those for tents are on a flatter grass area. All have shade.

The on-site restaurant serves family-friendly dishes. Bread and croissants can be ordered from reception for the morning, and there is an outdoor swimming pool where you can cool off. Children can also enjoy the use of the playground and games room. A sizeable commercial centre is just outside the site with hotels, restaurants, a supermarket and a petrol station. There is some road noise from the adjacent motorway.

One large, modern (Heated) sanitary block is in the central lodge, with two further blocks (solar heated) only open in high season. Facilities for babies. Accessible facilities, Washing machines. Motorhome services. Bar (All year, opens with a reception in low season). Snack/pizza and takeaway (July/Aug). Heated swimming and paddling pools (Seasonal). TV room. Games room. Reading room (books and local information). Playground. Table tennis, Boules. Picnic and barbecue area. Only gas and electric barbecues are allowed. Free Internet point at reception. WiFi in the bar (Free).

Key Features

📅 Book Online

📅 All Year

🐾 Pets allowed

♿ Accessible Facilities

♨ Outdoor Pool on Site

🎣 Childrens Play Area

🍸 Bar on Site

Find Out More
Visit ar.camp/fr69010
or scan the QR code.

Rhône, Rhône Alpes

Alan Rogers Ref: FR69020
Accommodations: 29
Pitches: 60
GPS: 46.18790, 4.69916
Post Code: F-69820

what3words:
fracas.mushy.pioneering

Contact:
info@beaujolais-camping.com
Tel: +33 4 74 69 80 07
www.beaujolais-camping.com

Open Dates:
Mid April - Early October.

La Grappe Fleurie

With easy access from the A6 autoroute and the N6, this attractive and welcoming site is perfect for overnight stops. But stay awhile and get to know this delightful region with its wine heritage, historical monuments and magical rolling landscape. This is a neat, well-ordered campsite situated in the heart of Beaujolais. It's surrounded by vineyards and just walking distance (within 1 km) of the pretty village of Fleurie (one of the premier Beaujolais crus). Here you'll find all the shops and amenities you'll need.

The winding lanes meander through the charming vineyards, with familiar names from the wine list all around - a great way to explore is by bike or on foot. This popular site has 60 generous, grassy and relatively level touring pitches delimited by substantial hedging and shady trees and with individual access to water, drainage and electricity connections (10A). The English-speaking owners arrange interesting wine tastings on-site twice weekly in the high season.

Two modern sanitary blocks. Accessible Facilities. Washing machine and dryer. Fridge. Bread to order. Snack bar with homemade pizza (May-Sept). Covered and heated swimming pool (15x7m). Playground. Tennis court. Large TV/games room. Pétanque. Regular wine tastings (No charge). Sauna. Gas barbecues only. Free WiFi.

Key Features

- Book Online
- Pets allowed
- Accessible Facilities
- Indoor Pool on Site
- Childrens Play Area

Find Out More
Visit ar.camp/fr69020
or scan the QR code.

📍 **Isère, Rhône Alpes**

Camping Belledonne

This spacious site is continually being improved and is owned by the RCN group. It has well-drained, level, generous, grassy pitches, most for touring, all with electricity (6-10A). Beech hedges and abundant mature trees provide ample privacy and shade. A bar/restaurant with a terrace is open all season next to the attractive pool complex, comprising two heated swimming pools, a paddling pool and an ample sunbathing space surrounded by gardens and grassy areas.

The site becomes lively in July and August with many organised activities and entertainment. Twin-axle caravans are not accepted, and large outfits should phone ahead. The site has five areas, each named after one of the local valleys.

Two well-appointed sanitary blocks, one renovated, include baby rooms and accessible facilities. Shop. Bar/restaurant and takeaway (All season). Two swimming pools and a paddling pool. Sauna. Hamman, Tennis. Good play area. Multisport pitch, Large meadow with fitness course. Football field. Entertainment team during the summer. WiFi throughout (Free), strongest at the main building.

Alan Rogers Ref: FR38100
Accommodations: 50
Pitches: 130
GPS: 45.11423, 6.00765
Post Code: F-38520

what3words:
grained.banishes.dazzle

Contact:
reservation@rcn.eu
Tel: +31 8 50 40 07 00
www.rcn.nl/en/camping/france/alpe-d-huez

Open Dates:
Early May- Late September & Mid December - Early March.

Key Features

📅 Book Online

🐾 Pets allowed

♿ Accessible Facilities

🏊 Outdoor Pool on Site

🛝 Childrens Play Area

🍸 Bar on Site

Find Out More
Visit **ar.camp/fr38100**
or scan the QR code.

Isère, Rhône Alpes

Camping le Champ du Moulin

Le Champ du Moulin is in the narrow Vénéon valley at an altitude of 960 m, so the days may be hot, but the nights are cool. It is open in summer and winter and has 83 level stone and grass pitches, 65 for touring. They are delineated by various trees that offer shade, and all have electricity (6/10A, long leads useful). Rock pegs are essential.

When the mountain snow melts in spring, the river beside the site changes from a trickle to an impressive torrent, so parents and dog owners need to be especially vigilant. Large units are accepted, but please book ahead. Even though the bustling town of Le Bourg-d'Oisans is only a 15-minute drive away, this peaceful campsite is enjoyed by visitors in both winter and summer. It is a good base for skiing and for exploring this beautiful region.

One heated, well-equipped sanitary block with washbasins in cabins. Accessible facilities (Key required). Laundry and drying room. Motorhome services. Small shop in reception stocks basics. Chalet restaurant/bar with home cooking. Small play area. TV room. Boules. Fishing. WiFi (Free 5hr/day).

Alan Rogers Ref: FR38110
Accommodations: 20
Pitches: 83
GPS: 44.98596, 6.11986
Post Code: F-38520

what3words:
tidally.layered.curls

Contact:
info@champ-du-moulin.com
Tel: +33 4 76 80 07 38
www.champ-du-moulin.com

Open Dates:
End May - Mid Sept. / Mid Dec. - Early Jan. / Early Feb. - Late April.

Key Features

- Book Online
- Pets allowed
- Accessible Facilities
- Childrens Play Area
- Bar on Site
- Fishing on Site

Find Out More
Visit **ar.camp/fr38110**
or scan the QR code.

📍 **Drôme, Rhône Alpes**

Camping Champ la Chèvre

This pleasant, unpretentious site has magnificent views across the western Alps. The campsite is just 200 m. from the village and 500 m. from the D1075. Formerly a farm (hence its name) and now under new management, Champ la Chèvre is undergoing a steady refurbishment process. Facilities such as an outdoor covered swimming pool and a restaurant and bar, which are open all day, are available on-site. WiFi is available across the entire campsite for those wanting to stay connected. Camping Champ la Chèvre is a popular family site. Children will love the games, activities, and creative crafts run during July and August.

There are 94 pitches, mostly sunny and spacious, and many with fine mountain views. Some pitches are sloping, and 70 pitches have 6A electrical connections. Adults can explore the region with free guided walks to see the vultures and orchids or to visit cheese makers and lavender distilleries.

Centrally located toilet block with accessible facilities and a second block by the entrance. Motorhome services. Bar, restaurant and takeaway (All season). Heated swimming pool (High season). Play area. Children's club (July/Aug). Minigolf. Mobile homes and chalets for rent.

Alan Rogers Ref: FR26270
Accommodations: 38
Pitches: 94
GPS: 44.66440, 5.70742
Post Code: F-26220

what3words:
ogle.early.treble

Contact:
info@campingchamplachevre.com
Tel: +33 4 92 58 50 14
campingchamplachevre.com

Open Dates:
Late April - Mid September.

Key Features

📅 Book Online

🐾 Pets allowed

♿ Accessible Facilities

🏊 Outdoor Pool on Site

🛝 Childrens Play Area

🍸 Bar on Site

Find Out More
Visit **ar.camp/fr26270**
or scan the QR code.

📍 **Ardèche, Rhône Alpes**

Le Ranc Davaine

In the heart of the Ardèche and close to the famous gorges, Sunêlia Le Ranc Davaine is a large, busy, family-oriented site with direct access to the River Chassezac and its pebble beach. There are approximately 500 pitches, 50 for touring, all with electricity (10/16A), for which very long leads are required (some may cross roads). Most pitches are scattered between static caravan and tour operator pitches on reasonably flat, stony ground under a variety of trees, some of which are pretty low, giving much-needed shade.

The site can get very busy for much of the season, with the extensive aqua park acting as a focal point, especially as the sun goes down and the evening's entertainment begins. New features have been added, including a covered pool area, more slides, a wave machine and an improved two-storey bar with a veranda.

Three sanitary blocks with facilities for visitors with reduced mobility. Washing machines and dryers. Large shop. Bar/restaurant, pizzeria, takeaway. Indoor swimming pool (heated), various pools, water slides and water park (All season, no shorts allowed). River beach. Large playground. Spa. Tennis. Football, volleyball, table tennis. Fishing, riding, golf, and quad biking nearby. Archery, Extensive entertainment programme and kids club (Jul/Aug). Discos. Bicycle hire, Fitness area. Free WiFi (partial coverage).

Alan Rogers Ref: FR07050
Accommodations: 310
Pitches: 500
GPS: 44.41410, 4.27290
Post Code: F-07120

what3words:
unsought.essentials.tars

Contact:
contact@rancdavaine.fr
Tel: +33 4 75 39 60 55
www.camping-ranc-davaine.fr

Open Dates:
Late April - Late September.

Key Features

- Book Online
- Pets allowed
- Accessible Facilities
- Indoor Pool on Site
- Childrens Play Area
- Bar on Site
- Bicycle Hire on Site
- Fishing on Site

Find Out More
Visit **ar.camp/fr07050**
or scan the QR code.

📍 **Ardèche, Rhône Alpes**

Alan Rogers Ref: FR07630
Accommodations: 264
Pitches: 70
GPS: 44.44470, 4.36630
Post Code: F-07120

what3words:
cuddles.bested.learnt

Contact:
contact@alunavacances.fr
Tel: +33 4 75 93 93 15
www.alunavacances.fr

Open Dates:
Early April - Late September.

Aluna Vacances

Situated on the doorstep of the Ardèche Gorges, Sunêlia Aluna Vacances is well-placed for all kinds of outdoor activities. The famous Pont d'Arc itself is only 15 km away, popular for canoeing excursions amidst spectacular scenery. The surrounding wooded hills offer wonderful cycling and hiking trails through the wild herbs of the garrigue landscape.

This leafy site is well laid out around an impressive pool complex, forming a natural focal point. Some pitches are grassier than others, but all are set among the trees, all with 10A electricity and decent shade to most, and they're at least 100m sq. Extra large pitches are also available, as well as some hardstandings. Nearby medieval Ruoms is attractive and handy for its shops and amenities. There are plenty of local natural attractions: Cocalière cave and chestnut museum are charming in various ways.

Four sanitary blocks with showers, private washing cubicles and facilities for babies and accessible facilities. Washing machines and dryers. Well-stocked shop. Bar with TV. Restaurant and takeaway. Waterpark with heated outdoor pools, indoor pool and slides. Aquagym. Spa. Sports and kid's club (seasonal). Tennis. Volleyball. Table tennis. Boules. Multisports field. Playground. Entertainment programme. Cycling, rafting, horse riding, and canoeing are nearby. WiFi (extra charge).

Key Features

📅 Book Online

🐾 Pets allowed

♿ Accessible Facilities

🏊 Indoor Pool on Site

🛝 Childrens Play Area

🍸 Bar on Site

Find Out More
Visit ar.camp/fr07630
or scan the QR code.

Ardèche, Rhône Alpes

Nature Parc l'Ardéchois

Camping Nature Parc l'Ardéchois is a very high-quality, family-run site within walking distance of the amenities of Vallon-Pont-d'Arc. It borders the River Ardèche, and hugely popular canoe trips are run directly from the site. The campsite is just 4 km from the famous Pont-d'Arc, a huge limestone arch spanning the river, and its river beach. A drive along the gorge is a must, with spectacular viewpoints.

Of the 250 well-maintained pitches, 225 for touring units are separated by trees and shrubs. All have electrical connections (6/10A), and, for an additional charge, 125 larger pitches have full services (22 include a fridge, patio furniture, hammock and free WiFi). This is an excellent choice for active families and anyone interested in good food and wine after some gentle exercise.

Two well-equipped toilet blocks, one superb with everything working automatically. Facilities are of the highest standard, very clean and include good facilities for babies and children and with accessible facilities. Laundry facilities. Four private bathrooms to hire. Well-stocked shop. Excellent restaurant, bar and takeaway. Heated swimming pool and paddling pool (No shorts). Wellness area with sauna, hammam, jacuzzi and 4 seasons-shower. Different types of massage and treatments. Yoga. Gym. Tennis. Very good play area. Organised activities and canoe trips. Bicycle hire. Only gas barbecues are permitted. Communal barbecue area. WiFi throughout (Charged).

Alan Rogers Ref: FR07120
Accommodations: 25
Pitches: 250
GPS: 44.39804, 4.39878
Post Code: F-07150

what3words:
soulful.lightheaded.seaweeds

Contact:
info@ardechois-camping.com
Tel: +33 4 75 88 06 63
www.ardechois-camping.com

Open Dates:
Early April - Mid October.

Alan Rogers Awards Won
2018

Key Features

- Book Online
- Pets allowed
- Accessible Facilities
- Outdoor Pool on Site
- Childrens Play Area
- Bar on Site
- Bicycle Hire on Site
- Fishing on Site

Find Out More
Visit ar.camp/fr07120
or scan the QR code.

📍 Gironde, Aquitaine

La Côte d'Argent

Camping de la Côte d'Argent is a large, well-equipped site set back a short walk from the sandy beach, part of a long ribbon of golden sand running from the Gironde to the Spanish border. The beach is just magnificent, with lots of water sports available too. The huge Landes pine forest encloses the site, so walkers and cyclists can explore over 100 km of trails and cycle paths. Hourtin-Plage itself is a pleasant little resort with a few shops and restaurants.

Aside from its proximity to the beach, the site's big draw is its pool complex, with wooden bridges connecting the pools and islands, sunbathing and play areas, plus an indoor heated pool. The site has 618 touring pitches (all with 10A electricity), not always clearly defined, arranged under shady trees with some on sand.

Sanitary blocks include accessible facilities. Washing machines. Motorhome services. Grocery store, restaurant, takeaway, pizzeria and bar. Four outdoor pools with slides and flumes (Seasonal). Indoor pool (All season). Fitness room. Massage (Institut de Beauté). Tennis. Multisport area. Beach volleyball. Pétanque. Play areas. Miniclub, fitness and organised entertainment in high season. Bicycle hire (Adults only). WiFi partial site (Charged). Charcoal barbecues are not permitted (Gas barbecue rental on site).

Alan Rogers Ref: FR33110
Accommodations: 522
Pitches: 618
GPS: 45.22372, -1.16318
Post Code: F-33990

what3words:
iteration.lamps.sneakily

Contact:
info@cca33.com
Tel: +33 5 56 09 10 25
camping-cote-dargent.com

Open Dates:
Mid May - Mid September.

Key Features

🐾 Pets allowed

♿ Accessible Facilities

🏖 Seaside Beach Nearby

🌊 Indoor Pool on Site

🛝 Childrens Play Area

🍸 Bar on Site

🚲 Bicycle Hire on Site

Find Out More
Visit ar.camp/fr33110
or scan the QR code.

Camping La Côte d'Argent
★★★★★

📍 **Gironde, Aquitaine**

Alan Rogers Ref: FR33050
Accommodations: 37
Pitches: 300
GPS: 45.18207, -1.07560
Post Code: F-33990

what3words:
hairbrush.tinkle.kitty

Contact:
info@lesourmes.com
Tel: +33 5 56 09 12 76
www.lesourmes.com

Open Dates:
Late April - Mid September.

Camping les Ourmes

Located just 500 metres from the largest freshwater lake in France, this level, well-maintained campsite is only a ten-minute drive from the beach and, with its own pool, is an attractive holiday site for those who enjoy watersports. Of the 300 pitches, 232 are for touring units. These are marked but not separated and arranged amongst tall pines and other trees that give good shade. All have electricity (10A).

The site's amenities are arranged around a pleasant entrance courtyard with an evening entertainment programme in season. In low season, this is a quiet site with the bonus of the bar and restaurant being open. Visits to many of the châteaux and vineyards in the area are possible, and the site owners will organise excursions to these.

Four refurbished toilet blocks. Accessible Facilities. Washing machine and dryer. Small shop (July/Aug). Bar/restaurant with outdoor tables, takeaway snacks and reasonably priced meals (Seasonal). Medium sized swimming pool, paddling pool (All season). Large leisure area, play area, Multisport pitch, volleyball. TV, table tennis, archery, football, games rooms. Boules. Entertainment, WiFi throughout (Charged). 37 mobile homes to rent.

Key Features

📅 Book Online

🐾 Pets allowed

♿ Accessible Facilities

⛱ Seaside Beach Nearby

🏊 Outdoor Pool on Site

🛝 Childrens Play Area

🍸 Bar on Site

Find Out More
Visit **ar.camp/fr33050**
or scan the QR code.

📍 **Dordogne, Aquitaine**

Alan Rogers Ref: FR24630
Accommodations: 17
Pitches: 85
GPS: 44.89402, 1.11382
Post Code: F-24200

what3words:
flint.evolutionary.twine

Contact:
lescharmescamping@gmail.com
Tel: +33 5 53 31 02 89
www.campinglescharmes.fr

Open Dates:
End April - Mid September.

Camping les Charmes

Les Charmes is a pleasant, rural site located amidst forest and farmland overlooking the valley of the Château de Puymartin. There are 85 large, level pitches, with 68 for touring units. Some are in clearings in a wooded area, and others are grassy and more open, with trees giving shade. Almost all pitches have 6A electricity, although some may need longer leads.

Les Charmes offers a quiet, friendly holiday with all the facilities needed to enjoy your time here. An on-site restaurant with splendid views over the surrounding hills provides a small but tasty menu. You can also buy fresh bread from the campsite shop each morning, which sells all the necessities needed to cook at your pitch. There is no entertainment programme here, but there are plenty of activities to keep everyone amused. There's an outdoor swimming pool with slides, a tennis court, a children's playground, and archery, to name but a few activities to enjoy.

Large, spotless toilet block, centrally located, houses all necessary facilities, including accessible facilities. Baby room. Laundry facilities. Indoor, heated pool plus jacuzzi (All season) and large outdoor pool (High season), including slides. Grocery store (July/Aug), bread to order. Bar, snack bar and takeaway (July/Aug). Restaurant (every evening). Refurbished play area. Board games. Library. Activities organised for children and adults include dancing and live music in the bar (High season). Tennis. Boules. Free WiFi.

Key Features

🗓 Book Online

🐾 Pets allowed

♿ Accessible Facilities

🏊 Indoor Pool on Site

🛝 Childrens Play Area

🍸 Bar on Site

Find Out More
Visit **ar.camp/fr24630**
or scan the QR code.

📍 **Dordogne, Aquitaine**

Camping Les Péneyrals

Within easy reach of all the attractions of the Périgord region, Sandaya has created an attractive and friendly family campsite at les Péneyrals. There are around 274 pitches, 122 of which are for touring. The pitches at the bottom of the hill tend to be quieter as they are further from the main facilities but are all level and grassy (some on terraces), with electricity (5/10A), and most have some shade.

An attractive bar and restaurant with a terrace overlook the excellent pool complex, and at the bottom of the site is a small fishing lake. Activities are organised over a long season, including archery, various sports tournaments, an aqua gym, discos and a children's club. On-site entertainment is provided in and around the bar and terrace area every night except Saturdays.

Three modern, unisex toilet blocks provide good quality facilities, including provision for babies and accessible facilities. Motorhome services. Good value shop, excellent restaurant and takeaway. The pool complex has two large pools (One heated), a paddling pool with games, and four slides with a splash pool. Indoor heated pool. Bicycle hire. Minigolf. Tennis (Charged). Badminton. Play area. Games room, Entertainment, WiFi over site (Charged), TV room and small library. Fishing.

Alan Rogers Ref: FR24320
Accommodations: 65
Pitches: 274
GPS: 44.95776, 1.27290
Post Code: F-24590

what3words:
socked.kidding.setting

Contact:
vacances@sandaya.fr
Tel: +33 5 53 28 85 71
www.sandaya.co.uk/our-campsites/peneyrals

Open Dates:
Early April - Late September.

Key Features

🗓 Book Online

🐾 Pets allowed

♿ Accessible Facilities

🏊 Indoor Pool on Site

🛝 Childrens Play Area

🍸 Bar on Site

🚲 Bicycle Hire on Site

🐟 Fishing on Site

Find Out More
Visit **ar.camp/fr24320**
or scan the QR code.

📍 **Lot-et-Garonne, Aquitaine**

Camping Moulin de Campech

This well-shaded, pretty site is run by Sue and George Thomas, who have owned it since 1999. On-site, there are 46 large-sized pitches divided mainly by hedges, and electric hook-up points are available (6A, long leads may be necessary for places but can be borrowed free of charge).

The main focus of this campsite is at the site's entrance, which is the trout lake surrounded by willow trees, and it runs under the restored mill house, which is home to where the owners live. The mill house is where you will find the campsite bar and restaurant. Enjoy the views of the lake on the terrace whilst enjoying the home-cooked food by Sue (Fresh trout is on the menu). Other on-site facilities include an outdoor swimming pool on an elevated area above the mill house. A small stream from the lake continues through both sides of the site.

Separate male and female toilet & shower facilities, with a dedicated accessible washroom for campers with reduced mobility. Washing machine and tumble dryer. Shop. Restaurant. Heated swimming pool (Access via steep steps or gentle grassy slope - Seasonal). Open grassy games area. Board games and English library. Boules. Quiz night (Wed) in high season. Torch useful. Free WiFi throughout.

Alan Rogers Ref: FR47050
Pitches: 46
GPS: 44.27179, 0.19093
Post Code: F-47160

what3words:
blackly.embrace.inlets

Contact:
camping@moulindecampech.co.uk
Tel: +33 5 53 88 72 43
www.moulindecampech.co.uk

Open Dates:
Early May - Late September.

Key Features

📅 Book Online

🐾 Pets allowed

♿ Accessible Facilities

🏊 Outdoor Pool on Site

🍸 Bar on Site

🐟 Fishing on Site

Find Out More
Visit **ar.camp/fr47050**
or scan the QR code.

Landes, Aquitaine

Alan Rogers Ref: FR40440
Accommodations: 173
Pitches: 317
GPS: 44.48160, -1.09380
Post Code: F-40460

what3words:
overbite.planets.salt

Contact:
vacances@sandaya.fr
Tel: +33 5 58 82 70 80
www.sandaya.co.uk/our-
campsites/sanguinet-plage

Open Dates:
Late June - Mid September.

Camping Lac de Sanguinet

Camping Sandaya Lac de Sanguinet is just 100 m. from the large lake of the same name. There are 317 pitches here, of which 144 are for touring. One hundred twenty have electrical connections (10/16A). Around 173 pitches are occupied by mobile homes, chalets and fully equipped bungalow tents, all available to rent, including some models specially adapted with accessible facilities.

Amenities include an attractive swimming pool, a volleyball court, and two playgrounds. A marquee is used for activities and entertainment during the peak season. The Lac de Sanguinet is one of Europe's largest lakes (6,800 hectares!) and is renowned for the clarity of its waters.

Three sanitary blocks have hot showers, washbasins in cabins and accessible facilities. Motorhome services. Laundry facilities. Snack bar and pizzas (July/Aug). Heated outdoor swimming pool (June-Sept). Games room. Bouncy castle. Play areas. Wellness area, Activities and entertainment programme. Mobile homes, equipped tents and chalets to rent. WiFi on the part of the site (Charged).

Key Features

- Book Online
- Pets allowed
- Accessible Facilities
- Outdoor Pool on Site
- Childrens Play Area
- Bar on Site
- Fishing on Site
- Sailing on Site

Find Out More
Visit **ar.camp/fr40440**
or scan the QR code.

Alan Rogers Ref: FR40050
Accommodations: 548
Pitches: 259
GPS: 43.90285, -1.31250
Post Code: F-40560

what3words:
repels.footpath.reflex

Contact:
vacances@sandaya.fr
Tel: +33 5 58 42 94 06
www.sandaya.co.uk/our-campsites/le-col-vert

Open Dates:
Late March - Mid September.

Camping Le Col Vert

Camping Sandaya le Col Vert is a large, well-maintained campsite, well-laid out on the shores of Lac de Léon, that offers 259 touring pitches and 548 mobile homes for rent. The pitches range from simple ones to those with water and a drain, and there are eight with private, well-designed, modern sanitary facilities.

It is a quiet site in the low season, and those pitches beside the lake offer a wonderful backdrop to relaxing pastimes. During the main season, it is a lively place for children of all ages, with entertainment and many sporting activities available. A pool complex offers a standard pool for swimming, a pool for children with a water canon and fountains, plenty of sunbeds and a heated indoor pool.

Four toilet blocks, one heated. Accessible facilities. Laundry facilities. Motorhome services. Shops, bar/restaurant, takeaway (seasonal; limited hours until June). Swimming pool complex with three pools (All season). Spa, fitness centre and sauna. Play area. Games room. Sports areas. Boules. Tennis. Bicycle hire. Minigolf. Fishing. Riding. Sailing school (High season). Communal barbecues only. WiFi throughout (Charged). Free bus to the beach (July/Aug).

Key Features

- Book Online
- Pets allowed
- Accessible Facilities
- Seaside Beach Nearby
- Indoor Pool on Site
- Childrens Play Area
- Bar on Site
- Bicycle Hire on Site

Find Out More
Visit **ar.camp/fr40050**
or scan the QR code.

📍 **Landes, Aquitaine**

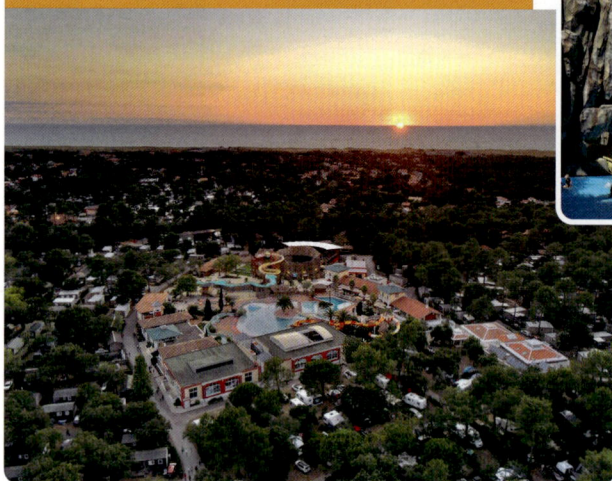

Alan Rogers Ref: FR40200
Accommodations: 380
Pitches: 600
GPS: 43.59570, -1.45638
Post Code: F-40530

what3words:
bikini.legislated.buzzy

Contact:
info@yellohvillage-sylvamar.com
Tel: +33 5 59 45 75 16
www.camping-sylvamar.com

Open Dates:
Early April - Late September.

Camping Le Sylvamar

Yelloh! Village le Sylvamar is just a kilometre from the endless sandy beach, just north of Bayonne on the southern edge of the Landes. There are around 600 pitches, of which 234 are for tourers, all level, numbered, and separated mainly by low hedges. Several newer pitches are less shaded. All have electricity (16A), water and drainage; some have private sanitary facilities, and premium pitches with pergolas are available.

The extensive pool complex is remarkable, featuring several pools, a wild water river, toboggans, slides and a spectacular 'volcano'. In a sunny setting, all are surrounded by ample sunbathing terraces and overlooked by the excellent bar/restaurant. An 800-seat amphitheatre hosts entertainment. Visit the local resorts of Capbreton and Hossegor, which have a marina and fishing port, museums and beaches, plenty of surf culture, and fantastic seafood.

Four modern toilet blocks have washbasins in cabins. Excellent accessible facilities and facilities for babies. Laundry. Fridge hire. Shop, bar/restaurant and takeaway. Swimming pool complex. Spa treatments. Yoga, aquagym, pilates. Play area. Games room. Cinema, TV and video room. Fitness centre. Wellness amenities. Tennis. Football pitch. Bicycle hire. Library. Extensive entertainment programme for all ages. WiFi over site (Charged). No charcoal barbecues.

Key Features

🐾 Pets allowed

♿ Accessible Facilities

⛱ Seaside Beach Nearby

🏊 Indoor Pool on Site

🛝 Childrens Play Area

🍸 Bar on Site

🚴 Bicycle Hire on Site

Find Out More
Visit **ar.camp/fr40200**
or scan the QR code.

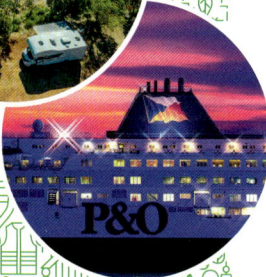

📍 **Pyrénées-Atlantiques, Aquitaine**

Camping le Pavillon Royal

Le Pavillon Royal is located in an excellent situation on raised ground overlooking the sea (100 m. from the beach), with good views along the coast to the south and the north coast of Spain. The site's centre has a large heated swimming pool and sunbathing area.

The camping area is divided into 325 marked, level pitches, many of a good size. Seventy-five are reserved for tents and are only accessible on foot. Asphalt roads connect the remainder. All have electric hook-up points available. Much of the campsite is in full sun, although the area for tents is shaded. Beneath the site – and only a very short walk down – stretches a wide sandy beach where the Atlantic rollers provide ideal conditions for surfing.

Good quality toilet blocks with baby baths and two accessible units. Washing facilities (Only two open at night). Washing machines, dryers. Motorhome services. Shop (incl. gas sales), restaurant and takeaway, bar, heated swimming and paddling pools, wellness facilities, fitness room (All season). Entertainment (High season) Bicycle hire, Playground. General room, TV room, games room, films. Fishing. Surf school. Dogs are not accepted. WiFi throughout (Charged).

Alan Rogers Ref: FR64060
Accommodations: 5
Pitches: 325
GPS: 43.45458, -1.57649
Post Code: F-64210

what3words:
griddles.rider.procession

Contact:
info@pavillon-royal.com
Tel: +33 5 59 23 00 54
www.pavillon-royal.com

Open Dates:
Mid May - Mid October.

🏅 **Alan Rogers Awards Won**
2012

Key Features

🗓 Book Online

♿ Accessible Facilities

⛱ Seaside Beach on Site

🌊 Outdoor Pool on Site

🛝 Childrens Play Area

🍸 Bar on Site

🚲 Bicycle Hire on Site

🐟 Fishing on Site

Find Out More
Visit **ar.camp/fr64060**
or scan the QR code.

📍 **Pyrénées-Atlantiques, Aquitaine**

Camping Beau Rivage

This well-cared-for site lies just outside the walls of the bastide town of Navarrenx. Many bushes and trees have been planted, and a total of 54 touring pitches are available either on hardstanding with full services or on grass, the latter having more shade. A traffic-free track leads to the town where all essential shops can be found.

Located within driving distance of the Atlantic coast and the Pyrenees, this is a good site for touring. The local area has many ancient towns and Navarrenx, just five minutes walk away, offers superb views across the countryside and down the river valley.

Two spotless sanitary blocks with good separate facilities for ladies and men include modern facilities for babies. Accessible facilities available. Laundry facilities. Locally produced good quality wines available in reception. Homemade pizzas. Bar in high season. Small swimming pool (Seasonal). Playground for small children. Max. 2 dogs. Chalets for rent. Caravan storage. WiFi throughout (Free).

Alan Rogers Ref: FR64120
Accommodations: 16
Pitches: 54
GPS: 43.32001, -0.76216
Post Code: F-64190

what3words:
fact.continuation.pageant

Contact:
beaucamping@orange.fr
Tel: +33 5 59 66 10 00
www.beaucamping.com

Open Dates:
Late March - Early October.

Key Features

📅 Book Online

🐾 Pets allowed

♿ Accessible Facilities

🏊 Outdoor Pool on Site

🛝 Childrens Play Area

🍸 Bar on Site

Find Out More
Visit **ar.camp/fr64120**
or scan the QR code.

📍 **Gers, Midi-Pyrénées**

Alan Rogers Ref: FR32010
Accommodations: 35
Pitches: 197
GPS: 43.98299, 0.50183
Post Code: F-32480

what3words:
accents.baroque.delimit

Contact:
info@lecampdeflorence.com
Tel: +33 5 62 28 15 58
www.lecampdeflorence.com

Open Dates:
Start April - Early October.

🎖 **Alan Rogers Awards Won**
2013

Le Camp de Florence

Castel Camp de Florence is an attractive and well-equipped site on the edge of a historic village in pleasantly undulating Gers countryside. The 197 large, part terraced pitches (110 for touring units) all have 10A electricity, 20 with hardstanding and 16 fully serviced. They are arranged around a large field with rural views, feeling spacious.

The 13th-century village of La Romieu is on the Santiago de Compostela pilgrims' route. The Pyrenees are a two hour drive, the Atlantic coast a similar distance. There is a 500m2 swimming pool perfect for relaxing and enjoying the games the animation team hold here during the day. There is a kids club with sporting activities, crafts, and hours of fun. During the evening, everyone can get involved with the activities and enjoy live music.

Three toilet blocks (one heated) provide all the necessary facilities, including accessible facilities. Washing machines and dryers. Motorhome services. Restaurant (Seasonal, also open to the public). Takeaway. Bread. Swimming pool area with water slide (Seasonal). Jacuzzi. Protected children's pool (Open to the public in afternoons). New playgrounds, games and an animal park. Bouncy castle. Trampoline. Outdoor fitness machines. Games room. Tennis. Pétanque. Bicycle hire. Discos, picnics, musical evenings. WiFi over site (Charged, free in bar). Max. 2 dogs.

Key Features

📅 Book Online

🐾 Pets allowed

♿ Accessible Facilities

🏊 Outdoor Pool on Site

🧒 Childrens Play Area

🍸 Bar on Site

🚲 Bicycle Hire on Site

Find Out More
Visit ar.camp/fr32010
or scan the QR code.

📍 **Lot, Midi-Pyrénées**

Camping Le Ventoulou

Sites et Paysages Le Ventoulou is a small, well-kept, peaceful site on the Périgord Walnut Route at the heart of the Quercy Causses Natural Park. The site is based around an ancient farmhouse between the quaint villages of Padirac and Thégra. On just over half a hectare, the site is compact, yet it does not seem crowded because of the careful spacing of pitches (10A Europlug electricity). You will receive a warm welcome from the French owners.

The Padirac Aquapark is just 3 km. away. There is a weekly soirée during the high season. The area's culture and history, including local châteaux, windmills, pigeon houses and ancient bread ovens, will keep you occupied during your stay.

Two modern sanitary blocks, one can be heated. Good accessible facilities. Baby room with bath. Laundry facilities. Shop. Bar with TV. Restaurant and takeaway. Heated, covered swimming pool and paddling pool. Bicycle hire. Boules. Play area with two trampolines. Games room and library. Multisports area. WiFi (Charged).

Alan Rogers Ref: FR46180
Accommodations: 30
Pitches: 34
GPS: 44.82690, 1.77890
Post Code: F-46500

what3words:
cooperates.bluntest.country

Contact:
contact@leventoulou.com
Tel: +33 5 65 33 67 01
www.camping-leventoulou.com

Open Dates:
Start April - End October.

📍 **Alan Rogers Awards Won**
2023

Key Features

📅 Book Online

🐾 Pets allowed

♿ Accessible Facilities

🌊 Indoor Pool on Site

🛝 Childrens Play Area

🍸 Bar on Site

🚲 Bicycle Hire on Site

Find Out More
Visit **ar.camp/fr46180**
or scan the QR code.

📍 **Hautes-Pyrénées, Midi-Pyrénées**

Alan Rogers Ref: FR65450
Accommodations: 35
Pitches: 98
GPS: 43.09566, -0.07468
Post Code: F-65100

what3words:
beamed.watching.puppy

Contact:
hello@camping-hautes-pyrenees.com
Tel: +33 5 62 94 04 38
www.camping-hautes-pyrenees.com

Open Dates:
End March - End October.

Camping la Forêt

As its name suggests, Camping la Forêt can be found in a peaceful, wooded valley just one kilometre from Lourdes. This 4.5-hectare site has a relaxed atmosphere and a popular restaurant serving traditional specialities. The 98 grass pitches are level and shaded; 68 are for touring and have 3 – 10A electricity (French plugs) and easy access. The remainder is occupied by tastefully arranged chalets and mobile homes for rent, and the owner has created a 'tents only' area where car owners leave their cars in a designated car park close by, making it a very safe place for campers with young children.

The farm animal area with its geese, hens and a pig, allowed out of their compound in the evening to get to know campers, is very popular with animals and humans alike. The heated swimming pool with jacuzzi and paddling pool area has splendid views of 'Le Grand Couvent' at the sanctuary of Lourdes.

The sanitary block has hot showers and washbasins in cubicles. Facilities for babies, children and accessible facilities. Washing machine and dryer. Motorhome services. Bread to order. Bar with TV. Restaurant (Evenings only in low season). Snack bar. Heated swimming pool, paddling pool and jacuzzi (Seasonal). Play area. Trampoline, volleyball, boules, basketball, junior football. WiFi throughout (Charged). No charcoal barbecues. Daily bus service to Lourdes. EV Charging stations,

Key Features

📅 Book Online

🐾 Pets allowed

♿ Accessible Facilities

🏊 Outdoor Pool on Site

🛝 Childrens Play Area

🍸 Bar on Site

Find Out More
Visit ar.camp/fr65450
or scan the QR code.

📍 **Hautes-Pyrénées, Midi-Pyrénées**

Alan Rogers Ref: FR65080
Accommodations: 11
Pitches: 54
GPS: 42.98822, -0.08900
Post Code: F-65400

what3words:
markets.eliminates.couplets

Contact:
info@yellohvillage-lavedan.com
Tel: +33 5 62 97 18 84
www.yellohvillage-lavedan.com

Open Dates:
Early March - Late October.

Camping du Lavedan

Yelloh! Village Camping du Lavedan is a well-established, family-owned site set in the Argelès-Gazost valley south of Lourdes, where a warm welcome and an impressive mountain view await you. There are 54 level touring pitches, all with electricity (3-10A), and most have shade from trees. They are set away from the 38 mobile homes, of which 11 are to rent. Planting of bushes and trees has been carefully considered.

The large, well-designed restaurant and bar area is the scene of some lively evening entertainment in the summer. Lourdes is an important pilgrimage town, and a bus goes from outside the campsite. The site is beside the main road, so some daytime traffic noise exists.

Recent well-maintained toilet block. Baby room. Accessible facilities. Washing machines and dryers are in a separate block heated in winter. Shop All year). Bread delivery (Seasonal). Restaurant with terrace, pizzeria and snacks (Seasonal). Bar, TV (All year). Swimming pool (Seasonal, can be covered). Entertainment and children's activities in high season, Paddling pool. Play area. Boules. WiFi over site (Charged).

Key Features

📅 Book Online

🐾 Pets allowed

♿ Accessible Facilities

🏊 Outdoor Pool on Site

🛝 Childrens Play Area

🍸 Bar on Site

Find Out More
Visit **ar.camp/fr65080**
or scan the QR code.

📍 **Haute-Garonne, Midi-Pyrénées**

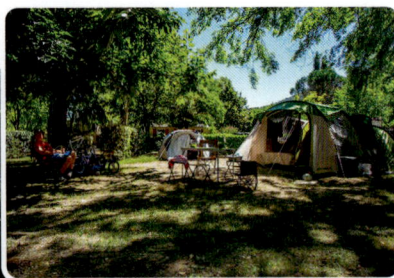

Alan Rogers Ref: FR31000
Accommodations: 24
Pitches: 60
GPS: 43.19048, 1.01788
Post Code: F-31220

what3words:
kicker.butterflies.rhino

Contact:
info@campinglemoulin.com
Tel: +33 5 61 98 86 40
www.campinglemoulin.com

Open Dates:
End March - Start October.

Alan Rogers Awards Won
2015

Camping Le Moulin

With attractive, shaded pitches and many activities, Sites et Paysages le Moulin is a family-run campsite incorporating 12 hectares of woods and fields beside the River Garonne. It is close to Martres-Tolosane, a fascinating medieval village.

Some of the 60-level and grassy pitches are super-size, and all have 6/10A electricity. There are also 24 chalets to rent. Summer brings opportunities for guided canoeing courses, archery and walking. A large sports field is available all season, with tennis, volleyball, basketball, boules and birdwatching on site. The site is very child-friendly and provides many amenities to occupy and entertain young visitors. There is slight road noise.

Large sanitary block with separate toilets for men and women. The communal area has showers and washbasins in cubicles. Separate heated accessible area with shower, WC and basin. Baby bath. Laundry facilities. Motorhome services. Outdoor bar. Restaurant (High season). Snack bar and takeaway (Seasonal). Bread to order. Modern heated pool complex with paddling pools, waterslide and jacuzzi area (High season). Fishing. Tennis. Canoeing. Archery. Fitness area. Two playgrounds. Games room. Bouncy castle. Entertainment programme and children's club (High season). Massage by arrangement (Charged). Car rental service. WiFi throughout (Charged).

Key Features

- Book Online
- Pets allowed
- Accessible Facilities
- Outdoor Pool on Site
- Childrens Play Area
- Bar on Site
- Bicycle Hire on Site
- Fishing on Site

Find Out More
Visit ar.camp/fr31000
or scan the QR code.

Aveyron, Midi-Pyrénées

Camping les Genêts

A real haven of peace, located at the shores of Lake Pareloup, the 5-star campsite of Les Genêts has lots in store for your stay in the Aveyron and offers for both families and watersports fanatics. The 163 pitches include 80 grassy, mostly individual pitches for touring units. These are in two areas, one on each side of the entrance lane, divided by hedges, shrubs and trees. All have 6A electricity (waste) water drainage.

The site slopes gently down to the beach and lake, with facilities for all water sports, including water skiing. There is also a full entertainment and activities programme available in high season. You'll find high-quality equipment and installations for sports activities in a well-maintained, scenic setting, offering a pleasant stay.

Two sanitary blocks are equipped with showers, private washing cubicles, and one accessible suite. Bar. Bicycle hire. (Motor) Boat. Washing machines. Dryers. Disco. Well-stocked shop. Restaurant. Grill/Pizzeria. Takeaway. Refurbished Heated outdoor pools. Paddling pool. Activities and entertainment programmes (July/August). Nursery. SUP. Canoe. Kayak and Pedalo hire. Fishing. Free WiFi. Private lakeside. Sandy beach. Lake. Facilities for watersports, including water skiing. Play area. Mini-golf. Mini sport area. TV. Free WiFi (All site).

Alan Rogers Ref: FR12080
Accommodations: 45
Pitches: 100
GPS: 44.18925, 2.76670
Post Code: F-12410

what3words:
hazed.unmapped.decades

Contact:
contact@camping-les-genets.fr
Tel: +33 5 65 46 35 34
www.camping-les-genets.fr

Open Dates:
Mid May - Mid September.

Alan Rogers Awards Won
2023, 2018

Key Features

- Book Online
- Pets allowed
- Accessible Facilities
- Outdoor Pool on Site
- Childrens Play Area
- Bar on Site
- Skiing on Site
- Bicycle Hire on Site

Find Out More
Visit ar.camp/fr12080
or scan the QR code.

📍 **Aude, Languedoc-Roussillon**

Alan Rogers Ref: FR11210
Accommodations: 15
Pitches: 45
GPS: 43.28308, 2.44152
Post Code: F-11600

what3words:
snails.soaped.urges

Contact:
contact@moulindesainteanne.com
Tel: +33 4 68 72 20 80
www.moulindesainteanne.com

Open Dates:
Start April - End October.

Le Moulin de Sainte Anne

Just a few years ago, Sites et Paysages le Moulin Sainte Anne was a vineyard, but with much hard work by the owners and the backing of the Mairie, there is now a flourishing campsite on the edge of the town. There are 45-level grass pitches of a good size separated by hedges. All have water and 10A electricity and are terraced where necessary and landscaped with growing trees and shrubs.

The facilities are modern, well-kept and in keeping with the area. They include a heated outdoor swimming pool, Multi-sport field, table tennis, trampoline and games room. A snack bar operates in July and August, and a daily bread service is available, too. There is close cooperation with the village, and villagers are welcome to the evening entertainment, including themed dinners, wine tastings and live music.

A modern toilet block is very well equipped. Accessible sanitary facilities. Washing machine. Motorhome services. Bar, snack bar with takeaway (High season). Heated swimming and paddling pools (Seasonal). Basket- and volleyball court. Games room. Play area. Entertainment (High season), Communal barbecue (No barbecues on pitches). Chalets to rent. WiFi throughout.

Key Features

📅 Book Online

🐾 Pets allowed

♿ Accessible Facilities

🏊 Outdoor Pool on Site

🛝 Childrens Play Area

🍸 Bar on Site

🐟 Fishing on Site

Find Out More
Visit **ar.camp/fr11210**
or scan the QR code.

📍 **Pyrénées-Orientales, Languedoc-Roussillon**

Camping Cala Gogo

This is an excellent, well-organised site in Catalan country with direct access to the sandy beach and warm waters of the Med. In addition, the site has an impressive pool complex, attractively laid out with palm trees and sunbathing areas. The large bar complex overlooking the pool area becomes very busy in the high season, with entertainment on some evenings. This vibrant family site offers sun, sea and sand and a lively holiday atmosphere for all ages.

There are around 650 pitches, with 378 good-sized, level pitches for touring, all with electrical connections (6/10A) and some shade. Twenty fully serviced pitches are available. There's no shortage of things to do on-site, but a day trip to Spain is an easy option, and the bustling resort of Argelès-Sur-Mer is close by, as is the historic city of Perpignan.

Fully equipped toilet blocks with some squat-style WCs. Accessible facilities. Motorhome services. A good supermarket and a small shopping mall. Sophisticated restaurant. Self-service restaurant. Takeaway. Bar. Small beach bar. Fridge hire. Disco. TV. Three swimming pools (Heated) plus one for children, water jets, jacuzzi, and waterfall. Play area. Tennis. Fishing. Diving club. Bicycle hire. Events, sports and entertainment are organised in season. Kids club, Boat launching. Torches useful. WiFi throughout (Charged). Only gas or electric barbecues are allowed.

Alan Rogers Ref: FR66030
Accommodations: 92
Pitches: 650
GPS: 42.59939, 3.03761
Post Code: F-66750

what3words:
painting.flexibility.misfit

Contact:
camping@calagogo66.fr
Tel: +33 4 68 21 07 12
www.camping-le-calagogo.fr

Open Dates:
Late April - End September.

Key Features

📅 Book Online

🐾 Pets allowed

♿ Accessible Facilities

⛱ Seaside Beach on Site

🌊 Outdoor Pool on Site

🛝 Childrens Play Area

🍸 Bar on Site

🚲 Bicycle Hire on Site

Find Out More
Visit ar.camp/fr66030
or scan the QR code.

📍 **Pyrénées-Orientales, Languedoc-Roussillon**

Camping Ma Prairie

Ma Prairie is an excellent site, and its place in this guide goes back over 30 years to when it was simply a field surrounded by vineyards. The trees planted then have matured and are home to mischievous red squirrels. More trees, along with colourful shrubs, continue to be planted, providing a comfortable, park-like setting with 208 touring pitches, 197 with 10A electricity and 15 with water and drainage. There are also 50 mobile homes available to rent and 10 privately owned.

It is a peaceful haven, some 3 km. back from the sea but within walking distance of Canet village itself. The restaurant and bar are across the road and overlook a modern, attractive pool complex and a wonderful old palm tree. You will also find the sports complex and gym here.

Fully equipped toilet blocks with accessible facilities, baby bath. Washing machines and dryers. There is no shop, but the baker calls every morning June-Sept. Covered snack bar and takeaway. Air-conditioned bar and restaurant. Large heated swimming pool, separate water chute and splendid children's pool (Seasonal). Multisports court. Gym. TV. Amusement machines. Busy daily activity and entertainment programme in season for children aged 6-12. WiFi over site (Charged). Bicycle hire. Charcoal barbecues are not permitted. Several small communal barbecue areas. Tourist train stops at the site (April-June and Sept).

Alan Rogers Ref: FR66020
Accommodations: 50
Pitches: 208
GPS: 42.70135, 2.99968
Post Code: F-66140

what3words:
gown.prestige.cobbles

Contact:
contact@maprairie.com
Tel: +33 4 68 73 26 17
www.maprairie.com

Open Dates:
Mid April - Late September.

Key Features

📅 Book Online

🐾 Pets allowed

♿ Accessible Facilities

🏖 Seaside Beach Nearby

🏊 Outdoor Pool on Site

🛝 Childrens Play Area

🍸 Bar on Site

🚲 Bicycle Hire on Site

Find Out More
Visit **ar.camp/fr66020**
or scan the QR code.

📍 **Pyrénées-Orientales, Languedoc-Roussillon**

Camping Le Brasilia

Situated across the yacht harbour from the Canet-Plage resort, Yelloh! Village Le Brasilia is an impressive, well-managed family site directly beside the beach. There's much to praise here, from the state-of-the-art reception to the sensational water park, excellent spa and park-like grounds. Although large, it is attractive and well kept with a remarkable range of facilities – with good reason, it's always a popular choice.

The 699 touring pitches are neatly hedged, most with electricity (6-10A) and 408 with water and drainage. They vary in size from 80 to 120 sq.m. with some of the longer pitches suitable for two families together. There is decent shade from pines and flowering shrubs, with less on pitches near the beach. A member of Yelloh! Village and the prestigious Leading Campings group.

Nine modern sanitary blocks with British-style WCs and washbasins in cabins. Good facilities for children and accessible facilities. Laundry room. Motorhome services. Range of shops. Gas supplies. Bars and a restaurant. Pool complex (heated). The wellness centre includes a jacuzzi, massage room, and beauty room. Play areas. Sports field. Tennis. Sporting activities. Library, games and video room. Hairdresser. Internet café and WiFi. Daily entertainment programme. Bicycle hire. Fishing. Post office. Weather forecasts. No charcoal barbecues. Free WiFi in the bar.

Alan Rogers Ref: FR66070
Accommodations: 262
Pitches: 699
GPS: 42.70830, 3.03552
Post Code: F-66141

what3words:
skilled.desire.accusations

Contact:
info@lebrasilia.fr
Tel: +33 4 68 80 23 82
www.brasilia.fr

Open Dates:
Mid April - Early October.

📍 **Alan Rogers Awards Won**
2023, 2016

Key Features

📅 Book Online

🐾 Pets allowed

♿ Accessible Facilities

⛱ Seaside Beach on Site

🏊 Outdoor Pool on Site

🛝 Childrens Play Area

🍸 Bar on Site

🚴 Bicycle Hire on Site

Find Out More
Visit ar.camp/fr66070
or scan the QR code.

Hérault, Languedoc-Roussillon

Alan Rogers Ref: FR34450
Accommodations: 707
Pitches: 55
GPS: 43.31300, 3.36517
Post Code: F-34450

what3words:
entrepreneur.retaken.lotus

Contact:
vacances@sandaya.com
Tel: +33 4 67 01 03 10
www.sandaya.fr/nos-campings/domaine-de-la-dragonniere

Open Dates:
Late March - Early October.

Domaine de la Dragonnière

Camping Sandaya Domaine de la Dragonnière offers an amazing selection of swimming pools and a wide range of sporting activities and entertainment, which amply makes up for it being set back from the sea. It is a busy holiday village, located between the popular resorts of Vias and Portiragnes, and very well organised.

In total, there are about 750 pitches split into two areas, most occupied by a range of smart mobile homes and chalets, but there are still 55 touring pitches with shade from trees and shrubs. All have electrical connections (10A) as well as water and drainage and a number of individual en-suite sanitary units. La Dragonnière lies 5 km. from the nearest sandy beach, and a free shuttle operates in peak season. This is a wonderful site for families with teenagers and young children, offering something for everyone.

Individual sanitary unit on every pitch. Accessible facilities, Baby room with bath and changing area. Laundry. Supermarket. Range of stalls selling local produce. Bar and restaurant complex with takeaway service. Two heated swimming pool complexes with children's pools. Indoor pool. Play areas. Sauna and gym. Multisports pitch. Sports competitions, children's clubs and evening entertainment in high season. Activity programme in low season. Bicycle hire. WiFi (Charged). Excursions are reserved at reception. Mobile homes and chalets for rent. Communal or gas barbecues only.

Key Features

- Book Online
- Pets allowed
- Accessible Facilities
- Seaside Beach Nearby
- Indoor Pool on Site
- Childrens Play Area
- Bar on Site
- Bicycle Hire on Site

Find Out More
Visit ar.camp/fr34450
or scan the QR code.

Hérault, Languedoc-Roussillon

Alan Rogers Ref: FR34070
Accommodations: 581
Pitches: 1026
GPS: 43.26340, 3.32000
Post Code: F-34410

what3words:
timid.sending.advocacy

Contact:
info@leserignanplage.com
Tel: +33 4 67 32 35 33
www.leserignanplage.com

Open Dates:
Late April - Early October.

Camping Le Sérignan-Plage

Yelloh! Village le Sérignan-Plage is a lively and vibrant Mediterranean site with direct access to a superb 600-metre sandy beach (including a naturist section). There's an impressive aqua park, a vast spa centre with lavish balnéotherapy pools, and all kinds of activities designed with youngsters in mind. This is a family-friendly site, and the bustling resort of Valras-Plage is close by.

There are over 1,000 pitches for touring units, all fairly level, on sandy soil and with 10A electricity. Most are well delimited by hedging and have moderate shade. Take bikes, explore the country lanes and local vineyards, visit historic Béziers or, further afield, head to the Camargue for a fascinating day out.

Seven modern sanitary blocks with facilities for guests with reduced mobility. Baby bathroom. Laundry. Motorhome services. Supermarket, bakery and newsagent. Other shops (High season). ATM. Restaurants, bars and takeaway. Hairdresser. Balnéo spa (Afternoons). Gym. Indoor heated pool. Outdoor pools, water playground and waterslides (all season). Tennis. Yoga. Multisport courts. Playgrounds. Trampolines. Children's clubs. Evening entertainment. Sporting activities. Bike rental. Bus to Sérignan village (Jul/Aug). Beach (Lifeguards, high season). Canoeing, water sports, adventure park nearby. WiFi (Charged). Gas barbecues only.

Key Features

- Pets allowed
- Accessible Facilities
- Seaside Beach on Site
- Indoor Pool on Site
- Childrens Play Area
- Bar on Site
- Bicycle Hire on Site

Find Out More
Visit **ar.camp/fr34070**
or scan the QR code.

📍 **Gard, Languedoc-Roussillon**

Alan Rogers Ref: FR30020
Accommodations: 404
Pitches: 532
GPS: 43.56307, 4.15888
Post Code: F-30220

what3words:
asserting.tablecloth.moped

Contact:
info@yellohvillage-petite-camargue.com
Tel: +33 4 66 53 98 98
www.yellohvillage-petite-camargue.com

Open Dates:
Late April - Mid September.

Camping La Petite Camargue

Yelloh! Village la Petite Camargue sets a high standard and is a well-organised site with much to offer. The fascinating Camargue on its doorstep, the medieval walled city of Aigues Mortes and the Mediterranean beaches close by make it an ideal holiday centre.

A large site (532 pitches) on 40 hectares, it has a swimming pool complex and other sporting amenities, including a riding school. There are 128 good-sized touring pitches (6/10A electricity) on level, sandy grass in shady avenues with colourful, flowering shrubs. They are interspersed among more than 300 mobile homes and several tour operator pitches.

Three toilet blocks provide modern facilities, including many combined showers and washbasins. Accessible facilities. Laundry facilities. Motorhome services. Shops, bar/restaurant with pizzeria and takeaway. Hairdresser and beauty centre. Large L-shaped swimming pool with jacuzzi. Aquagym. Scuba diving. Large, imaginative play area and children's club. Mini animal park. Tennis. New multisports court. Jogging circuit. Bicycle hire. Diving school. Free shuttle bus to the beach (July/Aug). Disco/nightclub (Over 16 yrs). WiFi throughout (Free). Facilities are open all season.

Key Features

- Book Online
- Pets allowed
- Accessible Facilities
- Seaside Beach Nearby
- Outdoor Pool on Site
- Childrens Play Area
- Bar on Site
- Bicycle Hire on Site

Find Out More
Visit ar.camp/fr30020
or scan the QR code.

Gard, Languedoc-Roussillon

Alan Rogers Ref: FR30120
Accommodations: 199
Pitches: 350
GPS: 43.99384, 4.81799
Post Code: F-30400

what3words:
translate.urban.boat

Contact:
vacances@sandaya.fr
Tel: +33 4 90 15 15 90
www.sandaya.co.uk/our-
campsites/l-ile-des-papes

Open Dates:
Early May - Late September.

Camping Ile des Papes

Camping Sandaya Ile des Papes is a large, open, well-equipped site. Avignon and its palace and museums are 8 km. away. The site has an extensive swimming pool and a fishing lake with beautiful mature gardens. The railway is quite near, but the noise is not too intrusive. The 350 pitches, 151 for touring (all with 10A electricity), are of a good size on level grass but with little shade.

Games and competitions for all ages are organised in the high season. This site is very popular with groups and is especially busy at weekends and in high season. In July and August, a minibus is available for transport to Avignon, the airport and the railway station; the local bus can take you directly to Avignon.

Sanitary facilities with toilets and showers and accessible facilities, restaurant, Shop, Bar, Take away food, 2 Outdoor swimming pools, children's play area, Bicycle hire on site, Fishing on-site, Kayaking, Entertainment (High season), Kids club, Multisports pitch, Badminton Basketball, Bouncy Castle, Football, Mini disco, Mini golf, Petanque, Ping-pong, Lively evenings, Volleyball. WiFi. Pets allowed.

Key Features

- Book Online
- Pets allowed
- Accessible Facilities
- Seaside Beach Nearby
- Outdoor Pool on Site
- Childrens Play Area
- Bar on Site
- Bicycle Hire on Site

Find Out More
Visit ar.camp/fr30120
or scan the QR code.

📍 **Alpes-de-Haute-Provence, Provence**

Alan Rogers Ref: FR05235
Accommodations: 32
Pitches: 260
GPS: 44.52312, 6.34092
Post Code: F-05230

what3words:
peacemakers.mats.owners

Contact:
reservation@
campinglapresquile.com
Tel: +33 4 92 50 62 63
www.campinglapresquile.com

Open Dates:
Mid May - Mid September.

Camping La Presqu'île

Sunelia La Presqu'île is in the mountains of the Hautes-Alpes, in the south of France. A beautiful road through the Alps leads you to the small mountain village of Prunières. Continue a little further, and you will see the site. It is in a beautiful location on a peninsula on the shores of Lake Serre Ponçon, one of the largest artificial lakes in Europe.

The view from the site is simply breathtaking. The pitches are all on terraces so that you can view the mountains and the lake around you. The most pleasant pitches are at the water's edge. The site has 260 grass /hardstanding pitches, of which 228 are for touring units, with 6-amp hook-up points. There are also 32 bungalows available to hire. There are plenty of activities to keep guests entertained. There's a swimming pool with a toddler pool, a multisport pitch and table tennis, which the older children can enjoy a game or two.

The toilet block has showers, washbasins, and WCs. Accessible facility. Chemical toilet point. Baby room. Dishwashing area. Laundry. Bread to order. Restaurant. Bar. Snack bar. Pizzeria. Takeaway. WiFi. Freezer for ice packs. Outdoor swimming pool. Toddler pool. Children's play area. Table tennis. Tennis court. Multi-sports court. Kids club and crafts (High season) TV room. Dogs allowed. Barbecues are permitted, gas and charcoal only. Lake swimming. Windsurfing nearby.

Key Features

- 📅 Book Online
- 🐾 Pets allowed
- ♿ Accessible Facilities
- 🛝 Childrens Play Area
- 🍸 Bar on Site
- 🐟 Fishing on Site
- ⛵ Sailing on Site

Find Out More
Visit **ar.camp/fr05235**
or scan the QR code.

Alpes-de-Haute-Provence, Provence

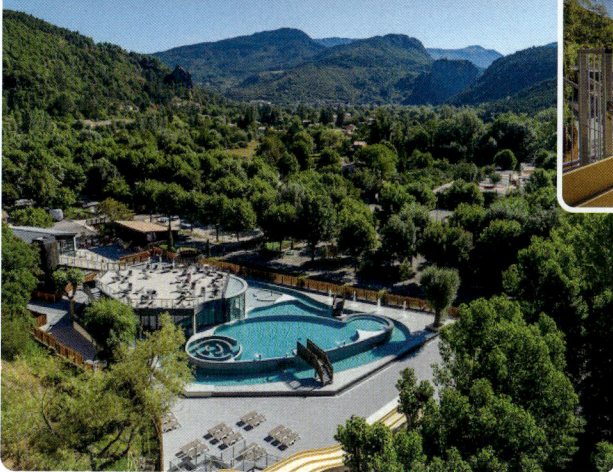

Domaine du Verdon

Close to the Route des Alpes and the Gorges du Verdon, Camping Sandaya Domaine du Verdon is a large, level site, part meadow, part wooded, with an attractive range of planting. There are 500 partly-shaded, rather stony pitches (183 for touring units), all with 16A electricity and many with water and drainage. Numbered and separated by bushes, they vary in size and are mostly separate from the mobile homes and pitches used by tour operators. Some overlook the unfenced Verdon River, so watch your children.

This is a very popular holiday area, the gorge and the associated canoeing and rafting being the main attractions. Two heated pools and numerous on-site activities during the high season help to keep non-canoeists here. This site is ideal for active families.

Refurbished toilet blocks include accessible facilities. Washing machines and dryers. Fridge hire. Motorhome services. Babysitting service. Supermarket. Restaurant, terrace, and log fire for cooler evenings. Pizzeria/crêperie. Takeaway. Heated swimming pools and a paddling pool with a fountain. All amenities are open all season. Fitness equipment. Organised entertainment (July/Aug). Play areas. Minigolf. Archery. Organised walks. Bicycle hire. Riding. Small fishing lake. Room for games and TV. Internet access. Communal barbecue (Charcoal not permitted on pitches). WiFi in some parts (Free). Mobile homes for rent.

Alan Rogers Ref: FR04020
Accommodations: 317
Pitches: 500
GPS: 43.83921, 6.49396
Post Code: F-04120

what3words:
warmer.cocktails.ultimatum

Contact:
vacances@sandaya.fr
Tel: +33 4 92 83 61 29
www.sandaya.co.uk

Open Dates:
Late May - Late September.

Key Features

- Book Online
- Pets allowed
- Accessible Facilities
- Indoor Pool on Site
- Childrens Play Area
- Bar on Site
- Bicycle Hire on Site
- Fishing on Site

Find Out More
Visit ar.camp/fr04020
or scan the QR code.

📍 Var, Côte d'Azur

Alan Rogers Ref: FR83120
Accommodations: 280
Pitches: 1040
GPS: 43.11779, 6.35176
Post Code: F-83230

what3words:
garages.reverb.westerner

Contact:
mail@campdudomaine.com
Tel: +33 4 94 71 03 12
www.campdudomaine.com

Open Dates:
Start April - End October.

🎖 **Alan Rogers Awards Won**
2013

Camp du Domaine

Camp du Domaine is located along the coast just outside the town of Bormes and is 3 km. south of Le Lavandou. The same family has run this large, attractive beachside site for 70 years. With 1040 touring pitches, 957 of which are level and have 10/16A electricity, you can pitch either in the shade in one of the pine forests or the most popular pitches beside the beach with a sea view. Pitches are generous (80-150sqm), but those located furthest from the beach are the largest with more shade. There are also 280 mobile homes/bungalows to rent situated on the hillside with superb views.

The on-site facilities include various bars and restaurants, six tennis courts, two multisport grounds, and play areas for the whole family to enjoy. There is also a programme of entertainment every day ranging from kid and teen clubs to sports competitions, wine tastings and live shows.

Ten modern, well-used, clean toilet blocks serve each area of the site. Accessible facilities. Baby room with showers, WC and changing facilities. Washing machines. Fridge hire. Well-stocked supermarket, bars, and pizzeria (All season). There is no swimming pool, but there is direct beach access. Wellness area. Several excellent play areas. Activities and entertainment for children and teenagers (July/Aug). 6 tennis courts. Kayak and paddle board hire. Wide range of watersports. Modern gym. Only gas and electric barbecues are allowed. Dogs are not accepted in high season. Free WiFi at the tennis bar.

Key Features

🐾 Pets allowed

♿ Accessible Facilities

⛱ Seaside Beach on Site

🛝 Childrens Play Area

🍸 Bar on Site

🐟 Fishing on Site

⛵ Sailing on Site

Find Out More
Visit ar.camp/fr83120
or scan the QR code.

📍 Var, Côte d'Azur

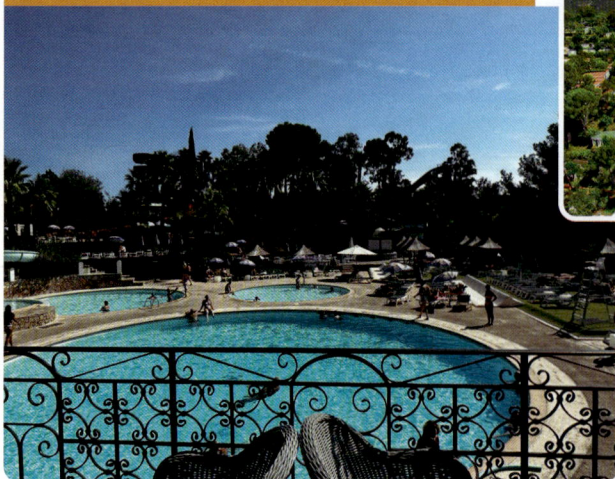

Alan Rogers Ref: FR83020
Accommodations: 331
Pitches: 164
GPS: 43.45378, 6.83282
Post Code: F-83530

what3words:
stipulate.yelps.earmuffs

Contact:
contact@esterel-caravaning.fr
Tel: +33 4 94 82 03 28
www.esterel-caravaning.co.uk

Open Dates:
Late March - Late September.

◎ **Alan Rogers Awards Won**
2023, 2016

Caravaning Esterel

Camping Caravaning Esterel is a quality caravan site east of Saint Raphaël, set among the hills beyond Agay. The site is 3.5 km. from the sandy beach at Agay, where parking is perhaps a little easier than at most places on this coast, but a shuttle from the site runs to and from the beach several times daily in July and August. It has 164 touring pitches (tents are not accepted) with 10A electricity and a water tap. Several 'deluxe' pitches are available with a heated bathroom, jacuzzi, dishwasher and washing machine. Pitches are on shallow terraces, attractively landscaped with good shade and various flowers, giving a feeling of spaciousness.

Access is excellent, and check-in is efficient with English spoken. This took less than 10 minutes from arrival to pitch. Facilities were very modern and cleaned several times a day. They are checked regularly by the team and the site owners, the Laroche family, who created the site over 50 years ago and are very proud of their achievements.

Heated toilet blocks (one refurbished with facilities for babies and children). New en-suite accessible facilities. Laundry room. Motorhome services. Small supermarket. Gift shop. Takeaway. Bar/restaurant. Swimming pool complex (two heated), separate 'jungle' pool for children (Covered, heated). Fitness centre. Spa with sauna. Disco. Archery. Minigolf. Tennis. Pétanque. Squash. Playground. Nursery (4 months to 3 years). Clubs for children and teenagers. Family activities. TV room/library. Bicycle hire. Internet access. Organised events in season. No barbecues. WiFi throughout.

Key Features

📅 Book Online

🐾 Pets allowed

♿ Accessible Facilities

⛱ Seaside Beach Nearby

🏊 Indoor Pool on Site

🎢 Childrens Play Area

🍸 Bar on Site

🚲 Bicycle Hire on Site

Find Out More
Visit **ar.camp/fr83020**
or scan the QR code.

📍 Corse-du-Sud, Corsica

Alan Rogers Ref: FR20415
Accommodations: 65
Pitches: 120
GPS: 41.69809, 8.89629
Post Code: F-20113

what3words:
ardently.disjointed.tastier

Contact:
vignamaggiore@gmail.com
Tel: +33 4 95 74 62 02
www.vignamaggiore.com

Open Dates:
Start May- End September.

Camping Vigna Maggiore

Set on 15 acres and shaded by olive, pine and eucalyptus trees, the pitches at Olmeto's Camping Vigna Maggiore in southern Corsica are simple enough in style. But everything else at this fantastic campsite is about effortless luxury and spectacular views – in fact, there's pretty much everything you could want when escaping reality for a few days. This campsite features 120 touring pitches between 70-180 m2 and are located on terraces.

The simple, avant-garde architecture combines with a hilltop location for fabulous views wherever you go. The restaurant, open in the evenings and for Sunday brunch, offers dining with romantic sea or valley views from the terrace. Enjoy some time in the swimming pool or play a game of table tennis or petanque, or escape to the adults-only wellness centre, a peaceful retreat with a lap pool, spa treatments and hammam baths overlooking the Gulf of Valinco.

Sanitary facilities with baby room and children's facilities, Accessible shower and toilet facilities in the same building as for the other campers, Bar, Restaurant, shop, Spa/Wellness facilities, Children's playground, table tennis, petanque, Entertainment, Outdoor swimming pool, Children's pool, pets allowed, WiFi.

Key Features

- 📅 Book Online
- 🐾 Pets allowed
- ♿ Accessible Facilities
- ⛱ Seaside Beach Nearby
- 🏊 Outdoor Pool on Site
- 🎠 Childrens Play Area
- 🍸 Bar on Site

Find Out More
Visit ar.camp/fr20415
or scan the QR code.

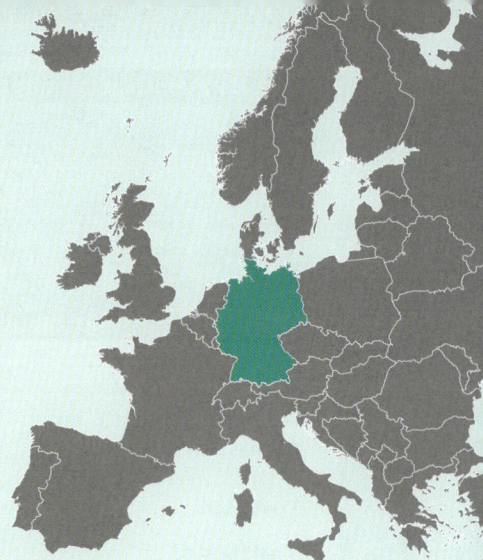

Capital Berlin
Currency Euro (€)
Language German
Time Zone CET (GMT+1)
Telephone Code +49
Emergency Number 112
Tourist Website germany.travel

Shops Supermarkets 8am to 8pm, other shops 10am to 8pm Mon-Sat. All stores including supermarkets close on Sun. Bakeries often open earlier until 6pm Mon-Sat and until midday on Sun.

Money ATMs are widespread in towns and cities and usually accessible 24 hours a day. Some have multilingual instructions. Major cards are accepted, but it's handy to carry cash as this is often the preferred payment method.

Travelling with Children Very children-friendly with a variety of attractions. Public transport is usually discounted for children. Most attractions will let under 18s in for free. Many restaurants offer a kids menu, but children are expected to behave.

Public Holidays 1 Jan New Year's Day; Mar/Apr Good Friday; Mar/Apr Easter Monday; 1 May Labour Day; May Ascension; May/Jun Whit Monday; 3 Oct Day of German Unity; 25 Dec Christmas Day; 26 Dec Boxing Day.

Accessible Travel Score

Access and assistance for wheelchair users and the less abled is widespread, largely standardised and of good quality.

Driving in Germany The country's network of toll-free and well-maintained autobahns is among the best in the world. Drink-driving and using your mobile whilst driving are illegal. You should overtake trams on the right unless there is not sufficient space. Camper vans and cars with caravans are not allowed to exceed 18.75 metres in length, 4 metres in height and 2.55 metres in width. Low Emission Zones exist in all major cities, foreign vehicles are required to register. The use of dashcams is legal, but speed camera detectors are not, so you should disable this features on sat navs or mobile devices before entering the country.

Germany

View all campsites in Germany
ar.camp/germany

See campsite map page 479

Climate Summers are warmer and winters are colder than the UK.	☀ **Avg. summer temp** 18°C (N), 19°C (S)	🌧 **Wettest month** Dec (N), Jul (S)

With its wealth of scenic, historical and cultural interests, Germany is a land of contrasts. From the flatlands of the north to the wooded mountains in the south, with forests in the east and west, regional characteristics are a strong feature of German life and present a rich variety of folklore and customs.

Each region has its own unique identity. Home of lederhosen, beer and sausages is Bavaria in the south, with small towns, medieval castles and Baroque churches. It is also home to the fairytale 19th-century Romanesque Revival castle of Neuschwanstein. In the southwest, Baden Württemberg is famous for its ancient Black Forest and its spas and boasts the most hours of sunshine. Further west is the stunningly beautiful Rhine Valley, where the river winds through steep hills dotted with castles, ruins and vineyards. Eastern Germany is studded with lakes, rivers, and undulating lowlands that give way to mountains. The north has busy cities such as Bremen and Hamburg and traditional North Sea family resorts. The capital city of Berlin, situated in the northeast of the country and once divided by the Berlin Wall, is an increasingly popular tourist destination, with its blend of old and modern architecture, zoos and aquariums, museums, art galleries, green spaces and lively nightlife.

Scan QR code to browse more campsites on our website

📍 **Flensburg, Schleswig-Holstein**

Camping Jarplund

Campingplatz Jarplund is located 2 km south of Flensburg. Despite being close to the town (Jarplund), the site is quiet and idyllic in the countryside. Flensburg can be reached quickly by public transport, bike or car and offers a beautiful old town and harbour in addition to the shopping centre.

The Flensburg Fjord and the Baltic Sea on the doorstep invite you to swim and hike. The site has leisure facilities, such as a swimming pool with a paddling pool (seasonal) and a playground with attractive play equipment for the children. There are 100 grass pitches, 60 of which are touring pitches suitable for caravans, motorhomes, or tents with 16 amp hook-up points. The site also has log cabins available to rent.

The toilet block has showers, washbasins, and WCs. Accessible facilities. Chemical toilet point. Laundry with washing machine and dryer. Dishwashing area. Dogs allowed. Dog walk. WiFi. BBQs allowed. Shop. Ice pack freezer. Children's play area. Outdoor swimming pool and toddler pool (Seasonal) Trampoline. Table tennis. Multi-sports area. Climbing wall. Late-night arrivals area. Earliest arrival time: 15.00.

Alan Rogers Ref: DE25700
Accommodations: 2
Pitches: 100
GPS: 54.74500, 9.43838
Post Code: D-24941

what3words:
overstay.waffled.assessed

Contact:
campingplatz.jarplund@web.de
Tel: +49 46 19 79 024
www.campingplatz-jarplund.de

Open Dates:
Mid March - Mid November.

Key Features

🐾 Pets allowed

♿ Accessible Facilities

🌊 Outdoor Pool on Site

🛝 Childrens Play Area

Find Out More
Visit **ar.camp/de25700** or scan the QR code.

Westoverledingen, Lower Saxony

Alan Rogers Ref: DE29380
Accommodations: 7
Pitches: 350
GPS: 53.17471, 7.42011
Post Code: D-26810

what3words:
paprika.captain.runway

Contact:
info@ostfriesland-camping.de
Tel: +49 49 55 92 00 40
ostfriesland-camping.de

Open Dates:
Start April - End October.

Camping Am Emsdeich

Comfort-Camping Freizeitpark Am Emsdeich is a large site in a beautiful location by the Freizeitssee. This is a natural, moderately sized lake near Westoverledingen (4 km away) with a large sandy beach. They have constructed a few wooden platforms that project over the water, ideal for sunbathing and jumping into the water. Also, it is handy for tying up your boat. Canoeing and kayaking are favourite pastimes here, as are fishing and windsurfing. There is a large restaurant ideally located next to the lake. It has a comprehensive menu including traditional East Frisian specialities dishes to try, all whilst enjoying the great views.

Here, you can also find a small camping shop that supplies the necessities to cook back at your pitch. The 350 touring pitches have 16-amp hook-up points, are well maintained and spacious with plenty of shade and privacy. This is from the neatly maintained hedges and bushes around each pitch. There are also 30 hardstanding motorhome pitches.

The heated toilet blocks have showers (charged), washbasins, and WCs. Accessible facilities. Baby room. Laundry with washing machine and dryer. Dishwashing by EasyBe, Chemical toilet point. Motorhome service point. Shop. Bread to order. Snack bar. Takeaway. Bar. Restaurant. Communal BBQ area. Freezer for ice packs. Bike hire. Children's play area. Dogs allowed. Wellness centre. Games room. Table tennis. Boules. Multi-sport pitch. Volleyball. TV room. Fitness equipment. Electric car charging.

Key Features

- Pets allowed
- Accessible Facilities
- Childrens Play Area
- Bar on Site
- Bicycle Hire on Site
- Fishing on Site

Find Out More
Visit ar.camp/de29380
or scan the QR code.

📍 **Hamburg, Hamburg**

Alan Rogers Ref: DE30050
Accommodations: 12
Pitches: 115
GPS: 53.65015, 9.92927
Post Code: D-22457

what3words:
clearly.ordering.rock

Contact:
hamburg@knauscamp.de
Tel: +49 40 55 94 225
www.knauscamp.de

Open Dates:
All year.

Camping Hamburg

Knaus Camping Hamburg is situated some 15 km. from the centre of Hamburg on the northern edge of the town; this is a suitable base either for visiting this famous German city or as a night stop before catching the Harwich ferry or travelling to Denmark. There is some traffic noise because the autobahn runs alongside (despite efforts to screen it out) and also some aircraft noise. However, the proximity of the A7 (E45) does make it easy to find. The 115 pitches for short-term touring are about 100 sq.m, on grass with access from gravel roads. All have 6A electricity and are marked out with small trees and hedges.

Only basic food supplies are stocked in reception as the site is about a 10-minute walk from the restaurants and shops in town. Apart from some road traffic 'hum', as previously mentioned, this is a quiet, well-laid-out site. A large number of trees and shrubs offer shade and privacy. Ten gravel roads are reserved for large motorhomes.

A deposit is required for the key to the single sanitary block, a well-constructed modern building with high-quality facilities and heated in cool weather. Accessible sanitary facilities, with allocated pitches close to the sanitary block. Washing machines and dryers. Dishwashing by EasyBe, Motorhome services. Shop with essentials. Playground. Dogs accepted. WiFi (charged).

Key Features

📅 All Year

🐾 Pets allowed

♿ Accessible Facilities

♿ Childrens Play Area

Find Out More
Visit **ar.camp/de30050**
or scan the QR code.

📍 Klein Rönnau, Schleswig-Holstein

Alan Rogers Ref: DE30080
Accommodations: 6
Pitches: 120
GPS: 53.96142, 10.33737
Post Code: D-23795

what3words:
bladed.start.brightening

Contact:
info@kluethseecamp.de
Tel: +49 45 51 82 368
www.kluethseecamp.de

Open Dates:
All year except February.

Klüthseecamp Seeblick

Klüthseecamp Seeblick is a modern, family-run site situated on a small hill between two lakes. It is an ideal location for a family holiday with activities on site for all ages and a useful base to explore the region. The large, open, grass touring part of the site has sunny, shaded and semi-shaded areas.

There are 120 touring pitches on reasonably level ground, all with electricity (10/16A) and 30 with water and drainage, and pitches for tents in natural surroundings. Klüthseecamp offers wellness, a swimming pool, food and drink, organised entertainment for young and old, and a sandy lakeside beach.

Two modern, heated sanitary blocks, some washbasins in cabins, five bathrooms to rent and free showers. Facilities for children and accessible facilities. Attractive baby room. Motorhome services. Gas supplies. Laundry. Shop with breakfast service. Bar and café in the main building, additional beer garden and restaurant by the lake. Outdoor swimming pool (heated May-Sept). Wellness. Sauna, steam bath, massage. Play room/kindergarten. Bouncy castle. Three outside play areas. Large projected TV. Bicycle hire. Go-kart hire. Minigolf. Way-marked paths around the lake. Kids' and teenagers' clubs, including weekly disco. Free WiFi at the small restaurant.

Key Features

- 📅 Book Online
- 🐾 Pets allowed
- ♿ Accessible Facilities
- ⛱ Seaside Beach Nearby
- 🏊 Outdoor Pool on Site
- 🎮 Childrens Play Area
- 🍸 Bar on Site
- 🚲 Bicycle Hire on Site

Find Out More
Visit ar.camp/de30080
or scan the QR code.

📍 **Ostseebad, Mecklenburg-West Pomerania**

Alan Rogers Ref: DE37900
Pitches: 340
GPS: 54.27960, 13.71379
Post Code: D-18586

what3words:
cramps.upstage.bearings

Contact:
campingplatz-thiessow@t-online.de
Tel: +49 38 30 86 69 585
www.campingplatz-thiessow.de

Open Dates:
All year. (Excluding November)

Campingplatz Thiessow

If you are looking for a holiday near the sea and the right atmosphere to relax and unwind, then Camping Thiessow in Thiessow is the place for you. It has a unique location between the Baltic Sea and the Zicker See on a narrow strip of coastline. It is just a few steps to the fine, one-kilometre-long sandy beach, one of the most beautiful beaches on Rügen island. The campsite is located in the Southeast Rügen Biosphere Reserve, perfect for nature lovers and those looking for a quiet and peaceful holiday.

The site, which is operated by the municipality of Mönchgut, has 340 pitches for tents, caravans and motorhomes. There are options for it to be located under pine trees or in open sunny pitches. The site offers excursion programmes, guided walks, and an entertainment programme. You can swim nearby in the sea or try windsurfing and paddle boarding. Other on-site facilities include a restaurant and snack bar open during high season and a children's play area.

The heated toilet block has showers (charged), washbasins, and WCs. Accessible facilities. Family toilet. Baby room. Dishwashing area. Laundry with washing machine and dryer. Chemical toilet point. Defibrillator. Cooking facilities. Freezer for ice packs. Small shop. Bread to order. Snack Bar Takeaway. Restaurant. Bar. Bike hire. Children's play area. Table tennis. Volleyball. Dogs and BBQs are allowed. Communal BBQ area.

Key Features

📅 All Year

🐾 Pets allowed

♿ Accessible Facilities

⛱ Seaside Beach Nearby

🛝 Childrens Play Area

🍸 Bar on Site

🚲 Bicycle Hire on Site

Find Out More
Visit **ar.camp/de37900**
or scan the QR code.

📍 **Munster, Lower Saxony**

Alan Rogers Ref: DE29220
Accommodations: 5
Pitches: 72
GPS: 52.91868, 10.12729
Post Code: D-29633

what3words:
sculpture.kingpin.populates

Contact:
info@oertzewinkel.de
Tel: +49 50 55 55 49
www.oertzewinkel.de

Open Dates:
All year.

Camping Zum Örtzewinkel

In the middle of the Lüneburger Heide, Camping Zum Örtzewinkel is directly next to the river Oertze. An idyllic location - right between the most beautiful points of the Heide and the major theme parks in the area. There are 72 touring pitches on-site with 16Amp electric hook-up points available and five wooden cabins to hire. Two sanitary blocks are easily reachable, with facilities being functional and comfortable. There are a couple of children's playgrounds in between pitches. For older children, there is table tennis, a football field, and a lounge with television.

You can rent bicycles and go-carts, or if you are into horses, you can bring your horse with you here as there are plenty of opportunities to explore the surrounding countryside or book a riding lesson on-site. For those who enjoy a spot of fishing, there are opportunities to do so on-site at the campsite's pond. The pond also offers guests the chance to have a refreshing dip in the summer months. The campsite also has a restaurant offering a range of traditional dishes from the region and modern classics.

Two heated sanitary buildings, Accessible facilities, Baby changing room, Shop (small) Children's play area, Restaurant, Bar, Bicycle hire, Lounge,Table tennis, Football field, TV, swimming pond, Fishing, Riding, BBQ's allowed, WiFi, Pets allowed,

Key Features

📅 Book Online

📅 All Year

🐾 Pets allowed

♿ Accessible Facilities

🎠 Childrens Play Area

🍸 Bar on Site

🚲 Bicycle Hire on Site

🐟 Fishing on Site

Find Out More
Visit ar.camp/de29220
or scan the QR code.

📍 **Münster, North Rhine-Westphalia**

Alan Rogers Ref: DE31850
Accommodations: 4
Pitches: 570
GPS: 51.94645, 7.68908
Post Code: D-48157

what3words:
plant.clinked.damp

Contact:
mail@campingplatz-muenster.de
Tel: +49 25 13 11 982
campingplatz-muenster.de

Open Dates:
All year.

Campingplatz Münster

This is a first-class site on the outskirts of Münster. Of a total of 570 pitches, 120 are for touring units, each with electricity, water, drainage, and TV sockets. The pitches are level, most with partial hardstanding, and others are separated into groups by mature hedges and trees providing shade.

The campsite reception has an extensive range of tourist brochures, many in English, full of useful tips. A small shop is next to the reception desk, and a comfortable bar/restaurant with a terrace is adjacent. Bicycles are available for hire on-site, too. There are plenty of opportunities to enjoy a day at the campsite, with a mini golf course, a tennis court and a multisport pitch. There is also an on-site sauna if you want to relax after spending the day exploring the area.

The two sanitary blocks are well-designed, modern and maintained to the highest standards. Controllable showers are token-operated. Two accessible units. Baby room. Cooking facilities. Washing machine, dryer and ironing facilities. Sauna. Hairdressing salon. Motorhome services. Shop. Bar/restaurant. Minigolf. Play area. Beach volleyball. Chess. Tennis. Playroom (under 8 yrs). Bicycle hire. Security barrier card deposit € 10. WiFi throughout.

Key Features

📅 All Year

🐾 Pets allowed

♿ Accessible Facilities

🏊 Outdoor Pool on Site

🛝 Childrens Play Area

🍸 Bar on Site

🚲 Bicycle Hire on Site

🎣 Fishing on Site

Find Out More
Visit **ar.camp/de31850**
or scan the QR code.

📍 **Potsdam, Brandenburg**

Alan Rogers Ref: DE38270
Accommodations: 9
Pitches: 240
GPS: 52.35857, 13.00633
Post Code: D-14471

what3words:
reinstated.email.lobe

Contact:
info@camping-potsdam.de
Tel: +49 33 19 51 09 88
www.camping-potsdam.de

Open Dates:
Start April - Early November.

Camping Sanssouci

Sanssouci is a good, if relatively expensive, base for visiting Potsdam and Berlin. It lies about 2 km. from Sanssouci Park on the banks of the Templiner See, in a quiet woodland setting. There are 240 pitches in total, 170 for touring with 6-16A electricity, and many also have their own water tap and drainage. Tall trees mark out these pitches; most have views overlooking the lake. There is a separate area for tents.

Reflecting the effort put into its development, the campsite has many facilities to make your stay comfortable. Enjoy delicious homemade food at the restaurant overlooking the lake or the spa facilities at the hotel 200m from the campsite. The campsite is located right on the water's edge, so there is plenty of water-filled fun. There are plenty of activities to get involved in with stand-up paddle boarding, kayaking and swimming. Or how about a Kite surfing lesson? Children between 9 and 14 can join a surfing camp during the high season on weekends.

Sanitary facilities are in two modern, heated blocks containing hot showers, washbasins in cabins and facilities for babies. Useful, accessible facilities. Bathrooms to rent. Laundry. Gas supplies. Kitchen. Motorhome services. Shop. Restaurant/bar. Swimming and sailing in the lake. Wellness. Rowing boats, motorboats, canoes and pedaloes for hire. Fishing. Play area. Bicycle hire (E-bikes on request). Table tennis, Hairdresser. Internet café and WiFi throughout (charged). Public transport tickets and discounts for Berlin attractions.

Key Features

- 📅 Book Online
- 🐾 Pets allowed
- ♿ Accessible Facilities
- 🛝 Childrens Play Area
- 🍸 Bar on Site
- 🚲 Bicycle Hire on Site
- 🐟 Fishing on Site
- ⛵ Sailing on Site

Find Out More
Visit **ar.camp/de38270**
or scan the QR code.

📍 **Eifel, North Rhine-Westphalia**

Eifel-Camp

This delightful campsite offers spaciously arranged pitches on terraces set amongst lush greenery. All pitches are equipped with 220V/16 A electricity connection, and the long-term pitches have access to the community antenna/common aerial. You will also find a drain and service station for caravans and campervans, as well as well-grounded pitches for campervans.

Located in the northern Eifel, Eifel-Camp is situated only a few kilometres away from Blankenheim and close to Lake Freilingen in the countryside.

Enjoy the comforts of this award-winning campsite with facilities including an accessible unit, spacious and superb bathroom/sanitary facilities with centrally heated showers providing free unlimited hot water. You may also book individual bathing units with washbasin, shower and toilet. Washing machines and tumble dryers. The popular "Waldläufer" restaurant with a sun terrace. On-site kiosk offering fresh rolls and croissants in the morning, as well as basic necessities. Playground. The leisure club " Geißbock-Stadel" on the first floor of the sanitary building offers various options for guests, e.g. as a lounge or recreation room, but it can also be used for mini-club activities, the mini-disco, indoor sports activities or cinema shows. An open barbecue facility with a separate fireplace on the outskirts of the campsite or a small complete BBQ cabin in the upper part of the "mountain pasture" offering room for up to 24 people. There are also two BBQ cabins (additional charge).

Alan Rogers Ref: DE31970
Accommodations: 34
Pitches: 185
GPS: 50.41508, 6.71869
Post Code: D-53945

what3words:
doses.quaver.aspire

Contact:
eifel-camp@freizeit-oasen.de
Tel: +49 26 97 282
www.eifel-camp.de

Open Dates:
All year.

🏅 **Alan Rogers Awards Won**
2019

Key Features

📅 Book Online

📅 All Year

🐾 Pets allowed

♿ Accessible Facilities

🧑‍🦽 Childrens Play Area

🚲 Bicycle Hire on Site

Find Out More
Visit **ar.camp/de31970**
or scan the QR code.

📍 **Olpe-Sondern, North Rhine-Westphalia**

Camping Biggesee

Situated on a gentle, south-facing slope that leads down to the water's edge, Vier Jahreszeiten - Camping Biggesee blends in well with its wooded surroundings. The 200 touring pitches, all with electricity, are arranged in circles at the top part of the site and on a series of wide terraces lower down. They are grassy with some hardstandings.

From the lower part of the site, there is access through a gate to a large open meadow that ends at the water's edge, where swimming is permitted. The attractive Biggesee, with arms branching out into the surrounding hills, is a watersports paradise where virtually all forms of watersports are available. These include schools for sailing, diving and windsurfing. Close by, hundreds of kilometres of paths and cycleways lead along the lakeside and through the surrounding forests.

Excellent heated sanitary facilities are in two areas. New building with cabins for hire. Many washbasins in cabins and special showers for children. Facilities for babies and accessible facilities. Laundry. Motorhome services. Cooking facilities. Shop. Restaurant. Bistro (including breakfast). Paintball. Water blob and Aquapark. Playroom and playground for smaller children. Grill hut. Fishing. Solarium and sauna. Entertainment and excursions. Dog shower.

Alan Rogers Ref: DE32100
Accommodations: 2
Pitches: 200
GPS: 51.07529, 7.85323
Post Code: D-57462

what3words:
students.smart.staked

Contact:
info@biggesee.com
Tel: +49 27 61 94 41 11
www.biggesee.freizeit-oasen.de

Open Dates:
All Year.

Key Features

📅 Book Online

📅 All Year

🐾 Pets allowed

♿ Accessible Facilities

🍼 Childrens Play Area

🍸 Bar on Site

🐟 Fishing on Site

🐴 Riding on Site

Find Out More
Visit **ar.camp/de32100**
or scan the QR code.

Trendelburg, Hessen

Alan Rogers Ref: DE33420
Accommodations: 4
Pitches: 120
GPS: 51.57289, 9.42403
Post Code: D-34388

what3words:
sinister.coroner.unforced

Contact:
kontakt@campingplatz-trendelburg.de
Tel: +49 5675 301
www.campingplatz-trendelburg.de

Open Dates:
All year.

Camping Trendelburg

Camping Trendelburg is located on the Mühlenanger, an island in the Diemel, surrounded by the Mühlengraben and the Diemel, idyllically situated at the foot of the Trendelburg. The site has 120 touring pitches, half occupied by seasonal units. There is a large tent meadow away from the other guests, ideal for groups, where campfires are allowed. There are also four apartments available to hire. The main pitches are located to the west of the campsite. The on-site facilities are centrally located where you will find the reception building, the campsite restaurant and the small shop. A table tennis table is available for a game or two, and rackets can be borrowed from reception.

Ideally located next to a weir, there are plenty of paddling opportunities for the younger children in the shallows below, whilst swimming is available above the wire. Some local companies offer canoe and kayaking trips along the river Diemel, but a slipway is available from the campsite if you bring your canoe or kayak. You can also fish directly from the campsite's river bank.

The toilet block has showers, wash basins, and WCs. Accessible Facilities. Laundry with washing machine and dryer. Baby room. Chemical toilet point. Dishwashing area. Children's play area. Games room. TV room. WiFi zone. Restaurant. Snack bar. Takeaway. Ice pack freezer. Dogs allowed. BBQs allowed. Bread to order. Fishing on site. Table tennis. Earliest arrival time: 14.00.

Key Features

- All Year
- Pets allowed
- Accessible Facilities
- Childrens Play Area
- Bar on Site
- Fishing on Site

Find Out More
Visit **ar.camp/de33420**
or scan the QR code.

📍 Quedlinburg, Saxony-Anhalt

Alan Rogers Ref: DE39120
Accommodations: 110
Pitches: 140
GPS: 51.68848, 11.11076
Post Code: D-06485

what3words:
rampages.guises.clip

Contact:
harz-camp-bremer-teich@
web.de
Tel: +49 39 48 56 08 10
www.harz-camp-gernrode.de

Open Dates:
All year.

Harz-Camp Bremer Teich

Adjacent to the four-hectare Bremer Teich Lake in Saxony-Anhalt and with views of the Harz mountains, this idyllic site has been extensively upgraded in recent years. There are 140 level touring pitches (80 sq.m), the majority with 16A electricity and 20 fully serviced. The main attraction is the lake, whose shallow banks make it suitable for paddling, and a lifeguard is present in high season.

It is an ideal base for visiting the local area, in particular, the medieval town of Quedlinburg, a UNESCO World Heritage town with half-timbered houses, a castle and a cathedral. Accommodation on site includes cottages and a hostel, making it a popular destination for groups and school trips.

Renovated sanitary blocks can be heated and have hot showers, private cabins, family shower room and facilities for children and accessible facilities. Washing machines. Motorhome services. Shop (Seasonal). Restaurant (Seasonal). Shop, Lake swimming. Playground. Fishing.

Key Features

🗓 Book Online

📅 All Year

🐾 Pets allowed

♿ Accessible Facilities

🏊 Outdoor Pool on Site

🤸 Childrens Play Area

🍸 Bar on Site

🐟 Fishing on Site

Find Out More
Visit **ar.camp/de39120**
or scan the QR code.

📍 Hohenfelden, Bavaria (N)

Alan Rogers Ref: DE40720
Accommodations: 41
Pitches: 194
GPS: 50.87208, 11.17874
Post Code: D-99448

what3words:
insides.iconic.butter

Contact:
info@stausee-hohenfelden.de
Tel: +49 36 45 04 20 81
www.campingplatz-hohenfelden.de

Open Dates:
All year.

Stausee Hohenfelden

Campsite Stausee Hohenfelden can be found in Hohenfelden, Thuringia, located in the woods and by a large lake/reservoir, which is the heart of the site. This large terraced site has 194 (100m2) marked-out touring pitches with plenty of shaded areas by mature trees. Electrical hook-up points (16A) are available. You will also find over 330 permanent pitches, bungalows, and holiday homes for rental. Stausee Hohenfelden is also located close to a lovely sandy beach. The staff at the reception desk are all friendly and helpful, ensuring a smooth check-in and providing valuable information during your stay.

First thing in the morning, you'll find a selection of freshly baked bread rolls available and adjacent to the site, you will find a restaurant serving various local dishes and quick bites to eat. Dog owners will appreciate the private dog field with direct access to the lake. The sanitary facilities are immaculate and well-maintained, reflecting the attention to detail throughout the campsite.

Hot showers, washbasins and heated toilet facilities. Family toilet facilities and baby room. Accessible facilities, Washing up sinks. Washing machines and dryers. Waste water drainage and water connection points. Restaurant (Apr-Dec). Fresh bread daily. Small grocery selection. Lake swimming. Children's playground. Multi-sports field. Table tennis. Fishing. Cycle and walking routes from the site. Max 2 dogs allowed. Barbecues are not permitted. WiFi.

Key Features

📅 All Year

🐾 Pets allowed

♿ Accessible Facilities

🧒 Childrens Play Area

🚲 Bicycle Hire on Site

🐟 Fishing on Site

⛵ Sailing on Site

Find Out More
Visit **ar.camp/de40720**
or scan the QR code.

Dresden, Saxony

Alan Rogers Ref: DE38330
Accommodations: 40
Pitches: 238
GPS: 51.12055, 13.98083
Post Code: D-01900

what3words:
nestled.rescues.pearls

Contact:
info@luxoase.de
Tel: +49 35 95 25 66 66
www.luxoase.de

Open Dates:
Start March - Mid December.

Alan Rogers Awards Won
2017

Camping LuxOase

This is a well-organised and quiet site located just northeast of Dresden, with easy access from the autobahn. The site has very good facilities and is arranged on grassland beside a lake, which is reached from the site through a gate. Although the site is fairly open, trees do provide shade in some areas.

There are 238 large touring pitches (plus 40 seasonal in a separate area), marked by bushes or posts on generally flat or slightly sloping grass. All have 10/16A electricity, and 132 have water and drainage. At the entrance is an area of hardstanding (with electricity) for late arrivals. A member of the Leading Campings group. You may swim, fish or use inflatables in the lake (at your own risk). A wide entertainment programme is organised for children in high season.

Two excellent buildings provide modern, heated facilities with private cabins, a family room, baby room, Accessible units and eight bathrooms for hire. Special facilities for children with novelty showers and washbasins. Kitchen. Gas supplies. Motorhome services. Shop and bar plus restaurant (Seasonal). Lake swimming. Jacuzzi. Sauna. Fitness room. Fishing. Play area. Sports field. Minigolf. Train, bus and theatre tickets from reception. Regular guided bus trips to Dresden, Prague, etc. Bicycle hire. Internet point. WiFi throughout.

Key Features

- Book Online
- Pets allowed
- Accessible Facilities
- Childrens Play Area
- Bar on Site
- Bicycle Hire on Site
- Fishing on Site

Find Out More
Visit ar.camp/de38330 or scan the QR code.

📍 Gemünden-Hofstetten, Bavaria (N)

Alan Rogers Ref: DE37350
Accommodations: 4
Pitches: 100
GPS: 50.05144, 9.65684
Post Code: D-97737

what3words:
waterfall.leaps.pleaser

Contact:
info@spessart-camping.de
Tel: +49 93 51 86 45
www.spessart-camping.de

Open Dates:
Start April - Early October.

Spessart Schönrain

Situated 4 km. west of the town of Gemünden, with views of forested hills bordering the Main river, this is a very friendly, well-organised, family-run site with excellent facilities. Frau Endres welcomes British guests and speaks a little English. There are 100 pitches, 70 of which are for touring. They vary in size (70-150 sq.m), and all have 10A electricity and 20 with water. Another area has been developed for tents.

The site has a pleasant bar with a terrace. Meals can be ordered from local restaurants for delivery, or the site's bus will provide transport. The campsite shop sells all the basic necessities, plus local schnapps and full-bodied Franconian wine.

A superb new heated sanitary building has card-operated entry – the card is prepaid and operates the showers, washing machines and dryers, gas cooker, baby bathroom, jacuzzi etc. Two private bathrooms (complete with wine and balcony!) to rent. Accessible facilities, Motorhome services. Bar. Shop. Swimming pool. Beauty and wellness programme. General room with play area for very young children, games and a TV. Upstairs library and Internet café, fitness room and solarium. Playground. Bicycle hire. Excursions.

Key Features

🐾 Pets allowed

♿ Accessible Facilities

🏊 Outdoor Pool on Site

🛝 Childrens Play Area

🍸 Bar on Site

🚲 Bicycle Hire on Site

Find Out More
Visit ar.camp/de37350
or scan the QR code.

Schwäbisch Hall, Baden-Württemberg

Alan Rogers Ref: DE35070
Accommodations: 33
Pitches: 67
GPS: 49.09827, 9.74230
Post Code: D-74523

what3words:
suspect.marker.vanish

Contact:
camping.sha-steinbach@t-online.de
Tel: +49 79 12 984
www.camping-schwabisch-hall

Open Dates:
Start April- Mid October

Camping Am Steinbacher See

Camping Am Steinbacher See is in Schwäbisch Hall, Baden-Württemberg near the Kocher River. At the foot of the former Benedictine monastery of Comburg. It is centrally located in a nature reserve directly on Lake Steinbach (unsuitable for swimming). It is a small site within walking or cycling distance of Schwäbisch Hall, which is worth taking a day to visit. The site has 67 grass touring pitches with 16-amp hook-up points available and 33 seasonal pitches.

This family-run site has set itself the goal of making guests' holidays as pleasant as possible; if you are looking for a quiet site without a large entertainment program and attractions, this is the right place for you. Simple but clean sanitary facilities are available, as well as a volleyball court and basketball hoop.

The heated toilet block has showers, washbasins, and WCs. Accessible facilities. Chemical toilet point. Dishwashing area. Laundry with washing machine and dryer. Motorhome service point. Bread to order. Bar. Communal BBQ area. WiFi. Dogs and BBQs are allowed. Freezer for ice packs. Children's play area. Table tennis. Bocce. Volleyball. TV room.

Key Features

🐾 Pets allowed

♿ Accessible Facilities

🧒 Childrens Play Area

Find Out More
Visit ar.camp/de35070
or scan the QR code.

📍 Nürnberg, Bavaria (N)

Campingpark Nürnberg

Knaus Campingpark Nürnberg is an ideal site for visiting the fascinating and historically important city of Nürnberg (Nuremberg). The site is 500 meters from the Grundig Stadium and 600 meters from the Nuremberg Exhibition Centre. There are 140 shaded pitches, 118 with 10A electrical connections and with water taps in groups. On mainly flat grass among the tall trees, some pitches are marked out with ranch-style boards, others still attractively 'wild', some others with hardstanding. There is sufficient space for them to be quite big, and many have the advantage of being drive-through. When there is an event at the Max-Morlock-Stadion, there can be a lot of noise, and road diversions are in place. It is well worth checking before planning an arrival.

There are also some mobile homes and a few long-term units. All the Knaus parks are well run, and they are pleased to welcome British tourers. Red squirrels are a common sight. Since acquiring this pleasantly situated site, the Knaus group have undertaken various improvements, and it now ranks as one of the best city sites.

A heated sanitary building offers first-class facilities, including free showers. Washing machines and dryers. Cooking facilities. Accessible facilities. Gas supplies. Motorhome services. Shop. Bar/bistro area with terrace and light meals served. Play area in woodland.

Alan Rogers Ref: DE36100
Accommodations: 14
Pitches: 140
GPS: 49.42318, 11.12154
Post Code: D-90471

what3words:
curtains.remix.laws

Contact:
nuernberg@knauscamp.de
Tel: +49 91 19 81 27 17
www.knauscamp.de

Open Dates:
All year.

Key Features

📅 Book Online

📅 All Year

🐾 Pets allowed

♿ Accessible Facilities

🚼 Childrens Play Area

🍸 Bar on Site

Find Out More
Visit **ar.camp/de36100**
or scan the QR code.

Staufen, Baden-Württemberg

Camping Belchenblick

This site stands at the gateway, via Münstertal, to the Black Forest. Not very high up itself, it is just at the start of the long road climb, which leads to the top of Belchen, one of the highest summits of the forest. The site has plenty of shade for the 230 pitches (182 for touring units), all with electrical connections (10/16A, some 2-pin) and TV (100 also have water). The site has recently undergone some modernisation, including improvements to some sanitary facilities.

The shop and café offer a limited selection, but the food was tasty. Charges include hot water and use of the inviting indoor pool. Staufen is a pleasant little town with character. A local train runs past the site during the day. Visitors are entitled to a Konus Card, allowing the user free bus and train travel throughout the Black Forest.

Three sanitary blocks are heated and have free hot water, individual washbasins (six private cabins), plus 21 family cabins with WC, basin and shower (some on payment per night for exclusive use). Accessible facilities, Dog shower. Washing machine. Gas supplies. Motorhome services. Shop (Seasonal). Bar (All year). Snacks and takeaway (Seasonal). Indoor pool. Sauna and solarium. Tennis. Playground with barbecue area. Table tennis and pool room. Bicycle, fun bike and skate hire. WiFi (charged).

Alan Rogers Ref: DE34450
Pitches: 230
GPS: 47.87178, 7.73667
Post Code: D-79219

what3words:
charts.firefighters.compose

Contact:
info@camping-belchenblick.de
Tel: +49 76 33 70 45
www.camping-belchenblick.de

Open Dates:
All year.

Key Features

- Book Online
- All Year
- Pets allowed
- Accessible Facilities
- Indoor Pool on Site
- Childrens Play Area
- Bicycle Hire on Site

Find Out More
Visit ar.camp/de34450
or scan the QR code.

📍 Bad Wildbad, Baden-Württemberg

Alan Rogers Ref: DE34060
Accommodations: 29
Pitches: 300
GPS: 48.73807, 8.57710
Post Code: D-75323

what3words:
loveable.hints.hubcaps

Contact:
info@kleinenzhof.de
Tel: +49 70 81 34 35
www.kleinenzhof.de

Open Dates:
All year.

Resort Kleinenzhof

In the northern Black Forest, popular with walkers and cyclists alike, this large and busy site runs along the bank of a small but safe stream in a dramatic wooded valley. Of the 300 or so pitches, 100 of which are for tourers, all with 16A electricity and water and most with drainage. The four shower blocks are of the highest quality. In the middle of the site is a hotel, bar and restaurant complex, which incorporates indoor and outdoor pools available free to campers.

There is also a small river that flows through the middle of the campsite, perfect for paddle boarding or rafting. During winter, the campsite is mainly geared towards winter sports enthusiasts as the area is suitable for cross-country skiing.

Four excellent sanitary blocks, all heated, are clean, with many washbasins in cabins and showers. Accessible Facilities. Baby changing. Children's bathroom. Family bathrooms to rent. Dog shower. Laundry facilities and dishwasher. Motorhome services. Gas. Shop. Bar and restaurant (at the hotel). Indoor pool. Outdoor pool (Seasonal) and paddling pool. Impressive indoor sports/games hall with toddler annexe. Petting zoo, Playgrounds. TV and games room. Fishing. Go-kart hire. WiFi over site (charged).

Key Features

- Book Online
- All Year
- Pets allowed
- Accessible Facilities
- Indoor Pool on Site
- Childrens Play Area
- Bar on Site
- Bicycle Hire on Site

Find Out More
Visit ar.camp/de34060 or scan the QR code.

📍 Erpfingen, Baden-Württemberg

Camping Schwäbische Alb

Azur Rosencamping Schwäbische Alb is situated in the verdant countryside of the Swabian Alb and within reach of the state capital, Stuttgart. This site may be a good choice for families seeking a quiet, relaxing holiday with some activities available for children. There are 150 level grassy touring pitches, some shaded, 120 with 16A Europlugs.

The campsite is set over extensive grounds, perfect for children to explore, run around, and let off some steam. There is also an outdoor swimming pool to splash around in and an activity and entertainment programme during July and August. Many of the facilities on site have been upgraded recently, including a modern reception with a shop and daily bread roll service. There is also a Children's play area and beach volleyball court.

Toilet facilities include provision for baby changing and accessible facilities. Launderette. Motorhome services. Supermarket. Restaurant with terrace. Outdoor swimming pool. Playground. Entertainment and animation programme, Garden chess. Beach volleyball. Pets allowed, WiFi.

Alan Rogers Ref: DE34070
Accommodations: 15
Pitches: 150
GPS: 48.36296, 9.18346
Post Code: D-72820

what3words:
toolbar.dislodge.tablecloths

Contact:
erpfingen@azur-camping.de
Tel: +49 71 28 466
www.azur-camping.com

Open Dates:
All year.

Key Features

📅 Book Online

📅 All Year

🐾 Pets allowed

♿ Accessible Facilities

🏊 Outdoor Pool on Site

🧒 Childrens Play Area

🍸 Bar on Site

Find Out More
Visit **ar.camp/de34070**
or scan the QR code.

📍 **Augsburg, Bavaria (S)**

Lech Camping

Situated just north of Augsburg, this beautifully run site, with its own small lake, is a pleasure to stay on. Gabi Ryssel, the owner, spends her long days working very hard to cater for every wish of her guests – from the moment you arrive and are given the key to one of the cleanest toilet blocks we have seen, plus plenty of tourist information, you are in very capable hands.

The 50 level, grass and gravel pitches are roomy and have shade from pine trees. Electricity connections are available (10/16A Europlug). This is an immaculate site with a separate area for those with reduced mobility to park near the accessible facilities provided. The site is located beside a busy main road. A key (deposit payable) is needed to access washrooms and water points.

The toilet block (cleaned several times daily) provides British-style WCs and good showers with seating areas and non-slip flooring. Baby room. Separate family bathroom to rent. Five-star accessible facilities. Separate room with washing machine and laundry sinks. Motorhome services. Small shop, lakeside restaurant/bar/takeaway (All season). Small playground (partially fenced). Bicycle hire. Free WiFi. Trampolines. Surfboards and rowing boats (free). Dog shower.

Alan Rogers Ref: DE36420
Pitches: 50
GPS: 48.43759, 10.92937
Post Code: D-86444

what3words:
lifeguards.candlestick.craning

Contact:
info@lech-camping.de
Tel: +49 82 07 22 00
www.lech-camping.de

Open Dates:
Mid April - Mid September.

🏅 **Alan Rogers Awards Won**
2016, 2014

Key Features

🗓 Book Online

🐾 Pets allowed

♿ Accessible Facilities

🛝 Childrens Play Area

🍸 Bar on Site

🚲 Bicycle Hire on Site

🐟 Fishing on Site

Find Out More
Visit **ar.camp/de36420**
or scan the QR code.

Ingolstadt, Bavaria (S)

Waldcamping Auwaldsee

With easy access from the nearby A9, Azur Waldcamping Auwaldsee lies along the northern banks of a small lake. There are 650 pitches, of which 350 are for touring units. These are level, grassed and have 16A electricity. Access roads (some overgrown when we visited) lead to large, open grass areas with unmarked pitches, which are shaded in places by mature trees. Opposite reception is a traditional Bavarian restaurant with a large beer garden – a good place to try the Bavarian speciality wheat beer.

With its location in the centre of Bavaria, the site is a useful base to tour the region or as a stopover point for those travelling further afield. First documented in 806, Ingolstadt, with its old town and fortified walls, is an interesting place to visit. It was the setting for Mary Shelley´s Frankenstein, and for those with strong nerves, a Frankenstein tour is offered.

Two heated sanitary blocks. Accessible facilities, Washing machines and dryers. Motorhome services. Shop and snack bar. Boating, swimming and fishing on Auwaldsee. WiFi, Pets allowed.

Alan Rogers Ref: DE36160
Accommodations: 16
Pitches: 650
GPS: 48.75397, 11.46416
Post Code: D-85053

what3words:
raced.rich.curries

Contact:
ingolstadt@azur-camping.de
Tel: +49 84 19 61 16 16
www.azur-camping.de

Open Dates:
All year.

Key Features

Book Online

All Year

Pets allowed

Accessible Facilities

Bar on Site

Bicycle Hire on Site

Fishing on Site

Find Out More
Visit **ar.camp/de36160**
or scan the QR code.

📍 **Neureichenau, Bavaria (S)**

Alan Rogers Ref: DE37050
Accommodations: 91
Pitches: 400
GPS: 48.74886, 13.81723
Post Code: D-94089

what3words:
nation.distribution.jock

Contact:
lackenhaeuser@knauscamp.de
Tel: +49 85 83 311
www.knauscamp.de

Open Dates:
Start January - Early November
& Xmas to New Year.

Campingpark Lackenhäuser

This extensive site is some 40 km. from Passau, right at the southeast tip of Germany – the border with Austria runs through one side of the site, and the Czech Republic is very close, too. It is a very popular site and reservations may be advisable from mid-June to September, and it is very busy in winter with skiing and other winter activities.

Mainly on sloping ground with good views from some parts, it has 400 pitches with terracing in some areas, nearly all for touring units, and 100 seasonal pitches. Electricity connections (16A) are available, and water points are fed from pure springs. An area provides 50 pitches for motorhomes, all with electricity and some fully serviced. The site is open all year and has much winter sports trade, with its own ski lift.

Three sanitary buildings are good quality, with some washbasins in cabins and underfloor heating. Baby room. Accessible facilities, Laundry. Gas supplies. Motorhome services. Cooking facilities. Dishwashing by EasyBe. Supermarket (Seasonal). Restaurant/bar (Seasonal). Hairdressing salon. General room for young. Caravan shop. Heated indoor pool (free) with a child's pool, sauna and fitness room, and an outdoor spring water pool. Small lake (ice sports in winter). Fishing. Bowling. Mini golf, Football, Archery, Church. Organised activities (July/Aug. and Xmas). Ski hire. Dog-free area.

Key Features

🗓 Book Online

🐾 Pets allowed

♿ Accessible Facilities

🏊 Indoor Pool on Site

🎪 Childrens Play Area

🍸 Bar on Site

⛷ Skiing on Site

🚴 Bicycle Hire on Site

Find Out More
Visit **ar.camp/de37050**
or scan the QR code.

Chieming, Bavaria (S)

Alan Rogers Ref: DE40890
Pitches: 200
GPS: 47.92953, 12.49181
Post Code: D-83339

what3words:
unveiling.spire.compass

Contact:
info@campingkupfersmied.de
Tel: +49 86 67 446
www.campingkupferschmiede.
de

Open Dates:
Start April - End October.

Camping Kupferschmiede

Camping Kupferschmiede is a family-run campsite in Arlaching, on the northern shore of the Chiemsee lake in Bavaria, Germany. Due to its location in the middle of a wooded area, guests can choose from both sunny and shaded pitches. The site has 200 grass pitches, of which 80 are for touring units, and has 16-amp hook-up points available.

The site has a pub, Kupferschmiede, and the adjoining restaurant offers local hot dishes. Guests could provide themselves with a well-stocked selection of food and beverages from the on-site shop. Around the lake, there is a varied range of leisure activities. Boat and surfboard rental, horseback riding, golfing and tennis are available nearby. The charming landscape invites you to take long walks or bike rides.

The toilet block has showers, individual washing cabins, and WCs. Accessible facilities. Laundry with washing machine and tumble dryer. Chemical toilet point. Motorhome service point. Dishwashing area. Small shop. Bread to order. Restaurant. Bar. Snack bar. Takeaway. Pizzeria. Freezer for ice packs. Public telephone. WiFi. Dogs and BBQs allowed. Dog walk. Lake swimming. Children's play area. Table tennis. Public transport nearby.

Key Features

🐾 Pets allowed

♿ Accessible Facilities

🛝 Childrens Play Area

🍸 Bar on Site

Find Out More
Visit **ar.camp/de40890**
or scan the QR code.

Capital London
Currency British Pound (£)
Language English
Time Zone GMT (BST)
Telephone Code +44
Emergency Number 999 or 112
Tourist Website visitbritain.com

Shops Generally 9am to 5.30pm weekdays and Sat, and 11am to 4pm on Sun. Smaller supermarkets usually stay open until 11pm.

Money ATMs are widespread and accessible 24hrs a day. Cards accepted almost everywhere, some places are cashless.

Driving in Britain Driving is on the left, speed is measured in miles per hour, and road signs use imperial measurements. In Scotland and Wales, road signs display regional languages alongside English. When using motorways, only use the hard shoulder if instructed to or if you break down. Smoking in a vehicle with minors present and using a mobile device whilst driving are illegal. Pedestrians and cyclists have priority.

Public Holidays 1 Jan New Year's Day; Mar/Apr Good Friday; Mar/Apr Easter Monday; May Early May Bank Holiday; 8 May King Charles III Coronation; May/June Late May Bank Holiday; Late Aug August Bank Holiday; 25 Dec Christmas Day; 26 Dec Boxing Day. Regional holidays are also observed.

Low Emission Zones Most major cities have Low Emission Zones in place. London and surrounding counties have a complex network of Low, Ultra Low and Zero Emission Zones, as well as congestion charges. Signs give information on charges and payment methods. Registration is required for all non-UK vehicles.

Accessible Travel Score
Mostly well-equipped, public buildings in cities and major towns are accessible. Disabled WCs are widespread. Efforts to improve and adapt are actively being made.

Wales Boasting a diverse landscape, from lakes, mountains and valleys to beautiful coastlines and rolling wooded countryside.

Scotland From gently rolling hills and rugged coastlines to dramatic peaks punctuated with beautiful lochs, Scotland is an untamed land steeped in history.

Northern Ireland From wild coastlines to green valleys, rugged mountains and shimmering lakes to the natural phenomenon of the Giant's Causeway, Northern Ireland is crammed full of sights.

EU Member | Schengen Area | Common Travel Area

Great Britain

View all campsites in Great Britain
ar.camp/england
ar.camp/northern-ireland
ar.camp/scotland
ar.camp/wales

See campsite map page 480

Climate Varied. Mild in the summer and cooler and wetter in the winter months.	☀ **Avg. summer temp** 15°C (N), 19°C (S)	🌧 **Wettest month** Oct (N), Nov (S)

The United Kingdom offers a wealth of extraordinary landscapes set against the backdrop of rich and vibrant history. In terms of character and stunning scenery, it offers an unsurpassed choice of holiday activities from coast to country.

Northern England A beautiful and varied region of rolling hills and undulating moors, along with a wealth of industrial heritage and undiscovered countryside. The Yorkshire Moors, Cumbrian lakes, Northumbrian ancient forts and fairytale castles are all highlights not to be missed.

Southern England Rich in maritime heritage and historical attractions, the southern region comprises tranquil English countryside replete with picture-postcard villages, ancient towns, formidable castles and grand stately homes, coupled with a beautiful coastline, white-faced cliffs and lively Victorian seaside resorts.

Heart of England Spanning central England, from the ancient borders of Wales in the west across to Lincolnshire on the east coast, the Heart of England is rich in glorious rolling countryside, magnificent castles and fine stately homes.

Eastern England A perfect mix of gentle countryside and sleepy villages, it's an unspoilt region with endless skies, inland waterways and traditional beach resorts.

Western England A region of contrasts, with windswept moorlands and dramatic cliffs towering above beautiful sandy beaches.

📍 **Saint Martin, Jersey**

Alan Rogers Ref: UK9710
Accommodations: 20
Pitches: 130
GPS: 49.23841, -2.05058
Post Code: JE3 6AX

what3words:
worried.windfalls.resembles

Contact:
enquiries@rozelcamping.com
Tel: +44 1534 855200
www.rozelcamping.com

Open Dates:
Early May - Early September.

Rozel Camping Park

Family-owned and run for over forty years, this attractive park has some beautiful views across the sea to the coast of France. The famous Durrell Wildlife Park is within walking distance, as is Rozel's pretty harbour and fishing village. The campsite provides four terraced, grass camping areas, all with differing characteristics – open and with views, sheltered at a lower level or with pitches in groups in hedged bays.

The welcoming owners will help you decide which will suit you best. There are 130 touring pitches, all with access to 16A electricity. A further 20 are used for fully equipped tents for hire. The site has provided easy access for caravans and motorhomes, and the Germains will meet you at the ferry to help you navigate to the park.

Two bright, heated sanitary buildings are kept clean and include some washbasins in cubicles. Accessible sanitary facilities. Family shower rooms Motorhome drain point (grey water only). Fully equipped laundry, also with hairdryers. Shop (opened and stocked acc. to season). Solar-heated swimming pool (June-Sept) with children's pool and sunbathing areas. Play area. Crazy golf. Games, reading and TV rooms. Torches useful. Fully equipped tents to rent. WiFi near reception (free).

Key Features

🐾 Pets allowed

♿ Accessible Facilities

⛱ Seaside Beach Nearby

🌊 Outdoor Pool on Site

🎠 Childrens Play Area

Find Out More
Visit ar.camp/uk9710
or scan the QR code.

La Bailloterie Camping

Arranged on a series of spacious, grassy meadows, each surrounded by attractive trees, La Bailloterie is a long-established Guernsey campsite run by friendly and welcoming owners. It is a very peaceful setting down a narrow, rural lane but is just minutes from the shops and services of the Vale and the beach. There is always plenty of room for around 100 tents or motorhomes, and 20 electricity connections are available (16A). Choose your pitch. Also provided are hire tents and simple log cabins to rent.

The site's amenities are in a large, converted granite barn with sanitary facilities on the ground floor and reception, a simple shop and a lounge with a relaxing balcony where you can enjoy a coffee overlooking the play area. The campsite can arrange a permit to bring your caravan or motorhome onto the island.

Sanitary facilities are modern and kept clean. Showers are free. Accessible sanitary facilities. Baby room. Washing machine and drier. Motorhome emptying point. Basic shop (pre-order bread high season). Coffee lounge and café with TV (seasonal). Takeaway (Seasonal). Organised barbecues and meals (twice weekly in high season). Play area. Tea garden and boules pitch. Bicycle hire. WiFi in the café area (free). Glamping tents and camping cabins to rent.

Alan Rogers Ref: UK9790
Accommodations: 8
Pitches: 100
GPS: 49.48926, -2.53110
Post Code: GY3 5HA

what3words:
reviews.sounding.parent

Contact:
info@campinginguernsey.com
Tel: +44 1481 243636
www.campinginguernsey.com

Open Dates:
Mid May - Mid September.

Key Features

- Pets allowed
- Accessible Facilities
- Seaside Beach Nearby
- Childrens Play Area
- Bicycle Hire on Site

Find Out More
Visit **ar.camp/uk9790**
or scan the QR code.

📍 **Cornwall, South West**

St Ives Bay Holiday Park

A large and spacious site with pitches laid out amongst undulating dunes leading down to its own three-mile-long sandy beach. Some of the pitches have lovely views over St Ives Bay, while others are more sheltered by the large dunes and may be some way from the beach.

There are over 1,000 pitches, with around half for touring. Three hundred have 16A electricity, but those near the sea lack electricity. The maximum footprint of all outfits is 8x5m. There is an on-site surf school for those wishing to learn to surf. Dogs are not accepted.

Several adequate toilet blocks with all necessary facilities, some catering for babies and accessible sanitary facilities. Launderette. Motorhome services. Comprehensive shop. Beach shop. Bars and Bistro. A small indoor pool and a separate shallow pool. Games room with electronic games. Mini golf, Multisport pitch, TV room. Pool table. Family entertainment. Large play area next to the bar. Surf School. WiFi near Bistro (free).

Alan Rogers Ref: UK0007
Accommodations: 550
Pitches: 550
GPS: 50.20049, -5.40233
Post Code: TR27 5BH

what3words:
openly.kitchens.dummy

Contact:
generalenquiries@awayresorts.co.uk
Tel: +44 1736 752274
awayresorts.co.uk/parks/cornwall/st-ives-bay

Open Dates:
Early May - Late September.

Key Features

🗓 Book Online

♿ Accessible Facilities

⛱ Seaside Beach on Site

🏊 Indoor Pool on Site

🛝 Childrens Play Area

🍸 Bar on Site

Find Out More
Visit **ar.camp/uk0007** or scan the QR code.

📍 **Cornwall, South West**

Carnon Downs CAMC Campsite

Carnon Down was acquired by the Caravan and Motorhome Club in 2021. The founder and former owners started this site from just a field. Looking at the site today, you will find that hard to believe. This site is beautifully landscaped with areas separated by well-trimmed box hedging, low natural stone walls and a variety of well-tended trees. This large site is spread over twenty acres and into different areas, but it never seems crowded.

Reception is shared with a well-stocked shop, information centre and refreshment area, with a lovely outside area with tables and chairs overlooking the park. There is an excellent children's play area, and around the site, there are several dishwashing areas.

Two excellent modern, light and airy heated toilet blocks include en-suite accessible units. Another well-maintained, heated block consists of some washbasins in cubicles and showers (unisex). Family room, two baby sinks and full-sized bath. Two laundries with freezers. Motorhome services (ask at reception). Good adventure-type play area. Football field. Gas, newspapers and caravan accessories. General room with TV. Good dog walks. Caravan storage. No late-night arrivals area. BBQs allowed gas, charcoal & electric. TV reception is good. Bus stop 300 metres. Train station 4 miles. Earliest arrival time: 1:00 pm. Tents accepted.

Alan Rogers Ref: UK0180
Pitches: 150
GPS: 50.22529, -5.08012
Post Code: TR3 6JJ

what3words:
caramel.slogans.ghosts

Contact:
UKSitesBookingService@camc.com
Tel: +44 1872 862283
www.camc.com

Open Dates:
All year.

Key Features

📅 Book Online

📅 All Year

🐾 Pets allowed

♿ Accessible Facilities

⛱ Seaside Beach Nearby

🛝 Childrens Play Area

Find Out More
Visit ar.camp/uk0180
or scan the QR code.

📍 **Cornwall, South West**

Trevella Holiday Park

Trevella has a longer season than most parks and is among the best-known and most respected Cornish parks. It has many colourful flowerbeds and is a regular winner of a Newquay in Bloom award. Well organised, the pitches are in a number of adjoining meadows. The 270 slightly sloping touring pitches are in three different categories, 170 of which have 10A electricity. Some of the super pitches are on hardstanding and are fully serviced. For an extra charge, some can be individually reserved.

Trevella is essentially a quiet family touring park. Ready-erected tents are available for hire. Access to two fishing lakes is free, (permits from reception); with some fishing instruction and wildlife talks for youngsters in season.

Three blocks provide good coverage with individual washbasins in cabins, hairdressing room, baby rooms and sizeable en-suite family rooms. Laundry. Freezer pack service. Well-stocked supermarket (Easter-Oct). Café (including breakfast) and takeaway. Heated outdoor pool. Crazy golf. Large adventure playground. Play and sports area. Pets' Corner. Fishing. Caravan storage. WiFi.

Alan Rogers Ref: UK0170
Accommodations: 76
Pitches: 270
GPS: 50.39730, -5.09613
Post Code: TR8 5EW

what3words:
shell.parsnips.named

Contact:
Trevella@parkholidays.com
Tel: +44 1637 830308
www.trevella.co.uk

Open Dates:
Mid March - Late October.

Key Features

🗓 Book Online

🐾 Pets allowed

♿ Accessible Facilities

⛱ Seaside Beach Nearby

〰 Outdoor Pool on Site

🛝 Childrens Play Area

🐟 Fishing on Site

Find Out More
Visit **ar.camp/uk0170**
or scan the QR code.

Devon, South West

Alan Rogers Ref: UK0819
Accommodations: 8
Pitches: 50
GPS: 50.30148, -3.78930
Post Code: TQ7 4AF

what3words:
towns.combines.crafts

Contact:
enquiries@parklandsite.co.uk
Tel: +44 1548 852723
www.parklandsite.co.uk

Open Dates:
All year.

Parkland

Parkland is in an area of outstanding natural beauty and ideally situated for exploring all the stunning South Hams area of South Devon has to offer. Open all year, the site is set within three acres of mature, landscaped grounds with panoramic views over Kingsbridge and Salcombe and the rolling countryside towards Dartmoor National Park.

Explore the market town of Kingsbridge and the historic towns of Dartmouth and Totnes. Ramble along the picturesque South West Coast path. Relax on fabulous beaches: Bantham, Thurlestone, Bigbury, Slapton Sands and Hope Cove. Enjoy an array of attractions, activities and water sports. Indulge in local produce, quality village pubs and fine dining eateries. The site has 50 grass & hard standing pitches with 16 amp electric hook-up and drinking water points for all pitches. Grey and Black waste disposal points (majority of pitches). The site is for adults only (aged 18 and over), and dogs are prohibited.

The site offers two heated amenity buildings with 'hotel' style washrooms with toilets, washbasins, and large walk-in showers or baths, all with lighted mirrors, hand dryers and hair dryers. Accessible facilities include a wet room shower, a low-level basin, and a high-rise toilet with grab rails and emergency pull cords. Private washrooms with large showers are also available - pre-booking essential. Indoor dishwashing rooms, complimentary dishwashers, modern coin-operated laundry machines. Campers' kitchen has a microwave, hot plate, kettle, toaster, fridge, and freezer. Arrivals are welcome from midday to 7pm.

Key Features

18+ Adults Only

365 All Year

Accessible Facilities

Seaside Beach Nearby

Find Out More
Visit ar.camp/uk0819
or scan the QR code.

Devon, South West

Alan Rogers Ref: UK0802
Accommodations: 25
Pitches: 40
GPS: 50.54490, -4.08417
Post Code: PL19 9JZ

what3words:
crumb.pothole.tributes

Contact:
jane@langstonemanor.co.uk
Tel: +44 1822 613371
www.langstonemanor.co.uk

Open Dates:
End March - End October.

**Alan Rogers
Awards Won**
2013

Langstone Manor Park

Situated on the southwest edge of Dartmoor, this holiday park has been developed on the grounds of the old Langstone Manor house. The touring pitches are tucked into various garden areas with mature trees and flowering shrubs or in the walled garden area with views over the moor. There are 40 level grass pitches, which vary in size (35 with 16A electricity). A popular camping area has been terraced with open views over farmland and the moor.

You pass by some holiday caravans on the way to reception and the touring pitches, where you will also find some holiday cottages and flats to rent. The 'pièce de resistance' is the unexpected traditional bar and restaurant in the Manor House, with a terrace that catches the evening sun. Open in high season and on-demand in low season, it has an open fire (if needed) and games room.

The facilities provided are to a very high standard and include a bathroom and private cabins. Laundry. Baby mats are changing in both the men's and ladies' rooms. A private bathroom is available. Basic supplies are kept in reception (order bread the day before). Bar & restaurant serving evening meals. Games room. Play area. Outdoor table tennis. Camping pods for hire.

Key Features

🗓 Book Online

🐾 Pets allowed

♿ Accessible Facilities

🧒 Childrens Play Area

🍸 Bar on Site

Find Out More
Visit **ar.camp/uk0802**
or scan the QR code.

📍 **Devon, South West**

Mill Park

Mill Park is a small family-run sheltered touring caravan and camping site set in an attractive wooded valley on the North Devon Coast. It has a shop, a takeaway, a games room, laundry, and many other facilities such as gas-changing and ice pack freezing. Several glamping options, including three bell tents and three glamping pods, are available on-site. There is also an on-site pub serving a modest menu. Mill Park is surrounded by attractive woodland and is an ideal family site as it's just a short walk to quiet sand and pebble beaches.

Bring your Fishing tackle to Mill Park and enjoy the Lake. A stream-fed 1.5-acre coarse fishing lake stocked with carp. Exmoor's unspoilt and breathtaking beauty is equally close by, and the nearest village, Berrynarbor, is just a five-minute walk from the site. This village dates back to the sixteenth century and earlier. There is a quaint old country pub, village stores and a post office.

Two Separate shower blocks - recently refurbished and kept impeccably clean, onsite bar, well-stocked shop, fishing lake, a small river flowing through the park, children's play area, games room, book swap, games library, free Internet in bar and restaurant, games room, Pool table. Close to beaches, secluded and quiet, and very peaceful.

Alan Rogers Ref: UK0681
Accommodations: 6
Pitches: 91
GPS: 51.20484, -4.06417
Post Code: EX34 9SH

what3words:
duos.finalists.oxidation

Contact:
enquiries@millpark.com
Tel: +44 1271 882647
www.millpark.com

Open Dates:
Start March - End October.

Key Features

🐾 Pets allowed

♿ Accessible Facilities

🛝 Childrens Play Area

🍸 Bar on Site

🐟 Fishing on Site

Find Out More
Visit **ar.camp/uk0681**
or scan the QR code.

📍 **Devon, South West**

Forest Glade Holiday Park

Forest Glade, immaculately managed, owned and run by the Wellard family, is set in a forest clearing on the Blackdown Hills (designated an Area of Outstanding Natural Beauty), deep in mid-Devon away from the hectic life on the coast.

A sheltered site set amongst woodland with extensive walking opportunities, there are 80 level touring pitches, 62 of which have 10 amp electricity connections, 2 with full services and 39 with hardstanding. Touring caravans and large motorhomes must be booked in advance when the most straightforward route will be advised (phone bookings accepted). Although set in the countryside, the beaches of East Devon are a reasonably easy drive away.

One main toilet block is heated in cold weather, with some washbasins in cubicles. Family shower room. Separate accessible suite. Laundry with washing machines and dryers. Facilities for babies. Extra prefabricated unit with toilets, washbasins and showers at the swimming pool. The stocked shop includes gas and a takeaway (evenings except Sun). Microwave in campers' kitchen. Heated swimming pool (free). Sauna (on payment). Extensive adventure play area with access to woodland. Games room. All-weather tennis court. WiFi over site (charged). Caravan storage. Wildlife information room.

Alan Rogers Ref: UK1000
Accommodations: 25
Pitches: 80
GPS: 50.85783, -3.27752
Post Code: EX15 2DT

what3words:
limes.outcasts.prelude

Contact:
enquiries@forest-glade.co.uk
Tel: +44 1404 841381
www.forest-glade.co.uk

Open Dates:
Mid March - End October.

Key Features

🗓️ Book Online

🐾 Pets allowed

♿ Accessible Facilities

⚓ Seaside Beach Nearby

🏊 Indoor Pool on Site

🧗 Childrens Play Area

Find Out More
Visit **ar.camp/uk1000**
or scan the QR code.

Somerset, South West

Alan Rogers Ref: UK1390
Accommodations: 6
Pitches: 100
GPS: 51.15263, -2.68030
Post Code: BA6 8JS

what3words:
bookshelf.couriers.flash

Contact:
info@theoldoaks.co.uk
Tel: +44 1458 831437
www.theoldoaks.co.uk

Open Dates:
Start March - Mid November.

Old Oaks Touring Park

The Old Oaks, an adults-only park, is tucked below the Glastonbury Tor in a lovely secluded setting with views across to the Mendip Hills. The grounds are immaculate, and much attention to cleanliness is given throughout. There are 100 large pitches in a series of paddocks, 91 with 16A electricity on hardstandings, and 50 are fully serviced. Mainly backing onto hedges, they are attractively arranged and interspersed with shrubs and flowers in a circular development or terraced with rural views.

There is a quiet orchard area for camping, and six camping cabins provide a luxurious alternative to tents but retain that 'outdoor feel'. A member of the Best of British group.

The two blocks are both of excellent quality, with fully fitted individual shower rooms. Accessible sanitary facilities in three rooms. Two fully equipped laundry rooms. Motorhome services. Fridge & freezers for ice packs (free). Useful dog wash. Licensed shop selling local produce, freshly baked cakes and bread (pre-ordered). Pool table. Fishing. Painting holidays. Toilet cassette cleaning machines. Coffee machine. Free and premium WiFi over site. A range of takeaway food is delivered to the site five nights a week. Free walking & cycling maps. Only adults (18 years and over) are accepted.

Key Features

18+ Adults Only

🐾 Pets allowed

♿ Accessible Facilities

🐟 Fishing on Site

Find Out More
Visit **ar.camp/uk1390**
or scan the QR code.

📍 **Dorset, South West**

Alan Rogers Ref: UK2060
Pitches: 90
GPS: 50.81670, -1.99040
Post Code: BH21 4HW

what3words:
splice.calibrate.gagging

Contact:
holidays@shorefield.co.uk
Tel: +44 1590 648333
www.shorefield.co.uk

Open Dates:
Start March - Late October.

Wilksworth Caravan Park

Wilksworth Caravan Park is a spacious, quiet park well-suited for families, with a heated outdoor pool designed in a beautiful Spanish style. The rural situation is lovely, just outside Wimborne and around 12 miles from the beaches between Poole and Bournemouth.

The park takes 60 caravans and 25 tents, mainly on grass. All pitches have electricity, and ten also have water and drainage. There are 77 privately owned caravan holiday homes in a separate area. With a duck pond at the entrance, the park has been well planned on good quality ground with fairly level grass and some views.

The central, well-equipped toilet block has underfloor heating, washbasins in cubicles, a family bathroom and a shower/bath for children with baby changing. Accessible sanitary facilities. Laundry room. Modern reception and shop (basics only, limited hours, seasonal). Gas supplies. Freezer for ice packs. Heated 40x20 ft. swimming pool (unsupervised, but walled and gated, May-Sept). Small paddling pool with slide. Upgraded play area. 'Tiny Town' playhouses (under 7 yrs). BMX track. One full and one short size tennis court. Winter caravan storage. WiFi (charged).

Key Features

🗓 Book Online

🐾 Pets allowed

♿ Accessible Facilities

⛱ Seaside Beach Nearby

🏊 Outdoor Pool on Site

🛝 Childrens Play Area

Find Out More
Visit **ar.camp/uk2060**
or scan the QR code.

📍 **Isle of Wight, South**

Whitecliff Bay Holiday Park

Whitecliff Bay is a very large complex divided by a main road, with a holiday home and chalet park on the right-hand side (230 units) and a large area on the left-hand side also dedicated to static caravans with a decreasing area at the bottom of the hill available to touring units.

Some 58 pitches are spread over two fields, which are pretty level. Most of the pitches have 16A electricity hook-ups, and there are some gravel hardstandings. Static caravan plots will likely increasingly reduce the number of touring pitches over the coming years.

One sanitary unit is not far from reception. Accessible shower and a suite (with shower). A second suite with a hip bath/shower is at the lower block with a similar facility to serve as a baby/family room. Motorhome services. Small shop at reception. Playground. At the holiday home park: launderette, hairdresser and second larger shop. The Culver Club. Snack bars. Swimming pool (18x18 m, Whitsun-end Aug). Indoor fun pool and soft play zone (under 8s). Most facilities are open Mar-Oct. Free WiFi on the main site. Full programme of activities and entertainment for all ages. Mini golf, Fully equipped tents to rent.

Alan Rogers Ref: UK2510
Accommodations: 230
Pitches: 58
GPS: 50.67498, -1.09606
Post Code: PO35 5PL

what3words:
writers.crumple.victor

Contact:
generalenquiries@awayresorts.co.uk
Tel: +44 1983 872671
awayresorts.co.uk/parks/isle-of-wight/whitecliff-bay

Open Dates:
Mid March - Start November.

Key Features

📅 Book Online

🐾 Pets allowed

♿ Accessible Facilities

⛱ Seaside Beach on Site

🏊 Indoor Pool on Site

🧗 Childrens Play Area

🍸 Bar on Site

🚲 Bicycle Hire on Site

Find Out More
Visit ar.camp/uk2510
or scan the QR code.

📍 **West Sussex, South East**

Alan Rogers Ref: UK2940
Accommodations: 53
Pitches: 97
GPS: 50.94864, -0.35274
Post Code: RH13 8NX

what3words:
alleges.clubbing.files

Contact:
enquiries@honeybridgepark.co.uk
Tel: +44 1403 710923
www.honeybridgepark.co.uk

Open Dates:
All year.

Honeybridge Park

This 15-acre park is situated amidst beautiful woodlands and countryside on the edge of the South Downs, within an Area of Outstanding Natural Beauty. Of the 150 pitches, 97 are for touring, some are on hardstandings, and all have 16A electricity. The remaining pitches are occupied by holiday homes but these are in a separate area. Some pitches are hedged for privacy, others are on slightly sloping grass, well spaced and generously sized.

A large wooden, adventure-style playground is provided for children away from the pitches, and simple family entertainment is organised on special occasions. A large games room provides table tennis, a pool, a library and a TV with Freeview channels.

Two modern toilet facilities are heated in cool weather and include spacious accessible facilities (Radar key). Laundry facilities. Motorhome services. Fridge and freezer for campers' use. Licensed shop and café (Seasonal). Play area. Games room with library. The security barrier (card access) is locked from 23.00 to 07.00. WiFi at café. Pets allowed.

Key Features

- 📅 All Year
- 🐾 Pets allowed
- ♿ Accessible Facilities
- ⛱ Seaside Beach Nearby
- 🛝 Childrens Play Area

Find Out More
Visit **ar.camp/uk2940**
or scan the QR code.

📍 **Berkshire, South**

Alan Rogers Ref: UK2690
Pitches: 87
GPS: 51.36001, -0.95513
Post Code: RG7 1SP

what3words:
slang.imparts.outgrown

Contact:
info@wellington-country-park.co.uk
Tel: +44 118 932 6444
www.wellington-country-park.co.uk

Open Dates:
Mid March - Early November.

Wellington Country Park

This campsite is situated within the very popular 350-acre Wellington Country Park, open to the public from March to November. The park contains a wide range of amenities: a shop, a café, play areas, twelve-hole minigolf, an animal farm and petting barn, a miniature railway (charged), four nature trails, a deer park and a host of play equipment. Entrance to the Park is included in the campsite fees.

There are 87 pitches, 57 with 6A electricity and 50 on hardstanding. Thirty non-electric pitches are for tents; a few premium pitches offer slightly more privacy. It is a charming setting, and once the park closes at 18.00, all is much quieter. It would be best if you aimed to arrive before 16.30 (low season) and 17.30 (high season) when the main reception centre closes.

The central toilet block provides washbasins and well equipped showers with good dry areas. Ample laundry. Shop stocks basics. Café (during park hours). Calor gas exchange. Country Park with nature walks, deer field, minigolf, play areas and miniature railway (£1.50 extra). Family events are held all year round. Twin-axle caravans by arrangement. WiFi over site (charged). Torch useful.

Key Features

🐾 Pets allowed

🎠 Childrens Play Area

Find Out More
Visit **ar.camp/uk2690**
or scan the QR code.

Kent, South East

Alan Rogers Ref: UK3055
Pitches: 150
GPS: 51.20073, 0.39333
Post Code: TN12 6PY

what3words:
regaining.tapers.prayers

Contact:
touring@thehopfarm.co.uk
Tel: +44 1622 870838
www.thehopfarm.co.uk/stay

Open Dates:
Start March - End November.

The Hop Farm Campsite

Set in 500 acres of the Garden of England, The Hop Farm Touring & Camping Park is the venue for many special events throughout the summer, including music festivals & shows. To one side, overlooking all this activity and the attractive cluster of oasts, is the touring park, which provides 150 pitches, of which 75 are hardstanding on flat, open fields. Electricity (16A) and water are available.

There is also space for up to 1000 tents. The main toilet block is clean and provides modern facilities; these are supplemented by prefabricated units when events bring extra campers.

New showers and washrooms have been added to the site. Small shop (in reception - Seasonal) for essentials. Nature walks. Boat launching. Fishing. Dogs are accepted but not permitted inside the visitor attraction. Activities and entertainment at the visitor attraction. No WiFi.

Key Features

- Pets allowed
- Accessible Facilities
- Childrens Play Area
- Bar on Site
- Fishing on Site

Find Out More
Visit **ar.camp/uk3055**
or scan the QR code.

Kent, South East

Broadhembury Caravan Park

Alan Rogers Ref: UK3040
Accommodations: 25
Pitches: 110
GPS: 51.10647, 0.86809
Post Code: TN26 1NQ

what3words:
squeaking.directive.dean

Contact:
holidaypark@broadhembury.co.uk
Tel: +44 1233 620859
www.broadhembury.co.uk

Open Dates:
All year.

Broadhembury Caravan & Camping Park is found in the quiet countryside just outside Ashford and within easy reach of London, Dover, Folkestone and the Kent coast. There are areas for family camping with play areas and amenities designed with children in mind and separate quiet meadows just for adults with modern luxury facilities.

In total, the park takes 110 touring units of any type. The well-kept pitches are on level grass, backed by tall, neat hedges, 105 with electricity connections (10/16A). In addition, six pitches are fully serviced, and ten more have double hardstanding plus a grass area for an awning. The welcome is friendly at this popular park, and it is often full in the main season.

Well-equipped toilet block for the family areas and ecologically considered block for the couples meadows. Underfloor heating. Private cabins. High-quality, accessible sanitary facilities. Sanitary facilities, especially for children, and a well-equipped laundry room. Good campers' kitchen, fully enclosed with microwaves, fridge and freezer, free of charge. Motorhome services. Well-stocked shop with local produce, wine and beer (butchers, bakery and papers to order). Internet access. Pool room, games room with video games, table football and table tennis. There are two play areas (one for children under seven years old) and one with an all-weather surface. Playing field adjacent to the touring area. WiFi over site (charged). Up to two dogs per pitch are accepted. Large units are accepted if pre-booked.

Key Features

18+ Adults Only

365 All Year

Pets allowed

Accessible Facilities

Seaside Beach Nearby

Childrens Play Area

Find Out More
Visit ar.camp/uk3040
or scan the QR code.

Gloucestershire, Heart of the Country

Alan Rogers Ref: UK4105
Pitches: 211
GPS: 51.71418, -1.98403
Post Code: GL7 1UT

what3words:
park.crunched.gained

Contact:
UKSitesBookingService@
camc.com
Tel: +44 1285 651546
www.camc.com

Open Dates:
Start March - Early January.

Cirencester Park CAMC Site

Cirencester Park Caravan and Motorhome Club site is set in beautiful Grade I listed parkland. The site is a peaceful oasis that forms part of the lovely Bathurst Estate. Great for walks in the surrounding natural landscapes or picnics under the shade of statuesque trees, the site is also close to the thriving market town of Cirencester, once the second-largest town in England during the Roman occupation.

The town offers attractions for the whole family, from shopping and sampling local food treats to visiting nostalgic landmarks such as its picturesque church and well-kept museum. There are 211 pitches (Hardstanding & Grass), all with 16 amp electricity. Some seasonal pitches.

Two toilet blocks provide accessible facilities. Laundry. Showers. Wash basins. Dishwashing. Motorhome service point. Small shop. Chemical toilet point. Gas sales. Children's play area adjacent. Wi-Fi is poor and charged. BBQs allowed gas, electric & charcoal. Defibrillator. TV reception booster system. Information room. Pets allowed. Dog walk. Dog pit stop. Twin axle caravans accepted. Late-night arrivals area. Bus stop 600 metres. Waitrose 0.5 miles. No Tents allowed. Earliest time of arrival: 1:00pm. Maximum outfit length 9 metres. Caravan storage.

Key Features

🗓️ Book Online

🐾 Pets allowed

♿ Accessible Facilities

🛝 Childrens Play Area

Find Out More
Visit **ar.camp/uk4105**
or scan the QR code.

Oxfordshire, South

Wysdom Touring Park

You'll have to go a long way before finding anything remotely like this site! Burford School owns the land, and the site was created to raise money for the school. It is like stepping into their own private garden. This adults-only park is screened from the main school grounds by trees and provides 25 pitches (six seasonal), separated by hedges, all with 16A electricity.

This is a lovely location for exploring the Cotswolds – Burford calls itself the 'Gateway to the Cotswolds.' The turn into the site, off the school drive, is narrow, and the site is not considered suitable for large motorhomes. It is best to avoid school pick-up and drop-off times when the school can be congested. Bookings are taken only via phone.

No on-site sanitary facilities (Max. 2 dogs per pitch). Chemical w/c disposal point (Elsan), grey water disposal point, 16 amp electric hook-up, ample fresh water taps, book swap.

Alan Rogers Ref: UK2620
Pitches: 15
GPS: 51.80198, -1.63937
Post Code: OX18 4JG

what3words:
tastier.buddy.eyeful

Contact:
Tel: +44 1993 823207
www.wysdomtouringpark.co.uk

Open Dates:
All year.

Key Features

18+ Adults Only

All Year

Pets allowed

Find Out More
Visit **ar.camp/uk2620**
or scan the QR code.

📍 **Abbey Wood, London**

Abbey Wood CAMC Campsite

Abbey Wood Caravan and Motorhome Club site feels positively rural when you reach this gently sloping verdant site. It has mature tree screening and spacious grounds, making this a 'green oasis'. It is hard to believe that this park is in London and the wardens have made every effort to create an attractive environment. There are 159 level pitches, all with 16A electricity and TV aerial connections; 95 are hardstanding. A tent area provides 35 pitches.

A secure fence around the perimeter is linked to CCTV, and just outside is a late arrivals area with electricity and toilets, also protected by cameras. This site's location makes it unique - good railway connections provide frequent services to central London in just 35 minutes, within walking distance of the site.

Three modern, fully equipped toilet blocks, two with underfloor heating, one designed to be open all year, including washbasins in cubicles, generous showers and a baby/toddler washroom. Private accessible sanitary facilities. Laundry facilities. Motorhome services. Gas. Bread, milk and cold drinks from reception (high season). Play area. Good travel and information centre. WiFi good, over site (charged). Chemical toilet point. Late-night arrivals area. Twin-axle caravans are allowed. Pets allowed. Dog walk. BBQs allowed Gas, Electric and Charcoal. Bus stop 270 metres. Sainsbury's 0.5 miles. Earliest time of arrival: 1:00pm. Maximum unit length 11.6 metres.

Alan Rogers Ref: UK3260
Accommodations: 5
Pitches: 159
GPS: 51.48635, 0.11971
Post Code: SE2 0LS

what3words:
socket.uses.bland

Contact:
UKSitesBookingService@camc.com
Tel: +44 20 8311 7708
www.camc.com

Open Dates:
All year.

Key Features

📅 Book Online

📅 All Year

🐾 Pets allowed

♿ Accessible Facilities

🧗 Childrens Play Area

Find Out More
Visit **ar.camp/uk3260**
or scan the QR code.

📍 **Essex, East of England**

Alan Rogers Ref: UK3305
Accommodations: 11
Pitches: 35
GPS: 51.82402, 1.10456
Post Code: CO16 9BP

what3words:
yield.cheering.savings

Contact:
booking@theprettything.co.uk
Tel: +44 1255 830374
www.theprettything.co.uk

Open Dates:
All year.

Pretty Thing Caravan Site

The Pretty Thing Caravan Site is the perfect place to relax and unwind during your stay, providing guests with a picturesque and calm atmosphere on peaceful grounds catering to camping, touring and glamping. You will find a choice of grass pitches, or you can spend your nights under the shelter of a stylish bell tent or camping pod.

The site is not far from the historic town of Colchester and within 20 minutes of the sandy beach and pier at Clacton-on-sea. Set on an acre of calm green space. The 35 touring pitches here are on grass, with 15 electric hook-ups available. The Blue Sari restaurant is located just 500 yards from the site, and it's a five-minute drive to St Osyth's town centre.

The small toilet block has showers, wash basins, and WCs. Dishwashing area. Chemical toilet point. BBQs allowed. Dogs welcome. Children's play area. Freezer for ice packs. Cycle hire. Earliest arrival time 1.00pm. Caravan storage facility. Public transport nearby.

Key Features

🐾 Pets allowed

⛱ Seaside Beach Nearby

🧒 Childrens Play Area

🚲 Bicycle Hire on Site

Find Out More
Visit **ar.camp/uk3305**
or scan the QR code.

Suffolk, East of England

Haw Wood Farm Camping

Alan Rogers Ref: UK3357
Pitches: 65
GPS: 52.28916, 1.55308
Post Code: IP17 3QT

what3words:
reverses.songs.implanted

Contact:
Info@hawoodfarm.co.uk
Tel: +44 1502 359550
www.hawoodfarm.co.uk

Open Dates:
Start March - End October.

Haw Wood Farm Caravans and Camping is nestled in 14 acres of picturesque countryside; this camping site in Suffolk boasts excellent facilities. With just a short five-minute distance to the nearest beach, you can enjoy the best of both worlds - a peaceful retreat in nature with easy access to the coast. Pitches here are generous and level, catering for motorhomes, caravans, campervans and tents. As well as fully serviced hardstanding pitches, there are also large grass pitches with or without electricity.

There is a heavy emphasis on being environmentally friendly here, evident in the biomass boiler that provides underfloor heating and constant hot water and in the gold awards from David Bellamy that praise the tremendous wildlife present in the park and the green manner in which the site is run. The site is open from March; grass pitches are bookable until the end of October. Hardstanding pitches are available until the end of the year. The site has 65 pitches, most of which have 10/16 amp hook-up points. Some pitches even have a view of a lovely pond.

The heated toilet block has showers, washbasins, and WCs. Accessible facilities. Laundry with washing machine and dryer. Dogs allowed. Dog walk area. Shop/café. Breakfast. BBQs and campfires are permitted. Children's play area. Excellent location for local beaches, and it's a dark sky site. WiFi. Table tennis. The earliest arrival time is noon.

Key Features

- All Year
- Pets allowed
- Accessible Facilities
- Seaside Beach Nearby
- Childrens Play Area

Find Out More
Visit **ar.camp/uk3357**
or scan the QR code.

Norfolk, East of England

Alan Rogers Ref: UK3387
Pitches: 108
GPS: 52.68009, 1.69795
Post Code: NR29 3SR

what3words:
supper.cabs.correct

Contact:
scratbyhall@aol.com
Tel: +44 1493 730283
www.scratbyhall.co.uk

Open Dates:
Mid April - End September.

Scratby Hall Caravan Park

Scratby Hall Caravan Park is a touring caravan and tent site. The perfect base to explore the stunning countryside, beaches and Broads of Norfolk. It is situated in a secluded, rural setting on the outskirts of the coastal village of Scratby, Norfolk. The site is surrounded by arable farmland and is less than one mile from the nearest beach. It is the perfect holiday location to relax and reflect.

The site has 108 level, grass pitches for your caravan, motorhome or tent. There are also many other facilities to ensure your stay is pleasant. There are also non-electric and electrical hook-up pitches available with 16amp electrical hook-up, water, grey water disposal, and T.V. connections.

A single toilet block provides showers, washbasins, and WCs. Accessible sanitary facilities. Family bathroom with large walk-in shower. Laundry Irons and hairdryers available. Chemical toilet disposal point. Food preparation and dishwashing room. Ice pack freezer. Well-stocked shop. Children's play area. Heated outdoor swimming pool (end July - end August). WiFi charged. Gas sales. Pets allowed. 4-acre rally field available for club bookings with dedicated shower and toilet facilities. Restaurant ½ mile. Bar 1 mile. Golf Course and Horse Riding nearby. Earliest arrival time: noon.

Key Features

- Pets allowed
- Accessible Facilities
- Seaside Beach Nearby
- Outdoor Pool on Site
- Childrens Play Area

Find Out More
Visit ar.camp/uk3387
or scan the QR code.

229

📍 **Herefordshire, Heart of England**

Alan Rogers Ref: UK4340
Accommodations: 180
Pitches: 15
GPS: 52.25286, -2.89083
Post Code: HR6 9NQ

what3words:
clicker.infants.images

Contact:
info@pearllake.co.uk
Tel: +44 1568 708326
www.pearllake.co.uk

Open Dates:
Start March - End November.

Pearl Lake Leisure Park

Principally, this is a large holiday home park spread over 80 acres, with some 180 units arranged around an attractive 15-acre lake. However, it does have a very small touring site with just 15 pitches and a modern sanitary unit located at the park entrance, adjacent to the road. Most of the pitches are on gravel hardstanding and are fully serviced, with 16A electricity, water and wastewater connections.

A variety of activities includes fishing in the lake, golf and a bowling green. Places to visit include The Black and White Village Trail, Lingen Nursery and Gardens, and the churches of Wigmore Abbey Parish.

The sanitary unit provides open washbasins and controllable hot showers, with a wide-door accessible cubicle (the outer door is only standard width). Club with bar/restaurant serving hot food and takeaways (weekends only in low season). Fishing. 9-hole golf course. Bowling green. Playing field and adventure-style playground. Pets allowed. Dog showers. WiFi.

Key Features

🐾 Pets allowed

♿ Accessible Facilities

🧒 Childrens Play Area

🍸 Bar on Site

🐟 Fishing on Site

⛳ Golf on Site

Find Out More
Visit **ar.camp/uk4340**
or scan the QR code.

Warwickshire, Heart of England

Harbury Fields Farm

This delightful, family-run caravan park is surrounded by a 222-acre arable and sheep farm. Peaceful and quiet, it is set in the unspoilt 'Shakespeare countryside'. Located well away from main roads, it is just a mile from the lively village of Harbury, an ancient, prehistoric settlement on a hill near the Fosse Way Roman Road in Warwickshire. There are 58 fully serviced pitches, all with 16 amp electricity. Tents are not accepted. The site has a newly built, cabin-style pinewood reception with WiFi and additional toilet facilities.

The surrounding area has many old quarries that were historically used to extract lyas, a form of limestone used to manufacture cement. These quarries now make for unique family excursions. Some of the material produced by this work now forms a Site of Special Scientific Interest and is home to one of the top butterfly habitats in the UK. Also within easy reach, the Chiltern Railway runs through Harbury and has the deepest railway cutting in Europe.

All the heated toilet facilities have shower cubicles with washbasins. Separate cubicles with WCs for men and similar for women. Accessible sanitary facilities. Washing machine and dryer. Dishwashing area. Security barrier. Motorhome services. No shop. Dog walks around the farm. No late-night arrivals area. WiFi hotspot, free. BBQs allowed. TV reception is good. No tents allowed. Bus stop 600 metres. Train Station 5 miles. The earliest arrival time is noon.

Alan Rogers Ref: UK4065
Pitches: 58
GPS: 52.23985, -1.48689
Post Code: CV33 9JN

what3words:
pumpkin.masks.nags

Contact:
info@harburyfields.co.uk
Tel: +44 1926 612457
www.harburyfields.co.uk

Open Dates:
Mid February - Late November.

Key Features

📅 Book Online

🐾 Pets allowed

♿ Accessible Facilities

Find Out More
Visit ar.camp/uk4065
or scan the QR code.

231

📍 **Cambridgeshire, East of England**

Alan Rogers Ref: UK3586
Pitches: 40
GPS: 52.63496, 0.15011
Post Code: PE14 0AZ

what3words:
cooking.cans.gravitate

Contact:
info@littleranchleisure.co.uk
Tel: +44 1945 860066
www.littleranchleisure.co.uk

Open Dates:
All year.

Little Ranch Leisure

Little Ranch Leisure site offers 40 large, level pitches with hard-standing bases, allowing for all-year touring. Each pitch has electricity, mains water, a TV point, and grey water wastage. American RVs are welcome. Dogs are welcome, provided they are always kept on a lead. Pitches with a lake-side view ensure scenery for everyone to enjoy.

It's a quiet site, though the A47 does provide background traffic noise. There is an excellent range of facilities in the well-provisioned central block. Electric hook-up is no problem to the extent that if you forget your lead, the site will lend you one! The delightful rural villages of Elm, Friday Bridge and the historic township of Wisbech surround this well-established, family-run touring park in the heart of Fenland countryside.

The modern centrally heated toilet block provides toilets and showers. Accessible sanitary facilities, Baby changing facility. Sinks for washing up and vegetable preparation. Washing machine and tumble dryer. Waste disposal point. Fishing, A chemical toilet point. Service point for motor homes. Some fully serviced pitches. The TV reception is good.

Key Features

📅 All Year

🐾 Pets allowed

♿ Accessible Facilities

🐟 Fishing on Site

Find Out More
Visit ar.camp/uk3586
or scan the QR code.

📍 Shropshire, Heart of England

Love2Stay

Love2Stay site is located on the outskirts of Shrewsbury, Shropshire. A touring site and 'glamping' village, set in 22 acres of landscaped grounds close to the England-Wales border, it boasts sleek, modern architecture and superb facilities. Whether you want to exercise, spend valuable time with family and friends, explore the area or relax and get away from it all, Love2Stay is a state-of-the-art site to suit all tastes.

The site has 122 fully serviced hardstanding pitches (some seasonal) and 11 glamping pods to rent. The site is a Caravan and Motorhome Club Affiliated Site Scheme member, but non-members are also very welcome.

A single toilet block provides facilities for visitors. Accessible sanitary facilities and showers. Wash basins. Laundry. Dishwashing area. Pets allowed. Dog walk adjacent. Chemical toilet point. Motorhome service point. Gas sales. WiFi is good, charged. The TV reception is good. Restaurant. Outdoor yoga. Pilates studio. Gym. Wellness centre. Small shop. Coffee shop. Pizzeria. Outoor barbecues and cooking fire pits. Jogging and walking paths and even barefoot trails. Adventure playground for children. On-site fishing. Natural swimming pool. Heated outdoor hot springs. Late-night arrivals area. Co-op 1.5 miles. Bus stop 600 metres. Train station 3 miles. The earliest arrival time is 13.00.

Alan Rogers Ref: UK4431
Accommodations: 11
Pitches: 122
GPS: 52.69146, -2.70943
Post Code: SY5 6QS

what3words:
cages.gentlemen.wool

Contact:
info@love2stay.co.uk
Tel: +44 1743 583124
www.love2stay.co.uk

Open Dates:
All year.

Key Features

- Book Online
- All Year
- Pets allowed
- Accessible Facilities
- Outdoor Pool on Site
- Childrens Play Area
- Bicycle Hire on Site
- Fishing on Site

Find Out More
Visit **ar.camp/uk4431**
or scan the QR code.

📍 Cheshire, North West

Alan Rogers Ref: UK5220
Accommodations: 1
Pitches: 67
GPS: 53.08731, -2.83033
Post Code: CH3 9EN

what3words:
splat.shelter.districts

Contact:
info@manorwoodcaravans.
co.uk
Tel: +44 1829 782990
cheshirecaravansites.co.uk

Open Dates:
All year.

Manor Wood Caravan Park

Arranged on well-maintained grass, on farmland with views towards the Welsh hills, this family-owned and orientated site has a small swimming pool for use in the summer months. There are 67 level touring pitches with 16A electricity, accessed via tarmac roads. Fifty-six have hardstandings, and 47 have water and drainage. The footpaths and bridle paths from the park will appeal to those interested in nature, walking and cycling. Pools on the site allow various activities, from serious fishing to pond dipping. Chester and its zoo are nearby, and the seaside can be reached in an hour.

The park has a David Bellamy Gold Award for conservation, and the nature theme is maintained with information boards across the park highlighting the wildlife that can be seen in the varied habitats.

Heated sanitary unit with showers and washbasins in cubicles. Accessible sanitary unit. Laundry. Basics can be purchased. Small swimming pool (heated May-Sept), adventure play area (6-14 yrs). Games room with pool and table tennis. Tennis court. Security barrier with unrestricted card access. WiFi (free). Dog walk (2 dogs per pitch) and wellie washing. Gas available. Small shop, Fishing £5 per rod. Separate, central car parking for several pitches.

Key Features

- 📅 All Year
- 🐾 Pets allowed
- ♿ Accessible Facilities
- 🏊 Outdoor Pool on Site
- 🛝 Childrens Play Area
- 🐟 Fishing on Site

Find Out More
Visit **ar.camp/uk5220**
or scan the QR code.

Derbyshire, Heart of England

Ashbourne Heights

Ashbourne Heights is set on high, flat ground in the Peak District National Park with marvellous views. The site provides 260 spacious and carefully positioned pitches, of which 170 are for touring units. On grass or with hardstanding, most have 16A electricity. Privately owned caravan holiday homes (30) and 60 seasonal units occupy further fields. Amenities include an indoor, heated swimming pool, which is open all season.

The park is in the heart of the National Park – Dovedale and Ilam are only a mile or two by footpath, and the Tissington Trail, with access to the High Peak Trail, passes by the park. The surrounding Derbyshire countryside provides breathtaking landscapes. Destinations for days out could include Buxton, Chatsworth House, the Crich Tram Museum or Alton Towers.

Two heated, stone-built toilet blocks are well-maintained and clean. Washing machine and dryer. Shop for basics and gas. Good play area. Heated indoor swimming pool (all season, charged). WiFi throughout (charged). Winter caravan storage. Torches useful.

Alan Rogers Ref: UK3800
Accommodations: 10
Pitches: 260
GPS: 53.05479, -1.74748
Post Code: DE6 1LE

what3words:
slimming.whizzed.contexts

Contact:
ashbourneheights@
ashbourne-heights.co.uk
Tel: +44 1335 218986
www.ashbourne-heights.co.uk

Open Dates:
Early March - Early November.

Key Features

- Book Online
- Pets allowed
- Indoor Pool on Site
- Childrens Play Area

Find Out More
Visit **ar.camp/uk3800**
or scan the QR code.

235

Alan Rogers Ref: UK3925
Accommodations: 1
Pitches: 50
GPS: 53.23576, -0.87978
Post Code: NG22 0JN

what3words:
conceals.diverts.upcoming

Contact:
bailey-security@freezone.co.uk
Tel: +44 1777 870264
www.greenacres-tuxford.co.uk

Open Dates:
All year.

Greenacres Touring Park

The site is set in a wonderful location and enjoys some of the region's most scenic countryside. It is also just a stone's throw from local amenities and only a short drive from regional areas of interest, including Sherwood Forest, Lincoln, Newark and other local landmarks. The site has 50 touring pitches (11 seasonal), of which 36 have electrical hook-up points. The recently renovated toilet block is cleaned throughout the day and is always warm and well-lit.

Greenacres Touring Park is the perfect place for some well-deserved peace away from the stresses of modern life. Each spacious pitch is designed to ensure that you have all the room you need to sit back and enjoy your break in comfort. It is an adult-only site. However, mobile homeowners occasionally may have young family members stay during the school holidays.

The modern toilet block has washbasins, toilets and showers (Paid). Hand dryers. A private accessible shower room. Laundry. Chemical toilet point. WiFi is available.

Key Features

18+ Adults Only

All Year

Pets allowed

Accessible Facilities

Find Out More
Visit **ar.camp/uk3925**
or scan the QR code.

Lincolnshire, Heart of England

5s

Captain Bluebells Farm Park

Alan Rogers Ref: UK3639
Pitches: 30
GPS: 53.25521, 0.27266
Post Code: PE24 5YF

what3words:
duplicity.trunk.reheat

Contact:
mailbox@bluebell.farm
Tel: +44 7450 232807
www.captainbluebells.com

Open Dates:
Mid March - End September.

Captain Bluebells Farm Caravan Park is an adult-only, dog-friendly site, handily placed between Sutton on Sea and Chapel St, Leonards, with two pubs and the sea (Anderby Creek) within a 5-minute drive. The site caters for couples and solo caravan and motorhome guests. It has 30 grass/hardstanding pitches with electric hook-up points. The farm is steeped in history with fields of ridge and furrow dating back to Viking times. Set on 8 acres on the grounds of a Victorian farm that dates to the 1860s. It has farm animals, a rare breed flock of sheep and some more four-legged friends such as llamas, alpacas, goats, chickens, and ducks.

The facilities are modern and clean and at no extra cost. On-site are a farm shop selling jams, chutneys, honey, and fresh farm eggs produced onsite or from friends in the local area. The site does not open the farm to the public, just to guests only, and staff are on-site to ensure a good night's sleep. The site has a policy of no unnecessary noise between 10.30 pm - 7 am. This means no group chatter, music not even on low volume, etc, between these hours. So, if you prefer a livelier night, this won't be the place for you.

The toilet block has showers, washbasins, and WCs. Dishwashing area. Dogs welcome. Dog shower. Two designated dog walk areas. BBQs allowed. Farm shop selling jams, chutneys, honey, and fresh farm eggs. Book swop. DVD library. 24-hour CCTV coverage on the entrance. Charging point for electric cars. WiFi part site.

Key Features

🐾 Pets allowed

⛱ Seaside Beach Nearby

Find Out More
Visit **ar.camp/uk3639**
or scan the QR code.

Mersey, North West

Willowbank Touring Park

Well situated for the Sefton coast and Southport, Willowbank Holiday Home & Touring Park is set on the edge of sand dunes amongst mature, windswept trees. Entrance to the park is controlled by a barrier, with a pass-key issued at the excellent reception building, which doubles as a sales office for the substantial, high-quality caravan holiday home development.

There are 79 touring pitches, 30 on gravel hardstandings, 16 on grass and a further 33 pitches, all with 10A electricity; these are on grass hardstanding using an environmentally friendly reinforcement system. Large units are accepted by prior arrangement. This lovely flat open site is very well maintained, with large pitches, all with electricity, and you have a choice of where you wish to pitch. Facilities were modern and clean in a central block with easy access. If you have mobility issues, this site is ideal as surfaces are smooth and the site is level.

The purpose-built, heated toilet block is of a high standard, including an excellent, accessible bathroom, although the showers are relatively compact. Baby room. Laundry. Motorhome services. Play area. A field for ball games. Beauty treatments. WiFi throughout (charged).

Alan Rogers Ref: UK5360
Pitches: 79
GPS: 53.58880, -3.04400
Post Code: PR8 3ST

what3words:
teams.gloves.buggy

Contact:
info@willowbankcp.co.uk
Tel: +44 1704 571566
www.willowbankcp.co.uk

Open Dates:
All year - Excl. February.

Key Features

🐾 Pets allowed

♿ Accessible Facilities

🏖 Seaside Beach Nearby

🛝 Childrens Play Area

Find Out More
Visit **ar.camp/uk5360**
or scan the QR code.

Lancashire, North West

Alan Rogers Ref: UK5272
Accommodations: 175
Pitches: 25
GPS: 53.94095, -2.82761
Post Code: LA2 0ES

what3words:
bulges.firebird.rapport

Contact:
info@mosswood.co.uk
Tel: +44 1524 791041
www.mosswood.co.uk

Open Dates:
Start March - End October.

Moss Wood Caravan Park

Moss Wood is a well-established park in a secluded rural location near the village of Cockerham. You can be sure of a friendly welcome from the park wardens when you arrive. A sheltered field has 25 touring pitches on level hardstandings (steel pegs required) with 16A electricity. Most also have water and drainage.

Screened from the touring area by a high fence so that they are not visually intrusive are 175 privately owned holiday homes. A purpose-built log cabin houses reception and a shop which sells basic supplies. Although there are passing places, the approach road to the park is narrow, so care should be taken.

The modern, centrally located sanitary block (key entry) is kept spotlessly clean and provides vanity-style washbasins and roomy, preset showers. Fully equipped accessible facilities. Undercover food preparation area, dishwashing and laundry facilities. Adventure playground. Large field for ball games. Fishing lake (fenced). Woodland dog walking. WiFi throughout (charged).

Key Features

Pets allowed

Accessible Facilities

Seaside Beach Nearby

Childrens Play Area

Fishing on Site

Find Out More
Visit **ar.camp/uk5272**
or scan the QR code.

📍 West Yorkshire, Yorkshire

Alan Rogers Ref: UK4787
Accommodations: 10
Pitches: 75
GPS: 53.81550, -1.93618
Post Code: BD22 9SS

what3words:
prevented.touches.dustbin

Contact:
info@upwoodpark.co.uk
Tel: +44 1535 644242
www.upwoodpark.co.uk

Open Dates:
Start March - End December.

Upwood Holiday Park

The owner's futuristic ideas and drive have made Upwood Holiday Park a pioneer in the camping arena. It has four glamping mega-pods, 3 Mongolian yurts, 80 mobile homes and a holiday cottage. The site overlooks the Bronte villages of Haworth and Oxenhope, just over a mile away.

The accommodation takes in the best of the stunning panoramic views. And, of course, there are 75 touring pitches, where you can take your pick from grass or hard-standing pitches with a hook-up 10 amp supply. Seasonal pitches and storage are also available. Visitors are well placed to drive to the Yorkshire Dales National Park for days out. Or maybe the Forest of Bowland Area of Outstanding Natural Beauty? How about both?

A large, fully centrally heated, modernised toilet and shower block with laundry is available, including an accessible wet room. Baby changing facility. Gas sales. Club House. Bar. Free WiFi. TV room. Games room. The TV reception is good. Resturant. Bar. Games room. Play Area. Tents allowed. Motorhome service point. Pets allowed. Dog walk. Late-night arrivals area. Caravan storage.

Key Features

🐾 Pets allowed

♿ Accessible Facilities

🛝 Childrens Play Area

🍸 Bar on Site

Find Out More
Visit **ar.camp/uk4787**
or scan the QR code.

Alan Rogers Ref: UK4497
Accommodations: 50
Pitches: 53
GPS: 53.90266, -0.31186
Post Code: YO25 8RU

what3words:
searched.petrified.timed

Contact:
info@bluerosepark.com
Tel: +44 1964 543366
www.bluerosepark.com

Open Dates:
All year.

Blue Rose Caravan Park

Blue Rose Country Caravan Park is an all-year site that is exclusively for adults, nestled between the sleepy villages of Brandesburton and Leven villages on the edge of the Yorkshire Wolds. These villages are within easy walking distance and have pubs serving excellent food, a delicatessen, Chinese takeaway and an award-winning fish and chip shop/restaurant.

Hornsea Freeport and the historic market town of Beverley are only a 15-minute drive away, or spend a day at the seaside in Bridlington, just 20 minutes away. Historic York and Whitby are only an hour away. The site has 60 touring pitches (some seasonal). There are also 50 privately owned mobile homes.

Fully heated toilet and shower block. Accessible wet room and launderette. Chemical toilet point. WiFi, charged. Dogs allowed. Dog walk. Beach near. Security barrier. Function room. Beer garden. Picnic area. Putting green. Public phone. Information area. Tents not accepted.

Key Features

- 18+ Adults Only
- All Year
- Pets allowed
- Accessible Facilities
- Seaside Beach Nearby

Find Out More
Visit **ar.camp/uk4497**
or scan the QR code.

📍 **North Yorkshire, Yorkshire**

Alan Rogers Ref: UK4596
Pitches: 119
GPS: 54.30790, -2.18801
Post Code: DL8 3PS

what3words:
tango.publisher.alcove

Contact:
UKSitesBookingService@
camc.com
Tel: +44 1969 667338
www.camc.com

Open Dates:
Mid March - Early January.

Hawes CAMC Campsite

The Hawes Caravan and Motorhome Club site is set in beautiful Wensleydale, where the famous cheese has been made for nearly a century and offers delightful views. The site is situated between the River Ure and the market town of Hawes and is within the boundary of the beautiful Yorkshire Dales National Park. It has 119 pitches, all hardstanding, ten are serviced, and all have 16 amp electricity.

With the beautiful Dales on the doorstep, walking enthusiasts will have hours of captivating landscapes to explore. The Pennine Way is another must - it still carries tracks made in previous centuries, so you can feel you are following in your ancestor's footsteps.

A single toilet block provides accessible facilities. Laundry. Showers. Wash basins. Dishwashing area. Motorhome service point. Chemical toilet point. Children's play area. Games room. Picnic area. WiFi is poor and charged. BBQs allowed gas, electric & charcoal. Defibrillator. TV reception booster system. Information room. Pets allowed. Dog walk. Twin axle caravans accepted. Late-night arrivals area. Bus stop 800 metres. Spar 0.25 miles. No tents allowed. The earliest time of arrival is noon. Maximum outfit length 8.5 metres.

Key Features

📅 Book Online

🐾 Pets allowed

♿ Accessible Facilities

🛝 Childrens Play Area

Find Out More
Visit ar.camp/uk4596
or scan the QR code.

North Yorkshire, Yorkshire

Rigg Farm Caravan Park

Alan Rogers Ref: UK4576
Accommodations: 30
Pitches: 9
GPS: 54.44267, -0.59155
Post Code: YO22 4LP

what3words:
scouted.bearable.museum

Contact:
davidswilkes@aol.com
Tel: +44 7969 064825
riggfarmcaravanpark.co.uk

Open Dates:
Start March - End October.

Rigg Farm Caravan Park is close to Whitby and Robin Hoods Bay. The site consists of thirty static caravan holiday homes and nine touring pitches; all the statics are privately owned. The site has been developed to attract those who appreciate the peace and tranquillity of this outstanding area of the North Yorkshire coastline. Whitby, Robin Hood's Bay, Goathland, and Grosmont (a bygone era of working steam trains) are all but a 10-20 minute drive away.

The pitches are spread over two sites and offer beautiful views of both Whitby Abbey and the North Sea. A short walk onto the Moors themselves allows guests even more spectacular views across Whitby Bay and beyond.

The toilet block has showers, washbasins, and WCs. Chemical disposal point. Electric hook-ups, Laundry. Dishwashing area. Games room. Children's play area. Pets allowed. Gas sales. Shop.

Key Features

🐾 Pets allowed

⛱ Seaside Beach Nearby

🛝 Childrens Play Area

Find Out More
Visit **ar.camp/uk4576**
or scan the QR code.

📍 **Ambleside, Cumbria**

Alan Rogers Ref: UK5520
Accommodations: 8
Pitches: 97
GPS: 54.41715, -2.99528
Post Code: LA22 0HX

what3words:
villager.learns.estimate

Contact:
info@skelwith.com
Tel: +44 15394 32277
www.skelwith.com

Open Dates:
Start March - Mid November.

Skelwith Fold

Skelwith Fold has been developed on the extensive grounds of a country estate, taking advantage of the wealth of mature trees and shrubs. Over 300 privately owned caravan holiday homes and 97 touring pitches are absorbed into this unspoilt natural environment, sharing it with red squirrels and other wildlife in several discrete areas branching off the central, mile-long main driveway. Touring pitches (no tents) are on gravel hardstanding, and metal pegs will be necessary for awnings. Electricity hook-ups (10-16A) and basic amenities are available in all areas.

You will find endless pleasure exploring over 130 acres of wild woodland, and if you are an early riser, it is possible to see deer, foxes, etc., at the almost hidden tarn deep in the woods. There are plenty of paths to follow, leading to a wealth of discoveries, including our mystical tarn, sculptures and breathtaking views of the Langdale Pikes and surrounding fells.

Three toilet blocks, well situated to serve all areas, have the usual facilities, including laundry, drying and ironing rooms. Accessible sanitary facilities. Motorhome services. Well stocked, licensed shop. Battery charging, gas and caravan spares and accessories. Adventure play area. Astroturf sports pitch. Library with computer. E-bicycle hire. Family recreation area with picnic tables and goalposts in the Lower Glade. WiFi. Dishwashing facilities by EasyBe

Key Features

🐾 Pets allowed

♿ Accessible Facilities

🧗 Childrens Play Area

Find Out More
Visit **ar.camp/uk5520**
or scan the QR code.

Alan Rogers Ref: UK5625
Pitches: 70
GPS: 54.64767, -2.73702
Post Code: CA10 2JB

what3words:
flicked.districts.explorer

Contact:
customerrelations@
pureleisuregroup.com
Tel: +44 1768 863631
www.lowther-holidaypark.co.uk

Open Dates:
Early March - Late November.

Lowther Holiday Park

Sitting on the banks of the River Lowther, this holiday park occupies 50 acres of rural, wooded parkland, home to the rare red squirrel. There are 400 caravan holiday homes and lodges around the park, together with 70 touring pitches. Seasonal lets take a proportion of these. Marked and numbered, on mostly level ground between mature trees, all have 10A electricity and hardstanding. A separate elevated grass area is available for tents, and two pods have been added.

A small touring office with 24-hour security is adjacent to the holiday home sales office. Here, too, is a well-stocked, licensed shop selling caravan accessories. The Squirrel Inn is open all season and serves restaurant meals and takeaways.

Two toilet blocks are central to the touring areas (key entry). They are very clean, and they provide large, preset showers. Fully equipped bathroom with baby changing. Drive-through motorhome service. Well-equipped laundry. Full Accessible sanitary facilities(Radar key). Licensed shop. Squirrel Inn has a restaurant, terrace, and games room. Play areas. Fly fishing on the river (permit from office). Activity weekends. Live entertainment and children's parties. Max. 2 dogs per unit.

Key Features

- Pets allowed
- Accessible Facilities
- Childrens Play Area
- Bar on Site
- Fishing on Site

Find Out More
Visit ar.camp/uk5625
or scan the QR code.

📍 **Northumberland, Northumbria**

Alan Rogers Ref: UK5810
Accommodations: 118
Pitches: 32
GPS: 55.00166, -2.09470
Post Code: NE46 4RP

what3words:
sped.left.rooster

Contact:
info@fallowfielddene.co.uk
Tel: +44 1434 603553
www.fallowfielddene.co.uk

Open Dates:
Mid March - Early November.

Fallowfield Dene Camping

Although only 2.5 miles from Hexham, Fallowfield Dene Caravan Park is very secluded, situated in mature woodland at the end of a no-through road. Set in woodland glades (formerly a Victorian lead mine), each with a Roman name (Hadrian's Wall is close), are 118 seasonal pitches and 32 touring pitches, all with 16A electricity. A further ten tent pitches have been added, suitable for smaller tents.

The park entrance, with a new reception and shop, is neat, tidy and very colourful. No play area or games field exists, but the surrounding woods are a paradise for children. Fallowfield Dene itself is a network of tracks, and there are footpaths from the site entrance.

Brick-built toilet blocks are central and heated in cool weather. Well-tiled and kept very clean, there are washbasins in cabins and free hairdryers. Separate, fully equipped, accessible room. Laundry room with dishwashing sinks. Baby bath. Motorhome services. Small shop for essentials, including gas. Small Coffee Bar. Barrier card £5 deposit. WiFi (charged; currently in the reception area with plans to extend over the site).

Key Features

🐾 Pets allowed

♿ Accessible Facilities

Find Out More
Visit **ar.camp/uk5810**
or scan the QR code.

Northumberland, Northumbria

South Meadows Caravan Park

South Meadows is set in the north Northumberland countryside, within walking distance of the village of Belford with its market cross and old coaching inn. The park is pleasantly landscaped, and two short walks lead into the adjacent bluebell woods. Covering 40 acres of level grass, there are 165 touring pitches (67 let seasonally) with 16A electricity, water and TV aerial points. Help is available from a team who will position and level your caravan for you. A further area can accommodate about 50 tents.

The manager is environmentally aware and encourages recycling. There is an area, especially for visitors, with accessibility requirements, with wider paths, and safety features. Just off the A1 road, this would be a convenient stopover, but Northumberland is an undiscovered county with castles and stately homes, the Farne Islands, Holy Island and long golden beaches, and you would be most welcome here for a longer stay.

The fully tiled toilet block is excellent, heated in cool weather, with washbasins in cabins and roomy showers (free). Three family shower rooms. An additional prefabricated sanitary unit is open in one area for the summer months. Hairdryers. Fully accessible facilities. Laundry with washing machines, dryers and iron plus a baby unit. Play area. Caravan storage and servicing. Free WiFi over site.

Alan Rogers Ref: UK5755
Accommodations: 112
Pitches: 165
GPS: 55.59097, -1.82258
Post Code: NE70 7DP

what3words:
stays.fattening.hangs

Contact:
info@southmeadows.co.uk
Tel: +44 1668 213326
www.southmeadows.co.uk

Open Dates:
All year.

Key Features

All Year

Pets allowed

Accessible Facilities

Seaside Beach Nearby

Childrens Play Area

Find Out More
Visit ar.camp/uk5755
or scan the QR code.

📍 **Carmarthenshire, West Wales**

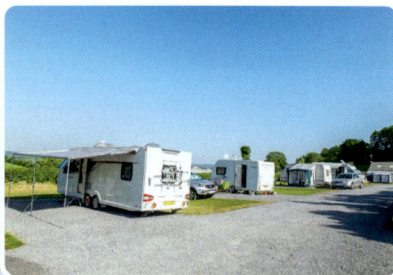

Alan Rogers Ref: UK5937
Pitches: 25
GPS: 51.70384, -4.09333
Post Code: SA14 8AX

what3words:
vision.humid. purple

Contact:
info@southwalescaravansite.
co.uk
Tel: +44 1554 820420
southwalescaravansite.co.uk

Open Dates:
All year.

South Wales Touring Park

South Wales Touring Park is an adult-only, all-year caravan park in South Wales. It is located on the outskirts of Llanelli. The hard-standing pitches are beautifully landscaped on a peaceful hillside, so you can enjoy country views over the Loughor Estuary.

Expect a warm welcome from Cathrin and Hywel, along with a host of thoughtful touches which set this site apart. The site will provide the opportunity to explore the South Wales coast, Gower Peninsula and the Brecon Beacons. It is a member of the Tranquil Sites Group. There are 25 touring pitches (some seasonal). The hardstanding touring pitches are carefully landscaped on three tiers across the hillside. This means every guest can enjoy countryside views.

The heated amenities building has showers, washbasins, WCs, and hair dryers. Laundry with washing machine and tumble dryer. Dishwashing area. Chemical toilet point. Motorhome service point. Free WiFi. Dogs allowed. Dog shower. Dog exercise field. Tourist information. Electric car charging point. Twin-axle caravans are permitted. BBQs allowed. Freezer for ice packs.

Key Features

18+ Adults Only

365 All Year

🐾 Pets allowed

Find Out More
Visit **ar.camp/uk5937**
or scan the QR code.

Pembrokeshire, West Wales

St Davids Lleithyr CAMC

St David's Lleithyr Meadow Caravan and Motorhome Club site is nestled between three headlands of the dramatic Pembrokeshire Coast. It offers swimming, surfing, windsurfing and sailing from Whitesands Bay, just over a mile from the site. Anglers can fish in the reservoirs or the sea. Dedicated to the outdoor lover, the site encourages you to explore the rich, luscious surroundings. The site has 115 grass pitches (some seasonal), all with 16 amp electricity.

In the unlikely event of boredom at the site's Whitesands location, daily trips are available to Ramsey from St Justinians and Skomer, Skokholm and Grassholm from Martin's Haven (about 20 miles down the coast from the site).

The toilet block provides accessible facilities. Laundry. Showers. Wash basins. Dishwashing. Motorhome service point. Small shop. Chemical toilet point. Gas sales. Children's play area. Wi-Fi is poor and charged. BBQs allowed, gas, electric & charcoal. Defibrillator. TV reception fair. Information room. Pets allowed. Dog walk adjacent. Dog pit stop. Twin axle caravans accepted. No late-night arrivals area. Bus stop adjacent. Shops 1.5 miles. No tents allowed. Earliest time of arrival: 1:00pm. Maximum outfit length 11.6 metres.

Alan Rogers Ref: UK5993
Pitches: 115
GPS: 51.89645, -5.27853
Post Code: SA62 6PR

what3words:
grabs.distracts.waiters

Contact:
UKSitesBookingService@camc.com
Tel: +44 1437 720401
www.camc.com

Open Dates:
Early April - Early October.

Key Features

🗓 Book Online

🐾 Pets allowed

♿ Accessible Facilities

⛱ Seaside Beach Nearby

🛝 Childrens Play Area

Find Out More
Visit ar.camp/uk5993
or scan the QR code.

📍 **Powys, Mid Wales**

Alan Rogers Ref: UK4351
Accommodations: 3
Pitches: 28
GPS: 52.09684, -3.13350
Post Code: HR3 5RX

what3words:
dime.monorail.river

Contact:
info@blackmountainview.co.uk
Tel: +44 7971 842997
www.blackmountainview.co.uk

Open Dates:
Early March - Mid October.

Black Mountain View

Black Mountain View is just 1½ miles from the popular border town of Hay-on-Wye. The site is situated in the beautiful Wye Valley on the Powys/ Herefordshire border. From here, you can take the short walk to The Offa's Dyke Path, fish on the River Wye or simply take in the breathtaking views of the Black Mountains. The area is an excellent destination for walking the Black Mountains and the Brecon Beacons National Park.

Over the border, Herefordshire and The Golden Valley has something to offer everyone; historic market towns and cultural attractions such as historic houses, museums and art galleries. This small, family run caravan park is set on an organic small holding. The site accepts touring caravans, motorhomes, campervans or tents. It has 28 spacious pitches, some serviced. Three mobile homes are available to rent.

A modern heated toilet/ shower block. Free hot showers. Separate accessible facilities/ Family room with baby changing. Electric shaving point. Coin-operated Hair Dryer. Washing up facilities. Chemical toilet disposal point. Motorhome grey water disposal point. There is an aerial point on most pitches for Freeview and Sky connection (BYO Sky Box - single lead connection only). Free WiFi access. Pets Welcome. Dog walking area. Arrivals from 2pm. Charging of electric cars not allowed on pitches, an electric point can be provided at £5 for 3 hours. TV reception is good. Charge for pets and awnings.

Key Features

🐾 Pets allowed

♿ Accessible Facilities

Find Out More
Visit **ar.camp/uk4351**
or scan the QR code.

Ceredigion, West Wales

Alan Rogers Ref: UK6019
Accommodations: 6
Pitches: 40
GPS: 52.15265, -4.41537
Post Code: SA44 6HB

what3words:
mute.scripted.sectors

Contact:
info@welshcoastalholidays.
co.uk
Tel: +44 7852 365796
welshcoastalholidays.co.uk

Open Dates:
All year.

Glyncoch Isaf Farm Camping

Glyncoch Isaf Farm is just three miles from Llangrannog's stunning sandy beaches. You will love wandering along the best of Ceredigion's coast and visiting stunning beaches nearby. This charming dog-friendly farm is an animal lover's dream with friends in the form of alpacas, horses, sheep and more. You'll be a short drive from several stunning beaches, cliff walks, woodlands and rivers.

The site has hardstanding or grass pitches, with up to ten electric hook-ups available between the pitches. Pitches are well sheltered, and the site has views north of the Cambrian and Snowdonia Mountain ranges. The site has 20 grass and 20 hardstanding touring pitches with optional electric hook-up points. There are also three bell tents, a yurt, a gypsy caravan and a shepherd's hut available to hire.

The site has coin-operated showers, washbasins and WCs. A family room. Laundry room. Chemical toilet point. Shared barn kitchen space. Phone charging. Ice pack freezing. Dogs allowed. WiFi. BBQs allowed. Public transport is within a mile of the site. There is a Londis and a local pub nearby. Earliest arrival time: 14.00.

Key Features

📅 All Year

🐾 Pets allowed

⛱ Seaside Beach Nearby

Find Out More
Visit ar.camp/uk6019
or scan the QR code.

📍 **Powys, Mid Wales**

Red Kite Touring Park

Alan Rogers Ref: UK6243
Pitches: 66
GPS: 52.45999, -3.55132
Post Code: SY18 6NG

what3words:
panoramic.mentioned.plodding

Contact:
info@redkitetouringpark.co.uk
Tel: +44 1686 412122
www.redkitetouringpark.co.uk

Open Dates:
Start March - Start January.

Red Kite Touring Park is an exclusively for adults site situated one mile from the historic market town of Llanidloes. It has a large amenity area with nature ponds, a coarse fishing pool, walking routes and dog walks. The site is on a gently sloping, south-facing side of the Clywedog Valley, easily accessible directly off the B4518 with a large tarmac entrance.

Within the park grounds are large dog walking areas, with a separate fenced-off dog training area. There are lovely walks from the park into town, or along the river Clywedog, and the Severn Way skirts the park; please ask reception for more information. On-site are sixty-six all-services touring pitches with 16amp electric hook-up points (some seasonal). The site is a member of the Tranquil Sites Group.

The modern toilet block has underfloor heating and provides showers, washbasins and WCs. Accessible wet room. Laundrette including washers, dryers and ironing board Dish washing room. Motorhome service point. Chemical toilet point. Free WiFi is available on all pitches. Dog washroom. Information area. Gas sales. Caravan & motorhome accessories are available. Pets welcome. Dog walking areas. Dog training area. Dog Wash. Late arrivals area with electric hook-up. Numberplate recognition security barrier.

Key Features

18+ Adults Only

🐾 Pets allowed

♿ Accessible Facilities

⛱ Seaside Beach Nearby

🐟 Fishing on Site

Find Out More
Visit **ar.camp/uk6243**
or scan the QR code.

Powys, Mid Wales

Alan Rogers Ref: UK6305
Accommodations: 60
Pitches: 26
GPS: 52.54422, -3.23872
Post Code: SY15 6ND

what3words:
outsmart.dancer.describe

Contact:
info@smithypark.co.uk
Tel: +44 1584 711280
www.smithypark.co.uk

Open Dates:
Start March - End October.

Smithy Park

Smithy Park is set in four acres of landscaped grounds bordered by the River Severn and the Shropshire Union Canal in the tranquil rolling countryside of central Wales. It has 60 privately owned caravan holiday homes, but beyond these is a separate touring area with the benefit of being closest to the river with the best views and a small picnic and seating area on the bank. This area has 26 fully serviced hardstanding pitches (16A electricity, water, wastewater and satellite TV hook-ups). A timber chalet provides all the sanitary facilities and is located in one corner of the touring area.

This is a well-run site under the same ownership as Westbrook Park (UK4390), with a resident manager on site. The village has two local pubs, a shop and Post Office, and a bus service – all within easy walking distance. American RVs are accepted with prior notice. Kite flying and cycling in the park are not permitted.

The heated, timber-clad chalet building provides two good-sized showers, washbasins in cubicles, and a family room doubling as accessible facilities (there is a step up to the building). Additional toilet and washbasin in a new building by reception. The utility room houses a laundry with a washing machine, dryer, and dishwashing sink. Fishing in the River Severn. Fenced playground. Gas stocked. WiFi.

Key Features

🐾 Pets allowed

♿ Accessible Facilities

🧒 Childrens Play Area

🐟 Fishing on Site

Find Out More
Visit **ar.camp/uk6305**
or scan the QR code.

📍 **Gwynedd, North Wales**

Islawrffordd Caravan Park

This site is ideal if you like to park up and have all amenities within easy access. Family-owned and run since being established in 1957, Islawrffordd Caravan Park offers the best quality, evident as you enter the park. There are 75 fully serviced touring pitches (some seasonal) and 30 tent pitches. The fully serviced pitches all have courtesy light, electricity, fresh and waste water points and chemical disposal.

The site has private access to a sandy beach with a slipway launching for small boats. The towns of Harlech, Barmouth and the Italianate village of Portmeirion are all a short drive away. Snowdonia National Park is virtually on the doorstep.

The immaculate, modern toilet facilities have underfloor heating and climate control, an Accessible toilet (Radar key) and a baby changing room. Launderette. The toilet block and the entrance and exit of the park are activated by a key fob (deposit required). Well-stocked minimarket. Bar/restaurant and takeaway. Indoor swimming pool with sauna, jacuzzi and tanning suite. Fully equipped playground with safety surface. WiFi throughout (charged).

Alan Rogers Ref: UK6385
Accommodations: 5
Pitches: 75
GPS: 52.77249, -4.10030
Post Code: LL43 2AQ

what3words:
acquaint.camp.hoops

Contact:
info@islawrffordd.co.uk
Tel: +44 1341 247269
islawrffordd.com

Open Dates:
All year.

Key Features

📅 All Year

🐾 Pets allowed

♿ Accessible Facilities

⛱ Seaside Beach on Site

🏊 Indoor Pool on Site

🛝 Childrens Play Area

🍸 Bar on Site

⛷ Skiing on Site

Find Out More
Visit **ar.camp/uk6385**
or scan the QR code.

Denbighshire, North Wales

Alan Rogers Ref: UK6337
Accommodations: 3
Pitches: 11
GPS: 53.03665, -3.46723
Post Code: LL21 9PP

what3words:
juggle.secondly.windmills

Contact:
info@parcpenybryn.co.uk
Tel: +44 7538 929771
www.parcpenybryn.co.uk

Open Dates:
All year.

Parc Pen Y Bryn Campsite

Parc Pen Y Bryn is situated on the edge of Clocaenog forest, a 15-minute drive from Llyn Brenig and 25 minutes from Betws-y-Coed. This laidback, small-scale holiday park on the edge of Snowdonia National Park is open all year.

There is hardly a house to be seen at this secluded spot, where you can admire valley views and, in the distance, watch wind turbines turning slowly in the breeze. Well-placed outdoor furniture is available for those looking to sit in the open air and take it all in. The site has 11 hardstanding touring pitches with electric hook-up points; there are also 3 log cabins available to hire.

The toilet block has showers, washbasins, and WCs. Dishwashing area. Chemical toilet point. A communal kitchen where you can prep packed lunches in the run-up to your next big explore. BBQs allowed. Fire pit available to hire. WiFi. Shop and community-run pub nearby. Corwen on the river Dee has shops and a pharmacy. Dogs welcome. Dog walk nearby.

Key Features

All Year

Pets allowed

Find Out More
Visit **ar.camp/uk6337**
or scan the QR code.

Denbighshire, North Wales

Alan Rogers Ref: UK6662
Pitches: 120
GPS: 53.28204, -3.36188
Post Code: LL17 0TY

what3words:
nurse.simulator.stealthier

Contact:
contact@penisarmynydd.co.uk
Tel: +44 1745 582227
penisarmynydd.co.uk

Open Dates:
Early March -Mid January.

Penisar Mynydd Caravan Park

Penisar Mynydd Caravan Park is a friendly site located in the beautiful open countryside of North Wales. The park is close to the coastline and the marvellous Snowdonia National Park. Attractive, mature beech hedges separate many generously sized pitches to increase privacy. The site has 120 grass or hardstanding pitches (some seasonal), most with 16amp electric hook-up points. Some are also serviced.

You can enjoy pleasant walks in the area, including Offa's Dyke. Approximately 3 miles away, the village of Dyserth features the astounding Dyserth Waterfalls. Less than 8 miles away, you can visit the peaceful coastal resorts of Rhyl and Prestatyn. Castle and Bodrhyddan Hall are within a few minutes drive from the park.

A modern amenities building provides toilet, washing, shower and laundry facilities. Limited accessible facilities, Power provided for electric shavers. Dishwashing area. Separate washing, drying and ironing laundry facility. Chemical toilet point. Pets welcome (on lead at all times). Caravan & motorhome storage. Gas sales. Ice pack freezer. WiFi charged.

Key Features

🐾 Pets allowed

♿ Accessible Facilities

⛱ Seaside Beach Nearby

Find Out More
Visit **ar.camp/uk6662**
or scan the QR code.

📍 Isle of Anglesey, North Wales

Alan Rogers Ref: UK6637
Pitches: 80
GPS: 53.36250, -4.27545
Post Code: LL70 9PQ

what3words:
kite.regarding.reverted

Contact:
mail@tyddynisaf.co.uk
Tel: +44 1248 410203
tyddynisaf.co.uk

Open Dates:
Mid March - Late September.

Tyddyn Isaf Camping Park

This warm, welcoming family site cascades down the hillside from the bar/restaurant at the top of the site to the beach. The site has had the same owners for over 40 years. Lligwy Bay, with its sandy beach and sheltered waters, is ideal for children to play on and is accessible from the site. There are 80 touring pitches (of which 40 are seasonal), all with 16A electricity. The tent pitches (some with 10A electricity) are on separate fields.

Children are catered for with a play area arranged neatly on one of the slopes which make up the site. The site has been influenced by the clients who have visited over the years. The owners insist that all visitors are escorted to their pitch and, if required, helped with sitting. While the Isle of Anglesey has many attractions to entertain the whole family, Ireland is only a 90-minute ferry ride across the Irish Sea.

Two toilet blocks with free electric showers (timed; activated by a key-fob) and hairdryers. Dishwashing sinks with plenty of hot water. The laundry room has a washing machine and tumble dryer in the lower toilet block. The upper toilet block can be overstretched in peak times. A third toilet block is next to the bar. Accessible sanitary facilities, Shop selling basics. The bar will serve snacks, main meals, and takeaway (Seasonal). Gym, WiFi (free). Pets allowed.

Key Features

🐾 Pets allowed

♿ Accessible Facilities

⛱ Seaside Beach on Site

🧒 Childrens Play Area

🍸 Bar on Site

Find Out More
Visit ar.camp/uk6637
or scan the QR code.

📍 **Dumfries and Galloway, Lowlands**

Hoddom Castle Caravan Park

The park around Hoddom Castle is landscaped, spacious and well laid out on mainly sloping ground with many mature and beautiful trees, originally part of an arboretum. The drive to the site is just under a mile long with a one-way system. Many of the 91 numbered touring pitches have good views of the castle and have gravel hardstanding with grass for awnings. Most have 16A electrical connections. In front of the castle are flat fields used for tents and caravans with a limited number of electricity hook-ups.

The oldest part of Hoddom Castle itself is a 16th-century Borders Pele Tower or fortified Keep. This was extended to form a residence for a Lancashire cotton magnate, became a youth hostel and was then taken over by the army during WW2. Since then, parts have been demolished, but the original Border Keep still survives, unfortunately in a semi-derelict state.

The main toilet block can be heated and is very well-appointed. Washbasins in cubicles, three en-suite cubicles with WC and basin (one with baby facilities) and an en-suite accessible shower unit. Two further tiled blocks are kept very clean and provide washbasins and WCs only. Well-equipped laundry room at the castle. Motorhome services. Licensed shop at reception (gas available). Bar, restaurant and takeaway (Easter-Oct). Games room. Large grass play area. Crazy golf. Mountain bike trail. Fishing. Golf. Guided walks (high season). WiFi in the bar. Caravan storage.

Alan Rogers Ref: UK6910
Accommodations: 11
Pitches: 91
GPS: 55.04137, -3.31100
Post Code: DG11 1AS

what3words:
marsh.goat.imagined

Contact:
enquiries@hoddomcastle.co.uk
Tel: +44 1576 300251
www.hoddomcastle.co.uk

Open Dates:
Start April - Late October.

Key Features

- 🐾 Pets allowed
- ♿ Accessible Facilities
- ⛱ Seaside Beach Nearby
- 🧗 Childrens Play Area
- 🍸 Bar on Site
- 🐟 Fishing on Site
- 🚩 Golf on Site

Find Out More
Visit **ar.camp/uk6910**
or scan the QR code.

Stirling, Heart of Scotland

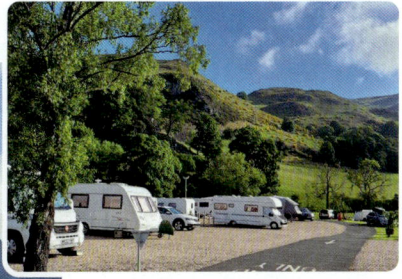

Witches Craig Caravan Park

Witches Craig is a neat and tidy park nestling under the Ochil Hills. All 60 pitches have 10A electricity and hardstanding, seven of these being large (taking American-style motorhomes easily). Reasonably level, the park covers five well-maintained acres with beautifully manicured grass Being by the A91, there is some daytime road noise. Trees have been planted to minimise this, but the further back onto the park you go, the less the traffic is heard.

The area has a wealth of historic attractions, starting with the Wallace Monument, which practically overlooks the park. Its 220 ft. tower dominates the surrounding area, and climbing up its 246 steps gives spectacular views. Stirling is known as the 'Gateway to the Highlands', and its magnificent castle is world-renowned.

The modern, heated toilet block is well maintained and includes one cubicle with a washbasin and WC each for ladies and men. Free controllable showers. Baby bath and mat. Good accessible sanitary unit. Drive-over motorhome service point. Laundry with free fridge/freezer facilities. Bread, milk, drinks and papers are available daily (supermarket 2.5 miles). Large fenced play area. Field for team games. Free WiFi.

Alan Rogers Ref: UK7320
Accommodations: 7
Pitches: 60
GPS: 56.14803, -3.89867
Post Code: FK9 5PX

what3words:
contain.farmer.playroom

Contact:
info@witchescraig.co.uk
Tel: +44 1786 474947
witchescraig.co.uk

Open Dates:
Start April - End October.

Key Features

- Pets allowed
- Accessible Facilities
- Seaside Beach Nearby
- Childrens Play Area

Find Out More
Visit ar.camp/uk7320
or scan the QR code.

📍 **Perth and Kinross, Heart of Scotland**

Alan Rogers Ref: UK7276
Pitches: 199
GPS: 56.62250, -3.85797
Post Code: PH15 2AQ

what3words:
trials.dishes.blogging

Contact:
info@aberfeldycaravanpark.co.uk
Tel: +44 1887 820662
aberfeldycaravanpark.co.uk

Open Dates:
Mid March – End October.

Aberfeldy Caravan Park

Aberfeldy Caravan Park is a popular and relaxed touring base in Highland Perthshire. The site has 134 grass pitches (some seasonal) for caravan and motorhome holidays, including a handful of hardstanding pitches. Some pitches have electric hookups – prepay card meter £10.00 deposit for card.

The site is the perfect base to explore the local area. The charming town of Aberfeldy is right on the doorstep, with plenty of local shops, cafes and bars within easy walking distance. You can look forward to stunning views and all the onsite essentials. Well-behaved pets are also welcome.

Toilet block with showers, washbasins, and WCs. Razor points. Dishwashing area. Accessible facilities. Chemical toilet point. Baby room. Laundry room with washing machine and tumble dryer. Dogs welcome. Dog walk. Restaurants and Bars in Aberfeldy. 24-hour security. WiFi. Children's play area. Ball games area. Gas Sales.

Key Features

🐾 Pets allowed

♿ Accessible Facilities

🛝 Childrens Play Area

🐟 Fishing on Site

Find Out More
Visit **ar.camp/uk7276**
or scan the QR code.

Aberdeenshire, Grampian

Alan Rogers Ref: UK7530
Accommodations: 16
Pitches: 23
GPS: 57.52475, -2.02612
Post Code: AB42 5FQ

what3words:
aura.sandbags.dockers

Contact:
wardens@
adencaravanandcamping.co.uk
Tel: +44 1771 623460
adencaravanandcamping.co.uk

Open Dates:
Easter - Late October.

Aden Country Park

The Aberdeenshire local authority owns Aden Country Park, which is open to the public. The caravan and camping site is on one side of the park. Beautifully landscaped and well laid out with trees, bushes and hedges, it is kept very neat and tidy. It provides 23 numbered pitches for touring units, with varying degrees of slope (some level) and all with 16A electrical hook-ups, plus an area for around 20 tents. There are also 16 caravan holiday homes and 12 seasonal pitches. The campsite is also leased by the council to private owners.

The park is in an attractive area, and one could spend plenty of time enjoying all it has to offer. Attractions for visitors include an Agricultural Heritage Centre, Wildlife Centre, Nature Trail and restaurant, and open and woodland areas with a lake for walking and recreation.

The modern toilet block is clean, with good accessible facilities. It can be heated and provides free, preset hot showers, a hairdryer, and a baby bath, but no private cabins. Dishwashing and laundry facilities (metered). Motorhome services. Gas supplies. Small shop in the reception area. Restaurant in the Heritage Centre. Games areas. Play equipment (safety surfaces). Dog exercise area.

Key Features

🐾 Pets allowed

♿ Accessible Facilities

🛝 Childrens Play Area

Find Out More
Visit **ar.camp/uk7530**
or scan the QR code.

📍 **Highland, Highlands and Islands**

Culloden Moor CAMC Campsite

Alan Rogers Ref: UK7639
Pitches: 87
GPS: 57.48601, -4.05748
Post Code: IV2 5EF

what3words:
degrading.cute.evolves

Contact:
UKSitesBookingService@camc.com
Tel: +44 1463 790625
www.camc.com

Open Dates:
Mid March - Early November

Culloden Moor Caravan and Motorhome Club site is a quiet and tranquil place ideally located for exploring the city of Inverness and the surrounding areas. Gently sloping to face a glorious, unspoilt view over the Nairn Valley, it has the asset of being sheltered on one side by an abundant belt of mature trees to afford extra privacy and wind protection. It has 87 mainly hardstanding pitches (some seasonal), and most have 16 amp electricity.

The site is only about 1.5 miles from the famous Culloden Battlefield, where Bonnie Prince Charlie was defeated, and Scottish history was rewritten. The site is also just six miles from the pretty city of Inverness - not only does it have more than enough choice for shopping treats and places to eat or drink, but it is also centrally situated for touring some of the most beautiful scenery in Scotland.

A single heated toilet block provides accessible facilities. Laundry. Dishwashing area. Dog walk. Motorhome Service Point. Information Room. No WiFi. TV reception via pitch bollard. BBQs allowed, charcoal, gas, electric. Children's play area. Small shop. Twin axle caravans accepted. Pets allowed. Calor Gas sales. Tents allowed. Late-night arrivals area. Defibrillator. Tesco 5 miles. Bus Stop 90 metres. Maximum outfit length 9 metres. No arrivals before noon.

Key Features

📅 Book Online

🐾 Pets allowed

♿ Accessible Facilities

🧗 Childrens Play Area

Find Out More
Visit ar.camp/uk7639
or scan the QR code.

📍 Isle of Skye, Highlands and Islands

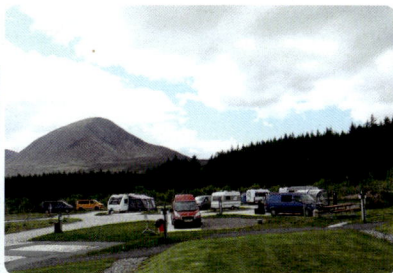

Camping Skye Broadford

Opened in June 2018, this site has been set up as a community campsite by the local community as a non-profit making enterprise. It is a lovely modern site in an amazing location with mountain views all around, yet it is just a five-minute walk from the village.

The site consists of twenty six hardstanding pitches all with 16 amp hook-up, as well as twenty six terraced camping pitches, with a community barbecue area, all pitches have mountain views. The modern facilities block has fully accessible facilities, a laundry/drying room, toilets, and showers. The site is in a good location on the South East side off the Island making it ideal to explore Skye, including Kilt Rock, Lealt Falls and 'The Old Man of Storr" and several local distilleries, a ferry to the Isle of Raasay is a 25 minutes drive away.

Accessible sanitary facilities, WiFi, TV reception (Good), Laundry, Dishwashing area, Toilets/Showers, Children's facilities, Drying room, Information Centre,

Alan Rogers Ref: UK7751
Pitches: 26
GPS: 57.24548, -5.91840
Post Code: IV49 9DF

what3words:
///passwords.stocked.collects

Contact:
mail@campingskye.com
Tel: +44 1471 550420
www.campingskye.com

Open Dates:
Late March - Early November and Christmas to New Year.

Key Features

🐾 Pets allowed

Find Out More
Visit ar.camp/uk7751
or scan the QR code.

📍 **Outer Hebrides, North Uist**

Alan Rogers Ref: UK7930
Accommodations: 2
Pitches: 36
GPS: 57.60484, -7.51932
Post Code: HS6 5DL

what3words:
happening.copes.subtitle

Contact:
info@
balranaldhebrideanholidays.
com
Tel: +44 1876 510 304
balranaldhebrideanholidays.
com

Open Dates:
End March - End October.

Balranald Holidays

Balranald Hebridean Holidays is a family-run site located on the picturesque west coast of North Uist in the heart of the RSPB's Balranald Nature Reserve. Situated beside a beautiful sandy beach, the site is an ideal base for exploring Uist. It is a bird watchers paradise with a wide variety of wading and farmland birds nesting on the flower-rich machair and croft land. Horseshoe Bay is only 40m from the site entrance and is excellent for walking, kite surfing, swimming, kayaking, paddle boarding and watching the sunset in the evening.

The site has 19 hardstanding pitches with 16A Electric Hook-up suitable for motorhomes or caravans, 12 Grass pitches with 16A Electric Hook-up suitable for tents or campervans and 5 Grass pitches without Electric Hook-ups– suitable for tents or campervans. Corncrake Pod and Kettle Cottage are also available to hire.

Two heated toilet blocks provide showers (£1 coin-operated), washbasins, and toilets. Accessible toilet and shower with full wheelchair access. Chemical toilet emptying point for use with green/organic toilet fluid only (Green Toilet fluid is on sale in the office). Drying Room. Laundry with washing machine and dryer. Dishwashing area. Small shop. Fridge. Microwave and Kettle. Free WiFi. Based on site from May to September, the Dunes Cabin serves delicious scallop and bacon rolls, homemade soups, filled sandwiches and rolls, and home baking. Dogs welcome.

Key Features

🐾 Pets allowed

♿ Accessible Facilities

⛱ Seaside Beach Nearby

Find Out More
Visit ar.camp/uk7930
or scan the QR code.

Highland, Highlands and Islands

Alan Rogers Ref: UK7666
Accommodations: 3
Pitches: 75
GPS: 57.73167, -5.70223
Post Code: IV21 2BX

what3words:
sunk.caused.trees

Contact:
info@gairlochcaravanpark.com
Tel: +44 1445 712373
www.gairlochcampsite.co.uk

Open Dates:
Start April- Start November.

Gairloch Holiday Park

Gairloch Holiday Park is a small family-run site with 75 touring pitches; 35 are hardstanding, 25 have hook-ups, and there are also 35 non-electric tent pitches. Two modern static holiday homes and a six-bedroom holiday cottage are for hire. All pitches and the cottage have spectacular views across Loch Gairloch to The Isle of Skye.

Nearby Strath is the main crafting township in the historical parish of Gairloch. The park is ideally situated as a touring centre for Wester Ross. It is also located within 6 miles of the world-famous Inverewe Gardens. The village of Gairloch is within easy walking distance from the park and features a wide array of amenities, including a quality butcher, grocery store, and provisions. The location makes it an excellent stopover for the N500 coastal route as well as a relaxing holiday destination.

Modern toilets, showers & accessible facilities, Chemical, grey & general waste disposal, Laundry, Dishwashing, WiFi, Dog friendly

Key Features

- Pets allowed
- Accessible Facilities
- Seaside Beach Nearby

Find Out More
Visit **ar.camp/uk7666**
or scan the QR code.

📍 **Highland, Highlands and Islands**

Altnaharra CAMC Campsite

Nestled on the tranquil shores of Loch Naver with direct views of Ben Klibreck, Altnaharra Caravan and Motorhome Club site in Lairg is ideal for those wanting to get away from it all - the closest shops are 20 miles away. This site does not have a toilet block.

Walkers, anglers and birdwatchers will love the unspoilt natural wonders on offer in and around the site. Flyfish for free from the lakeshore; attempt to spot over 70 different species of birds or admire the red deer roaming in the wild. Those staying on-site have non-motorised boating rights on Lake Naver (conditions apply), which is ideal for those with small rowing boats and dinghies.

There is no toilet block. No Motorhome service point. Chemical toilet point. No children's play area. Gas sales. No WiFi. BBQs allowed gas, electric & charcoal. Defibrillator. TV reception is poor. Pets allowed. Dog walk adjacent. No children's play area. Twin axle caravans accepted. No Late night arrivals area. Spar supermarket 25 miles away. No tents allowed. The earliest time of arrival: 1:00pm. Maximum outfit length of 8.5 metres.

Alan Rogers Ref: UK7725
Pitches: 24
GPS: 58.29650, -4.37700
Post Code: IV27 4UE

what3words:
nowadays.erupt.share

Contact:
UKSitesBookingService@camc.com
Tel: +44 1549 411226
www.camc.com

Open Dates:
Mid March - Mid October.

Key Features

🗓 Book Online

🐾 Pets allowed

🐟 Fishing on Site

Find Out More
Visit **ar.camp/uk7725**
or scan the QR code.

Shetland, Highlands and Islands

Alan Rogers Ref: UK7975
Pitches: 34
GPS: 60.18621, -1.43830
Post Code: ZE2 9NY

what3words:
limelight.tasteful.dignitary

Contact:
josephinescott68@gmail.com
Tel: +44 1595 860287
www.skeldcaravanpark.co.uk

Open Dates:
Start April - End October.

Skeld Caravan Park

Skeld Caravan Park and Campsite is a well-kept, sheltered, flat, grassy park that accommodates 15 tent pitches and 19 hard-standing pitches for caravans, motorhomes and campervans. The picturesque village of Skeld is on the West side of Shetland, and the views are spectacular. The shorescape varies from the dramatic cliffs of the outer coast to long voes (sea inlets), which extend far into the heathery hills and green croft land. Whatever the wind direction, you can always find a sheltered beach.

The old village of Skeld was bustling in the nineteenth century. Fish was landed at Skeld, salted, dried and then exported to Spain. This led to 50-60 men being employed as sailmakers, carpenters, coopers and blacksmiths. At the head of Skeld Voe is the congregational church built in 1863. You can also buy fresh shellfish from the local fishermen who often land crabs, lobsters and scallops at the pier. A local bus service which leaves once a day and connects to the main service at Bixter. This will then take you to Lerwick.

The toilet block has showers, washbasins, and WCs. Accessible facility. Chemical toilet point. The kitchen area has a toaster, kettle, microwave, and fridge. Laundry room with washing machine and dryer. Hairdryer. Indoor board games. Electric power is provided for each pitch. Dogs allowed.

Key Features

🐾 Pets allowed

♿ Accessible Facilities

⛱ Seaside Beach Nearby

Find Out More
Visit ar.camp/uk7975
or scan the QR code.

Newry, Co. Down

Alan Rogers Ref: UK8415
Pitches: 12
GPS: 54.10541, -5.90361
Post Code: BT34 4TZ

what3words:
slept.voter.nearly

Contact:
info@chestnuttholidayparks.com
Tel: +44 28 4376 8248
chestnuttholidayparks.com

Open Dates:
Mid March - End October.

Annalong Caravan Park

Set between the torrs of Slieve Binnian and the sea, the proprietors of this well-appointed park have reserved 12 pitches near the sea exclusively for touring caravans. The park has grown over several years and has become a pleasant location, primarily for privately owned caravan holiday homes. Like many Irish caravan parks, Annalong has few trees, but with most of these being Cordyline palms, the park has a semi-tropical look.

A low sea wall and a pedestrian footpath beside the shore form the only barrier between the park and the Irish Sea. This path makes a delightful stroll to Annalong's picturesque old fishing harbour, a historic corn mill and a nearby licensed restaurant. Tourists will enjoy visits to the Silent Valley reservoir and park, Kilkeel's commercial fishing harbour and the delights of the Mountains of Mourne. Many footpaths lead into the mountains for those keen to explore.

Modern toilet block (fob access) has individual bathrooms with showers (token) and accessible facilities. Laundry facilities (extra charge). Safe and well-maintained playground. Small football field. WiFi throughout (charged).

Key Features

- Accessible Facilities
- Seaside Beach on Site
- Childrens Play Area
- Fishing on Site

Find Out More
Visit **ar.camp/uk8415**
or scan the QR code.

📍 Larne, Co. Antrim

Curran Caravan Park

Alan Rogers Ref: UK8320
Pitches: 44
GPS: 54.84995, -5.80818
Post Code: BT40 1DD

what3words:
coder.fizzle.outnumber

Contact:
info@caravanparksni.com
Tel: +44 28 2827 3797
www.currancaravanpark.com

Open Dates:
Easter - End October.

Perfect as a stopover for the Larne to Cairnryan ferry route, the attractive garden areas add to the charm of this small, neat park. It is conveniently situated near the ferry terminal and only a few minutes walk from the sea. The owner has been making upgrades and provides four hardstanding pitches for motorhomes. The 44 pitches, all with 14A electricity connections, give reasonable space off the tarmac road, and there is a separate tent area of 1.5 acres.

Larne market is on Wednesdays. You may consider using this site as a short-term base for discovering the area and an ideal overnight stop, especially for early or late ferry crossings. The warden can usually find room for tourists, so reservations are generally unnecessary.

The toilet block is clean and adequate without being luxurious. Laundry room with dishwashing facilities. Bowls and putting adjacent and also play areas with good equipment and safety surfaces. Late arrivals can call the garage if it is open. WiFi is available.

Key Features

🐾 Pets allowed

♿ Accessible Facilities

⛱ Seaside Beach Nearby

🛝 Childrens Play Area

Find Out More
Visit ar.camp/uk8320
or scan the QR code.

Dungannon, Co. Tyrone

Dungannon Park

This small touring park nestles amid a 70-acre park with a multitude of tree varieties, brightly coloured flower beds and a charming 12-acre fishing lake. The touring pitches, some with lake views, are on hardstanding, each with dedicated water, waste and 16A electricity connections. Hedging provides some separation. There is also an unmarked grass area for tents. Run by Dungannon Council, the park, which also incorporates tennis courts and football and cricket pitches, lies about one mile south of Dungannon town.

The site has an excellent range of facilities incorporating a mixed coarse/game fishery, café and gift shop, tennis courts, football & cricket pitches, a children's play area and a barbeque site. At the same time, walkers can enjoy the miles of interesting pathways that circumscribe the parkland, which from the high ground have splendid viewpoints of Dungannon Town and the surrounding countryside. The modern visitor amenity caters to extensive needs with quality sanitary facilities and washing/laundry amenities onsite.

Sanitary facilities are to the rear of the Amenity Centre and include showers (by token), washbasins, a baby changing mat and a spacious accessible unit. Laundry room with washing machine and dryer. Excellent play area. TV lounge. Tennis. Fishing. Walking. Orienteering.

Alan Rogers Ref: UK8550
Pitches: 24
GPS: 54.48933, -6.75735
Post Code: BT71 6DY

what3words:
squeezed.forkful.offices

Contact:
parks@midulstercouncil.org
Tel: +44 28 8772 8690
www.midulstercouncil.org/
DungannonPark

Open Dates:
Start March - End October.

Key Features

🐾 Pets allowed

♿ Accessible Facilities

🧷 Childrens Play Area

🐟 Fishing on Site

Find Out More
Visit **ar.camp/uk8550**
or scan the QR code.

Portrush, Co. Antrim

Alan Rogers Ref: UK8395
Accommodations: 7
Pitches: 12
GPS: 55.19696, -6.59651
Post Code: BT56 8NE

what3words:
washroom.skin.outline

Contact:
margaretagn@btinternet.com
Tel: +44 7763 167828
www.highviewholidaypark.
co.uk

Open Dates:
Mid March - Start October.

Highview Holiday Park

Highview Holiday Park has twelve hardstanding touring pitches with electric hook-up points; nine are fully serviced. There are also four log cabins, two mobile homes and a self-catering holiday cottage. Tents are not accepted at this park. The site is just minutes from Northern Ireland's premier resort, Portrush.

The list of easy days out around here reads like Ireland's list of the most popular attractions in Northern Ireland. The World-famous Giants Causeway, Bushmills Distillery, Carrick-a-Rede rope bridge, Game of Thrones Dark Hedges and Dunluce Castle. Portrush (a minute's drive) is a good place to start, whether you are off there to hit the beach, tee off at Royal Portrush Golf Club or take a turn on the rides at the legendary Barry's (Curry's) Amusements.

The toilet block has showers, wash basins, and WCs. Accessible sanitary facilities. Laundry. Dishwashing area. Motorhome service point. Chemical toilet point. Children's play area. Gas sales. Dogs allowed. BBQs allowed. Small shop. The earliest arrival time is 14.00. Public transport nearby. Bike hire.

Key Features

- Pets allowed
- Accessible Facilities
- Seaside Beach Nearby
- Childrens Play Area

Find Out More
Visit **ar.camp/uk8395**
or scan the QR code.

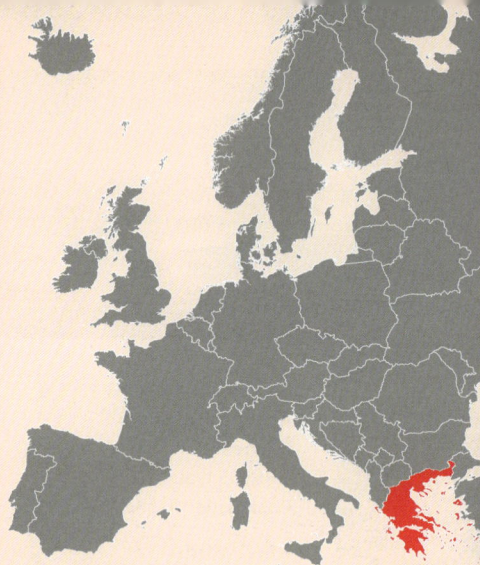

Capital Athens
Currency Euro (€)
Language Greek
Time Zone EET (GMT+2)
Telephone Code +30
Emergency Number 112
Tourist Website visitgreece.gr

Shops Hours vary throughout the year, with many shops operating on shorter hours in low and shoulder seasons. In high season 8am to 2pm Mon, Wed, Sat and 8am to 2pm and 5pm to 9pm Tues, Thurs, Fri.

Money ATMs are widespread, mostly open 24/7 and have multilingual instructions. Major cards are accepted but it's handy to have cash as it is often preferred.

Travelling with children Greece has plenty of green spaces, historical attractions and sandy beaches. Greek culture is all about sharing so restaurants will always be accommodating towards kids.

Public Holidays 1 Jan New Year's Day; 6 Jan Epiphany; Mar Orthodox Ash Monday; 25 Mar Independence Day; Apr/May Orthodox Good Friday; Apr/May Orthodox Easter Sunday; Apr/May Orthodox Easter Monday; 1 May Labour Day; Jun Orthodox Whit Sunday; Jun Orthodox Whit Monday; 15 Aug Assumption; 28 Oct Ochi Day; 25 Dec Christmas Day; 26 Dec Boxing Day

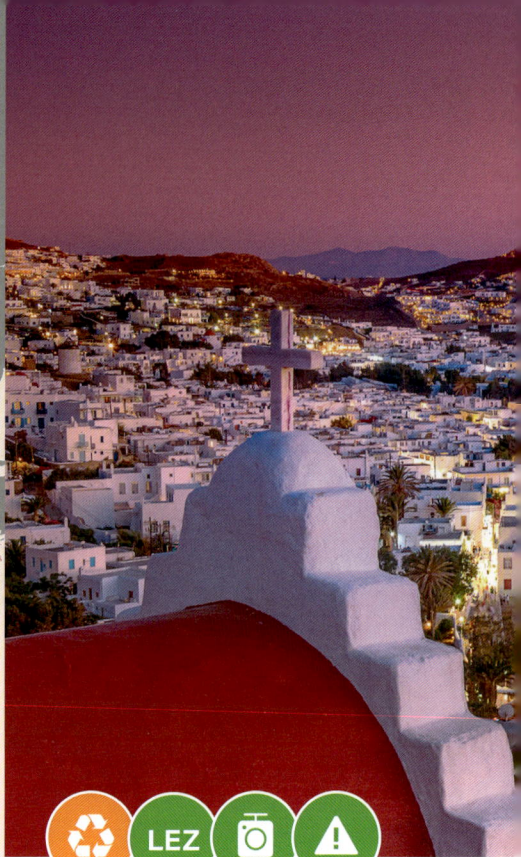

Accessible Travel Score

Although improving, especially in cities, much of Greece is difficult to navigate due to its historic nature. Public buildings often cater for wheelchair users and the less abled.

Driving in Greece Road signs are written in Greek and English. Some roads have distance-based tolls. Parking in Athens is prohibited within the Green Zone unless signposts state otherwise. If towing a caravan, the total length of the car and caravan cannot exceed 18m, 4m in height or 2.55m in width. Drink-driving and using your mobile whilst driving are illegal. Low Emission Zones don't currently affect foreign vehicles. The use of dashcams is legal, but using footage for insurance purposes is prohibited. Speed camera detectors are legal.

Greece

View all campsites in Greece
ar.camp/greece

See campsite map page 481

Climate Plenty of sunshine, mild temperatures and limited rainfall.	☀ **Avg. summer temp** 26°C (N), 29°C (S)	🌧 **Wettest month** December

Greece is made up of clusters of islands with idyllic sheltered bays and coves, golden stretches of sand with dunes, pebbly beaches, coastal caves with steep rocks and black volcanic sand and coastal wetlands. Its rugged landscape is a monument to nature with dramatic gorges, lakes, rivers and waterfalls.

Nestling between the Aegean, Ionian and Mediterranean waters, Greece has over 13,000 km of coastline. A largely mountainous country, its backbone is formed from the Pindus range, which extends as far as Crete, the largest of Greece's 6,000 islands, themselves peaks of the now-submerged landmass of Aegeis.

Mount Olympus in the north of the country, known from Greek mythology as the abode of the gods, is the highest mountain (2,917 m).

The Greek islands have something to offer every visitor – the vibrant nightlife of Mykonos, the 'honeymoon' island of Santorini, Rhodes, where the modern city sits alongside the medieval citadel, and Corfu, with its Venetian and French influences. The mainland is home to some of the most important archaeological sites, including the Acropolis, the Parthenon and Delphi.

Scan QR code to browse more campsites on our website

Plataria, Epirus

Alan Rogers Ref: GR8384
Pitches: 42
GPS: 39.46031, 20.26149
Post Code: GR-46100

what3words:
flirtation.sidebar.hive

Contact:
info@campingelena.gr
Tel: +30 26 65 07 14 14
www.campingelena.gr

Open Dates:
Start April - Mid October.

Camping Elena's Beach

Elena's Beach Camping is a traditional site, family-run by the owners, Vasilios and his wife, Katerina. The site is near the small fishing village of Plataria and has been running for over 30 years. As its name suggests, the campsite has its own beach overlooking the Ionian Sea. The campsite provides 42 touring pitches with an on-site taverna run by Katerina, offering authentic Greek food and homemade dishes for you to try. This has become the favourite spot to chill out during the summer for many locals and tourists alike.

The campsite has been carefully thought out, with many traditional fruit and olive trees throughout, offering plenty of shade for campers. There are various opportunities to explore the area with attractions and points of great interest, such as Sivota, Parga, the Acheronts River, the island of Corfu, Lefkada and Paxos nearby. Starting from the campsite, you will have the opportunity to get to know a different, alternative side of Greece.

Sanitary block with accessible facilities, Bar, Snack bar, Restaurant, Shop, Fresh bread available daily, Disposal and treatment of chemical toilet waste, Available to hire on site: Pedal boats, Motor boats, Diving equipment hire, Scooters. Kayaking, fishing, Sailing, Small children's playground, TV on site, WiFi, Pets allowed.

Key Features

- Pets allowed
- Accessible Facilities
- Seaside Beach on Site
- Childrens Play Area
- Bar on Site
- Fishing on Site
- Sailing on Site

Find Out More
Visit **ar.camp/gr8384**
or scan the QR code.

Delphi, Central Greece

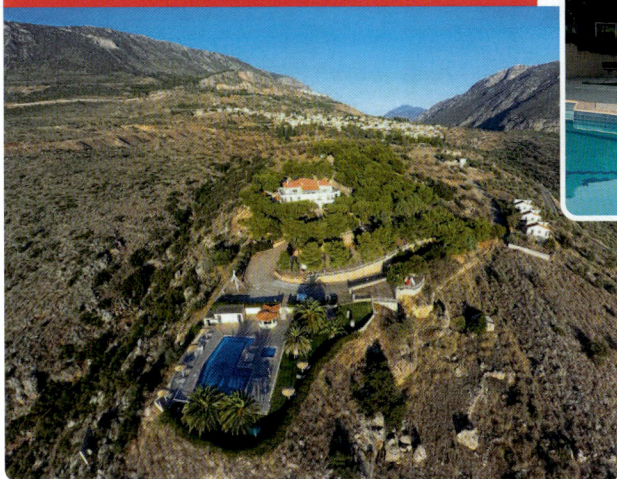

Chrissa Camping

Chrissa Camping is located on a hill with stunning views across vast olive groves to the Gulf of Corinth and beyond. There are 55 pitches with electric hook-up points available (10A). They are well-shaded and mainly terraced, which means that everyone can enjoy the spectacular views of the surrounding countryside.

On-site facilities include a restaurant serving traditional Greek food and local wine. Some of the ingredients even come straight from the kitchen garden. An outdoor swimming pool is available on site with plenty of sun loungers and umbrellas if you wish to relax in the shade. You can also find a small shop with essential supplies and a children's play area. There is also a football and a basketball court that can be found 300 metres away.

Modern, well-maintained toilet block with British-style WCs, open washbasins and controllable showers. Family shower rooms. Motorhome services. Laundry room with sinks, washing machine and dryer. Shop (Seasonal). Bar, restaurant and takeaway (weekends only in winter). Outdoor pool and paddling pool. Barbecues are not allowed. Internet point. WiFi (charged).

Alan Rogers Ref: GR8525
Accommodations: 12
Pitches: 55
GPS: 38.47407, 22.46023
Post Code: GR-33054

what3words:
autographs.printed.pruning

Contact:
info@chrissacamping.gr
Tel: +30 22 65 08 20 50
www.chrissacamping.com

Open Dates:
Start April - End October.

Key Features

- Pets allowed
- Seaside Beach Nearby
- Outdoor Pool on Site
- Childrens Play Area
- Bar on Site

Find Out More
Visit **ar.camp/gr8525**
or scan the QR code.

Poros, Ionian Islands

Alan Rogers Ref: GR8420
Accommodations: 10
Pitches: 53
GPS: 38.64168, 20.69598
Post Code: GR-31100

what3words:
influxes.barges.haunted

Contact:
irene@porosbeach.com.gr
Tel: +30 26 45 09 54 52
www.porosbeach.com.gr

Open Dates:
Start May - End September.

Camping Poros Beach

The Poros Beach Camping and Bungalows is a resort located in the southern part of the island of Lefkada. It is built on the side of a hill and is 60-150m away from the beach. The site is at the end of a steep, winding, narrow lane (3 km long with ten hairpin bends). The owners have made a massive investment in building apartments to rent at the top of the site. Here, you will find the on-site facilities, which include the reception and a small shop where bread and croissants are delivered daily.

An outdoor swimming pool and a traditional taverna serve local dishes and traditional Greek cuisine. The renovations, however, have been at the expense of access to the campsite, which is 40 meters lower down the hill at beach level. There are 53 pitches for touring units, set amongst olive and pine trees. Using the site's internal road for vehicles is now almost impossible, so having stopped at reception, you continue down the hill to a second entrance.

Sanitary facilities include hot showers, vanity-style washbasins and WCs. Laundry facilities. Shop, bar and restaurant at the higher level. Swimming pool (High season). Communal barbecue area. Some WiFi access.

Key Features

🏖 Seaside Beach on Site

🏊 Outdoor Pool on Site

🍸 Bar on Site

🐟 Fishing on Site

Find Out More
Visit **ar.camp/gr8420**
or scan the QR code.

Kefallonia, Ionian Islands

Karavomilos Beach

Camping Karavomilos Beach is just 1 km from the village of Sami, which has many shops, tavernas, bars, a post office, an ATM, medical facilities, and a pharmacy. The region of Sami, still untouched by the invasion of mass tourism, is a perfect place to have a wonderful holiday, either at one of the charming beaches or enjoying nature, the famous Melissani and Drogarati caves or the traditional villages.

All the pitches are separated by bushes and flowers, offering you maximum privacy and comfort, and shade is provided by poplar, eucalyptus and mulberry trees. Here you will find all the facilities of a modern and well-kept site, perfect organization and friendly service. The site has 253 grass/hardstanding touring pitches with 16amp hook-up points. There are also 8 Safari Tents available to hire.

The site has three toilet blocks with showers, washbasins, and WCs. Accessible facilities. Dishwashing area. Laundry with washing machine and dryer. Motorhome service point. Chemical toilet point. Communal kitchen. Freezers for ice packs. Safety deposit boxes. Public telephone. First aid box. Children's playground. Volleyball. Dogs allowed. Credit cards accepted. Free WiFi. BBQs allowed. Twin-axle caravans are allowed. Minimarket. Bread to order. Outdoor swimming pool. Restaurant. Bar. Snack bar. Pizzeria. Takeaway. Multi-sports pitch. TV room.

Alan Rogers Ref: GR8434
Accommodations: 8
Pitches: 253
GPS: 38.25088, 20.63803
Post Code: GR-28080

what3words:
screeches.corals.atoning

Contact:
campingkaravomilos@gmail.com
Tel: +30 26 74 02 24 80
www.camping-karavomilos.gr

Open Dates:
Start April - Mid October.

Key Features

- Pets allowed
- Accessible Facilities
- Seaside Beach on Site
- Outdoor Pool on Site
- Childrens Play Area
- Bar on Site
- Fishing on Site

Find Out More
Visit **ar.camp/gr8434**
or scan the QR code.

Gythion, Peloponnese

Camping Gythion Bay

Gythion Bay is based in the southeast of Peloponnese, on the 5km long sandy beach of Mavrovouni. The real draw to this site is the immaculate beach, ideal for swimming and watersports. The area is well known for endangered sea turtles, where they choose to lay their eggs. This four-star campsite is perfect for the family to come on their camping holiday as it is a clean, relaxing campsite with a wide choice of facilities and activities for all ages.

On-site, there are 300 touring pitches set amongst olive, fig and orange trees, still giving you that sense that you are staying in a traditional Greek campsite. You will be spoilt for choice when it comes to food; situated next to the swimming pool is the campsite's restaurant where the renovated kitchen offers a tempting menu with a variety of traditional Greek food and tasty snacks starting in the morning by serving breakfast and brunch with a wide variety of choices. There is also a cosy bar where you can enjoy local wine and beer on the beach or by the pool.

Four toilet blocks include accessible facilities. Laundry with washing machines. Motorhome services. Small shop (High season) including gas. Communal cooking facilities, Bar, restaurant and takeaway (High season.) Outdoor swimming pool. Play area. Table tennis, Bicycle hire, Fishing, windsurfing storage, and limited boat launching. Entertainment during high season, Small beach. Free WiFi (Partial site.)

Alan Rogers Ref: GR8685
Accommodations: 28
Pitches: 330
GPS: 36.73014, 22.54520
Post Code: GR-23200

what3words:
brains.glassware.swabs

Contact:
contact@gythiocamping.gr
Tel: +30 27 33 02 25 22
www.gythiocamping.gr

Open Dates:
Start April - End October.

Key Features

- Pets allowed
- Accessible Facilities
- Seaside Beach on Site
- Outdoor Pool on Site
- Childrens Play Area
- Bar on Site
- Bicycle Hire on Site
- Fishing on Site

Find Out More
Visit **ar.camp/gr8685**
or scan the QR code.

Iria/Argolis, Peloponnese

Camping Iria Beach

Situated close to the beach in a rural spot, Camping Iria Beach is a family site, although more basic than other Greek sites. However, the site offers a good selection of facilities, including a Greek taverna, a bar serving Greek cuisine, and an outdoor swimming pool, giving the site a relaxed atmosphere.

There are 66 pitches, most of which have electric (16A), a good variety of shaded pitches and some with hard standing. Families return to this site year after year due to its traditional charm. During the summer, various entertainment is held in the taverna with Greek music and traditional dances. There are also many games and other artistic activities held here.

The sanitary block is kept clean and has hot water. Facilities for families, including a baby changing room. Washing machine. Dryer. Ironing facilities. Snack bar (high season). Bar. Shop (high season). Bakery (high season, mornings only). Outdoor swimming pool with toddler's pool. Children's playground. Games room. TV. Sea fishing. Windsurfing and waterskiing are permitted. Snorkelling. Small library. Dogs allowed (on lead). BBQs permitted (charcoal or gas). WiFi (throughout).

Alan Rogers Ref: GR8620
Accommodations: 27
Pitches: 66
GPS: 37.49775, 22.99039
Post Code: GR-21060

what3words:
cliff.cottons.crystals

Contact:
info@iriabeachcamp.gr
Tel: +30 27 52 09 42 53
www.iriabeachcamp.gr

Open Dates:
All year.

Key Features

- Pets allowed
- Seaside Beach on Site
- Outdoor Pool on Site
- Childrens Play Area
- Bar on Site
- Fishing on Site

Find Out More
Visit **ar.camp/gr8620**
or scan the QR code.

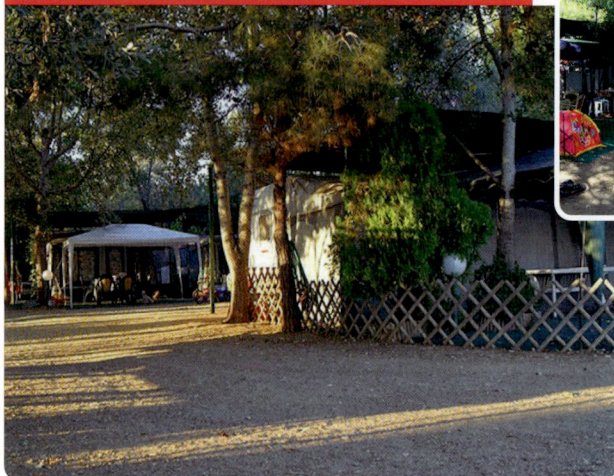

Eretria, Attica

Alan Rogers Ref: GR8450
Accommodations: 59
Pitches: 40
GPS: 38.39108, 23.77519
Post Code: GR-34008

what3words:
breezy.mushroom.aware

Contact:
info@campingmilos.gr
Tel: +30 22 29 06 04 20
www.campingmilos.gr

Open Dates:
Start April - End September.

Camping Milos

The island of Evia could easily be mistaken for part of the mainland, given that it is connected to Attica by two bridges and several ferries. It is, however, the second-largest Greek Island, Crete being that much bigger. Camping Milos is situated on the coast, just over 1.5 km. west of Eretria and provides 100 pitches. Forty touring pitches provide space for caravans and motorhomes under screens of varying heights.

This campsite is the perfect place to wake up with a coffee at the bar and enjoy a cocktail or two in the sun after cooling off in the campsite's pool. Evening entertainment, such as live shows and dance parties, is held here during the summer. The campsite beach is around 200 metres long and has spectacular views of the Euboean Gulf. If you wish, you can take your boat with you as a boat launch is available on the beach. The area around Chalkida is bustling and is a popular seaside resort for the Greeks from Athens and its suburbs.

Separate sanitary facilities for men and ladies include hot showers. Accessible Facilities. Laundry with washing machines. Two kitchens with sinks, gas hobs and fridges. Small shop. Outdoor pool with bar for drinks and snacks. Play area. Boat ramp. Free WiFi. Pets allowed.

Key Features

- Pets allowed
- Accessible Facilities
- Seaside Beach on Site
- Outdoor Pool on Site
- Childrens Play Area
- Bar on Site
- Fishing on Site

Find Out More
Visit **ar.camp/gr8450**
or scan the QR code.

📍 **Halkidiki, Central Macedonia**

Alan Rogers Ref: GR8087
Pitches: 93
GPS: 40.21624, 23.31838
Post Code: GR-63200

what3words:
activism.ovation.century

Contact:
info@ouzounibeach.gr
Tel: +30 69 77 40 40 40
www.ouzounibeach.gr

Open Dates:
Start May - Mid October.

Camping Ouzouni Beach

Camping Ouzouni Beach is a family-run site proudly owned by Dimitris Ouzounis, and you can expect a warm and friendly greeting when you arrive. This is a simple site with 93 touring pitches available, which are grassy and individually divided by hedges and shrubs; large trees or canopies shade them, and each pitch ranges from 65 sq.m. up to 80 sq.m. The campsite has a small shop where you can get your essentials and some traditional Greek dishes and pizza made by Andrea, one of the family members.

The beach is perfect for relaxing in the sun, strolling along the beach, and cooling off under umbrellas after dipping in the sea. There is also a small boat launch available directly from the site. Plenty of water sports are available nearby, including windsurfing and water skiing.

One sanitary block contains hot showers and a mixture of British and squat-style WCs, cleaned regularly. Accessible sanitary facilities (only open when needed), sinks for crockery and utensils, washing machines, electric washing machines, irons, electric hobs and cooking ovens, food storage fridges and a freezer for ice packs. Plenty of hot water 24 hours a day. Chemical toilet disposal, Shop, Fresh bread available, WiFi, Pets allowed.

Key Features

🐾 Pets allowed

♿ Accessible Facilities

⛱ Seaside Beach on Site

🍸 Bar on Site

🐟 Fishing on Site

Find Out More
Visit ar.camp/gr8087
or scan the QR code.

Capital Dublin
Currency Euro (€)
Language English and Gaelic
Time Zone GMT
Telephone Code +353
Emergency Number 112
Tourist Website ireland.com

Shops Most shops will open between 9am and 10am and close between 5pm and 6pm Mon to Sat, sometimes later in cities, and noon to 6pm Sun.

Money ATMs are widespread and accessible 24hrs a day. Major cards are widely accepted, Amex less so. Rural areas are often more reliant on cash.

Travelling with children Children are welcomed in Ireland, although family facilities aren't always accessible in rural spots. Most restaurants allow children although some high-end establishments may not. Children under 5 years of age travel free on all public transport.

Public Holidays 1 Jan New Year's Day; 17 Mar St Patrick's Day; Mar/Apr Easter Monday; Early May May Day; Early Jun June Bank Holiday; Early August Bank Holiday; Late Oct October Bank Holiday; 25 Dec Christmas Day; 26 Dec Boxing Day

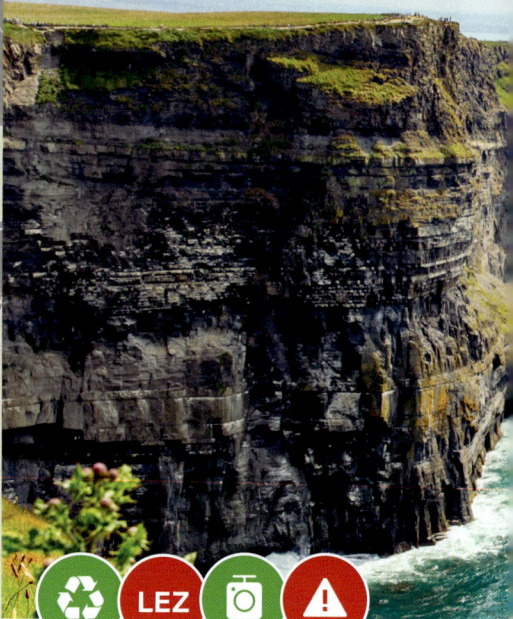

Accessible Travel Score

All new buildings are wheelchair-friendly. In cities, most buses have low-floor access and trains are accessible.

Driving in Ireland Driving is on the left-hand side, and roads are generally well-maintained. Tolls exist on some routes, most toll stations accept cards, although the East Link Bridge doesn't, so make sure to carry change. Signposts are in both Gaelic and English in most areas. Drink-driving and using your mobile whilst driving are illegal. There are no Low Emission Zones in place. The use of dashcams is legal, but speed camera detectors are not, so make sure to disable this feature on sat navs and mobile devices before entering the country.

Ireland

View all campsites in Ireland
ar.camp/ireland

See campsite map page 480

Climate Cool to mild summers. Winters are cold rarely freezing, often rainy.

☀️
Avg. summer temp
15°C

🌧️
Wettest month
Dec (N), Jan (S)

Ireland is made up of four provinces: Connaught, Leinster, Munster and Ulster, comprising 32 counties, 26 of which lie in the Republic of Ireland.

Famed for its folklore, traditional music and friendly hospitality, Ireland offers spectacular scenery within a relatively compact area. With plenty of beautiful areas to discover and a relaxed pace of life, it is an ideal place to unwind.

It is the perfect place to indulge in a variety of outdoor pursuits while taking in the glorious scenery. Plenty of waymarked footpaths lead through woodlands, across cliffs and past historical monuments. With its headlands, secluded coves and sandy beaches, the dramatic coastline is fantastic for watersports or simply relaxing and watching the variety of seabirds that nest on the shores. The Cliffs of Moher, in particular, is a prime location for birdwatching and Goat Island, just offshore, is where puffins make their nesting burrows.

In the south, the beautiful Ring of Kerry is one of the most visited regions. This 110-mile route encircles the Inveragh Peninsula and is surrounded by mountains and lakes. Other sights include the Aran Islands, the Rock of Cashel and the bustling cities of Dublin, Galway and Cork.

Scan QR code to browse more campsites on our website

📍 Letterkenny, Co. Donegal

Alan Rogers Ref: IR8635
Pitches: 26
GPS: 55.23357, -7.79571
Post Code: F92 W965

what3words:
stairway.opponents.oatmeal

Contact:
rosguillholidaypark@yahoo.ie
Tel: +353 74 915 5766
www.rosguillholidaypark.com

Open Dates:
Mid March - Early November.

Rosguill Holiday Park

Rosguill Holiday Park is a quiet, family-owned park on a stunning peninsula on the rugged and beautiful North West Donegal coast. It is surrounded by six long, clean, sandy beaches within walking distance and several other beaches nearby in Downings. It is no wonder that this part of Donegal is fast becoming one of Ireland's best locations for water sports and outdoor activities.

Privately owned mobile homes predominantly occupy the site but offer 26 touring pitches, 12 of which have concrete hardstanding, 10A electricity and water; the remainder are on grass without services. Every pitch on the park affords a view of Mulroy Bay and the surrounding rugged, varied scenery. An onsite café offers various ice creams, freshly brewed coffee, soft drinks & cakes. Nestled amidst breathtaking scenery, the idyllic beaches of Tra na Rossan and Murder Hole lie just a stone's throw from the site, providing an ideal haven for outdoor enthusiasts and those seeking tranquillity.

Well-appointed en-suite sanitary block in the touring area. Accessible Facilities. Family shower rooms. Modern campers' kitchen. Laundry facilities. Tennis. Multisports field. Pitch and putt. Bicycle hire. Play area.

Key Features

🐾 Pets allowed

♿ Accessible Facilities

⛱ Seaside Beach on Site

🛝 Childrens Play Area

🚲 Bicycle Hire on Site

🐟 Fishing on Site

Find Out More
Visit **ar.camp/ir8635**
or scan the QR code.

📍 Mullingar, Co. Westmeath

Alan Rogers Ref: IR8965
Accommodations: 120
Pitches: 49
GPS: 53.46611, -7.37528
Post Code: N91 P798

what3words:
workloads.cuties.infuriate

Contact:
eamon@caravanparksireland.com
Tel: +353 44 934 8101
www.caravanparksireland.com

Open Dates:
Start April - End September.

Lough Ennell Camping Park

Lough Ennell Camping Park is a tranquil campsite nestled amidst 18 acres of mature woodland on the shores of Lough Ennell, a scenic lake in County Westmeath, Ireland. The park is a haven for nature lovers and outdoor enthusiasts, offering a variety of activities and amenities to suit all ages and preferences. This park is run by a family who live on the site. They receive a blend of visitors – seasonal residents in camping holiday homes (private and to rent), caravanners and motorhome owners, and there are ample areas for tents. Pitches are varied and sheltered with trees and natural shrubbery.

There are 49 touring pitches with electricity (7A Europlug), 25 of which are hardstanding with water points conveniently located throughout the site. On-site facilities include a fully equipped campers' kitchen for guests, providing cooking hobs, ovens, microwaves, and sinks to prepare meals. A games room is available for guests of all ages, with various games and TV. A well-equipped playground is on-site, providing swings, slides and climbing frames.

The toilet block provides toilets, washbasins and hot showers (€ 1 coin). Additional dishwashing areas are around the park. Laundry. Small shop (all season). Café and coffee shop with takeaway. TV and games room. Play areas and an area for ball games. Small lakeside beach. Fishing. Late arrivals area outside. Security, including CCTV. Some breeds of dog are not accepted.

Key Features

🐾 Pets allowed

🛝 Childrens Play Area

🚲 Bicycle Hire on Site

🎣 Fishing on Site

⛵ Sailing on Site

Find Out More
Visit ar.camp/ir8965
or scan the QR code.

📍 **Clondalkin, Co. Dublin**

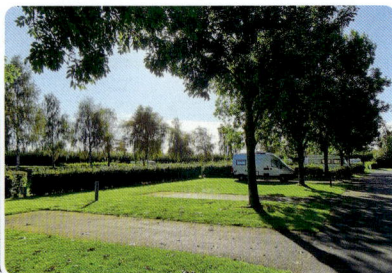

Alan Rogers Ref: IR9100
Pitches: 113
GPS: 53.30445, -6.41533
Post Code: D22 DR60

what3words:
harsh.ridge.insect

Contact:
reservations@camacvalley.com
Tel: +353 14 640 644
www.camacvalley.com

Open Dates:
All year.

Camac Valley Camping

Opened by the local council in 1996, this campsite is well placed for Dublin and offers a welcome stopover if travelling to the more southern counties from the north of the country, or vice versa. Despite its proximity to the city and the constant noise from the dual carriageway, being in the 300-acre Corkagh Park gives it a 'heart of the country' atmosphere.

There are 113 pitches on hardstanding for caravans, laid out in bays and avenues, all fully serviced (10A Europlug). Mature trees and shrubs separate pitches, and roads are of tarmac. Beyond the entrance gate and forecourt stands a timber-fronted building housing the site amenities. The reception building includes information on the local area, a small book exchange and a communal TV. Plus, a shop sells the essentials needed to cook on-site and some sanitary facilities. Some facilities show their age but are well-kept and cleaned regularly.

Heated sanitary facilities include good-sized showers (token). Accessible Facilities. Baby room. Laundry. Shop (basic) and coffee machine. Playground with wooden play frames and safety base. Fishing. The electronic gate is controlled by reception and 24-hour security. TV, WiFi (free).

Key Features

📅 All Year

🐾 Pets allowed

♿ Accessible Facilities

🛝 Childrens Play Area

🐟 Fishing on Site

Find Out More
Visit **ar.camp/ir9100**
or scan the QR code.

Rathdrum, Co. Wicklow

Hidden Valley Camping

This pleasant, level park occupies over seven hectares on both banks of the pretty Avonmore River near the small town of Rathdrum. It has 110 pitches arranged around a boating pond. The pitches are primarily concrete hardstanding, with a few on grass. All have 16A Europlugs and close access to a water tap and waste drainage. Across a fine footbridge is a large, flat area for tents – most used by families during high season.

This site boasts one of the best outdoor adventure play areas in Ireland, offering hours of entertainment for children of all ages. There is an extensive outdoor adventure play area, Football pitch, Archery, digital paintballing and crazy golf rowing boats and canoes available for hire on the park's shallow lake as well as the inflatable aqua park. The Lakehouse restaurant is on-site and offers a full menu, kid's meals, drinks, desserts, a coffee bar and ice cream. The site also has a shop selling basic supplies.

Well-equipped and very modern toilet block finished in local slate. Accessible facilities and motorhome services. Laundry. Hobs for cooking. Small shop, bar, restaurant and takeaway (all April-Sept). Fishing in the river may be arranged, combat laser tag, junior splash park (from late April), arts & crafts, adventure mini golf, kayaking, bumper boats, paddle boats, cinema, kid's disco, bingo, football, water balls (u12's), playgrounds, space net, giant tube slides and downhill tubing. Bicycle hire. Log cabins to rent. Dogs must be kept on a lead. WiFi.

Alan Rogers Ref: IR9155
Accommodations: 10
Pitches: 110
GPS: 52.93869, -6.22898
Post Code: A67 XY56

what3words:
strongly.lisped.riverside

Contact:
info@irelandholidaypark.com
Tel: +353 86 727 2872
www.hiddenvalley.ie

Open Dates:
Mid March - End September.

Key Features

- Book Online
- Pets allowed
- Accessible Facilities
- Childrens Play Area
- Bar on Site
- Bicycle Hire on Site
- Fishing on Site

Find Out More
Visit ar.camp/ir9155
or scan the QR code.

Redcross Village, Co. Wicklow

Alan Rogers Ref: IR9150
Accommodations: 98
Pitches: 211
GPS: 52.88840, -6.14528
Post Code: A67 H799

what3words:
stubble.swanky.manipulate

Contact:
info@rivervalleypark.ie
Tel: +353 40 441 647
www.rivervalleypark.ie

Open Dates:
Mid March - Late September.

**Alan Rogers
Awards Won**
2017

River Valley Park

This is a first-rate, family-run park in the small country village of Redcross, in the heart of County Wicklow. It is within easy reach of beauty spots such as the Vale of Avoca (Ballykissangel), Glendalough and Powerscourt, plus Brittas Bay, a 3.5-mile stretch of beautiful white dunes and clean beaches. The 211 touring pitches (many fully serviced) are divided into separate, well-landscaped areas with a separate adults-only section. All have 6/10 amp electricity connections and offer a choice of hardstanding or grass. A further 26 pitches are given over to seasonal tourers.

The Williams family continue to develop and make improvements to this park. There is an adventure playground and a vintage playground for smaller children. Mickey Finns Bar and Restaurant on site with a conservatory is inviting, offering weekly traditional Irish music and log fires; it also serves excellent homemade, traditional dishes and a selection of beers brewed on-site.

Modern, high-quality toilet blocks. Excellent, accessible facilities. Showers (€1 token). Baby & toddler washroom. Laundry area. Campers' kitchen. Motorhome services. Gas supplies. Full bar and restaurant. Entertainment twice per week. TV and games room. Three tennis courts. Beer garden with entertainment for children (July/August). Sports complex. Foot-golf course. Go-kart track. Remote control boats and cars. Movie nights. Adventure and toddlers' playgrounds. Caravan storage. WiFi (free). Archery range. Mini wildlife walk. Glampotel onsite. Late-night arrivals area. Pets allowed. Dog walk. BBQs allowed. Tents allowed.

Key Features

- Book Online
- Pets allowed
- Accessible Facilities
- Seaside Beach Nearby
- Childrens Play Area
- Bar on Site
- Golf on Site

Find Out More
Visit **ar.camp/ir9150**
or scan the QR code.

Ferrybank, Co. Wexford

Ferrybank Camping Park

Ferrybank Caravan & Camping Park is a family-friendly campsite overlooking Wexford harbour and is a short walk from Wexford's town centre in Ireland. The campsite is open all year and offers 52 spacious hardstanding touring with electric hook-up points available. The site is well-maintained and has various facilities to entertain the whole family while staying here. This includes a large children's playground with a swing, slide and climbing frame. There's a games room for the older kids with an air hockey table, table tennis and a pool table.

A TV room with a large screen offers a cosy atmosphere and a place to unwind after a day of exploring the surrounding area. Guests can also take full advantage of the leisure centre right next to the campsite, which offers a discounted rate for those staying onsite and can enjoy the indoor swimming pool, sauna, steam room, and gym.

Two sanitary blocks (€2 Tokens available at reception), Accessible WC and Shower, Laundry facilities (€4 Washing & Dryer tokens available at reception), Motorhome services, Outdoor washing up area, Communal kitchen, games room with a pool table, air hockey table, and table tennis table. Indoor swimming pool, Gym, Sauna, Steam room at the leisure centre, Security, WiFi, Pets allowed.

Alan Rogers Ref: IR9305
Pitches: 52
GPS: 52.34638, -6.45145
Post Code: Y35 Y184

what3words:
eyesore.faulty.comply

Contact:
info@ferrybankcaravanpark.ie
Tel: +353 53 918 5256
wexfordswimmingpool.ie

Open Dates:
All year.

Key Features

- All Year
- Pets allowed
- Accessible Facilities
- Seaside Beach Nearby
- Indoor Pool on Site
- Childrens Play Area

Find Out More
Visit ar.camp/ir9305
or scan the QR code.

289

📍 **Dunmore East, Co. Waterford**

Alan Rogers Ref: IR9345
Accommodations: 12
Pitches: 54
GPS: 52.15927, -6.99234
Post Code: X91 FY79

what3words:
vertical.occupying.listens

Contact:
info@dunmoreholiday.ie
Tel: +353 87 702 2566
www.dunmoreholiday.ie

Open Dates:
Start March - End October.

Dunmore East Holiday Park

Dunmore Holiday Park is a modern purpose-built touring park catering to caravans and motorhomes. It is set in over five acres of meadow surrounded by woodland, overlooking the village and coves of Dunmore East. There are 68 pitches (54 for touring equipped with electricity 16A) and wastewater with a shared tap on each pair of pitches.

On-site facilities include an on-site restaurant and an 18-hole championship golf course. South of the park, there are views across the estuary to Hook Head lighthouse, where the River Suir meets the Atlantic Ocean. The motorhome grounds are a short walk from all the amenities at the resort and in the village of Dunmore East. Tents are not accepted.

Sanitary block with hot showers (€ 1), family room and accessible facilities. Launderette. Motorhome services. Campers' kitchen. Restaurant, Golf course, Children's Playground. Pets allowed, WiFi.

Key Features

🐾 Pets allowed

♿ Accessible Facilities

⛱ Seaside Beach Nearby

🧒 Childrens Play Area

🍸 Bar on Site

⛳ Golf on Site

Find Out More
Visit **ar.camp/ir9345**
or scan the QR code.

Cahir, Co. Tipperary

The Apple Camping Park

Alan Rogers Ref: IR9410
Pitches: 32
GPS: 52.37663, -7.84262
Post Code: V94 E2C4

what3words:
diverging.expenditure.latching

Contact:
con@theapplefarm.com
Tel: +353 52 744 1459
www.theapplefarm.com

Open Dates:
Start May - End September.

This working fruit farm with campsite facilities offers an idyllic country holiday venue in one of the most delightful situations imaginable. For touring units only, it is located midway between Clonmel and Cahir with 32 pitches in a secluded situation behind the barns, set among trees and shrubs. They are mostly grass with 14 hardstanding and 28 electricity connections (13A Europlug).

Guests are free to stroll around the paths on the farm and can buy fresh fruit picked in season, jam, and cordials in the farm shop. Reception is housed with the other site facilities, including a communal campers kitchen with fridge, freezer and seating in a large farmyard barn. Although a rather unusual arrangement, it is central and effective. There is also a tennis court free to use for campers staying on-site.

Heated toilet facilities are kept very clean and comprise showers and washbasins in functional units. Accessible facilities. Also in the barn are dishwashing sinks, a washing machine and a fridge/freezer for campers. Good drive-over motorhome service point. Good tennis court (free). Play area. Dogs are not accepted. WiFi (free).

Key Features

Accessible Facilities

Childrens Play Area

Find Out More
Visit ar.camp/ir9410
or scan the QR code.

Clogheen, Co. Tipperary

Alan Rogers Ref: IR9380
Accommodations: 6
Pitches: 64
GPS: 52.28158, -7.98998
Post Code: E21 A377

what3words:
converting.uncalled.unwavering

Contact:
parsonsgreeninfo@gmail.com
Tel: +353 52 746 5290
www.parsonsgreen.ie

Open Dates:
Mid March - Start October.

Parsons Green Holiday Park

Parsons Green Holiday Park is in the Galtee Vee Valley in south Tipperary. This small, family-run park commands panoramic views toward the Vee Gap and Knockmealdown Mountains. The campsite is open style, surrounded by low ranch fencing offering 34 pitches with hardstanding for caravans and motorhomes and ten on grass, all with 6A electrical connections, plus 20 pitches for tents.

There is a range of things to do on-site, including indoor and outdoor playgrounds, Pony rides, an animal farm with rare breed animals and birds, crazy golf, an extensive farm museum, boating on the small lake and trout fishing on the river, which runs alongside the site. Bring a picnic or enjoy a snack from the coffee shop. Parsons Green offers the ideal venue for the entire family. There is something enjoyable and interesting around every corner.

Toilet facilities are near the top right of the site, close to reception, kept clean and include good accessible facilities (shower and toilet). The laundry area has washing machines, a dryer, and sinks. Campers' kitchen with cooker and fridge. Coffee shop and takeaway. Outdoor playground and indoor play area. Minigolf. Fishing. Animal farm, Museum, TV/games room.

Key Features

♿ Accessible Facilities

🧒 Childrens Play Area

🎣 Fishing on Site

Find Out More
Visit **ar.camp/ir9380**
or scan the QR code.

Glen of Aherlow, Co. Tipperary

The Glen of Aherlow

The owners of one of Ireland's neatest parks, George and Rosaline Drew, are campers themselves and have created an idyllic park in a stunning location. This three-hectare park is set in one of Ireland's most picturesque valleys. From every pitch, there are beautiful views of the wooded and hilly areas of Slievenamuck and the Galtee Mountains.

There are 48 large and level touring pitches, on both hardstanding and grass, each pair sharing a double 10amp Europlug post and water point. The Drew family welcomes large groups and rallies, and larger units can be accommodated, though the approach is narrow in places. The modern stone-built reception and shop beside the gate is a super addition to the site and includes a seasonal coffee shop. Excellent facilities are located in a purpose-built toilet block, which also houses a games room with table tennis and pool, perfect for those wetter days. The site is a member of the Caravan and Motorhome Club Affiliated Site Scheme, but visitors who are not club members are also very welcome.

The modern toilet block includes free showers and accessible facilities. Motorhome services. Laundry room with ironing facility. Campers' kitchen. Recreation and TV rooms. Shop. Gas sales. Coffee shop. Bicycle hire (delivered to site). WiFi (free). Chemical toilet point. Ice pack freezing facility. BBQs allowed. The TV reception is good. Late-night arrivals area. Battery charging facility. Tents allowed. Train station 5 miles. Tesco 5 miles. The earliest arrival time is noon.

Alan Rogers Ref: IR9400
Accommodations: 2
Pitches: 48
GPS: 52.41998, -8.18787
Post Code: E34 NH58

what3words:
appetite.sulks.shapeless

Contact:
rdrew@tipperarycamping.com
Tel: +353 62 565 55
www.tipperarycamping.com

Open Dates:
Mid March - End September.

Alan Rogers Awards Won
2022

Key Features

📅 Book Online

📅 All Year

🐾 Pets allowed

♿ Accessible Facilities

🚲 Bicycle Hire on Site

Find Out More
Visit ar.camp/ir9400
or scan the QR code.

293

📍 **Blarney, Co. Cork**

Alan Rogers Ref: IR9480
Pitches: 40
GPS: 51.94787, -8.54622
Post Code: T23 R85R

what3words:
welfare.goals.gaps

Contact:
info@blarneycaravanpark.com
Tel: +353 21 451 6519
www.blarneycaravanpark.com

Open Dates:
Mid March - End October.

📍 **Alan Rogers Awards Won**
2023

Blarney Camping Park

There is a heart-of-the-country feel about this 'on the farm' site, yet the city of Cork is only an 8 km. drive. What makes this friendly, family-run park so appealing is the welcome you receive on arrival and the friendliness throughout your stay from owner Con. Its secluded location and neat, spacious pitches add to its appeal. The terrain on the three-acre park is elevated and gently sloping, commanding views towards the world-famous Blarney Castle and the surrounding mountainous countryside.

The 80 serviced pitches, 40 of which have hardstanding and 10A Europlug, are with caravans near the entrance with tents pitched slightly further away. There are gravel roads, well-tended shrubs and a screen of mature trees. Tidy hedging marks the park's perimeter. The Faerie Garden and playing fields are popular with young campers.

Clean toilet facilities are housed in converted farm buildings. Reception and a small shop are at the entrance. Good accessible facilities. Laundry room. Campers' kitchen. Motorhome services. Shop (Start June - End August). TV lounge. Playground. WiFi throughout (free). Delightful 18-hole golf and pitch and putt course.

Key Features

📅 Book Online

🐾 Pets allowed

♿ Accessible Facilities

🛝 Childrens Play Area

⛳ Golf on Site

Find Out More
Visit ar.camp/ir9480
or scan the QR code.

📍 Skibbereen, Co. Cork

Alan Rogers Ref: IR9505
Pitches: 60
GPS: 51.54167, -9.26008
Post Code: P81 EV78

what3words:
wakes.mousetrap.recess

Contact:
skibbereencamping@gmail.com
Tel: +353 28 222 54
www.campingireland.ie

Open Dates:
Late April - Mid September.

The Hideaway Caravan Park

A sister park to The Meadow at Glandore (IR9500), the Hideaway is ideally situated as a touring base for the West Cork region. It is a well-run site under the supervision of the owners. Although it enjoys tranquil surroundings, including preserved marshland, it is only a ten-minute walk from the busy market town of Skibbereen.

The Hideaway is a two-hectare, touring-only park with 60 pitches, including 50 with hardstanding and 6A electric hook-ups. The tent field is nicely secluded, separate from the touring area, and well-sheltered by hedgerows and trees. One long building houses reception, toilet facilities and a games room. The size of the Campsite means plenty of open space with games and other activities constantly proving popular among families staying at the site. A large playground also offers hours of fun for the children staying on site.

The modern toilet block has non-slip floors, well equipped showers (on payment). Baby room with bath. En-suite accessible unit. Laundry. Camper's dining room. Motorhome services. Adventure play area. Football and cycling are not permitted in the park. Electric barbecues are not permitted. WiFi on the part of the site.

Key Features

🐾 Pets allowed

♿ Accessible Facilities

⛱ Seaside Beach Nearby

🧗 Childrens Play Area

Find Out More
Visit ar.camp/ir9505
or scan the QR code.

📍 **Killarney, Co. Kerry**

Alan Rogers Ref: IR9620
Accommodations: 6
Pitches: 86
GPS: 52.05595, -9.47458
Post Code: V93 HW56

what3words:
beings.mainly.hypnotist

Contact:
info@killarneycamping.com
Tel: +353 64 663 1590
www.killarneycamping.com

Open Dates:
Mid March - End October.

Fleming's White Bridge

The main road from Cork to Killarney (N22) runs through the gentle valley of the River Flesk. Between the two sits Fleming's White Bridge camping park. Its 15-acre site is within comfortable walking distance of Killarney Centre. Surrounded by mature, broad-leafed trees, the park is flat, landscaped and generously adorned with flowers and shrubs. It comprises 92 pitches, the majority for touring caravans, on well-kept grass pitches with electricity hook-ups, although some have concrete hardstanding and some are reserved for tents. Well distributed around the park are three well-appointed toilet blocks.

This is a site of which the owners are very proud. Hillary, Moira and Breda Fleming personally supervise the reception and grounds, maintaining high hygiene standards, cleanliness and tidiness. During the main season, they even find time to organise on-site activities that keep children and parents relaxed. The park's location makes it an ideal base to explore Killarney and the southwest.

Toilet blocks are of a high standard, including showers, toilets and baby changing. Accessible facilities. Dishwashing area. Chemical toilet point. Motorhome services. Campers' drying room and two laundries. Small shop (seasonal). Information room. Two TV rooms and a games room. Fishing (advice and permits provided). Canoeing (own canoes). Bicycle hire. Woodland walks. WiFi free. Outdoor Picnic Area. Bicycle Hire. Dog Walking Area. Late-night arrivals area. Bus stop adjacent. Train station 2 miles. Tents allowed.

Key Features

📅 Book Online

🐾 Pets allowed

♿ Accessible Facilities

🧍 Childrens Play Area

🚲 Bicycle Hire on Site

🐟 Fishing on Site

Find Out More
Visit ar.camp/ir9620
or scan the QR code.

Curraheen Little, Co. Kerry

Glenross Camping Park

Alan Rogers Ref: IR9600
Accommodations: 6
Pitches: 37
GPS: 52.05887, -9.93198
Post Code: V93 HF64

what3words:
housewares.departures.brisk

Contact:
glenrosscaravanpark@gmail.com
Tel: +353 66 976 8451
www.campingkerry.com

Open Dates:
Early April - Early October.

With a location set right in the heart of Co. Kerry, Glenross Caravan, Camping & Motorhome Park is situated on the spectacular Ring of Kerry and the Kerry Way footpath. It's an ideal base for touring Killarney and Dingle, and the scenery is epic as Glenbeigh approaches. The park commands stunning views of Rossbeigh Strand (within walking distance) and the Dingle Peninsula.

With a peaceful location on the edge of the village, the park is well-screened from the road and has 37 hardstanding touring pitches, mostly with 10 amp electricity (Europlug). There's a dedicated small tent area. Village shops are near, as is the Kerry Bog Village, a reconstructed pre-famine village. Watersports, fishing, riding and fell walking are all within a short distance, and there's golf at the Dooks and Killorglin courses.

Well-maintained and modern toilet block with showers (€1) includes accessible facilities. Laundry facilities. Motorhome services. Shelter for campers and dining area. Bar and restaurant next to site gates. Games room. Free WiFi throughout. Late-night arrivals area. BBQs allowed. Pets allowed. Dog walk adjacent. The TV reception is good. Bus stop adjacent. Shop 100 metres. Tents allowed. The earliest arrival time is noon. Maximum outfit length 9.5 metres.

Key Features

- Book Online
- Pets allowed
- Accessible Facilities
- Seaside Beach Nearby
- Bicycle Hire on Site

Find Out More
Visit ar.camp/ir9600 or scan the QR code.

297

Salthill, Co. Galway

Salthill Caravan Park

Salthill Caravan Park was opened in 1960 and has been run by the O'Malley family ever since. The park comprises five mobile homes and a three-acre campsite near the water's edge. The park has superb views over Galway Bay and has access to a shingle beach, just 100 m. distant. The 49 touring pitches are grassy and open, all with 10A electrical connections and 35 hardstanding. Salthill Caravan and Camping Park has several facilities, including a communal camper kitchen Complete with cookers, microwave, coffee tea facilities, sinks with hot & cold running water, and table and chairs for dining, which is beside the reception available 24 hours for all guests to use. There is also a children's playground and games room for the younger campers.

There is also access to the strand at the end of the park, just 20 meters away. With excellent bus and taxi service and a dedicated walk and bike lane into Salthill Village, it is just a 20-minute walk or 10-minute cycle. Adjacent to the site is a pleasant coastal pathway leading to Galway City and sandy beaches (800 m). There is a friendly pub (200 m) and a large, well-stocked supermarket (600 m) off-site.

One toilet block in the middle of the touring pitches also contains a washing machine, dryer (€ 5 each), and sinks (hot water charged). Showers by reception (on payment). Limited grocery items in reception. Communal kitchen, Children's playground. Games room. WiFi throughout (free).

Alan Rogers Ref: IR8870
Pitches: 49
GPS: 53.25680, -9.10491
Post Code: H91 K941

what3words:
angel.tiny.beats

Contact:
info@salthillcaravanpark.com
Tel: +353 91 523 972
www.salthillcaravanpark.com

Open Dates:
Start April - Mid October.

Key Features

- Pets allowed
- Seaside Beach Nearby
- Childrens Play Area

Find Out More
Visit **ar.camp/ir8870**
or scan the QR code.

Alan Rogers Ref: IR8860
Accommodations: 4
Pitches: 80
GPS: 53.38381, -9.95354
Post Code: H91 DTW8

what3words:
backfired.unfounded.mowers

Contact:
info@gurteenbay.ie
Tel: +353 95 358 82
facebook.com/gurteenbay1975

Open Dates:
End March - End September.

Gurteen Bay Camping Park

Gurteen Bay Caravan and Camping Park is just 50 m. from the beach and the sea, with fantastic views of the bay and a beautiful surrounding area. It offers 80 touring pitches, which occupy three sections throughout the site. All have 6A electricity, and water taps are provided throughout the site. There are also two apartments and two houses available to rent here.

On-site facilities include a shop providing the necessities, a communal kitchen and a dining area for all campsite guests. The site owners also organise group activities during the summer months to keep the whole family entertained. A lifeguard is on duty in July and August for those looking to relax and swim in the sea when the weather allows. If you are looking for a beach holiday without a large resort's 'all singing, all dancing' facilities, this park is a good choice.

Spotlessly clean, central toilet block includes hot showers (token operated) and washbasins. Accessible facilities, Campers' kitchen. Laundry facilities. Motorhome services. Shop (May-Sept) selling groceries, ice-cream and beach toys with a games and TV room at the rear. Bicycle hire. Organised group activities. WiFi throughout.

Key Features

- Pets allowed
- Accessible Facilities
- Seaside Beach on Site
- Bicycle Hire on Site
- Fishing on Site
- Sailing on Site

Find Out More
Visit ar.camp/ir8860
or scan the QR code.

Achill Island, Co. Mayo

Keel Sandybanks

This park offers a taste of island life and the opportunity to relax in dramatic, scenic surroundings. Achill, Ireland's largest island, is 24 km. long and 19 km. wide and is connected to the mainland by a bridge. The wide-open site is situated beside the Blue Flag beach near Keel Village. Although static holiday mobile homes are on this site, the 84 touring pitches are kept separate. There are 50 pitches with hardstanding, and some are located at the perimeter fence overlooking the beach. Although sand-based, the ground is firm and level. Roads are tarmac, and there is direct access to the beach, which lifeguards supervise.

Achill Island is an outdoor playground for all ages, with surfing, kitesurfing, kayaking, horse riding, mountain walking, cycling, golfing, angling and a number of blue flags beaches for revitalising sea swims and refreshing walks; the campsite is located next to a children's playground, there are also local shops, cafes, pubs and restaurants within walking distance.

Two modern toilet blocks serve the site, one at the entrance gate beside reception and the other in a central position. Heated facilities include WCs, washbasins and hot showers (payment required). Hairdryers. Laundry with irons and ironing boards. En-suite accessible facilities at the reception block. Campers' kitchen and dining room. Motorhome services. Play area. TV/games room. Watersports enthusiasts can enjoy kite surfing, canoeing and board sailing on Keel Strand and Lough. Fishing trips can be arranged. WiFi throughout (charged).

Alan Rogers Ref: IR8730
Accommodations: 16
Pitches: 84
GPS: 53.97535, -10.07790
Post Code: F28 EA47

what3words:
choppers.attached.valid

Contact:
info@keelcamping.ie
Tel: +353 87 255 5689
keelcamping.ie

Open Dates:
Easter - Start October.

Key Features

- Pets allowed
- Accessible Facilities
- Seaside Beach on Site
- Childrens Play Area

Find Out More
Visit **ar.camp/ir8730**
or scan the QR code.

Rosses Point, Co. Sligo

Greenlands Park

Just off the N15 road and 8 km. west of Sligo town, this is a well-run park at Rosses Point, in the sand hills adjoining a championship golf course. The 120 pitches (100 for touring units, all with 10A electricity) are thoughtfully laid out with small tents placed to the front of reception and the hardstanding touring pitches separated from the trailer tent pitches, which occupy the rear. The ground is undulating and adds interest to the overall appearance. Your view depends on where you are pitched – look towards Coney Island and the Blackrock lighthouse, which guards the bay, take in the sight of Benbulben Mountain or appreciate the seascape and the water lapping the resort's two bathing beaches.

On-site facilities include a games room with a TV and a children's playground with a sandpit. Families can enjoy a competitive game with a giant chess set and a draught set available to use. There is also a communal camper kitchen, and during the summer, an ice cream van and mobile coffee shop will stop at the campsite every day. The County Sligo Golf Club is beside the site, while the Yacht Club is just 100m away.

Modern toilet facilities are kept exceptionally clean, with hot showers (€ 1 token). Accessible facilities, Washing machine, dryer and iron. Motorhome services. Campers' kitchen. Information point and TV room beside reception. Play area and sand pit for children. Outdoor chess and draughts set. Internet in reception. Night security.

Alan Rogers Ref: IR8690
Accommodations: 20
Pitches: 120
GPS: 54.30628, -8.56889
Post Code: F91 TC64

what3words:
internet.matchmaker.darning

Contact:
rossespoint@
sligocaravanandcamping.ie
Tel: +353 71 917 7113
www.sligocaravanandcamping.
ie/rosses-point-park

Open Dates:
Start April - End September.

Key Features

🐾 Pets allowed

♿ Accessible Facilities

⚓ Seaside Beach on Site

🛝 Childrens Play Area

Find Out More
Visit **ar.camp/ir8690**
or scan the QR code.

Capital Rome
Currency Euro (€)
Language Italian
Time Zone CET (GMT+1)
Telephone Code +39
Emergency Number 112
Tourist Website italia.it

Shops Hours vary throughout the year, with many shops operating shorter hours in low and shoulder seasons. In high season 9am to 1pm and 3.30pm to 7.30pm Mon to Sat. Outside of cities, most close on Sun. Some also close on Mon morning.

Money ATMs are widespread and arc accessible 24hrs a day, some have multilingual instructions. Major cards are widely accepted, some smaller shops and trattorias may not take them.

Travelling with Children Very kid-friendly. Beaches are generally safe. Few restaurants open before 7.30pm although pizzerias usually open earlier.

Public Holidays 1 Jan New Year's Day; 6 Jan Epiphany; Mar/Apr Easter Sunday; Mar/Apr Easter Monday; 25 Apr Liberation Day; 1 May International Workers' Day; 2 Jun Republic Day; 15 Aug Assumption; 1 Nov All Saints; 8 Dec Immaculate Conception; 25 Dec Christmas Day; 26 Dec Boxing Day.

Accessible Travel Score
Largely under-equipped. Public buildings are slowly upgrading and awareness is gradually growing.

Driving in Italy Tolls are payable on the Autostrada network. A pre-paid Via card or cash can be used to pay, or an electronic Telepass tag can be purchased. An overhanging load must be indicated by a large red/white hatched warning square. An unladen weight of over 50% of the weight of the towing vehicle must have service brakes on all wheels. Drink-driving and using your mobile whilst driving are illegal. Low Emission Zones are in place in most major cities but differ from place to place, so check before travelling. The use of dashcams is legal, but speed camera detectors are not, so make sure to disable this feature on sat navs or mobile devices before entering the country.

Italy

View all campsites in Italy
ar.camp/italy

See campsite map page 482

Climate Hot summers, mild winters in the south. Cooler in the north.	☀ **Avg. summer temp** 25°C (N), 28°C (S)	🌧 **Wettest month** Apr (N), Dec (S)

Once the capital of the Roman Empire, Italy was unified as recently as 1861; thus, regional customs and traditions have been preserved. Its enviable collections of art, literature and culture have had worldwide influence and continue to be a magnet for visitors who flock to cities such as Venice, Florence and Rome.

In the north, the vibrant city of Milan is the fashion capital of the world and home to the famous opera house La Scala, as well as Da Vinci's 'The Last Supper. It is also a good starting-off point for the Alps; the Italian Lake District, incorporating Lake Garda, Lake Como and Lake Maggiore; the canals of Venice and the lovely town of Verona.

The hilly towns of central Italy are especially popular, with Siena, San Gimignano and Assisi among the most visited. The historic capital of Rome, with its Colosseum and Vatican City, is not to be missed.

Naples is an ideal base for visiting Pompeii and the breathtaking scenery of the Amalfi coast. The city also has a charm of its own – winding narrow streets and crumbling façades inset with shrines sit alongside boutiques, bars and lively street markets amid chaotic traffic and roaring scooters.

Scan QR code to browse more campsites on our website

📍 **Feriolo di Baveno, Piedmont**

Camping Orchidea

Camping Orchidea is an immaculate family-owned site on the western bank of Lake Maggiore, 35 km. south of the Swiss border and 8 km. from Stresa. This site has direct access to the lake and the banks of the River Stronetta and has a sandy beach. Orchidea has a good range of modern amenities, including a shop, bar and restaurant. Watersports are understandably popular here, and pedaloes and kayaks can be rented on-site.

The 234 touring pitches are grassy and generally well-shaded, with 6A electrical connections. Some pitches are available facing the lake (a supplement is charged in mid and peak season). There are apartments and mobile homes available for rent.

Two toilet blocks are kept clean and have hot and cold water throughout. Special facilities for children and accessible facilities. Laundry facilities. Shop. Restaurant. Bar. Takeaway. Direct lake access. Pedalo and kayak hire. Fishing. Boat launching. Playground. Children's club. Football pitch, Table tennis, Entertainment, Mobile homes for hire. Bicycle hire. WiFi on the part of the site (charged).

Alan Rogers Ref: IT62465
Accommodations: 15
Pitches: 234
GPS: 45.93340, 8.48120
Post Code: I-28831

what3words:
unsubtle.microwave.concrete

Contact:
info@campingorchidea.it
Tel: +39 0323 28 257
www.campingorchidea.it

Open Dates:
Mid March - Early October.

Key Features

🗓 Book Online

🐾 Pets allowed

♿ Accessible Facilities

🛝 Childrens Play Area

🍸 Bar on Site

🚲 Bicycle Hire on Site

🐟 Fishing on Site

Find Out More
Visit ar.camp/it62465
or scan the QR code.

Spigno Monferrato, Piedmont

Alan Rogers Ref: IT64045
Accommodations: 15
Pitches: 72
GPS: 44.48898, 8.34713
Post Code: I-15018

what3words:
needier.embargo.thrusters

Contact:
info@tenutasquaneto.it
Tel: +39 0144 91 744
www.tenutasquaneto.it

Open Dates:
Late April - Late September.

Alan Rogers Awards Won
2015

Camping Tenuta Squaneto

After years of experience in the camping industry, Barbara and Pieter Witschge have built their dream – Tenuta Squaneto, a natural camping with brilliant facilities. Its location is deep in the countryside with no villages, shops or restaurants in the immediate area. The 72 grassy, level touring pitches (100-120 sq.m) have wonderful views, and 35 have water, wastewater and TV connections. There are also 15 Lodge tents for rental.

The site is in a small valley with trees all around; there is a river to walk along, fish or simply swim and play in. A lovely lake is central to the site, and the nearby swimming pool is stunning with a large whirlpool and a children's shallow play pool with wonderful frogs and turtles that spray water.

Two modern sanitary blocks offer full and luxurious facilities, including accessible facilities. Some pitches have private facilities, including a cooker, fridge and luxury facilities (small extra daily charge). Fresh bread is available to order. Quality restaurant and bar. Attractive swimming pool and paddling pool. Large children's play area. Beach volleyball. Barbecues are allowed subject to local restrictions. Cooking groups in low season, weekly wine tastings. River swimming. WiFi in reception (free).

Key Features

- Book Online
- Pets allowed
- Accessible Facilities
- Outdoor Pool on Site
- Childrens Play Area
- Bar on Site
- Bicycle Hire on Site
- Riding on Site

Find Out More
Visit **ar.camp/it64045**
or scan the QR code.

📍 Idro, Lombardy

Alan Rogers Ref: IT62580
Accommodations: 6
Pitches: 190
GPS: 45.75418, 10.49821
Post Code: I-25074

what3words:
recover.suitcase.prolong

Contact:
info@idrosee.eu
Tel: +39 0365 83125
www.lakeidro.com

Open Dates:
Start April - End October.

⊙ Alan Rogers Awards Won
2017

Sportcamping Rio Vantone

Lake Idro, one of the smaller northern Italian lakes, is tucked away in the mountains west of Lake Garda. Rio Vantone is on the lake's southeast shore with marvellous views across the water to the villages on the opposite bank and surrounding mountains.

The ground slopes gently down to the water's edge, with many of the 190 touring pitches in level rows divided by hedges, with others between tall trees. All have 6A electricity, and there are 46 with water and drainage. The ones nearest the lake attract a higher charge. The lake is ideal for windsurfing, and the surrounding countryside is good for walking and climbing.

The main, heated sanitary block occupies the ground floor of a large building and is of excellent quality, including cabins (WC, washbasin and shower). A smaller block is also open in high season. Accessible facilities. No hot water 22.00-06.00. Washing machines and dryer. Motorhome services. Gas supplies. Cooking rings. Shop. Bar. Excellent restaurant (High season). Swimming pools. Lake swimming. Windsurf school. Boat and mountain bike hire. Play area. Torches are useful in some areas. WiFi throughout (charged).

Key Features

🗓 Book Online

🐾 Pets allowed

♿ Accessible Facilities

🌊 Outdoor Pool on Site

🛝 Childrens Play Area

🍸 Bar on Site

🚲 Bicycle Hire on Site

🐟 Fishing on Site

Find Out More
Visit **ar.camp/it62580**
or scan the QR code.

San Felice del Benaco, Lake Garda

Alan Rogers Ref: IT62800
Accommodations: 79
Pitches: 248
GPS: 45.59318, 10.53088
Post Code: I-25010

what3words:
temp.establishing.indulges

Contact:
info@weekend.it
Tel: +39 03 6543 712
www.weekend.it

Open Dates:
Mid April - Early October.

Weekend Resort

Created among the olive groves and terraced vineyards of the Château Villa Louisa, which overlooks it, this modern, well-equipped site enjoys superb views over the small bay that forms this part of Lake Garda. On reaching the site, you will pass through a most impressive pair of gates.

There are 248 pitches, all with 6/10A electricity, of which 79 are used by tour operators and for mobile homes. The touring pitches are in several different areas, many enjoying superb views. Some pitches for larger units are set in the upper terraces on steep slopes, so manoeuvring can be challenging and low olive branches may cause problems for long or high units.

Three sanitary blocks, one below the restaurant/shop, are modern and well-maintained. They mainly have British-style WCs, a few washbasins in cabins, and accessible facilities. Private sanitary facilities are available on some pitches. Baby room. Laundry. Shop. Bar/restaurant. Takeaway. Supervised swimming pool and paddling pool. Entertainment programme all season. TV. Barbecues. All facilities are open throughout the season. Two playgrounds. English spoken. WiFi in some areas (charged).

Key Features

- Book Online
- Pets allowed
- Accessible Facilities
- Outdoor Pool on Site
- Childrens Play Area
- Bar on Site
- Bicycle Hire on Site
- Riding on Site

Find Out More
Visit **ar.camp/it62800**
or scan the QR code.

Moniga del Garda, Lake Garda

Alan Rogers Ref: IT62770
Accommodations: 50
Pitches: 166
GPS: 45.52530, 10.54340
Post Code: I-25080

what3words:
suspending.outpaces.factually

Contact:
info@campingfontanelle.it
Tel: +39 03 6550 2079
www.campingfontanelle.it

Open Dates:
Late March - Early October.

Camping Fontanelle

Camping Fontanelle, a member of the HG Hotels group, is situated near the historic village of Moniga and enjoys excellent views across the lake. The site sits on the southwest slopes of Lake Garda and has 166 touring pitches on slightly sloping and terraced ground. Tour operators use a further 50 pitches, but there is minor impingement. All are marked and have 6A electricity connections (36 are fully serviced) and some enjoyable lakeside pitches (at extra cost).

Some tent and touring pitches are very secluded, distant from the campsite facilities, although small blocks with toilets are nearby. The campsite boasts a range of amenities and facilities to enhance your stay. There are two swimming pools for the adults with water slides and a paddling pool alongside (closed from 13.00-15.00).

The site has two large toilet blocks, which are modern and clean, with hot water throughout, though both may become busy during the high season. Accessible Facilities. Washing machines and dryers. Motorhome services. Well-stocked shop on site. Pleasant restaurant/bar. Takeaway. Swimming pools with slides (High season, supervised.) Tennis. Multi sport pitch, Mini golf, Play area. Entertainment (High season). Fishing. Boat launching. Charcoal & gas barbecues are permitted (subject to regular safety checks.) WiFi throughout (free.)

Key Features

- Book Online
- Pets allowed
- Accessible Facilities
- Outdoor Pool on Site
- Childrens Play Area
- Bar on Site
- Fishing on Site

Find Out More
Visit **ar.camp/it62770**
or scan the QR code.

Ca'Savio, Veneto

Alan Rogers Ref: IT60440
Accommodations: 256
Pitches: 1500
GPS: 45.44543, 12.46127
Post Code: I-30013

what3words:
showy.figure.sideboard

Contact:
info@casavio.it
Tel: +39 04 1966 017
www.casavio.it

Open Dates:
Late April - Early October.

Alan Rogers Awards Won
2018

Camping Ca'Savio

Ca'Savio is an extensive, family-owned site that is almost 50 years old. It is in the traditional Italian style and is set on a wide, sandy, Blue Flag beach that is safe for swimming. The beach is separated from the pitches by a pleasant open area and a row of bungalows. There are many activities here, some requiring additional payment.

There are 800 touring pitches (all with 10A electricity), 256 mobile homes/bungalows and around 400 tour operator pitches. Rows of pitches lead off a bustling central avenue, and they are shaded, mostly flat and varying in size (90-100 sq.m). Many are a long way from water and sanitary facilities. Customers can find their own pitches, so leave someone there while you fetch your unit!

Three large toilet blocks include many shower, toilet and washbasin units. The toilets are in cabins with showers and washbasins, so there may be a long wait during busy periods. Accessible facilities, Supermarket, bazaar and other shops. Restaurants, pizzeria, café and pub. Two very large pool complexes (free). Miniclub. Bicycle hire. Minigolf. Good adventure-style playground. Car hire. Internet and WiFi (at the restaurant; charged). Dogs are not accepted.

Key Features

- Book Online
- Accessible Facilities
- Seaside Beach on Site
- Outdoor Pool on Site
- Childrens Play Area
- Bar on Site
- Bicycle Hire on Site
- Fishing on Site

Find Out More
Visit ar.camp/it60440
or scan the QR code.

📍 **Trieste, Friuli - Venézia Giúlia**

Alan Rogers Ref: IT60000
Accommodations: 118
Pitches: 500
GPS: 45.77250, 13.62444
Post Code: I-34011

what3words:
spoil.vibrating.shaded

Contact:
info@marepineta.com
Tel: +39 04 0299 264
www.marepineta.com

Open Dates:
Start April - Mid October.

Camping Mare Pineta

Camping Village Mare is 18 km. Northwest of Trieste, at the top of an 80-metre cliff, has superb views over the Sistiana Bay. The campsite is situated in a peaceful spot amongst trees that line the coastline and offers stunning views of the Adriatic Sea. Of the 500 pitches, 340 are reserved for touring units, all with 4/6A electricity and water nearby. Some are in light woodland. Everyone is friendly, and English is spoken.

The campsite has a wide range of facilities and amenities to keep guests entertained and relaxed during their stay. A large swimming pool complex has a separate children's pool, a playground, and a mini market. The campsite also offers a variety of activities and entertainment programs, including live music, karaoke, and bingo. Enjoy a drink or food at the campsite cliff-top restaurant, which overlooks the pool complex and has fabulous bay views.

Five toilet blocks have been thoughtfully refurbished (two with solar panels for hot water), and some washbasins are offered in the cabins. WCs are of both British and squat style. Accessible facilities. Laundry. Motorhome services. Shop (all season). Bars. Pizzeria with terrace. Entertainment and disco. Swimming pool (Seasonal). Fitness studio. New playground. Tennis. Multisport pitch, Bicycle hire. Fishing. Organised entertainment in season. WiFi (charged). Information point. Dogs are permitted in certain areas only and not allowed on the beach.

Key Features

📅 Book Online

🐾 Pets allowed

♿ Accessible Facilities

⛱ Seaside Beach Nearby

🏊 Outdoor Pool on Site

🛝 Childrens Play Area

🍸 Bar on Site

🚴 Bicycle Hire on Site

Find Out More
Visit **ar.camp/it60000**
or scan the QR code.

📍 **Salsomaggiore Terme, Emília-Romagna**

Camping Arizona

Camping Arizona is a green site with a zero carbon rating, set on steep slopes 500 m from the pretty town of Tabiano, with its thermal springs dating back to the Roman era. The focus on water is continued within this pleasant, family-run site by a complex of four large pools, water slides, a jacuzzi, and a play area, all set on open landscaped grounds with superb views (open to the public).

The 270 level pitches with electricity (3A solar-generated on-site) vary from 50-90 sq.m. Those on terraced pitches enjoy shade from mature trees; others have no shade. Cars must be parked in the large adjacent car park. Trolleys are provided.

Two modern toilet blocks provide good facilities, including accessible facilities. Solar-heated water. Washing machines and dryers. Small, well-stocked shop, bar/restaurant with patio (all 1/4-6/10). Swimming pools, slides and jacuzzi (Seasonal, also open to the public but free for campers). Table Tennis. Boules. a basketball court, two volleyball courts, beach volleyball court, sand football pitch, synthetic grass five-a-side football pitch, synthetic grass tennis court, Two covered bowling greens, New outdoor fitness, New mountain bike training track, Large play centre. WiFi throughout (charged).

Alan Rogers Ref: IT60900
Accommodations: 32
Pitches: 300
GPS: 44.80621, 10.00980
Post Code: I-43039

what3words:
warming.conjurer.dips

Contact:
info@camping-arizona.it
Tel: +39 05 2456 5648
www.camping-arizona.it

Open Dates:
Start April - Mid October.

Key Features

🗓 Book Online

🐾 Pets allowed

♿ Accessible Facilities

🏊 Outdoor Pool on Site

🛝 Childrens Play Area

🍸 Bar on Site

🏇 Riding on Site

Find Out More
Visit **ar.camp/it60900**
or scan the QR code.

📍 **Lido Estensi, Emília-Romagna**

Alan Rogers Ref: IT60800
Accommodations: 1290
Pitches: 1300
GPS: 44.65583, 12.24527
Post Code: I-44029

what3words:
farmworkers.seat.depositors

Contact:
info@campingmarepineta.com
Tel: +39 05 3333 0110
www.campingmarepineta.it

Open Dates:
Mid April - Mid September.

Camping Mare e Pineta

Camping Mare e Pineta is a vast site located within a pinewood at the heart of the Adriatic Riviera. The site enjoys direct access to a gently shelving sandy beach. There are 1,300 shady pitches (110 for touring), all with 6A electricity. A large number of permanent pitches are distributed throughout the site. This is a lively site in high season with a large and varied entertainment programme, including yoga, fitness classes, dance courses and live shows. There are also activities on the beach, such as volleyball, beach tennis, beach soccer, basketball and bowls.

The campsite's private beach has plenty of sun loungers and umbrellas available for rent, so you can find the perfect spot to soak up the summer sun. There is also a water park for younger children with fountains and a giant bucket waterfall. The adults won't miss out either, as there is a large semi-Olympic outdoor swimming pool and a separate pool next to the waterpark with hydro massage stations.

Six centrally located sanitary blocks are of a high standard and include accessible facilities. Laundry facilities. Motorhome services. Bar. Restaurant/pizzeria. Shopping centre. Swimming pool (free in low season, small charge for use in high season) and children's pool. Wellness centre with gym, sauna and solarium, Tennis. Archery. Gym. Football pitch. Hairdresser and beautician. Games room. Playground. Entertainment and activity programme, beach activities. WiFi (charged). Bungalows and mobile homes to rent. Direct access to the sea.

Key Features

📅 Book Online

🐾 Pets allowed

♿ Accessible Facilities

⛱ Seaside Beach on Site

🏊 Outdoor Pool on Site

🛝 Childrens Play Area

🍸 Bar on Site

🚲 Bicycle Hire on Site

Find Out More
Visit **ar.camp/it60800**
or scan the QR code.

📍 **San Baronto di Lamporecchio, Tuscany**

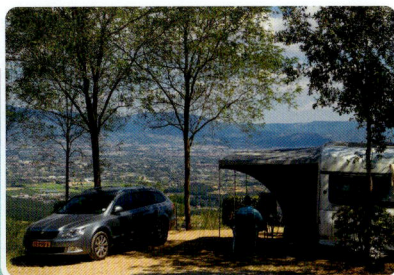

Alan Rogers Ref: IT66000
Accommodations: 30
Pitches: 274
GPS: 43.84190, 10.91130
Post Code: I-51035

what3words:
postcard.clogs.results

Contact:
info@barcoreale.com
Tel: +39 05 7388 332
www.barcoreale.it

Open Dates:
Start April - Late September.

Camping Barco Reale

Just forty minutes from Florence and an hour from Pisa, this site is beautifully situated high in the Tuscan hills, close to the fascinating town of Pistoia. Part of an old walled estate, there are impressive views of the surrounding countryside.

It is a quiet site of 15 hectares, and the 274 terraced pitches enjoy shade from mature pines and oaks. Some pitches are huge, with great views, and others are very private. Most are for touring units, although some have difficult access (the site provides tractor assistance). All 274 touring pitches have electricity, and 40 are fully serviced. A member of the Leading Campings group.

Three modern sanitary blocks are well-positioned and kept very clean; one block is heated. Good accessible facilities (dedicated pitches close by). Baby room. Laundry facilities. Fridge hire. Motorhome services. Dog shower. Shop, restaurant and bar. Supervised swimming pools (10.00-18.00, caps required). Ice cream shop. Playgrounds. Bowls. Riding. Disco. Entertainment. Animation for teens and children (high season). Cooking lessons for Tuscan-style food. Excursions. Bicycle hire. Internet point. WiFi over part of the site.

Key Features

🗓 Book Online

🐾 Pets allowed

♿ Accessible Facilities

🏊 Outdoor Pool on Site

🛝 Childrens Play Area

🍸 Bar on Site

🚲 Bicycle Hire on Site

Find Out More
Visit **ar.camp/it66000**
or scan the QR code.

📍 **Scarlino, Tuscany**

Alan Rogers Ref: IT66700
Accommodations: 200
Pitches: 17
GPS: 42.91291, 10.85253
Post Code: I-58020

what3words:
assists.energies.blip

Contact:
info@vallicellaglampingresort.com
Tel: +39 05 6637 229
www.vallicellaglampingresort.com

Open Dates:
Mid May - Start October.

Vallicella Glamping Resort

Cleverly set into two sides of a valley like an amphitheatre, some of the pitches here have glorious views over Tuscany to the sea and across the mountains to incredible hilltop villages. Stone walls and wooden safety rails are features around the site – these are essential as there are very uneven heights to many of the steps.

This site is mainly made up of glamping accommodation, but there are 17 touring pitches, mostly shaded and relatively flat, with a gravel/sand surface and 6A electricity. Cars are parked away from pitches. The site is unsuitable for those with mobility problems, and families with pushchairs may find the 800 m. height of the site is difficult.

Three blocks (one older, two modern) have squat and British-style toilets. A very difficult site for those with accessibility issues because of the steep terrain, but thoughtfully designed, good facilities are near a long terrace, giving easy access to the hub of the site. Shop. Bar. Restaurant. Wine bar. Pizzeria. Communal BBQ area, Swimming pools. Hydro-massage. Entertainment, Play area (supervision required). Kids club, Tennis, Multisport pitch, Bicycle and scooter hire. Internet point. EV charging points, Pet allowed.

Key Features

🗓 Book Online

🐾 Pets allowed

♿ Accessible Facilities

🏊 Outdoor Pool on Site

🛝 Childrens Play Area

🍸 Bar on Site

🚲 Bicycle Hire on Site

🎧 Riding on Site

Find Out More
Visit **ar.camp/it66700**
or scan the QR code.

📍 Pian di Boccio, Umbria

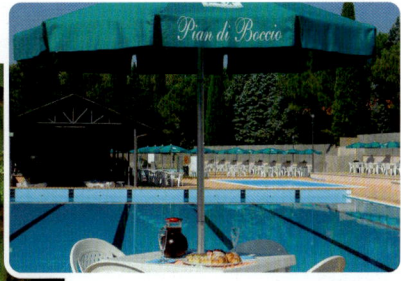

Alan Rogers Ref: IT66515
Accommodations: 23
Pitches: 70
GPS: 42.91242, 12.58674
Post Code: I-06031

what3words:
reloads.them.bloomer

Contact:
info@piandiboccio.com
Tel: +39 07 4236 0391
www.piandiboccio.com

Open Dates:
Start April - End September.

Camping Pian di Boccio

Pian di Boccio is a small-scale campsite in the heart of Umbria. It is situated near the fortress town of Bevagna and within a radius of 60 kilometres from the most critical cities in Umbria. The campsite is uniquely located in the middle of an olive orchard with views of the mountainous landscape. Pian di Boccio has plenty of activities, such as football, tennis, volleyball, and archery. It also has a playground. With bicycle hire available from reception, they can tell you where all the best cycle routes are in the region.

The large swimming pool and children's pool are the hub for a lot of the activities here. In high season, there is an entertainment team with an extensive programme for both children and adults. For example, the team organises pizza workshops, dance evenings, theatre, and water sports activities in the swimming pool. There is also a sunbathing terrace here with loungers and a cosy bar serving cold drinks and ice cream that overlooks the pool. For those that enjoy a spot of fishing 200m from the main facilities, you will find a fishing lake.

Sanitary block with Accessible facilities, Tennis court, Bicycle rent, Sports field, Football field, Volleyball field, Table football, Archery, Jeu de boules, Table tennis, Playground, Mini club, Entertainment for adults and children, Camping shop, Restaurant, Bar, 2 Outside pools, fishing, WiFi, Pets allowed.

Key Features

🗓 Book Online

🐾 Pets allowed

♿ Accessible Facilities

🏊 Outdoor Pool on Site

🧗 Childrens Play Area

🍸 Bar on Site

🚲 Bicycle Hire on Site

🐟 Fishing on Site

Find Out More
Visit **ar.camp/it66515**
or scan the QR code.

Otricoli, Umbria

Capitello Camping

Capitello Camping is an attractive and peaceful family site set near the curving River Tiber. It is efficiently run by the dynamic young owner, Alberto. The 35 slightly sloping pitches (80-120 sq.m) have electricity (5A), water and shade and enjoy great views of the medieval hilltop town of Otricoli. The swimming pool complex is a superb place for all the family with a variety of swimming and paddling pools, large soft slides and an area for relaxation.

A fascinating archaeological site is next to the campsite: the ruins of what was once a Roman city. The site is well-placed for exploring the surrounding Umbrian countryside and is only an hour's drive from the centre of Rome.

Single sanitary block with accessible facilities. Laundry. Bar, restaurant, snack bar, pizzeria and takeaway (High season). Fresh bread. Swimming pool complex (lifeguard - high season). Playground. Sports field. Games room. Table tennis. Beach volleyball. Canoes and kayaks to rent. Organised excursions (Seasonal). WiFi zone (free). Pets allowed.

Alan Rogers Ref: IT66482
Accommodations: 6
Pitches: 40
GPS: 42.40901, 12.46223
Post Code: I-05030

what3words:
enchanting.gobble.soulmate

Contact:
infocapitello@gmail.com
Tel: +39 04 0979 0652
www.capitellocamping.com

Open Dates:
Mid March - Late September.

Key Features

- Book Online
- Pets allowed
- Accessible Facilities
- Outdoor Pool on Site
- Childrens Play Area
- Bar on Site
- Fishing on Site

Find Out More
Visit **ar.camp/it66482**
or scan the QR code.

Roma, Lazio

Alan Rogers Ref: IT68110
Accommodations: 145
Pitches: 38
GPS: 42.15580, 12.57320
Post Code: I-00065

what3words:
flitting.wedged.devastate

Contact:
ipini@huopenair.com
Tel: +39 07 6545 3349
www.ipini.huopenair.com

Open Dates:
Late May - Early September.

I Pini Camping

Camping hu I Pini was built a few years ago by a family of experienced campers and is now part of the Homair group. The 30 pitches, with 6-10A electricity, are set on shaded, grassy terraces, some with views of the nearby hills. The beautifully designed restaurant, with a huge terrace, is typical of the thought that has gone into making I Pini a place where you can relax.

The pool complex is buzzing with the sound of happy children using the novel slides. This tranquil site is 45 minutes from Rome, where buses are available daily, and the site offers plenty of excursions.

The single excellent sanitary block is spotless throughout, and hot water is free. Two well-equipped accessible units and a separate child's shower. Washing machines and dryers. Motorhome services. Bar. Restaurant with a large terrace. Snack bar and pizza oven. Pleasant market. Bazaar. Lagoon-style swimming pools (with lifeguard). Pool bar. Tennis. Play area. Mini golf, Entertainment (High season). Buffet or traditional dinner and pool party (both weekly). Free WiFi. Torches are required in some areas. Excursions organised.

Key Features

- Book Online
- Pets allowed
- Accessible Facilities
- Outdoor Pool on Site
- Childrens Play Area
- Bar on Site
- Bicycle Hire on Site

Find Out More
Visit ar.camp/it68110
or scan the QR code.

📍 **Via di Castel Fusano, Lazio**

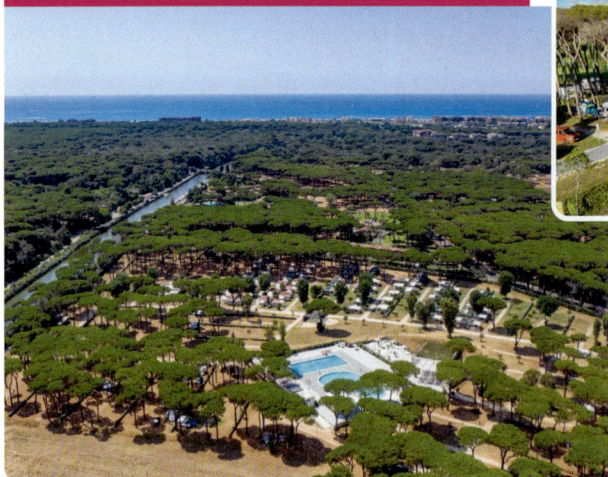

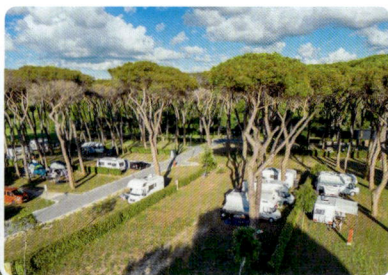

Alan Rogers Ref: IT67795
Accommodations: 216
Pitches: 700
GPS: 41.74387, 12.31411
Post Code: I-00124

what3words:
relating.dressy.nail

Contact:
info@baiaholiday.it
Tel: +39 06 2019 0700
www.campingcapitol.com

Open Dates:
Start April - Start November.

Camping Village Roma Capitol

Camping Village Roma Capitol is located in the heart of the Castel Fusano Pinewood Protected Nature Reserve in Ostia Antica. This site is ideal for those wanting to visit Rome and discover the surrounding area, such as the hills of the Castelli Romani and the coast of Ostia.

This is a large campsite comprising 700 touring pitches situated under the pine trees to allow shade in the height of summer. There are also 216 accommodation units to rent. On-site, you will find various activities to keep the whole family occupied, including three large outdoor swimming pools, one Olympic-sized. There are multiple restaurants and bars, including takeaway pizza. During high season, an animation team is on hand with morning gymnastics and water aerobics in the pool, and during the day, there are games and tournaments at the tennis courts and multi-sport pitch. Enjoy a lively line-up of evening shows and performances at the campsite's dedicated entertainment stage.

Heated Sanitary blocks with accessible facilities, Baby changing facilities, Private sanitary facilities available, Bar, Restaurant, Snack Bar, Takeaway food, Shop, Pizzeria, 3 Outdoor swimming pools, children's play area, Entertainment for the whole family during high season, Table tennis, Tennis courts, Multisports pitch, bicycle hire. WiFi, Separate camping area for those with pets.

Key Features

- 📅 Book Online
- 🐾 Pets allowed
- ♿ Accessible Facilities
- ⛱ Seaside Beach Nearby
- 🏊 Outdoor Pool on Site
- 🛝 Childrens Play Area
- 🍸 Bar on Site
- 🚲 Bicycle Hire on Site

Find Out More
Visit **ar.camp/it67795**
or scan the QR code.

📍 **Roseto degli Abruzzi, Abruzzo**

Camping Village Eurcamping

Eurcamping is about 2 km. south of the small town of Roseto degli Abruzzi. This is a pleasant and relatively quiet site, situated beside the sea, with 159 well-defined pitches. All pitches have 6A electricity, some are very large, and many have shade. There are good facilities which are grouped around the reception area including a very pleasant swimming pool with plenty of sun loungers and there is an entertainment area at the far end of the site.

For the more active, there are tennis courts, beach volleyball courts, and a football field. Eurcamping provides all the essentials to make your stay enjoyable. A well-stocked supermarket caters to your culinary needs, while a bakery ensures you start your day with freshly baked bread.

Three sanitary blocks with free hot showers. Accessible facilities. Baby rooms. Motorhome services. Laundry. Bar, restaurant, takeaway, pizzeria, shop (all high season). Swimming pools (hats must be worn) with solarium terrace (Seasonal). Play area. Outdoor fitness area. Tennis. Table tennis, Bicycle hire. Artificial grass football ground. Entertainment in high season. Clubs for children and teenagers. Communal BBQ area, WiFi throughout (charged). Pets are restricted to assigned pitches. Bungalows to rent. Free shuttle bus to Roseto Beach. Security bracelets are compulsory.

Alan Rogers Ref: IT68040
Accommodations: 84
Pitches: 159
GPS: 42.65770, 14.03530
Post Code: I-64026

what3words:
humans.takers.bedroom

Contact:
info@eurcamping.it
Tel: +39 08 5899 3179
www.eurcamping.it

Open Dates:
Mid June - Start November.

Key Features

- 📅 Book Online
- 🐾 Pets allowed
- ♿ Accessible Facilities
- 🏖 Seaside Beach on Site
- 🌊 Outdoor Pool on Site
- 🛝 Childrens Play Area
- 🍸 Bar on Site
- 🚲 Bicycle Hire on Site

Find Out More
Visit **ar.camp/it68040**
or scan the QR code.

Eboli Mare, Campania

Alan Rogers Ref: IT68410
Accommodations: 74
Pitches: 480
GPS: 40.49117, 14.94458
Post Code: I-84025

what3words:
beads.thickening.manipulates

Contact:
info@campingpaestum.it
Tel: +39 08 2869 1003
www.campingpaestum.it

Open Dates:
Mid May - Early September.

Camping Village Paestum

Camping Village Paestum is an excellent campsite on Italy's west coast. This large, family-owned site is set some way back from the beach near Paestum and the important ancient Greek temples of ancient Poseidon, built by the Greeks in the sixth century BC, taken by the Romans and renamed in 273 BC. Fast becoming a popular tourist resort, the town of Paestum is some way south of the site, enjoying a quiet, rural environment.

With 480 level and well-defined pitches situated in pine woodland, it has 200 allocated for international touring units, and these are in a special area maintained for non-Italian guests on the basis that they prefer more peace and quiet.

Five toilet blocks are well-finished and provide 75% squat and 25% British-style WCs. Free hot showers and hot and cold washbasins. Accessible facilities. Motorhome services. Washing machines. Small shop. Bar and restaurant. Swimming pool, children's pool and slide (swimming caps compulsory). Tennis. Entertainment and children's club. Disco. Shuttle bus to the beach. WiFi (charged). Bungalows to rent. Pets are not accepted.

Key Features

- Book Online
- Accessible Facilities
- Seaside Beach Nearby
- Outdoor Pool on Site
- Childrens Play Area
- Bar on Site
- Bicycle Hire on Site

Find Out More
Visit **ar.camp/it68410**
or scan the QR code.

Vieste, Puglia

Alan Rogers Ref: IT68460
Accommodations: 76
Pitches: 170
GPS: 41.91195, 16.12408
Post Code: I-71019

what3words:
meowing.bands.eyewitness

Contact:
info@lediomedee.com
Tel: +39 08 8470 6472
www.lediomedee.it

Open Dates:
Start May - Late September.

Camping le Diomedee

Diomedee is situated at the far end of the Gargano peninsula, close to the Foresta Umbra, and is part of a chain. The site has 170 level touring pitches (6A). Some shade is obtained from mature trees and screens, and some flat, beachside pitches are available. A beach-front restaurant/pizzeria offers a varied menu of Italian cuisine and international dishes catering for tourists. It is a great spot to watch the sunset in the summer evenings.

Games, sports tournaments, shows, group dances and disco evenings are activities organised daily by the campsite's entertainment team. The Mini Club entertains children from 4 years upwards with fun games and friendly sporting challenges throughout the day. The outdoor swimming pool is the perfect space to relax when the beach is too windy; centrally located makes it an ideal space for adults to be able to keep an eye on children playing as it is located next to many of the campsite facilities, including the children's play area and sports field.

The large, modernised toilet block has hot water throughout, showers, British-style WCs and washbasins. Accessible Facilities. Washing machines. Motorhome services. Shop and fruit stall. Bar. Restaurant/pizzeria/takeaway. Large swimming pool with loud music. Windsurfing school. Multi-sports pitch. Tennis, Beach volleyball. Children's entertainment (high season). Free WiFi in the pool area. Charcoal barbecues are not permitted.

Key Features

- Book Online
- Pets allowed
- Accessible Facilities
- Seaside Beach on Site
- Outdoor Pool on Site
- Childrens Play Area
- Bar on Site
- Fishing on Site

Find Out More
Visit **ar.camp/it68460**
or scan the QR code.

📍 **Alberobello, Puglia**

Alan Rogers Ref: IT68700
Accommodations: 8
Pitches: 90
GPS: 40.80128, 17.25122
Post Code: I-70011

what3words:
share.respected.cooker

Contact:
info@campingdeitrulli.it
Tel: +39 08 0432 3699
www.campingdeitrulli.it

Open Dates:
Start April - Start November.

Camping Dei Trulli

Camping Dei Trulli is just 17 km from the UNESCO-listed site at Alberobello. Staying Inland from the coast offers the chance to see the unusual Trulli properties. It is a dry, almost arid landscape here covered with olive groves, orchards, vineyards, and not forgetting the Trulli (strange circular buildings with conical roofs and domed within, built from local limestone without mortar).

This is a short-stay site offering visitors a chance to explore the area. It has 90 touring pitches surrounded by oak and pine trees, all with 6A electricity. Bungalows and caravans are available to rent. There is an outdoor swimming pool for guests to use whilst staying here, with plenty of umbrellas and sun loungers. The campsite also has a restaurant on-site, perfect for relaxing and enjoying a bite to eat after exploring the Trulli.

The very basic and dated toilet block includes accessible facilities, also houses the washing machine and is used for emptying chemical toilets. Small shop. Restaurant, Bar. Swimming pool and children's pool (Seasonal). Pool table, Tennis courts, Table tennis, and electronic games. Indoor disco during the winter months. WiFi over site (free).

Key Features

🐾 Pets allowed

♿ Accessible Facilities

🏊 Outdoor Pool on Site

🛝 Childrens Play Area

🍸 Bar on Site

🚲 Bicycle Hire on Site

Find Out More
Visit **ar.camp/it68700**
or scan the QR code.

Gallipoli, Puglia

Alan Rogers Ref: IT68655
Accommodations: 56
Pitches: 350
GPS: 40.07417, 18.00889
Post Code: I-73014

what3words:
thudded.shams.school

Contact:
info@lamasseria.net
Tel: +39 08 3320 2295
www.lamasseria.net

Open Dates:
All year.

Camping La Masseria

Nestled amidst a lush pine forest and just a stone's throw from the crystal-clear waters of the Salento Sea in Gallipoli. Camping La Masseria is renowned for its facilities, friendly staff, and picturesque setting, making this campsite the perfect destination for a camping holiday. The site provides 350 touring pitches with electric hook-up points available. During the low season, most pitches are unmarked in two significant areas, and in the high season, high net screens come into use to offer shade from the summer sun.

The heart of Camping La Masseria revolves around its swimming pool complex, surrounded by terraces and landscaped gardens. The pool offers ample space for leisurely swims and water games arranged by the site's entertainment team. There is a varied entertainment programme available on-site for both adults and children. In the high season, they will organise team matches and tournaments; there is a kids' and teens' club, dance evenings, and live music in the campsite's central square.

Five sanitary blocks and 36 private bathrooms (to rent) provide ample toilets, showers and washbasins. Washing machines and laundry service. Motorhome services. Bar, restaurant and shop. Large swimming pool complex. Entertainment (High season). Kids clubs, Tennis, football, Table tennis, Playground, Hairdressers, Free Shuttle bus to Gallipoli in high season. Wine and oil tasting on site. BBQs allowed. WiFi, Pets allowed.

Key Features

- Book Online
- All Year
- Pets allowed
- Seaside Beach Nearby
- Outdoor Pool on Site
- Childrens Play Area
- Bar on Site
- Bicycle Hire on Site

Find Out More
Visit ar.camp/it68655
or scan the QR code.

📍 **Roccelletta, Calabria**

Alan Rogers Ref: IT68925
Accommodations: 46
Pitches: 140
GPS: 38.79469, 16.58958
Post Code: I-88021

what3words:
timely.armfuls.twinge

Contact:
info@campingcalabrisella.it
Tel: +39 09 6139 1207
www.campingcalabrisella.it

Open Dates:
End May - Start November.

Camping Calabrisella

Camping Villaggio Calabrisella is located within a beautiful pine forest overlooking the sea in the pristine Gulf of Squillace, between Catanzaro Lido and Soverato. With its well-maintained facilities and loads of activities, the site provides the perfect setting for an unforgettable Italian getaway. There are 140 pitches, shaded by trees and located on an area of about 17,000 square metres with direct access to the beach, and some have a sea view. All pitches have an electricity hook-up point of 3/6 amps. Some pitches also have a tap and wastewater drain. There are also apartments available to hire.

Guests can take advantage of a well-stocked supermarket, a pizzeria serving authentic Italian cuisine, and a lively bar where you can unwind with a refreshing drink. For those seeking entertainment, Camping Calabrisella hosts various events and activities throughout the season, including themed evenings, live music performances, and children's animation programs.

The toilet block has showers, washbasins, and WCs. Accessible facilities. Laundry with washing machine and dryer. Baby room. Chemical toilet point. Bar. Restaurant. Snack bar. Takeaway. Pizzeria. Shop. Bread to order. Defibrillator. Dogs allowed. BBQs allowed. Tourist information. Water aerobics. Boules pitch. Multisport pitch. Volleyball. Table tennis. Games room. WiFi zone. Children's play area. TV room.

Key Features

🐾 Pets allowed

♿ Accessible Facilities

⛱ Seaside Beach on Site

🛝 Childrens Play Area

🍸 Bar on Site

🎣 Fishing on Site

Find Out More
Visit **ar.camp/it68925**
or scan the QR code.

Finale di Pollina, Sicily

Camping Rais Gerbi

Rais Gerbi provides very good quality camping, with excellent facilities, on the beautiful Tyrrhenian coast, not far from Cefalu. This attractive terraced campsite is shaded by well-established trees, and the 216 good-sized touring pitches (6A electricity) vary from informal areas under the trees near the sea to gravel terraces and hardstandings. Most have stunning views, many with their own sinks and with some artificial shade to supplement the trees.

From the mobile homes to the unusual white igloos, everything here is being established to a high quality. The large pool with its entertainment area and the restaurant, like so much of the site, overlooks the beautiful rocky coastline and aquamarine sea.

Excellent sanitary blocks, free hot showers in generous cubicles. Accessible facilities, Laundry. Small shop, bar, restaurant/pizzeria and takeaway (all seasonal). Communal barbecue. Entertainment area and pool near the sea. Tennis. WiFi over site (charged). High-quality accommodation and tents for rent. Rocky beach on the site. The small village of Finale is 500 m from site, and here you will find shops, a bank, a post office, a pharmacy and a doctor. Dogs are not accepted in August.

Alan Rogers Ref: IT69350
Accommodations: 45
Pitches: 216
GPS: 38.02278, 14.15389
Post Code: I-90010

what3words:
significant.revive.forefathers

Contact:
camping@raisgerbi.it
Tel: +39 09 2142 6570
www.raisgerbi.it

Open Dates:
All year.

Key Features

- Book Online
- Pets allowed
- Accessible Facilities
- Seaside Beach on Site
- Outdoor Pool on Site
- Childrens Play Area
- Bar on Site
- Fishing on Site

Find Out More
Visit ar.camp/it69350
or scan the QR code.

📍 **Mazara del Vallo, Sicily**

Alan Rogers Ref: IT69160
Accommodations: 69
Pitches: 90
GPS: 37.63647, 12.61631
Post Code: I-91026

what3words:
musician.sigh.imported

Contact:
info@sportingclubvillage.com
Tel: +39 09 2394 7230
www.sportingclubvillage.com

Open Dates:
Start April - Early October.

Sporting Club Village

Sporting Club Village & Camping can be found on Sicily's southwest coast. As the crow flies, Tunisia is not far, and the town has a distinct Arabic influence in its winding streets. The site is 2.5 km. from Mazara and boasts some good amenities, including a large swimming pool surrounded by tall palm trees. Pitches here (90 for touring) are grassy and generally well-shaded.

This is a lively site in high season with a wide range of activities, including mini golf, football, tennis and a regular entertainment programme. A pre-loaded card system is in operation, available from reception, as the site does not accept cash in the bar/restaurant. Sporting Club's focal point is its restaurant, which offers typical Sicilian dishes, notably locally caught fish.

Heated sanitary block with small shower cubicles (could be stretched at busy times). Accessible Facilities. Washing machine. Motorhome services. Shop (Seasonal). Restaurant, bar and large reception/function room. Play area with bouncy castles. Good sports club with a swimming pool, floodlit football pitches, tennis and volleyball. Mini golf, Fishing. Bicycle hire. Free WiFi throughout. Charcoal barbecues are permitted.

Key Features

🐾 Pets allowed

♿ Accessible Facilities

⛱ Seaside Beach Nearby

🏊 Outdoor Pool on Site

🧒 Childrens Play Area

🍸 Bar on Site

🚴 Bicycle Hire on Site

🎣 Fishing on Site

Find Out More
Visit **ar.camp/it69160**
or scan the QR code.

San Croce Camerina, Sicily

Camping Scarabeo

Camping Scarabeo is a beautiful site in Punta Braccetto, a little fishing port in Sicily's southeast corner. It is a perfect location with exceptional facilities to match. Split into two separate sites (just 50 m. apart) with a total of 70 pitches, it is being constantly improved with care by Angela di Modica. All pitches are well shaded, some naturally and others with an artificial cane roof and have 3/6A electricity.

Scarabeo lies adjacent to a sandy beach, and the little village is nearby. The site layout resembles a Sicilian farm courtyard divided into four principal areas. The ancient Greek ruins of Kamerina and Caucana are just a few kilometres from the site, and their ruins can be reached by bicycle. The Riserva Naturale at the mouth of the River Irminio is also a popular excursion.

Exceptional sanitary blocks provide personal WC compartments (personal key access). Ample hot showers (free low season). Accessible Facilities. Washing machine. Excellent motorhome service point. Takeaway. Herb garden for campers. Direct access to the beach. Playground. Entertainment programme in high season. Dog washing area. Excursions are arranged all year. Bicycle hire, WiFi over site (charged). Mobile homes to rent. No gas or electric barbecues.

Alan Rogers Ref: IT69190
Accommodations: 10
Pitches: 70
GPS: 36.81645, 14.46964
Post Code: I-97017

what3words:
crooned.unroll.cabarets

Contact:
info@scarabeocamping.it
Tel: +39 09 3291 8096
www.scarabeocamping.it

Open Dates:
All year.

Key Features

- All Year
- Pets allowed
- Accessible Facilities
- Seaside Beach on Site
- Bar on Site
- Bicycle Hire on Site
- Fishing on Site
- Sailing on Site

Find Out More
Visit ar.camp/it69190
or scan the QR code.

327

📍 **Alghero, Sardinia**

Alan Rogers Ref: IT69950
Accommodations: 193
Pitches: 339
GPS: 40.64230, 8.19060
Post Code: I-07041

what3words:
vastly.friendships.clinker

Contact:
info@torredelporticciolo.it
Tel: +39 07 9919 010
www.torredelporticciolo.it

Open Dates:
Mid May - Early October.

Camping Torre del Porticciolo

Torre del Porticciolo is set high on a peninsula with fabulous views from some parts of the site over the sea and old fortifications. It is family-owned, with striking traditional old buildings and attractive landscaping. Spread over a large area, pine trees mainly surround the site. A few pitches enjoy limited sea views. The campsite is located high above the beach, giving you a beautiful view of the rocky coast and the sea. A long staircase leads you to the private beach, an ideal location for snorkelling. The swimming pool is also a wonderful place to enjoy your holiday.

The campsite shop has freshly baked bread rolls every day. The campsite also features a restaurant and a bar, where you can enjoy drinks and traditional Sardinian dishes, such as filled pasta, fish dishes, and cheeses. There is also a snack bar and a beach bar. Torre del Porticciollo Campsite has a playground where you can play football, (table) tennis, exercise, and participate in Pilates.

The two older sanitary blocks have exclusively squat-style toilets. The few British-style toilets are in locked cabins with a key on request. Hot showers are free. Washing machines. Motorhome services. Supermarket. Restaurant. Good supervised pool and paddling pool. Aerobics. Fitness centre. Play areas. Bicycle hire. Miniclub. Entertainment (July/Aug). Excursion service. Beach 100 m. down a very steep slope. Excellent diving. WiFi in the restaurant (charged).

Key Features

📅 Book Online

🐾 Pets allowed

⛱️ Seaside Beach on Site

🏊 Outdoor Pool on Site

🏮 Childrens Play Area

🍸 Bar on Site

🚲 Bicycle Hire on Site

🐟 Fishing on Site

Find Out More
Visit ar.camp/it69950
or scan the QR code.

📍 **Bari Sardo, Sardinia**

Camping La Pineta

Camping La Pineta is a lovely small campsite run by the delightful couple, Tziania and Guliano Carraeoi, who live on-site. The touring pitches are level and clean, equipped with 6A electricity connections, and are shaded by pine and eucalyptus trees. The beautiful beach is 400 m. walk alongside a safe river complete with waterbirds. The pretty restaurant, bar/café, pizzeria and mini market offer a great choice of fare.

La Pineta gives excellent value for money, and if you enjoy cosy sites where you are treated as a friend, this will be a little piece of heaven for you. In a quiet, rural location, this would make a good base for exploring the varied coastline and Saracen towers. Much information is provided by the staff, and they will assist with ferry bookings.

One spotlessly clean sanitary block with a mixture of British and squat toilets, hot showers, baby room and Accessible facilities. Laundry. Motorhome services. Shop. Bar. Café/bar. Restaurant and pizzeria. Play area. Kayaking. Barbecue. Diving organised. Dog beach. Activities for children (July/Aug). Rental accommodation. Bicycle hire. WiFi in the bar. Torches useful.

Alan Rogers Ref: IT69715
Accommodations: 15
Pitches: 70
GPS: 39.82028, 9.67032
Post Code: I-08042

what3words:
confederate.enclave.albatrosses

Contact:
info@campingbungalowlapineta.it
Tel: +39 07 8229 372
campingbungalowlapineta.it

Open Dates:
Early April - End October.

Key Features

🐾 Pets allowed

⛱ Seaside Beach Nearby

🛝 Childrens Play Area

🍸 Bar on Site

🚲 Bicycle Hire on Site

Find Out More
Visit **ar.camp/it69715**
or scan the QR code.

Capital Luxembourg City
Currency Euro (€)
Language Luxembourgish, French, German
Time Zone CET (GMT+1)
Telephone Code +352
Emergency Number 112
Tourist Website visitluxembourg.com

Shops 9am to 6pm Mon to Sat. Shops are closed Sun except on the run up to Christmas. Supermarkets and shopping centres often stay open longer. Some shops are closed Mon morning.

Money ATMs are widespread in urban areas and arc accessible 24hrs a day. Major cards are widely accepted. Amex is rarely accepted.

Travelling with children A very family-friendly country. Some attractions will offer free admission for young children. Most restaurants will cater for children.

Public Holidays 1 Jan New Year's Day; Mar/Apr Easter Monday; 1 May Labour Day; 9 May Europe Day; May Ascension; May/Jun Whit Monday; 23 Jun National Day; 15 Aug Assumption; 1 Nov All Saints; 25 Dec Christmas Day; 26 Dec Boxing Day.

Public Transport Since 2020, all public transport in Luxembourg has been free to use including buses, trains and trams. You don't need a ticket but you may be required to show ID.

Accessible Travel Score

Hilly but generally wheelchair-friendly. Buses and trams are fitted with ramps, assistance offered elsewhere, public buildings are accessible.

Driving in Luxembourg There are no road tolls. Many holidaymakers travel through Luxembourg to take advantage of lower fuel prices, thus creating traffic congestion, especially in summer. Dipped headlights are recommended during daylight hours. Drink-driving and using your mobile whilst driving are illegal. On steep roads, traffic driving uphill has priority. Avoid parking in urban areas; use park-and-ride schemes or public transport. There are no Low Emission Zones in place. The use of dashcams and speed camera detectors is legal.

Luxembourg

View all campsites in Luxembourg
ar.camp/luxembourg

See campsite map page 473

Climate Summers are mild and long, lasting into Oct. Winters are cold and wet.

☀ **Avg. summer temp**
18°C

🌧 **Wettest month**
December

The Grand Duchy of Luxembourg is a sovereign state lying between Belgium, France and Germany. Divided into two areas: the spectacular Ardennes region in the north and the rolling farmlands in the south, bordered on the east by the wine-growing area of the Moselle Valley.

Most attractions are within easy reach of Luxembourg's capital, Luxembourg-Ville, a fortress city perched dramatically on its rocky promontory overlooking the Alzette and Petrusse Valleys. The verdant hills and valleys of the Ardennes are a maze of hiking trails, footpaths and cycle routes – ideal for an activity holiday.

The Moselle Valley, famous for its sweet wines, is just across the river from Germany; its charming hamlets can be discovered by bicycle or boat. Popular wine-tasting tours take place from late spring to early autumn. Echternacht is a good base for exploring the Mullerthal region, known as 'Little Switzerland'. Lying on the banks of the River Sûre, its forested landscape is dotted with curious rock formations and castle ruins, notably those at Beaufort and Larochette. The pretty Schießentümpel cascade is the highest waterfall in the country and is worth a visit.

Scan QR code to browse more campsites on our website

📍 Troisvierges, Diekirch

Alan Rogers Ref: LU7510
Accommodations: 13
Pitches: 151
GPS: 50.11889, 6.00152
Post Code: L-9912

what3words:
deflate.aviators.president

Contact:
info@visittroisvierges.lu
Tel: +352 99 71 41
www.camping-troisvierges.lu

Open Dates:
Start April - End September.

Camping Troisvierges

Camping Troisvierges (formerly Camping Walensbongert) is just 300 metres from all the facilities of Troisvierges, a large village with pleasant bars, restaurants and shops. The local tourist office owns the site, and the village swimming pool, with its restaurant and bar, is located at the heart of the site – campers enjoy a daily concessionary rate. The 151 level, grass touring pitches are separated by hedges and vary in size from 80-100 sq.m. They are in both open and shady areas, and all have 10A electricity.

A staircase must be used to access the main sanitary block, but new, well-equipped, accessible facilities are provided at ground level. This site, with its waymarked walks, will suit anyone who wants to enjoy the tranquillity of the countryside, although the campsite can be lively in the high season. There is a bus stop within 300 m. and a railway station within 600 m. of the entrance.

Unusual rotunda-style building (one flight of stairs) contains hot showers, toilets, laundry and washing-up facilities. Accessible facilities are at ground level (key access and unmarked door). Heated indoor and outdoor swimming pools (July/Aug); indoor pool closed in high season. Playing field adjacent. Play area. Activity programme (July/Aug). Beach volleyball court, basketball, petanque, tennis court, squash court, Multi-purpose sports field. Table tennis. WiFi throughout (charged).

Key Features

📅 Book Online

🐾 Pets allowed

♿ Accessible Facilities

🏊 Indoor Pool on Site

🛝 Childrens Play Area

Find Out More
Visit **ar.camp/lu7510**
or scan the QR code.

📍 **Heiderscheidergrund, Diekirch**

Alan Rogers Ref: LU7450
Accommodations: 17
Pitches: 70
GPS: 49.90516, 5.95631
Post Code: L-9659

what3words:
incursion.flown.consoles

Contact:
info@camping-bissen.lu
Tel: +352 83 90 04
www.camping-bissen.lu

Open Dates:
Start April - Early October.

Camping Bissen

Camping Bissen is a family-owned site on two levels, stretching along the banks of the River Sûre within the idyllic Upper-Sûre nature park. The higher level contains privately owned static caravans, with the 70 touring pitches (10A electricity) on the lower level immediately adjacent to the river. There is a well-stocked shop, and a new building houses a bar/snack bar with a terrace overlooking the river. A restaurant owned by the same family is just across the road and offers a comprehensive menu.

During the high season, a six-day activity programme has something for the whole family, including creative crafts, sports tournaments, and live shows. Those who wish to relax and unwind can enjoy the campsite's wellness facilities, which include two saunas and a whirlpool. Camping Bissen is also an excellent spot for fishing enthusiasts; a permit is needed, but many fish species can be caught here, including trout, pike, perch, eel and carp.

Three heated sanitary blocks with free hot water to showers and sinks. Good facilities for children and accessible facilities in two blocks. Family shower room. Laundry area with washing machine and tumble dryer. Well-stocked shop. Bar and snack bar with terrace. Grass area for ball games. New indoor and outdoor play areas. Entertainment, kids club (high season) Table tennis, (July/Aug). Free WiFi.

Key Features

📅 Book Online

🐾 Pets allowed

♿ Accessible Facilities

🛝 Childrens Play Area

🍸 Bar on Site

🚲 Bicycle Hire on Site

🐟 Fishing on Site

Find Out More
Visit ar.camp/lu7450
or scan the QR code.

📍 **Walsdorf, Diekirch**

Alan Rogers Ref: LU7540
Accommodations: 36
Pitches: 100
GPS: 49.91698, 6.17850
Post Code: L-9465

what3words:
promotes.frown.task

Contact:
walsdorf@beter-uit.nl
Tel: +352 83 44 64
www.beteruitholidayparks.com/walsdorf

Open Dates:
Mid March - End August
(accommodation to 1 October).

Vakantiepark Walsdorf

Beter-Uit Walsdorf is a beautifully presented site set in a quiet wooded valley. The 100 touring pitches are set in terraces alongside a small stream. The pitches are a good size at 100 to 170 sq.m, each with mature hedges and 4/6A electricity. The site buildings are modern and very well maintained. There are 36 mobile homes for rent, and these are discreetly placed on the upper terracing.

This is a very popular site which becomes lively in high season but quiet and peaceful at other times. A Christian travel group manages the site, and they have made this a delightful place to stay. Christian values are promoted throughout the campsite along with associated activities; you are welcome to participate or not, as you choose. A small bar and basic restaurant are available, as well as a shop providing you with what you would need to cook back at your pitch. There is also a youth area with a pool, darts and table football, as well as sports tournaments held at the volleyball court and playing field.

Immaculate, well-equipped sanitary block with facilities for children and Accessible facilities, Hot showers (first 5 minutes free). Small shop (limited hours in low season). A pleasant bar with a terrace, restaurant and takeaway. Club room with TV. Full entertainment programme (July/Aug). Field for ball games. Volleyball. Youth room with darts, table football and pool table. Trampoline. Free WiFi in restaurants.

Key Features

🗓 Book Online

🐾 Pets allowed

♿ Accessible Facilities

🛝 Childrens Play Area

🍸 Bar on Site

🚲 Bicycle Hire on Site

Find Out More
Visit **ar.camp/lu7540**
or scan the QR code.

📍 Diekirch, Diekirch

Alan Rogers Ref: LU7870
Pitches: 204
GPS: 49.86602, 6.16477
Post Code: L-9234

what3words:
deploying.overtones.framework

Contact:
info@camping-diekirch.lu
Tel: +352 80 87 80 701
www.camping.diekirch.lu

Open Dates:
Mid March - Mid December.

Camping de la Sûre

The municipal Camping de la Sûre is within walking distance of the centre of Diekirch, a town brimming with things to see and do. Located on the banks of the Sûre, this site offers 204 flat grass pitches, of which 175 are for touring, most with 10A electricity. One large building close to the entrance houses the reception and excellent sanitary facilities, all of which were in pristine condition.

In high season, there is a weekly entertainment programme for youngsters. There is also a large children's playground with table tennis and a leisure corner for the older kids with a pool table and table football. You will also find a bar on site with an outdoor seating area that serves various snacks, including pizza, during high season. There is also a daily bread roll service here.

Heated modern facilities, including showers and communal washbasins. Baby room and accessible facilities. Laundry. Bar and snack bar. Large play area. Children's entertainment (July/Aug). Boules. Fishing. Bicycle hire. Pool table. Table football, Table tennis, Internet access and WiFi in the bar area. Pets allowed.

Key Features

🐾 Pets allowed

♿ Accessible Facilities

🛝 Childrens Play Area

🍸 Bar on Site

🚲 Bicycle Hire on Site

Find Out More
Visit **ar.camp/lu7870**
or scan the QR code.

335

📍 **Tarchamps, Diekirch**

Alan Rogers Ref: LU7500
Accommodations: 19
Pitches: 90
GPS: 49.94651, 5.80102
Post Code: L-9689

what3words:
pesky.happening.friday

Contact:
umbierg@pt.lu
Tel: +316 21 26 78 28
www.umbierg.lu

Open Dates:
Mid March – End October.

Camping Um Bierg

This small site is set on a hillside overlooking the small village of Tarchamps, and although tidy, it looks somewhat dated. The upper area has two terraces with around 90 generously sized, level grass pitches for tourers, all with 6A electricity. Once pitched, cars must be left at the car park by the entrance. On-site facilities include a children's playground, trampoline, volleyball court, and football pitch, offering endless play.

There is also a restaurant with a terrace that overlooks the swimming pool. Open for breakfast, lunch, and dinner, the menu features a selection of dishes prepared with fresh vegetables from the campsite's organic garden. The friendly and helpful owners bake their own bread, which is sold on-site, too. This site is ideally suited to couples looking for a peaceful holiday in a good walking country in the low season. It is very popular in high season with families with young children.

The toilet block in the touring area has clean showers and toilets. A second block is available adjacent to the reception. Both can be heated and are accessed by steps. Laundry facilities. Heated swimming pool (July/Aug). Entertainment for children. Children's playground, trampoline, volleyball court, football pitch, WiFi (charged on-site, free at reception and on the terrace).

Key Features

📅 Book Online

🐾 Pets allowed

🏊 Outdoor Pool on Site

🛝 Childrens Play Area

🍸 Bar on Site

Find Out More
Visit **ar.camp/lu7500**
or scan the QR code.

📍 **Larochette, Luxembourg District**

Birkelt Village

This is very much a family site with a great range of facilities provided. It is well organised and laid out, set in an elevated position in attractive, undulating countryside. A tarmac road runs around the site with around 450 large grass pitches (Appx. 120 for touring); almost all pitches have electricity, either 10A or 16A, some slightly sloping, many with a fair amount of shade on either side of gravel access roads in straight rows and circles.

The main activities take place adjacent to the large, circular, all-weather family pool. There is also an outdoor pool in the high season, and the covered one is heated in cooler weather. Several play areas are dotted all over the site, including mini golf, tennis courts and a multisport pitch. Entertainment for children is arranged in high season, from mini discos and creative crafts for the younger campers and a junior club where a programme of sports tournaments are arranged during the day. There's also a programme of fitness activities for adults, including aqua aerobics, and live shows and musicals are performed in the evenings.

Three modern heated sanitary buildings well situated around the site include mostly open washbasins (6 cabins in one block). Baby baths. Accessible Facilities (including accommodation to rent). Washing machines and dryers. Motorhome services. Shops. Coffee bar. Restaurant with terrace. Swimming pool with a sliding cupola (heated all season). Outdoor pool for toddlers. Play areas. Trampolines. Volleyball. Minigolf. Tennis. Multisport pitch, Bicycle hire. Riding. Internet points. Free WiFi.

Alan Rogers Ref: LU7610
Accommodations: 326
Pitches: 450
GPS: 49.78508, 6.21033
Post Code: L-7633

what3words:
dissolves.clearing.narrate

Contact:
birkelt@huopenair.com
Tel: +352 87 90 40
www.birkelt.huopenair.com

Open Dates:
Late April - Mid September.

Key Features

📅 Book Online

🐾 Pets allowed

♿ Accessible Facilities

🏊 Indoor Pool on Site

🛝 Childrens Play Area

🍸 Bar on Site

🚲 Bicycle Hire on Site

🎠 Riding on Site

Find Out More
Visit **ar.camp/lu7610**
or scan the QR code.

337

📍 **Nommern, Luxembourg District**

Europacamping Nommerlayen

Situated in the lovely wooded hills of central Luxembourg, this is a top-quality site with fees to match, but it has everything! A large, central building housing most of the services and amenities opens onto a terrace around an excellent swimming pool complex with a large fun pool and an imaginative water playground. This peaceful area has many excellent walking and cycle trails, and day trips to Luxembourg, Vianden Castle and the Mosel Valley are accessible from here.

The 359 pitches (100 sq.m) are on grassy terraces with electricity (2/16A) and water taps. Pitches are grouped beside age-appropriate play areas, and the campsite facilities particularly reflect the attention given to families. Interestingly enough, the superb sanitary block is called Badtemple (having been built in the style of a Greek temple).

A large, high-quality sanitary unit provides washbasins in cubicles, Accessible facilities, family and baby rooms and a sauna. Twelve private bathrooms for hire. Laundry. Motorhome services. Supermarket, restaurant, snack bar, bar (all usually Mar-Nov). An excellent swimming pool complex and heated pool with a sliding roof (High season). Fitness programmes. Bowling. Playground. Large screen TV. Entertainment in the high season. Bicycle hire. WiFi (free over part of the site).

Alan Rogers Ref: LU7620
Accommodations: 32
Pitches: 359
GPS: 49.78472, 6.16519
Post Code: L-7465

what3words:
grunt.models.followers

Contact:
info@nommerlayen-ec.lu
Tel: +352 87 80 78
www.nommerlayen-ec.lu

Open Dates:
Start March - Early November.

📍 **Alan Rogers Awards Won**
2023, 2018, 2015

Key Features

🗓 Book Online

🐾 Pets allowed

♿ Accessible Facilities

🏊 Indoor Pool on Site

🎠 Childrens Play Area

🍸 Bar on Site

🚲 Bicycle Hire on Site

Find Out More
Visit **ar.camp/lu7620**
or scan the QR code.

Rosport, Grevenmacher

Camping du Barrage Rosport

Camping Du Barrage Rosport is on the bank of the Sauer River and the border of Germany and Luxembourg. It has well-maintained pitches on grassy fields directly by the water. Your stay here will be amidst greenery with a splendid river view. Du Barrage Rosport is a family site that attracts mainly sport-minded visitors as it is ideal for fishing enthusiasts.

Du Barrage Rosport has about 70 seasonal pitches and 110 grass-touring pitches with 16/12amp hook-up points. There are also 2 log cabins and two mobile homes available to hire. The pitches are along straight, hardened pathways on well-maintained, level grassy fields. A few deciduous trees offer shade, but most pitches are in the sun. The pitches by the water are ideal for those who want to fish straight from the river bank. (fishing licence is required)

The heated toilet block has showers, washbasins, and WCs. Accessible facilities. Family room. Baby room. Chemical toilet point. Laundry with washing machine and dryer. Dishwashing area. Shops in Rosport or Echternach. In high season, a baker visits. Restaurant. In high season, there is a bar and terrace. Snack bar. Entertainment (high season-children at least x2 a week): Live music and themed dinners. Defibrillator. Dogs allowed. WiFi. Heated outdoor swimming pool. Toddler pool. Cycle hire. Electric bike hire. Table tennis. Boules area. Kayaking, Paddleboarding, Multisports court. Beach volleyball.

Alan Rogers Ref: LU7790
Accommodations: 67
Pitches: 111
GPS: 49.80902, 6.50314
Post Code: L-6406

what3words:
credentials.cautiously.tuneless

Contact:
campingrosport@pt.lu
Tel: +352 73 01 60
www.camping-rosport.lu

Open Dates:
All year.

Key Features

- All Year
- Pets allowed
- Accessible Facilities
- Outdoor Pool on Site
- Childrens Play Area
- Bar on Site
- Bicycle Hire on Site
- Fishing on Site

Find Out More
Visit **ar.camp/lu7790**
or scan the QR code.

339

Capital Amsterdam
Currency Euro (€)
Language Dutch. French, German
Time Zone CET (GMT+1)
Telephone Code +31
Emergency Number 112
Tourist Website holland.com

Shops Hours vary throughout the year, with many shops operating shorter hours in low and shoulder seasons. In high season 10am to 6pm Tues to Fri, 10am to 5pm Sat and Sun and noon to 5pm or 6pm on Mon (if at all). Supermarkets are open 8am to 8pm.

Money ATMs are widespread and are accessible 24hrs a day. Major cards accepted widely though cash is still a popular payment method.

Travelling with children Among Europe's most child-friendly destinations. We recommend you stay clear of the Red Light District. Beaches are safe. Restaurants are kid-friendly, nearly all offer children's menus and colouring crayons.

Public Holidays 1 Jan New Year's Day; Mar/Apr Good Friday; Mar/Apr Easter Sunday; Mar/Apr Easter Monday; 27 Apr King's Day; 5 May Liberation Day; May Ascension Day; May/Jun Whit Sunday; May/Jun Whit Monday; 25 Dec Christmas Day; 26 Dec Boxing Day.

Accessible Travel Score

Generally very good. Public buildings and transport are well-equipped. Outdoor public spaces vary.

Driving in the Netherlands There is a comprehensive motorway system, but due to the high population density, all main roads can become very busy, particularly in the morning and evening rush hours. Trams should be overtaken on the right unless unsafe. Drink-driving and using your mobile whilst driving are illegal. Low Emission Zones exist in all major cities, affecting different vehicles, so check before travelling. In Amsterdam, diesel cars registered before 2006 are affected. The use of dashcams is legal, but speed camera detectors are not, so make sure to disable this feature on sat navs and mobile devices before entering the country.

340

Netherlands

View all campsites in Netherlands
ar.camp/netherlands

See campsite map page 483

Climate Slightly warmer, drier summers and colder, drier winters than the UK.	☀ **Avg. summer temp** 18°C	🌧 **Wettest month** October

With vast areas of the Netherlands reclaimed from the sea, nearly half of the country lies at or below sea level. The result is a flat, fertile landscape crisscrossed with rivers and canals. Famous for its windmills and bulb fields, it also boasts some of Europe's most impressive coastal dunes.

No visit to the Netherlands would be complete without experiencing its capital city, Amsterdam, with its maze of canals, bustling cafés, museums and summer festivals.

The fields of South Holland are an explosion of colour between March and May when the world's biggest flower auction takes place at Aalsmeer.

The Vecht valley and its towns of Dalfsen, Ommen and Hardenberg are best explored by bicycle, while Giethoorn, justly dubbed the 'Venice of Holland', has to be seen from a boat. The Kinderdijk windmills on the Alblasserwaard polder are a UNESCO World Heritage Site.

The islands of Zeeland are home to beautiful old towns such as Middelburg, the provincial capital, Zierikzee, with its old harbour and the quaint old town of Veere.

Scan QR code to browse more campsites on our website

📍 Franeker, Friesland

Alan Rogers Ref: NL6075
Accommodations: 33
Pitches: 85
GPS: 53.18968, 5.55333
Post Code: NL-8801 PG

what3words:
liberating.varied.hunk

Contact:
info@bloemketerp.nl
Tel: +31 517 395 099
www.bloemketerp.com

Open Dates:
All year.

Camping Bloemketerp

Camping Bloemketerp can be found within walking distance of the interesting and historic town of Franeker. There are about 85 sheltered and good-sized pitches here. These are dispersed around several camping fields. The park also has a range of holiday homes to rent. There is a well-equipped sports centre adjacent, with a sub-tropical indoor swimming pool, canoe rental and bicycle hire. Campers are allowed free access to this centre (fitness, tennis, squash, racquetball, sauna and massage). The park boasts an attractive, friendly restaurant (with a sun terrace) offering both a set menu and buffet options.

Franeker is one of Friesland's famed Eleven Cities. The town is famous for its unique Eisinga planetarium, which dates back to the 18th century. Franeker was formerly a town of great note, with the second university in The Netherlands and home to the Duke of Saxony. Nowadays, it is a tranquil place surrounded by delightful Frisian countryside. This is best explored on foot or by bicycle, and the site managers will be pleased to recommend routes.

Key Features

📅 Book Online

📅 All Year

🐾 Pets allowed

♿ Accessible Facilities

🏊 Indoor Pool on Site

🧒 Childrens Play Area

🍸 Bar on Site

🚲 Bicycle Hire on Site

One large toilet block with controllable, hot showers (paid), open-style washbasins and accessible facilities. Laundry. Motorhome services. Restaurant (with buffet option). Takeaway meals. Sports centre full facilities. Play area. Ten-pin bowling. Recreation team (High season). Canoe hire. WiFi over site (charged). Accommodation to rent.

Find Out More
Visit **ar.camp/nl6075**
or scan the QR code.

📍 **Noordwolde, Friesland**

Camping Rotandorp

Get ready for leafy walks, hikes and bike rides: the North Netherlands site Camping Rotandorp is in a part of Friesland known for its forests and is close to the Drents-Friese Wold National Park, one of the biggest in the country. The campsite is about a mile from the recreational lake, the Spoekeplas, which has a swimming pool just outside.

This is a particularly peaceful area in spring. Still, suppose you're around during the school holidays. In that case, all the Camping Rotandorp facilities are up and running, such as its many activities and the sale of freshly baked bread and newspapers each morning at the cafeteria. Other amenities include a modern shower block with baby changing facilities, a pétanque and sports court, and a play area with a sandpit, swings and a slide. Several shops and restaurants are in the neighbouring village of Noordwolde.

Sanitary block with baby changing facilities and children's facilities, Bar, Snack bar, Children's play area, sports field, Table tennis, Entertainment (High season), Pétanque, bicycle hire, Pets allowed. WiFi.

Alan Rogers Ref: NL6025
Accommodations: 2
Pitches: 75
GPS: 52.88432, 6.16583
Post Code: NL-8391 MB

what3words:
irritating.crossroads.caretakers

Contact:
info@campingrotandorp.nl
Tel: +31 561 431 227
www.campingrotandorp.nl

Open Dates:
Mid March - End October.

Key Features

🗓 Book Online

🐾 Pets allowed

🧒 Childrens Play Area

🍸 Bar on Site

🚲 Bicycle Hire on Site

🐟 Fishing on Site

Find Out More
Visit **ar.camp/nl6025**
or scan the QR code.

343

📍 Groningen, Groningen

Alan Rogers Ref: NL5770
Pitches: 150
GPS: 53.20090, 6.53570
Post Code: NL-9727 KH

what3words:
pipeline.formal.hinted

Contact:
info@campingstadspark.nl
Tel: +31 505 251 624
www.campingstadspark.nl

Open Dates:
Mid March - End October.

Camping Stadspark

Camping Stadspark Groningen is a 6 ha. Large campsite in the Groningen City Park, approximately 3.5 km from the city centre. The site has 150 pitches, 130 of which are for touring units and have 6A electricity and 30 are fully serviced with electricity, water and drainage. Hardstanding is available for large units and motorhomes. The separate tent area is supervised directly by the manager. Cars may not be parked on the fields due to the soft ground; Caravans are placed by a campsite employee using a tractor.

The site is surrounded by water & has one entrance located at the campsite. On-site facilities include two toilet blocks and a snack bar where you can order sandwiches and breakfast for the next day. There is also a large petting zoo within the park. There is also a large children's playground located here.

Two sanitary blocks provide hot showers, washbasins and toilets. One is modern, and the other has been refurbished to a good standard. Family shower and baby room. Accessible facilities. Motorhome services. Café, bar and takeaway (Seasonal). Bicycle hire. Volleyball. Fishing. Canoeing. Children's playground, Petting zoo, WiFi (free).

Key Features

🐾 Pets allowed

♿ Accessible Facilities

🛝 Childrens Play Area

🍸 Bar on Site

🚲 Bicycle Hire on Site

🐟 Fishing on Site

Find Out More
Visit **ar.camp/nl5770**
or scan the QR code.

📍 **Sellingen, Groningen**

Camping De Bronzen Eik

Alan Rogers Ref: NL6104
Accommodations: 7
Pitches: 90
GPS: 52.95440, 7.13805
Post Code: NL-9551 VT

what3words:
dragged.sawn.underwear

Contact:
recepttie@debronzeneik.nl
Tel: +31 599 322 006
www.debronzeneik.nl

Open Dates:
All year.

This site is perfect for families with young children and those who enjoy cycling and walking in a peaceful and natural environment. Camping De Bronzen Eik is a small, family-friendly campsite with 90 fully equipped pitches with 6A electricity, water and drainage. Twelve pitches are without electricity and a further five fields are available for tents, ideal for group camping. The heated municipal swimming pool nearby is free to use. The restaurant with a terrace offers an extensive menu ranging from a cup of coffee and a snack to à la carte dishes.

Just a stone's throw from the Westerwolde nature reserve, there are over 200 km. of walking, cycling and riding trails to choose from. Two thousand three hundred hectares of woodland flora and fauna are waiting to be discovered, an ideal area for hide and seek and where children can play safely.

Modern sanitary block with underfloor heating, free hot showers and facilities for children. Bar, Restaurant, Launderette with dryers. 'FootGolf' pitch. Play area. WiFi (free). Pets allowed.

Key Features

📅 Book Online

🐾 Pets allowed

🧒 Childrens Play Area

🍸 Bar on Site

Find Out More
Visit **ar.camp/nl6104**
or scan the QR code.

📍 **Diever, Drenthe**

Alan Rogers Ref: NL6148
Accommodations: 10
Pitches: 90
GPS: 52.82497, 6.31836
Post Code: NL-7986 PL

what3words:
garden.attribute.inlet

Contact:
info@wittelterbrug.nl
Tel: +31 521 598 288
www.campingwittelterbrug.nl

Open Dates:
Start April - End October.

Camping Wittelterbrug

Camping Wittelterbrug is a well-established, family-friendly site with a central location between the Drents-Friese Wold and the Dwingelderveld. This is an excellent cycling and walking country (cycle hire is available on-site). Pitches are in long lanes off paved access roads on good-sized, grassy fields. All are equipped with electricity (10A), water and drainage (a small charge is made for hot showers).

On-site amenities include two indoor heated pools and a convivial café/snack bar serving takeaway meals. In the peak season, there is a lively activity and entertainment programme, including a kids' club with special activities such as creative crafts, workshops, dancing, and sports tournaments. The campsite is close to the villages of Dwingeloo (best known for its radio telescope, the largest in the world at the time of completion in 1956) and Diever, at the heart of southwestern Drenthe.

Two blocks for tourers with controllable hot showers and open-style washbasins. Baby room. The bar provides meals, takeaways, drinks and ice. Covered swimming pool and children's pool. Playground. Entertainment, Pool table, table tennis, Bicycle hire. WiFi (charged). Accommodation to rent.

Key Features

🗓 Book Online

🐾 Pets allowed

🌊 Indoor Pool on Site

🛝 Childrens Play Area

🍸 Bar on Site

🚲 Bicycle Hire on Site

🐟 Fishing on Site

Find Out More
Visit **ar.camp/nl6148**
or scan the QR code.

📍 **Zorgvlied, Drenthe**

Park Drentheland

This park is aimed very much at those who enjoy riding. The site has 35 stables available, so you can bring your own horse, but there is no livery service. Groot Bartje has 100 touring pitches on three circular, grassy fields and two smaller fields. The middle field has 36 spacious, level pitches on grass, with shade from mature trees. All are equipped with 16A electricity, water, wastewater and cables.

To the front of the site is an open-air pool with a separate paddling pool and a small water slide. Behind reception are training facilities for horses, including two dressage schools. The site is on the edge of the Drents Friese Wold National Park, where you can enjoy riding, walking and cycling.

One good toilet block with underfloor heating, toilets, washbasins and preset hot showers (5 minutes free). Baby room. Accessible Facilities. Laundry with washing machines and dryers. Basics and bread from reception. Snack bar (daily in season). Pool (15x10 m) with slide and paddling pool. Tennis. Riding. Stables, Bicycle hire. Playground. Mini Golf, Torch useful. Animation (high season). WiFi (free around reception and comfort pitches).

Alan Rogers Ref: NL6165
Accommodations: 21
Pitches: 100
GPS: 52.92359, 6.25061
Post Code: NL-8437 PE

what3words:
dipper.perceptual.prosper

Contact:
info@parkdrentheland.nl
Tel: +31 521 388 136
www.parkdrentheland.nl

Open Dates:
Start April - Start November.

Key Features

🗓 Book Online

🐾 Pets allowed

♿ Accessible Facilities

🏊 Outdoor Pool on Site

🧒 Childrens Play Area

🍸 Bar on Site

🚲 Bicycle Hire on Site

🧲 Riding on Site

Find Out More
Visit ar.camp/nl6165
or scan the QR code.

📍 **Texel, Noord-Holland**

Alan Rogers Ref: NL6881
Pitches: 165
GPS: 53.05872, 4.75959
Post Code: NL-1791 PE

what3words:
faunas.planet.depictions

Contact:
receptie@woudtexel.nl
Tel: +31 222 313 080
www.maakjeklaarvoortexel.nl

Open Dates:
Early April - Early October.

Camping Woud Texel

Kampeerterrein Woud Texel can be found on the island of Texel and is a pleasant site with 165 large pitches (minimum 120 sq.m). All pitches have electrical connections (6-16A). The spacious camping area comprises several fields surrounded by trees. The emphasis is very much on the quality of the natural environment, and there are few amenities on site. Additionally, cars may only be parked on site for arrival and departure. At all other times, they must be left at the spacious car park at the site entrance. Several luggage carts are available for transporting groceries and the like.

A large field is provided for various sports, including football, volleyball and basketball, and there is also a good play area for children. Dogs are welcomed on-site, and one field is reserved for campers with dogs (they are not allowed elsewhere).

Centrally located sanitary facilities include provision for babies and accessible facilities. Play area. Football. Volleyball. Basketball. Excursions into the forest. Ferry offers for low season holidays (Sept/Oct). Free WiFi.

Key Features

🐾 Pets allowed

♿ Accessible Facilities

⛱ Seaside Beach Nearby

🛝 Childrens Play Area

🚲 Bicycle Hire on Site

Find Out More
Visit **ar.camp/nl6881**
or scan the QR code.

📍 **Julianadorp aan Zee, Noord-Holland**

Camping 't Noorder Sandt

Close to the marine city of Den Helder and about 600 m. from a wide, sandy beach is Camping 't Noorder Sandt. Adjacent to the site is the Duinvliet, a route for hikers, cyclists and horse riders – you can even do the route in a canoe! Some 180 open and shady touring pitches are available here. They are comfortable and are all equipped with 10A electricity; 60 also have water, drainage and cable connections.

Also worth noting is the friendly atmosphere and well-maintained sanitary facilities. For many, the site's main attraction is its pool complex. In the early mornings, it is only open for older people to start the day, and after 10 a.m. it is open to all. Clean air, space and relaxation are only a few of the site's advantages.

Two good toilet blocks with controllable hot showers and open-style washbasins. Accessible Facilities. Laundry with washing machines and dryers. Well-equipped campers' kitchen. Kiosk for basics. Restaurant. Indoor pool with fun pool and slide. Fishing. Riding. Bicycle hire. Canoes for hire. Dog showers, Entertainment team in high season. Free WiFi over site.

Alan Rogers Ref: NL6866
Accommodations: 237
Pitches: 180
GPS: 52.90667, 4.72499
Post Code: NL-1787 CX

what3words:
smart.mindlessly.reds

Contact:
noordersandt@ardoer.com
Tel: +31 223 641 266
www.noordersandt.ardoer.com

Open Dates:
Mid March - Mid October.

Key Features

🐾 Pets allowed

♿ Accessible Facilities

🏖 Seaside Beach Nearby

🏊 Indoor Pool on Site

🛝 Childrens Play Area

🍸 Bar on Site

🚲 Bicycle Hire on Site

🐟 Fishing on Site

Find Out More
Visit ar.camp/nl6866
or scan the QR code.

📍 **Amstelveen, Noord-Holland**

Alan Rogers Ref: NL5660
Pitches: 400
GPS: 52.29357, 4.82297
Post Code: NL-1187 NZ

what3words:
blanket.lunging.cove

Contact:
info@campingamsterdam.com
Tel: +31 206 416 868
www.europarcs.nl

Open Dates:
Mid March - Mid December.

Het Amsterdamse Bos

Het Amsterdamse Bos is a large park to the southwest of Amsterdam, one corner of which has been specifically laid out as the city's municipal campsite and is now under family ownership. Close to Schiphol Airport (expect some noise), it is a walk/bus and a metro ride into central Amsterdam.

The site is well laid out alongside a canal, with open pitches on separate flat lawns, mostly backing onto pleasant hedges and trees, with several areas of paved hardstandings. It takes 400 touring units, with 100 electrical connections (10A) and some with cable TV. An additional area is available for tents and groups. Some pitches can become very wet in the rain. The site has a modern reception, the former restaurant is now a cooking and dining area, and there are modern cabins to rent.

Three modern sanitary blocks are light and airy with showers (on payment). Facilities for babies and accessible facilities. Laundry facilities. Motorhome services. Gas supplies. Small shop with basics. Fresh bread from reception. Cooking and dining area. Play area. Bicycle hire. Internet and free WiFi over site. Twin-axle caravans are not accepted.

Key Features

📅 Book Online

🐾 Pets allowed

♿ Accessible Facilities

⛱ Seaside Beach Nearby

🛝 Childrens Play Area

🚲 Bicycle Hire on Site

🐟 Fishing on Site

Find Out More
Visit **ar.camp/nl5660**
or scan the QR code.

Zeewolde, Flevoland

Camping Het Groene Bos

Camping Het Groene Bos is a pleasant rural site located at the edge of a vast forest, the Horsterwold, in the province of Flevoland. There is a real sense of space and nature here. This immaculately kept site has 80 large, grassy touring pitches (well distributed over the site and up to 200 sq.m), most with 6-10A electricity.

The forest is ideal for walking, cycling and riding, with many miles of marked tracks. Unusually, it is possible to bring your own horse to the site and explore the Zeebodemtrail, a route of over 80 km. with horse facilities along the way. On-site, the children's farm is undeniably a popular feature. Zeewolde (3 km. distant) is an attractive town that provides good water opportunities with a fine beach and a marina.

One central, modern toilet block has preset hot showers, family rooms, baby room and accessible facilities, Motorhome services. Play area. Giant chess. Bar with library, TV and children's games. Boules. Children's farm. Stabling for horses. Bicycle and go-kart hire. WiFi (charged).

Alan Rogers Ref: NL6214
Accommodations: 2
Pitches: 45
GPS: 52.34012, 5.50547
Post Code: NL-3896 LS

what3words:
shortfalls.soaked.outbid

Contact:
info@hetgroenebos.nl
Tel: +31 365 236 366
www.hetgroenebos.nl

Open Dates:
Start April - Mid October.

Key Features

🐾 Pets allowed

♿ Accessible Facilities

🛝 Childrens Play Area

🍸 Bar on Site

🚲 Bicycle Hire on Site

🎠 Riding on Site

Find Out More
Visit **ar.camp/nl6214**
or scan the QR code.

📍 **Leerdam, Utrecht**

Alan Rogers Ref: NL5857
Accommodations: 11
Pitches: 45
GPS: 51.90592, 5.06162
Post Code: NL-4143 LP

what3words:
deflect.padding.jokers

Contact:
info@campingterleede.nl
Tel: +31 653 754 944
www.campingterleede.nl

Open Dates:
Start April - Start October.

Camping Ter Leede Leerdam

Camping Ter Leede Leerdam is located in a nature reserve In the polder landscape of Zuid-Holland close to the river Linge. This small, charming campsite is nestled within an orchard with many spacious pitches, giving you lots of privacy wherever you decide to pitch up. There is a well-kept sanitary block, which includes hot showers and laundry facilities.

The friendly campsite owner, John-Paul, is on hand to make your stay as relaxing and carefree as possible. There may not be a shop or bar on site, but you will find all the facilities you would need in the nearby village, Leerdam, which is 3.5km away and known for its glass and Leerdammer cheese. This area is perfect for those wanting to explore south Holland with its flat open landscapes, picturesque villages, and old windmills, and then there is Betuwe with its beautiful blossom trees. There are well-maintained cycle paths and footpaths which link to the villages. Utrecht and Kinderdijk are also a 35-minute drive away, which is perfect for a day trip.

Sanitary block with hot showers, Fresh bread delivered daily, Washing up facilities, Laundry facilities, Children's playground, Fishing on-site, WiFi, Pets allowed.

Key Features

📅 Book Online

🐾 Pets allowed

🛝 Childrens Play Area

🐟 Fishing on Site

Find Out More
Visit **ar.camp/nl5857**
or scan the QR code.

Renswoude, Utrecht

Alan Rogers Ref: NL6805
Accommodations: 9
Pitches: 125
GPS: 52.08466, 5.55130
Post Code: NL-3927 CJ

what3words:
krill.seldom.battle

Contact:
info@campingdegrebbelinie.nl
Tel: +31 318 591 073
www.campingdegrebbelinie.nl

Open Dates:
End March - Mid October.

Camping De Grebbelinie

Camping Grebbelinie is a friendly, family-run, environmentally green campsite in Utrechtse Heuvelrug National Park. The pitches are large and grassy, and all have 6/10A electricity, water, drainage, WiFi and TV connections. Several pitches run along a riverbank, with other pitches more centrally located and with shade from tall trees. There is a pleasant café/snack bar and a good playground. Opposite the site, Fort Daatselaar has an interesting history dating back to the mid-18th century and merits a visit. There are many delightful walks along the Gelderlei Valley, and the site owners will be pleased to recommend options.

A bed and breakfast service is available here, appealing to backpackers passing through the region. Fully equipped safari tents and mobile homes are also available for hire. Camping Grebbelinie is well located for exploring the broader reach, with the Hoge Veluwe National Park and the Utrechtse Heuvelrug within easy reach.

Several heated sanitary facilities, the most recent with underfloor heating, provide washbasins and showers, including provision for children and accessible facilities. Snack bar/café. Play area. Small petting zoo. Bicycle hire. Safari tents and mobile homes to rent. Bed and breakfast service. Table tennis, Entertainment (High season) WiFi throughout.

Key Features

- Book Online
- Pets allowed
- Accessible Facilities
- Childrens Play Area
- Bar on Site
- Bicycle Hire on Site

Find Out More
Visit **ar.camp/nl6805**
or scan the QR code.

353

📍 **Rheeze, Overijssel**

Alan Rogers Ref: NL6498
Accommodations: 5
Pitches: 250
GPS: 52.54685, 6.57155
Post Code: NL-7794 RA

what3words:
shift.running.quintet

Contact:
info@campingtveld.nl
Tel: +31 523 262 286
www.campingtveld.nl

Open Dates:
Start April - Start October.

Camping 't Veld

Camping 't Veld is situated in the Vecht Valley and is surrounded by forests and lakes. Of the 250 pitches, 110 are available for touring, all with 6/10A electricity. Five pitches are fully serviced, and four have private sanitary units. The site is well laid out, and the grassy touring pitches are divided between eight small, hedged fields. There are also two safari tents for hire and three mobile homes.

On-site facilities include a shop, bar and restaurant, all of which are first-class and open all season. The all-weather pool at the entrance is a bonus to this beautifully located site that would particularly suit families with young children and pre-teens. There is a designated children's pool with play equipment; the older kids can find a 48-metre slide adjoining the adult's pool.

One central, modern and heated sanitary block with hot showers, private cabins, a baby bathroom and accessible facilities. Laundry facilities. Motorhome service point. Shop, bar and restaurant. Swimming pool with a retractable roof for use in all weather. Paddling pool. Play area on each of the touring fields. Indoor play area, Sports field. Fishing. Kayaking, Bicycle hire. WiFi throughout (charged).

Key Features

🗓 Book Online

🐾 Pets allowed

♿ Accessible Facilities

🏊 Indoor Pool on Site

🧗 Childrens Play Area

🍸 Bar on Site

🚲 Bicycle Hire on Site

🐟 Fishing on Site

Find Out More
Visit **ar.camp/nl6498**
or scan the QR code.

Nijverdal, Overijssel

Camping De Noetselerberg

Camping De Noetselerberg is located in Nijverdal, Overijssel, Netherlands. It is a beautifully situated campsite with plenty of facilities for campers of all ages. The 200 grass touring pitches are spacious and arranged on open fields, surrounded by trees and shrubs. All have 10A electricity, water and drainage. Good quality facilities include a well-equipped toilet block and a fine restaurant, De Oale Sté, with a terrace.

There is an outdoor swimming pool and an indoor swimming pool with a pirate ship and a 35m water slide. A recreation team provides hours of organised fun for children during the high season. This is a true paradise for children. The campsite has several play areas and fields and a splendid covered play area for when the weather is unpleasant.

Three well-located toilet blocks provide washbasins (open style and in cabins), toilets and controllable hot showers. Facilities for children. Family shower room. Accessible Facilities. Laundry with washing machines, dryer and spin dryer. Shop. Bar/restaurant. Indoor and outdoor pools with slide and fun pool (Seasonal). Bicycle hire. Indoor playground. Multisport pitch, football field, bounce pad, Table tennis, Full entertainment programme in high season. WiFi (charged).

Alan Rogers Ref: NL6464
Accommodations: 11
Pitches: 200
GPS: 52.34991, 6.45458
Post Code: NL-7441 DK

what3words:
gratify.concretely.pins

Contact:
info@noetselerberg.nl
Tel: +31 548 612 665
www.noetselerberg.nl

Open Dates:
End March - Late October.

Key Features

- Book Online
- Pets allowed
- Accessible Facilities
- Indoor Pool on Site
- Childrens Play Area
- Bar on Site
- Bicycle Hire on Site

Find Out More
Visit ar.camp/nl6464
or scan the QR code.

📍 **Zuna/Nijverdal, Overijssel**

Alan Rogers Ref: NL5815
Accommodations: 30
Pitches: 75
GPS: 52.32633, 6.51873
Post Code: NL-7466 PD

what3words:
mooring.evidence.daring

Contact:
info@molke.nl
Tel: +31 548 512 743
www.molke.nl

Open Dates:
Early April - End October.

Vakantiepark Mölke

You will receive a warm welcome at Overijssel Vakantiepark Mölke, located on the banks of the lovely River Regge, around 5 km. south of Nijverdal. This river is ideal for canoeing and boat trips (hire available on-site), and there are endless opportunities for cycling and walking in this region.

This family site has much to do for children of all ages, with its excellent new indoor play area and ten-pin bowling alley. The 75 touring pitches (all with electricity (4-16A) are divided into three categories: standard, comfort (with water and drainage) and super comfort (with private wash/toilet unit). A variety of high-quality rental accommodation is available. The shop, bar, sizeable friendly restaurant and reception are closed on Sunday.

Two toilet blocks are relatively modern and very clean. Free showers. Accessible Facilities (key access). Small laundry. Shop. Bar. Child-friendly restaurant. Café with terrace overlooking harbour. Snack bar. Indoor pool (12x8 m) and paddling pool. Indoor playground. Playgrounds. Activity and entertainment programme (High season). Canoe hire. Boat trips on the Regge. Air trampoline. Tennis. Sports field. Archery. 10-pin bowling. WiFi over site (charged).

Key Features

🗓 Book Online

🐾 Pets allowed

♿ Accessible Facilities

🌊 Indoor Pool on Site

🛝 Childrens Play Area

🍸 Bar on Site

🚲 Bicycle Hire on Site

🎣 Fishing on Site

Find Out More
Visit **ar.camp/nl5815**
or scan the QR code.

Enschede, Overijssel

Alan Rogers Ref: NL6455
Accommodations: 86
Pitches: 32
GPS: 52.17105, 6.82428
Post Code: NL-7546 PS

what3words:
imagining.recharged.stubble

Contact:
info@ostana.nl
Tel: +31 534 282 723
www.ostana.nl

Open Dates:
Start April – End October.

Naturisten-vereniging Ostana

Naturistenvereniging Ostana is a Naturist site located at the Oude Buurserdijk in Enschede. The site has 32 touring pitches and 86 seasonal pitches with electricity. The site has a swimming pond, a children's beach, an on-site play forest, and a sauna. A children's playground is on site with a trampoline, swings and climbing frame. Other facilities on-site include a cosy common room with books and board games, and there is also a bar that is occasionally open for ice cream and snacks; a youth club is also available during high season.

Not only does the site offer plenty of opportunities, but the nature in the vicinity is also definitely worth a visit. The cycling and walking opportunities are enormous with the Witteveen, the Buurserzand, the Haaksbergerveen, and the nature areas just across the border in Germany.

Two toilet blocks with showers, washbasins, and WCs. Accessible facilities. Laundry with washing machine and dryer. Dishwashing area. Chemical toilet point. Free WiFi. Library. Games room. Bar. Youth club. Boules area. Dogs allowed. Defibrillator. Sauna. Children's play area. Trampoline. Car charging facility.

Key Features

- Naturist
- Pets allowed
- Accessible Facilities
- Childrens Play Area
- Bar on Site

Find Out More
Visit ar.camp/nl6455
or scan the QR code.

Wassenaar, Zuid-Holland

Alan Rogers Ref: NL5620
Accommodations: 400
Pitches: 750
GPS: 52.14642, 4.38737
Post Code: NL-2242 JP

what3words:
bumpy.december.immunity

Contact:
info@duinrell.nl
Tel: +31 705 155 255
www.duinrell.com

Open Dates:
All year.

Vakantiepark Duinrell

A vast site, Duinrell's name means 'well in the dunes', and the water theme continues in the adjoining amusement park and the extensive indoor pool complex. The campsite itself is huge, with 750 touring places on several flat, grassy areas (60-140 sq.m), and it can become very busy in high season. As part of a continuing improvement programme, the marked pitches have electricity, water and drainage connections, and some have cable TV.

Amenities shared with the park include restaurants, takeaways, a pancake house, a supermarket and a theatre. Entry to the popular pleasure park is free for campers – indeed, the camping areas surround and open out from the park. The Tiki Tropical Pool complex has many attractions, which include 21 slides ranging from quite exciting to terrifying (depending on your age!), whirlpools, and many other features.

Six heated toilet blocks serve the touring areas. One block has accessible facilities. Laundry facilities. Amusement park and Tiki tropical pool complex. Restaurant, cafés, pizzeria and takeaways (weekends only in winter). Supermarket. Entertainment and theatre with shows in high season. Rope Challenge trail and training circuit. Bicycle hire. Mini-bowling. All activities have extra charges. WiFi over site (charged).

Key Features

- Book Online
- All Year
- Pets allowed
- Accessible Facilities
- Seaside Beach Nearby
- Indoor Pool on Site
- Childrens Play Area
- Bar on Site

Find Out More
Visit ar.camp/nl5620
or scan the QR code.

Delft, Zuid-Holland

Vakantiepark Delftse Hout

This well-run, modern site is pleasantly situated in Delft's park and forest area on the city's eastern edge. It has 200 touring pitches formally arranged in groups of four to six and surrounded by attractive trees and hedges. All have sufficient space and electrical connections (10A Europlug).

Modern buildings near the entrance house the site amenities. A modern sanitary block and a new reception and entrance have been developed (2021). A more recent, smaller restaurant is available where basic snacks are for sale. Walking and cycling tours are organised, and there is a recreation programme in the high season.

Modern, heated toilet facilities include a spacious family room and children's section. Accessible Facilities. Laundry. Motorhome services. Shop for basic food and camping items (All season). Snack bar and takeaway (High season). Small heated outdoor swimming pool (mid-May - mid-Sept.) Adventure playground. Recreation room. Entertainment, Bicycle hire. Gas supplies. Max. 1 dog. WiFi (500 MB/day included).

Alan Rogers Ref: NL5600
Accommodations: 42
Pitches: 200
GPS: 52.01767, 4.37908
Post Code: NL-2616 LJ

what3words:
minder.bake.smokers

Contact:
info@delftsehout.nl
Tel: +31 152 130 040
www.delftsehout.nl

Open Dates:
End March - Start November.

Alan Rogers Awards Won
2022, 2017

Key Features

- Book Online
- Pets allowed
- Accessible Facilities
- Seaside Beach Nearby
- Outdoor Pool on Site
- Childrens Play Area
- Bicycle Hire on Site

Find Out More
Visit ar.camp/nl5600
or scan the QR code.

📍 **Rockanje, Zuid-Holland**

Alan Rogers Ref: NL6975
Accommodations: 50
Pitches: 340
GPS: 51.87999, 4.05398
Post Code: NL-3235 CC

what3words:
dashed.ruby.windmill

Contact:
waterbos@molecaten.nl
Tel: +31 181 401 900
www.molecaten.nl/waterbos

Open Dates:
Start April - Late October.

Park Waterbos

Molecaten Park Waterbos is a small, friendly campsite located behind dunes on the island of Voorne. The site is within easy walking distance of the broad sandy beach at Rockanje. This beach slopes gradually and is ideal for young children. There are 340 pitches here, of which 140 are for touring units, shaded by large trees and located on several grassy fields, often with play areas at the centre. There is a choice of basic, comfort and comfort-plus pitches, all with electricity (6/10A). The latter group comprises deluxe pitches, each equipped with a shower, toilet, and washbasin. There are also mobile homes, luxury accommodations and fully equipped tents for hire.

Molecaten Park Waterbos has all the facilities needed to enjoy your holiday here. There are fishing opportunities, a bar, a snack bar and a camping shop. Children can enjoy themselves at the large playground and outdoor children's pool with fountains and play equipment. Adults can also enjoy a refreshing swim in the larger pool. During high season, the entertainment team organises various games, creative crafts and activities for all ages.

Accessible sanitary facilities, Restaurant with bar and terrace, takeaway. Small shop for bread and basics. Heated outdoor swimming pool (Seasonal). Fishing pond. Play area. Bicycle and go-kart hire. Entertainment and activity programme. WiFi throughout (charged). Dogs are not accepted.

Key Features

♿ Accessible Facilities

🏊 Outdoor Pool on Site

🛝 Childrens Play Area

🍸 Bar on Site

🚲 Bicycle Hire on Site

🐟 Fishing on Site

Find Out More
Visit ar.camp/nl6975
or scan the QR code.

📍 **Voorthuizen, Gelderland**

Recreatiepark De Boshoek

Alan Rogers Ref: NL6337
Accommodations: 121
Pitches: 116
GPS: 52.18756, 5.63098
Post Code: NL-3781 NJ

what3words:
corals.fished.distantly

Contact:
info@deboshoek.nl
Tel: +31 342 471 297
holidayparkdeboshoek.com

Open Dates:
Late March - Late October.
Accommodation all year.

Recreationpark De Boshoek is a spacious, family-oriented campsite that forms part of a large leisure park with bungalows to rent and private chalets. There are 130 touring pitches of 100-120 sq.m., all equipped with 10A electricity, water, drainage and cable TV connections. They are in various fields, each with its own play area and two car-free areas, with a central area for general use. There are eight pitches reserved for campers.

Children will enjoy the playground with its giant 7.5-metre slide. There is also a pony club and a children's farm. State forests surround the site, and from the site, there are excellent opportunities for cycling or hiking. The site owners are happy to help you plan your trip.

One big and clean, heated sanitary building with heated showers. Children sanitary. Some washbasins in cubicles. Dishwashers. Separate laundry building. Shop with a variety of products. Good facilities for children and accessible facilities. Private sanitary facilities to rent on some pitches. Shop. Restaurant. Bar. Snack bar. Takeaway. Large swimming complex with heated indoor and outdoor pool. Spa with sauna and Turkish steam bath. Large adventure play area. Pony and horse riding lessons. Minigolf. 10-pin bowling. Short golf. Tennis. Football. Basketball. Children's farm. Entertainment and children's club. Hairdresser. Bicycle hire. Free WiFi in accommodation.

Key Features

📅 Book Online

📅 All Year

🐾 Pets allowed

🏊 Indoor Pool on Site

🧒 Childrens Play Area

🍸 Bar on Site

🚴 Bicycle Hire on Site

🎧 Riding on Site

Find Out More
Visit **ar.camp/nl6337**
or scan the QR code.

Winterswijk, Gelderland

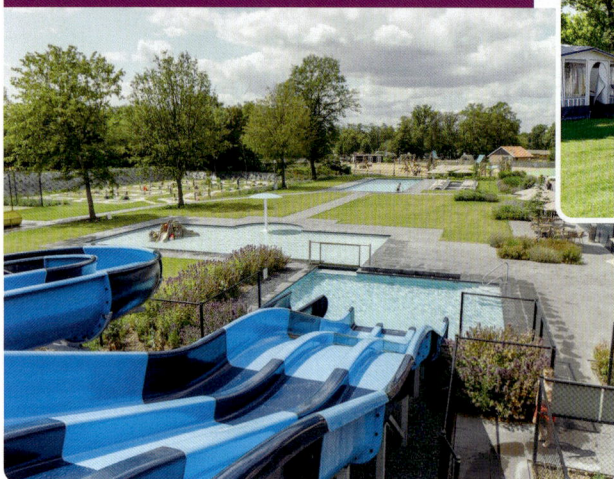

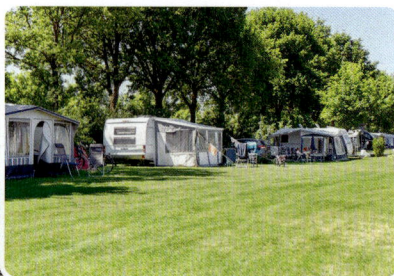

De Twee Bruggen

De Twee Bruggen is a spacious recreation park set in the Achterhoek countryside. The 350 touring pitches (all with 10/16A electricity) are divided between varying-sized fields. Although tall trees surround the fields, the ground is open and sunny. Beyond the touring area, 71 chalets set in well-tended grounds are for rent.

Children and adults can enjoy indoor and outdoor swimming pools. At the indoor pool, there is a covered terrace and, for relaxation, a sauna and jacuzzi. Adjacent to the pool is a small, open-air theatre, where shows are staged in high season. This campsite is suited to families looking for a relaxing holiday with many leisure activities. The restaurant at the entrance to the site is of high quality and attracts many outside visitors.

Three modern, well-maintained sanitary buildings include showers and washbasins in private cabins. Fourteen pitches have private sanitary facilities. Washing machines and dryers. Motorhome services. Supermarket, bar, restaurant and takeaway (All year). Heated outdoor pool (Seasonal). Heated indoor pool (All year). Paddling pool. Sauna. Jacuzzi. Solarium. Sports field. Gym, Tennis courts. Bicycle hire. Minigolf. Bowling. Playground. Bouncy castle. Deer field. Free WiFi over site. Max. 2 dogs.

Alan Rogers Ref: NL6425
Accommodations: 71
Pitches: 350
GPS: 51.94961, 6.64770
Post Code: NL-7109-AH

what3words:
vaccinated.pigtails.hardly

Contact:
info@detweebruggen.nl
Tel: +31 543 565 366
www.detweebruggen.nl

Open Dates:
All year.

Key Features

- Book Online
- All Year
- Pets allowed
- Indoor Pool on Site
- Childrens Play Area
- Bar on Site
- Bicycle Hire on Site

Find Out More
Visit **ar.camp/nl6425**
or scan the QR code.

Kamperland, Zeeland

De Schotsman

De Schotsman is located on the island of Noord-Beveland, on the shores of Veerse Meer. Benefiting from recent renovations throughout the site, it has a marina with a slipway and a good selection of boats for hire for all abilities. In the high season, there is a full programme of windsurfing and sailing lessons.

There is also a large, heated outdoor pool with a separate children's pool and an inviting restaurant with a terrace overlooking the lake. It is within reach of the ports of Hook of Holland, Zeebrugge, and Dunkerque and two and a half hours from Calais, so it may also be ideal for a short break in the low season.

Four spacious sanitary units are spotless and well-equipped and have accessible facilities. The largest block contains a launderette. Bakery and well-stocked supermarket. Bar, restaurant with lake view terrace, and takeaway. Heated outdoor pool with separate children's pool, slides, water chute and paddling pool (all season). Heated indoor swimming pool, Sports hall. Play area. Gym, Bicycle and go-kart hire. Fishing. Windsurf, pedalo and canoe hire. Lake beach. Marina with slipway. WiFi (free). Mobile homes, chalets, bungalows and apartments to rent.

Alan Rogers Ref: NL6924
Accommodations: 233
Pitches: 435
GPS: 51.56853, 3.66279
Post Code: NL-4493 ZG

what3words:
alright.pill.taps

Contact:
reservation@rcn.eu
Tel: +31 850 400 700
www.rcn.nl

Open Dates:
Late March - Late October.

Key Features

- Book Online
- Pets allowed
- Accessible Facilities
- Seaside Beach Nearby
- Indoor Pool on Site
- Childrens Play Area
- Bar on Site
- Bicycle Hire on Site

Find Out More
Visit ar.camp/nl6924
or scan the QR code.

📍 **Retranchement, Zeeland**

Alan Rogers Ref: NL5502
Accommodations: 105
Pitches: 110
GPS: 51.36613, 3.38583
Post Code: NL-4525 LW

what3words:
undergrad.fairy.migrants

Contact:
info@cassandriabad.nl
Tel: +31 117 392 300
www.cassandriabad.nl

Open Dates:
Late March - Late October.

Camping Cassandria Bad

Cassandria Bad was established in 1992, lying very close to the Belgian border and the resort of Cadzand Bad, just under 2 km. from the nearest North Sea beach. Pitches are grassy and spacious; some are privately let for the entire season. All pitches are equipped with 10A electricity and free cable TV connections.

Cars are not allowed in the camping area except for loading and unloading, but a large parking area is provided. On-site amenities include a bar, snack bar, shop services and games room. During the peak season, various activities are organised, including karaoke, bingo and sports tournaments.

Two clean and well-maintained sanitary units with free showers and two family bathrooms in the main block. Good laundry facilities. Small shop (fresh bread daily). Bar with LCD projector and screen. Snack bar. Sports fields with volleyball and two football pitches. Games room with table football, air hockey and electronic games. Trampoline. Several well-appointed and interesting play areas, including an indoor play area. Multisport pitch, Entertainment team, Bicycle hire. WiFi over site (charged). One dog is allowed per pitch.

Key Features

🗓 Book Online

🐾 Pets allowed

🧗 Childrens Play Area

🍸 Bar on Site

🚲 Bicycle Hire on Site

Find Out More
Visit **ar.camp/nl5502**
or scan the QR code.

Vinkel, Noord-Brabant

Alan Rogers Ref: NL5880
Accommodations: 337
Pitches: 381
GPS: 51.70472, 5.43048
Post Code: NL-5382 JX

what3words:
possessive.coasts.careless

Contact:
receptie@dierenbos.nl
Tel: +31 735 343 536
www.dierenbos.nl

Open Dates:
Mid March - Late October.

Camping Dierenbos

Dierenbos is a large site with motel accommodation, a bungalow park, and approximately 700 pitches. These are divided into grassy areas, many in an attractive wooded setting. There are 381 pitches for touring units, all with electrical connections (4-10A) and some with full services (water and TV connection).

A small, landscaped lake has sandy beaches and is overlooked by a large, modern play area. Some of the touring pitches also overlook the water. Campers are entitled to free entry to several attractions. The varied amenities are located in and around a modern, central complex. They include heated outdoor swimming pools, an indoor sub-tropical pool with slide and jet stream, and a ten-pin bowling alley.

Eight toilet blocks are well situated with a mixture of clean and simple facilities (some unisex) with some warm water for washing and some individual washbasins. Accessible facilities, Baby room. Supermarket. Bar. Modern restaurant. Snack bar/takeaway (high season). Free outdoor heated swimming pools (seasonal). Indoor pool (on payment). Ten-pin bowling. Tennis. Minigolf. Boules. Sports field. Bicycle hire. Petting farm, Pedaloes. Fishing. Barbecue area. Play areas on sand. Many organised activities in season. Conference facilities. Max. 1 dog per pitch.

Key Features

- Book Online
- Pets allowed
- Accessible Facilities
- Indoor Pool on Site
- Childrens Play Area
- Bar on Site
- Bicycle Hire on Site
- Fishing on Site

Find Out More
Visit ar.camp/nl5880
or scan the QR code.

Panningen, Limburg

Alan Rogers Ref: NL6525
Accommodations: 29
Pitches: 370
GPS: 51.34897, 5.96101
Post Code: NL-5981 NX

what3words:
apartment.bagger.skipped

Contact:
info@beringerzand.nl
Tel: +31 773 072 095
www.beringerzand.nl

Open Dates:
All year.

Camping Beringerzand

The history of this friendly site dates back more than 100 years to when it was established as a holiday resort for members of the Lazarist religious congregation. The park and its historic building (now the Patershof restaurant) have, for the last 40 years, been developed as a holiday paradise for young families. Beringerzand is set amongst the lovely villages and small lakes of the wooded area between the De Peel Natural Park and the Muse River.

The 21-hectare site offers 370 spacious touring pitches, all with electricity (10A), TV, water and wastewater, arranged around the edges of green fields. There are currently also 130 privately owned chalets. The fields have been well-designed and include various activity areas appropriate to different age groups.

Four heated toilet blocks include bathrooms for children and a fully equipped launderette. Accessible facilities, Well stocked supermarket, bar, restaurant and takeaway (all open all season). Games and TV rooms. Indoor and outdoor swimming pools (not guarded). Minigolf. Pétanque. Adventure play areas. Football pitch, Table tennis, Bicycle hire. Small BMX track. Outdoor chess. Riding. Fishing. Children's club and evening entertainment. WiFi throughout (charged). Max. 2 dogs per pitch.

Key Features

- Book Online
- All Year
- Pets allowed
- Accessible Facilities
- Indoor Pool on Site
- Childrens Play Area
- Bar on Site
- Bicycle Hire on Site

Find Out More
Visit **ar.camp/nl6525**
or scan the QR code.

📍 **Valkenburg, Limburg**

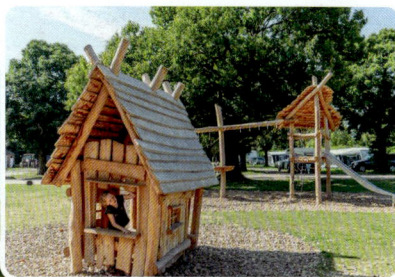

Alan Rogers Ref: NL6555
Accommodations: 68
Pitches: 340
GPS: 50.88063, 5.83349
Post Code: NL-6301 WP

what3words:
handing.wickets.corporate

Contact:
info@camping-debron.nl
Tel: +31 454 059 292
www.camping-valkenburg.com

Open Dates:
Start April- End December.

Camping Valkenberg-Maastricht

Camping Valkenburg - Maastricht is situated in Valkenburg, close to Recreatiepark De Valkenier and VVV Valkenburg. On-site, you can choose between 340 comfortable pitches, 255 for touring, which are nestled harmoniously with the surrounding nature. The on-site amenities include everything you would need to enjoy a holiday here, Featuring a bar with a terrace and a cosy lounge with table football. There is a food truck where you can enjoy some tasty treats and a small grocery shop selling all the basics.

Two fully renovated and heated swimming pools also await you for a well-deserved break. Less than 2km from the campsite you can discover Valkenburg and its many historical sites. Visit the ruins of the only hilltop castle in The Netherlands and the caves of Valkenburg. Want to relax and unwind? Head to the town's thermal baths.

Sanitary block with Children's facilities, Accessible facilities, Bar, Restaurant, Takeaway pizza (High season), Shop (Small), Multisport field, Children's playground (Small), Outdoor swimming pool, Games room, Television, Pets Allowed, and WiFi.

Key Features

📅 Book Online

🐾 Pets allowed

♿ Accessible Facilities

🏊 Outdoor Pool on Site

🛝 Childrens Play Area

🍸 Bar on Site

Find Out More
Visit **ar.camp/nl6555**
or scan the QR code.

Capital Oslo
Currency Norwegian Krone (NOK)
Language Norwegian
Time Zone CET (GMT+1)
Telephone Code +47
Emergency Number 110 Fire & Rescue, 112, Police, 113 Ambulance
Tourist Website visitnorway.com

Shops Hours vary throughout the year, with many shops operating shorter hours in low and shoulder seasons. In high season 10am to 5pm Mon to Sat and until 7pm on Thurs. Supermarkets 9am to 11pm Mon to Fri and until 10pm Sat.

Money ATMs are widespread and accessible 24hrs a day. Major cards are widely accepted. Largely cashless society though cash is still accepted in most places.

Travelling with children Norway is great for children. Attractions are often free for kids under 6 and discounted for those under 16.

Public Holidays 1 Jan New Year's Day; Mar/Apr Maundy Thursday; Mar/Apr Good Friday; Mar/Apr Easter Sunday; Mar/Apr Easter Monday; 1 May Labour Day; 2 Jun Constitution Day; May Ascension; May/Jun Whit Sunday; May/Jun Whit Monday; 25 Dec Christmas Day; 26 Dec Boxing Day.

Accessible Travel Score

Extremely well-equipped. Older buildings apapting, assistance given where access isn't easy, public transport is universally accessible except trams.

Driving in Norway Be prepared for long tunnels and hairpin bends. Some roads are closed to caravans. It may be necessary to use winter tyres with or without chains. Use dipped headlights during the day. Drink-driving and using a mobile whilst driving are illegal. Low Emission Zones are in place in Bergen, Kristiansand and Oslo, and all vehicles must pay a toll to enter (EVs are no longer exempt). The use of dashcams is legal, but speed camera detectors are not, so make sure to disable this feature on sat navs and mobile devices before entering the country.

Norway

View all campsites in Norway
ar.camp/norway

See campsite map page 486

Climate Winters are cold and snowy. Summers are warm, dry with 24hr daylight.

☀️
Avg. summer temp
12°C (N), 18°C (S)

🌧️
Wettest month
Oct (N), Aug (S)

A land full of contrasts, from magnificent snow-capped mountains, dramatic fjords, vast plateaux with wild, untamed tracts to huge lakes and rich green countryside. With nearly one-quarter of the land above the Arctic Circle, Norway has the lowest population density in Europe.

Norway is made up of five regions. In the heart of the eastern region, Oslo has everything one would expect from a major city and is the oldest of the Scandinavian capitals. The west coast boasts some of the world's most beautiful fjords, with plunging waterfalls and mountains.

In the heart of central Norway, Trondheim is a busy university town with many attractions, notably the Nidarosdomen Cathedral. The sunniest region is the south; its rugged coastline with white wooden cottages is popular with Norwegians and ideal for swimming, sailing and scuba diving.

The north is the Land of the Midnight Sun and the Northern Lights. It is home to the Sami, the indigenous people of Norway. The scenery varies from forested valleys and narrow fjords to icy tundra. Several cities are worth visiting, including Tromsø, with the Fjelheisen cable car, Polaria aquarium with bearded seals, and the Arctic Cathedral.

Scan QR code to browse more campsites on our website

📍 **Skibotn, Troms**

Alan Rogers Ref: NO2443
Accommodations: 11
Pitches: 90
GPS: 69.38057, 20.29574
Post Code: N-9143

what3words:
arranges.tenders.yoga

Contact:
firmapost@olderelv.no
Tel: +47 77 71 54 44
www.olderelv.no

Open Dates:
Mid May - Start September.

Olderelv Camping

Olderelv Camping is located in Skibotn, a village with a population of about 500 people. The town is approx. 110 km from Tromsø or 50 km from the border to Finland along E8 and the Northern Light Route. Olderelv Camping has been a quiet family-run site for almost 50 years and offers 90 touring pitches screened by pine trees. There are also 11 cabins available to hire.

Olderelv Camping is a great place to stay if you want a relaxing and scenic camping experience in Norway. The campsite is well-maintained and has a variety of amenities to make your stay comfortable. A café serves light meals, including home-baked cakes, freshly baked waffles and delicious coffee. There are also larger meals available, including pizza. You will find most essentials at the on-site shop to cook back at your pitch and freshly baked bread. In addition, they do sell some hiking equipment. There are plenty of activities to keep the younger guests active whilst staying on-site, with a nine-hole mini golf course and a children's playground to enjoy. For the older guests, there is a solarium with a sauna available when the water turns terrible.

Modern sanitary buildings with showers and sauna, laundry with washing machines and tumble dryer, Accessible shower and toilet, Communal kitchen with stoves, microwaves, dishwasher and dining area, Shop, Café, Mini Golf, Children's playground, WiFi, Pets allowed.

Key Features

🐾 Pets allowed

♿ Accessible Facilities

⚓ Seaside Beach Nearby

🧒 Childrens Play Area

🍸 Bar on Site

Find Out More
Visit **ar.camp/no2443**
or scan the QR code.

Kleppstad, Nordland

Alan Rogers Ref: NO2465
Accommodations: 10
Pitches: 165
GPS: 68.22481, 14.21661
Post Code: N-8313

what3words:
froth.brownish.weekend

Contact:
lofoten.bobilcamping@outlook.com
Tel: +47 76 07 77 78
www.lofoten-bobilcamping.no

Open Dates:
Start May - Late September.

Lyngvær Lofoten Bobilcamping

Lyngvær Lofoten Bobilcamping is located on the island of Austvågøy, just a short drive from the town of Svolvær, the largest town in the Lofoten Islands. This established site is very popular, with many customers returning for the well-maintained facilities and easy access to fishing and boating. The setting and location are pretty idyllic in the centre of Lofoten, alongside a tidal fjord with mountains all around.

Large terraces provide fine views for most of the 165 touring pitches, mainly on grass, some with hardstanding, all with 16A electricity. There are also cabins and rooms to rent at the site, all sleeping up to five people. Boat hire is available (canoes, rowing and motor boats), and the site has its own waters for salmon and trout fishing, which is free. The owners also bake their own bread and rolls to order.

Toilet facilities are spotless and cleaned regularly. Two heated sanitary units include showers in cubicles (on payment). Well-equipped motorhome service point. Two communal kitchens with cooking, sinks and fish freezer (free). BBQ area, Laundry facilities. Large sitting area with satellite TV. Play areas. Boat hire. Fishing (good fish cleaning area). Pets allowed, WiFi (free).

Key Features

🐾 Pets allowed

🧒 Childrens Play Area

🐟 Fishing on Site

⛵ Sailing on Site

Find Out More
Visit **ar.camp/no2465**
or scan the QR code.

📍 **Namsos, Nord-Trøndelag**

Alan Rogers Ref: NO2499
Accommodations: 31
Pitches: 54
GPS: 64.47531, 11.57898
Post Code: N-7805

what3words:
cakes.condense.waxer

Contact:
booking@namsos-camping.no
Tel: +47 74 27 53 44
www.namsos-camping.no

Open Dates:
All year.

Namsos Camping

Namsos Camping is located near teh outlet of the Namsen River, about a 5-minute car ride from the centre of Namsos. The site is in scenic surroundings, and the pitches are right next to the site's beach, some a little further away. The campsite has 54 touring pitches and 31 log cabins available to hire; 52 hardstanding pitches have 16 amp electric hook-ups. Water and wastewater drains are available on some of them.

Namsos Camping is committed to providing a family-friendly atmosphere, catering to the needs of both children and adults. The campsite features a well-equipped playground and mini-golf course, and fishing is available from the river's shores, providing activities for the whole family. After a day of exploring, Namsos Camping's shop offers access to essential supplies. Additionally, the campsite features a barbecue area where you can gather with friends and family and cook a delicious meal.

The heated toilet block has showers, washbasins, and WCs. Dishwashing area. Laundry with washing machine and dryer. Chemical toilet point. Motorhome service point. Defibrillator. Wi-Fi. Dogs, twin-axle caravans, and BBQs are allowed. Communal BBQ area. Children's play area. Mini golf, Microwave. Freezer for ice packs. Bread to order. Small shop (Seasonal) TV room. Games room. Electric car charging. Late-night arrivals area.

Key Features

📅 All Year

🐾 Pets allowed

🛝 Childrens Play Area

🐟 Fishing on Site

Find Out More
Visit **ar.camp/no2499**
or scan the QR code.

Åndalsnes, Møre og Romsdal

Alan Rogers Ref: NO2451
Accommodations: 20
Pitches: 93
GPS: 62.54474, 7.72150
Post Code: N-6300

what3words:
losses.method.slanting

Contact:
post@mjelvacamping.no
Tel: +47 71 22 64 50
www.mjelvacamping.no

Open Dates:
Start May - End September.

Mjelva Camping Og Hytter

Mjelva Camping Og Hytter has been a family-run site since 1964 in Nord-Fron, Norway. It is situated near the shore of the Mjølvatn lake, surrounded by stunning mountains and forests. The campsite had 93 pitches, 55 for touring, with 16 amp electric hook-up points available. There are also 20 cabins to rent. The campsite is a great place to relax and enjoy the outdoors. There are plenty of hiking, fishing, swimming, and boating opportunities. The campsite is also close to several other attractions, including the Jotunheimen National Park and the Rondane National Park.

The Mjølvatn lake is a popular fishing destination. There are a variety of fish species in the lake, including trout, salmon, and pike. You will also find a boat ramp nearby where you can rent boats or bring your own to explore the lake. Several activities are available on-site for the whole family, including a nine-hole mini golf course, giant chess set, children's playground and bicycle hire. There is also a communal BBQ area for those who want to cook their day's catch.

Sanitary block with accessible facilities, Laundry facilities, Washing up services, Daily bread service, limited shop, Own boats permitted, Fishing, Swimming, Bicycle rental, Mini golf, Children's playground, outdoor chess Communal BBQ area, Pets allowed, WiFi.

Key Features

- Pets allowed
- Accessible Facilities
- Childrens Play Area
- Bicycle Hire on Site
- Fishing on Site

Find Out More
Visit ar.camp/no2451
or scan the QR code.

📍 **Lærdal, Sogn og Fjordane**

Alan Rogers Ref: NO2375
Accommodations: 58
Pitches: 100
GPS: 61.10037, 7.46986
Post Code: N-6886

what3words:
spots.done.pulled

Contact:
info@laerdalferiepark.com
Tel: +47 57 66 66 95
www.laerdalferiepark.com

Open Dates:
Mid January - Mid December.

Lærdal Ferie & Fritidspark

This site is beside the famous Sognefjord, the longest fjord in the world. It is ideally situated if you want to explore the region's glaciers, fjords and waterfalls. The 100 pitches (all with 16A electricity) are level with well-trimmed grass, connected by tarmac roads are suitable for tents, caravans and motorhomes.

The fully licensed restaurant serves traditional, locally sourced meals, snacks, and pizzas. You can hire boats on the site for short trips on the fjord. Guided hiking, cycling, and fishing trips are also available, with waymarked cycling and walking trails running through the park. Climbing excursions can be arranged on request. The site also provides 29 traditional Norwegian cabins, flats and rooms to rent, plus a motel, all very modern and exceptionally tastefully designed.

Two modern and well-decorated sanitary blocks with washbasins (some in cubicles), showers on payment, and toilets. Accessible Facilities. Children's room. Washing machine and dryer. Kitchen. Motorhome services. Small shop, bar, restaurant and takeaway (all high season). TV room. Playground. Fishing. Motorboats, rowing boats, canoes, bicycles and pedal cars for hire. Go-kart sales. Free WiFi over site.

Key Features

🐾 Pets allowed

♿ Accessible Facilities

🛝 Childrens Play Area

🍸 Bar on Site

🚲 Bicycle Hire on Site

🐟 Fishing on Site

⛵ Sailing on Site

Find Out More
Visit **ar.camp/no2375**
or scan the QR code.

📍 Oslo, Østlandet

Bogstad Camping

Alan Rogers Ref: NO2581
Accommodations: 56
Pitches: 800
GPS: 59.96267, 10.64220
Post Code: N-0766

what3words:
lays.fans.chemistry

Contact:
bogstad@topcamp.no
Tel: +47 22 51 08 00
www.topcamp.no/topcamp-bogstad

Open Dates:
All year.

Located in the pleasant suburbs about 15 minutes from central Oslo, TopCamp Bogstad is an attractive all-year campsite to use as a base for exploring the historic city. Bogstad is Norway's largest campsite, with about 800 pitches, 300 of which are touring pitches with electric hook-up points available, and 38 are fully serviced.Located right next to a lake and golf course, it's easy to relax at this site if you need a break from city life. A bus service frequently serves the campsite, so there is no need to tackle parking in the city centre.

Bogstad campsite offers guests a blend of convenience and recreational opportunities, with two well-maintained sanitary facilities, a communal kitchen, and a volleyball court. A charming children's village with a playground and a bouncy castle provides endless hours of entertainment for families with children. There is a five-minute walk to the idyllic Bogstadvannet lake, with a beach and a swimming pier.

Two sanitary blocks, Accessible sanitary facilities, Dogs permitted. WiFi Hotspot. Laundry with washing machine, dryer and iron. Gas exchange. Communal BBQ area. Communal kitchen, Pizza and takeaway are available. Good shop. Children's playground. Volleyball, Crazy Golf.

Key Features

📅 All Year

🐾 Pets allowed

♿ Accessible Facilities

🛝 Childrens Play Area

Find Out More
Visit ar.camp/no2581
or scan the QR code.

Haugesund, Rogaland

Alan Rogers Ref: NO2656
Accommodations: 15
Pitches: 100
GPS: 59.42788, 5.25850
Post Code: N-5515

what3words:
agenda.curious.dissolve

Contact:
booking@hhcamping.no
Tel: +47 52 72 80 77
www.hhcamping.com

Open Dates:
All year.

Haraldshaugen Camping

Haraldshaugen Camping is an attractive campsite with fantastic sea views and interesting historic surroundings, yet only 2km from the centre of Haugesund. The site is large, with 100 touring pitches available, 37 of which are hardstanding, and there is accommodation available to hire. The site offers hardstanding caravan/motorhome pitches and pitches on grass, which are more suited to tents.

Several cabins on site are free to use, including one made up of glass, giving an appealing panoramic view over the bay. A house with a communal fire and a TV lounge/dining room is a great place to enjoy a meal prepared in the communal kitchen. They are perfect for when the weather draws in, and all can be accessed by requesting a key from reception. There is also a small children's playground and a giant chess set available to use.

Heated Sanitary block with individual showers and toilets, Laundry facilities, washing up area, Communal kitchen with TV and sofas, Communal room with fire, Children's playground, Giant chess, Fishing nearby, Pets allowed, WiFi.

Key Features

📅 All Year

⛱ Seaside Beach Nearby

🛝 Childrens Play Area

Find Out More
Visit **ar.camp/no2656**
or scan the QR code.

Lillesand, Aust-Agder

Tingsaker Familiecamping

Tingsaker Family Camping has been a family-run site since 1935, now run by the father and son. The campsite is located in the middle of Norway, 5 minutes walk from the town of Lillesand. You will find 150 touring pitches on site, all with electric hook-up points situated 150 metres from the beach, giving great sea views from every pitch, making this site a relaxing and enjoyable stay.

For those looking for activities to do whilst staying here, there are plenty of options for all ages; there is the free rental of kayaks and paddle boards and a jumping pillow and play area for the kids. Plenty of restaurants and supermarkets are within walking distance, but you can find a small shop on-site to grab your necessities. During high season, you will also find a snack bar on site with takeaway pizza.

Modern toilet block with accessible facilities, Shop, Laundry area, Snack bar and pizzeria during high season, Communal BBQ area, Communal kitchen area, Free rental of kayaks, paddleboards and canoes, Sailing, Fishing, Children's play area, Jumping pillow, Beach and sea swimming, WiFi, Pets allowed.

Alan Rogers Ref: NO2599
Accommodations: 16
Pitches: 150
GPS: 58.25629, 8.38956
Post Code: N-4790

what3words:
investors.trailer.devotion

Contact:
post@tingsakercamping.no
Tel: +47 37 27 04 21
www.tingsakercamping.no

Open Dates:
Start May - Start September.

Key Features

- Pets allowed
- Accessible Facilities
- Seaside Beach on Site
- Childrens Play Area
- Fishing on Site

Find Out More
Visit **ar.camp/no2599**
or scan the QR code.

Capital Lisbon
Currency Euro (€)
Language Portuguese
Time Zone GMT
Telephone Code +351
Emergency Number 112
Tourist Website visitportugal.com

Shops Hours vary throughout the year, with many shops operating shorter hours in low and shoulder seasons. In high season 9.30am to noon and 2pm to 7pm Mon to Fri. 10am to 1pm Sat.

Money ATMs are widespread, are accessible 24hrs a day and most have multilingual instructions. Major cards are accepted in some places but cash is still the most popular way to pay.

Travelling with children Portugal has a lot to offer children. Lisbon has a good choice of attractions. The Algarve is one of the best destinations for kids with its long sandy beaches, zoos, water parks and boat trips.

Public Holidays 1 Jan New Year's Day; Mar/Apr Good Friday; Mar/Apr Easter Sunday; 25 Apr Liberation Day; 1 May Labour Day; 10 Jun National Day; May/Jun Corpus Christi; 15 Aug Assumption; 5 Oct Republic Day; 1 Nov All Saints; 1 Dec Independence Restoration Day; 8 Dec Immaculate Conception; 25 Dec Christmas Day.

Accessible Travel Score

Access is improving. All public buildings provide level access. Some public transport is accessible though there is no universal standard.

Driving in Portugal The standard of roads is very variable; even some of the main roads can be very uneven. Tolls are levied on some auto-estradas. An electronic tag called Via Verde can be purchased for repeat trips. Drink-driving and using a mobile whilst driving are illegal. Parked vehicles must face the same direction as moving traffic. Lisbon has implemented a Low Emission Zone, which affects all vehicles (excl EVs). The use of dashcams and speed camera detectors is illegal, make sure to disable the latter on sat navs and mobile devices before you enter the country.

EU Member | Schengen Area

Portugal

View all campsites in Portugal
ar.camp/portugal

See campsite map page 484

Climate Hot summers and mild winters with varying rainfall between north/south.

☀ **Avg. summer temp**
23°C

🌧 **Wettest month**
December

Portugal is the westernmost country of Europe, situated on the Iberian peninsula, bordered by Spain in the north and east, with the Atlantic coast in the south and west. Despite its relatively small size, the country offers a tremendous variety, both in its way of life and its history and traditions.

Every year the Algarve is the destination for some ten million sunseekers and watersports enthusiasts who love its sheltered sandy beaches and clear Atlantic sea. In contrast, central Portugal's lush hills and forests are home to historic buildings and monuments, particularly the capital city of Lisbon, adjacent to the estuary of the River Tagus. Lisbon's history can still be seen in the Alfama quarter, which survived the devastating earthquake of 1755;

at night, the city comes alive with vibrant cafés, restaurants and discos.

The land becomes rather impoverished to the southeast of Lisbon, consisting of stretches of vast undulating plains dominated by cork plantations. Most people head for Evora, a medieval walled town and UNESCO World Heritage Site. The Minho area in the north is said to be the most beautiful part of Portugal, home to the country's only National Park and vineyards producing the famous Port wine.

Scan QR code to browse more campsites on our website

📍 Campo do Gerês, Braga

Alan Rogers Ref: PO8370
Accommodations: 16
Pitches: 200
GPS: 41.76310, -8.19050
Post Code: P-4840-030

what3words:
dethrone.hotness.sunflower

Contact:
info@parquecerdeira.com
Tel: +351 253 351 005
www.parquecerdeira.com

Open Dates:
All year.

 **Alan Rogers Awards Won**
2018

Parque Cerdeira

Located in the Peneda-Gerês National Park amidst spectacular mountain scenery, this excellent, well-run site offers modern facilities in a truly natural area. The national park is home to all manner of flora, fauna and wildlife, including the roebuck, wolf and wild boar. There's plenty of scope in the immediate area for fishing, riding, canoeing, mountain biking and climbing, so outdoorsy types take advantage of the quality mountain hospitality and enjoy the clear, fresh air and activities amidst the dramatic scenery.

The well-fenced, peaceful site offers 200 good-sized, unmarked, mostly level, grassy pitches in a shady woodland setting. Electricity (5/10A) is available for the touring pitches, though some long leads may be required. A large timber complex, tastefully designed with granite and wood - provides a superb restaurant with a comprehensive menu. A pool with a separated section for toddlers is a welcome cooling relief in the height of summer.

Three clean, sanitary blocks provide mixed-style WCs, controllable showers and hot water. Good accessible facilities. Laundry. Gas supplies. Shop. Restaurant/bar. Outdoor pool (High season). Playground. TV room (satellite). Medical post. Good tennis courts. Minigolf. Adventure park. Car wash. Barbecue areas. Torches useful. English spoken. Attractive bungalows to rent. WiFi in reception/bar area.

Key Features

📅 Book Online

📅 All Year

🐾 Pets allowed

♿ Accessible Facilities

🏊 Outdoor Pool on Site

🛝 Childrens Play Area

🍸 Bar on Site

🚲 Bicycle Hire on Site

Find Out More
Visit **ar.camp/po8370**
or scan the QR code.

📍 **Bragança, Trás-os-Montes**

Cepo Verde

Parque de Campismo Cepo Verde is a quiet and family-oriented campsite with an extraordinary landscape within the Montesinho National Park. Its beautiful surroundings make it an ideal site for keen hikers, with clearly marked walking trails nearby and maps available from reception. The site has around 40 touring pitches with 6 amp electric hook-up points available. Choose to rest your head at this peaceful and tranquil site, and you will be treated to quiet pitches in the open woods, shaded by impressive chestnut, cherry and oak trees.

The restaurant specialises in affordable regional dishes such as wild boar, local cheeses and a tasty chestnut pudding, making it the perfect place to gather and dine with family and friends. A bus service operates from just outside the site, taking you to nearby Bragança with its impressive medieval castle, or take a drive to the stunning Azibo lake and take a dip or soak up the sun on its beaches.

Toilet block with showers and wash basins. Accessible facilities. Laundry. Late arrivals area, without electric hook-up. Motorhome service point. Bar. Restaurant. Swimming pool. Children's play area. Takeaway. WiFi charged. Pets welcome. BBQs are not permitted on pitches. BBQ point. Supermarket 8 kilometres. Chalets are available to rent.

Alan Rogers Ref: PO8391
Accommodations: 11
Pitches: 42
GPS: 41.84612, -6.86033
Post Code: P-5300-516

what3words:
inland.dinky.lawn

Contact:
cepoverde@montesinho.com
Tel: +351 273 999 371
www.montesinho.com

Open Dates:
Start March - End October.

Key Features

🗓 Book Online

🐾 Pets allowed

♿ Accessible Facilities

🏊 Outdoor Pool on Site

🛝 Childrens Play Area

🍸 Bar on Site

Find Out More
Visit ar.camp/po8391
or scan the QR code.

📍 **Angeiras/Lavra, Porto**

Camping Angeiras

A pleasant little seaside village, Angeiras has a good beach with the occasional restaurant and bar, several shops and a small supermarket. The campsite is close to the heart of the village and is probably the most attractive Orbitur site we have visited. It is well kept, and pitches are under trees, separated by neatly trimmed hedges. Manoeuvring larger units might be tricky in places, but some areas are not marked where you can find a spot under pine trees or in the open. There is space for some 404 touring units among the many seasonal caravans. Electrical connections (6A) are available throughout.

A drive along the coast road will take you to more beaches and other villages, or you can take the motorway, toll-free, to Porto. Alternatively, a regular bus service from the campsite gates gets to the city centre in an hour and a quarter.

Three toilet blocks, one recently reconstructed and a second refurbished, are kept very clean: hot water to preset showers but cold water to open-style washbasins. Baby rooms. En-suite accessible units. Washing machines and dryer. Motorhome service point. Small supermarket (High season, basic supplies in reception other times). Pleasant bar and an excellent restaurant (all year, popular with locals). Swimming and paddling pools (Seasonal). Multisports courts. Sports field. Minigolf. Lounge with TV. Play area. Chalets and mobile homes to rent. WiFi in the reception area (free).

Alan Rogers Ref: PO8033
Accommodations: 98
Pitches: 404
GPS: 41.26718, -8.71996
Post Code: P-4455-039

what3words:
titles.mountaineer.liberally

Contact:
infoangeiras@orbitur.pt
Tel: +351 229 270 571
www.orbitur.pt

Open Dates:
All year.

Key Features

🗓 All Year

🐾 Pets allowed

♿ Accessible Facilities

⛱ Seaside Beach Nearby

🏊 Outdoor Pool on Site

🛝 Childrens Play Area

🍸 Bar on Site

Find Out More
Visit **ar.camp/po8033**
or scan the QR code.

Arganil, Coimbra

Camping Arganil

This peaceful inland site is attractively located on the edge of the village of Sarzedo, some three kilometres from the town of Arganil. It is on a hill among pine trees above the River Alva, where you can paddle, fish or canoe. A spacious and well-planned site, it is of high quality for a municipal, and prices are very reasonable. There are no marked pitches, but young trees define where you can park, and there is space for about 120 units, mainly on a flat, sandy grass terrace. There are 75 electrical connections (5-15A). The site is beautifully clean and neat, and access roads are tarmac.

Below the campsite, with gated access from the site via a steepish path and steps, is a municipal swimming pool, a tennis court and a riverside terrace/beach. From the site, you look across at the hill-top village of Sarzedo with its interesting church, and a ten-minute walk takes you to its highly recommended restaurant and bar. Down the road is the pleasant little town of Arganil, with several shops, bars and restaurants, a bank and a post office.

Sanitary facilities are clean and well maintained, with controllable hot showers, washbasins (mainly cold water) in semi-private partitioned cabins and a hairdressing area. Note: the block is on the edge of the top terrace, and access from the lower part is via steps or a brisk walk. Accessible facilities, Shop (July-Sept). Bar. Washing machines. TV and leisure room. WiFi over part of the site (free).

Alan Rogers Ref: PO8330
Accommodations: 5
Pitches: 120
GPS: 40.24165, -8.06772
Post Code: P-3300-432

what3words:
supermarket.nieces.snug

Contact:
camping@cm-arganil.pt
Tel: +351 235 205 706
www.visitarganil.pt

Open Dates:
Start March - End October.

Key Features

- Pets allowed
- Accessible Facilities
- Indoor Pool on Site
- Bar on Site
- Bicycle Hire on Site

Find Out More
Visit **ar.camp/po8330**
or scan the QR code.

📍 **Marinha Grande, Leiria**

Alan Rogers Ref: PO8100
Accommodations: 102
Pitches: 400
GPS: 39.75810, -9.02583
Post Code: P-2430-532

what3words:
loonies.sobered.midwinter

Contact:
infospedro@orbitur.pt
Tel: +351 244 599 168
orbitur.pt/en/destinations/
region-center

Open Dates:
All Year.

🏅 **Alan Rogers Awards Won**
2013

Camping São Pedro de Moel

This very attractive and well-kept site is situated under tall pines on the edge of the rather select, small resort of São Pedro de Moel. It is a shady and peaceful place in low season but can be crowded in July and August. There is space for some 400 touring units, including a few small marked pitches; otherwise you choose a place between the trees in one of two large camping areas; one has plentiful 6/10A electrical connections, the other a very limited provision.

A few pitches are used for permanent units, and an area to one side has 120 chalets and mobile homes, mostly for hire. The attractive, sandy beach is a short walk downhill from the site (you can take the car, although parking may be difficult in the town) and is sheltered from the wind by low cliffs.

Four clean toilet blocks (not all opened in low season) have mainly British-style toilets, hot showers and mainly open-style washbasins (some with hot water). Accessible facilities, Washing machines and dryer. Motorhome services. Gas supplies. Simple shop (Seasonal). Supermarket, restaurant and bar with terrace (High season). Excellent pool complex with paddling pool and large slide (High season). Satellite TV. Games room. Playground. Tennis. Table tennis, WiFi in some areas (free).

Key Features

📅 All Year

🐾 Pets allowed

♿ Accessible Facilities

⛱ Seaside Beach Nearby

🏊 Outdoor Pool on Site

🛝 Childrens Play Area

🍸 Bar on Site

Find Out More
Visit **ar.camp/po8100**
or scan the QR code.

Cascais, Lisbon

Camping Guincho

Attractively laid out among low pine trees, some twisted by the wind into interesting shapes, Orbitur Camping Guincho is located behind dunes and a wide, sandy beach. With a railway and motorway connection to Lisbon, the site provides a good base for combining a seaside holiday with a sightseeing visit to Portugal's fascinating capital.

There is space for over 400 touring units alongside seasonal pitches and rental accommodation. They are generally small, although larger units can be accommodated. Manoeuvring amongst the trees may be tricky, particularly when the site is full. Electrical connections (6A) are available throughout. Cascais is an interesting seaside town with plenty of shops, supermarkets, bars and restaurants.

Three sanitary blocks, one refurbished, are in the older style and could do with some refurbishment, but they are clean and tidy. Open-style washbasins with cold water but hot showers. Accessible Facilities. Washing machines and dryers. Motorhome services. Gas. Supermarket. Bar with excellent restaurant and takeaway (all year). Terrace. Swimming pool (Seasonal). General room with TV. Tennis. Playground. Entertainment in summer. WiFi on part of the site (free). Chalets to rent.

Alan Rogers Ref: PO8130
Accommodations: 71
Pitches: 400
GPS: 38.72117, -9.46667
Post Code: P-2750-053

what3words:
stopped.disables.extends

Contact:
infoguincho@orbitur.pt
Tel: +351 214 870 450
orbitur.pt/en/destinations/
region-lisboa/orbitur-guincho

Open Dates:
All year.

Alan Rogers Awards Won
2017

Key Features

- Book Online
- All Year
- Pets allowed
- Accessible Facilities
- Seaside Beach Nearby
- Outdoor Pool on Site
- Childrens Play Area
- Bar on Site

Find Out More
Visit **ar.camp/po8130**
or scan the QR code.

📍 Lisboa, Lisbon

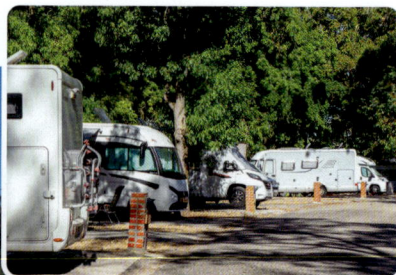

Alan Rogers Ref: PO8140
Accommodations: 70
Pitches: 189
GPS: 38.72477, -9.20737
Post Code: P-1400-061

what3words:
cake.elevator.sticky

Contact:
info@lisboacamping.com
Tel: +351 217 628 200
www.lisboacamping.com

Open Dates:
All year.

Lisboa Camping & Bungalows

Arriving at this large site in the suburbs of Lisbon, first impressions are good. Beyond the wide entrance with its ponds and fountains, the trees, lawns and flowering shrubs lead to the attractive swimming pool area. Positive impressions continue: on sloping ground, the site's many terraces are well shaded by trees and shrubs, and all 189 touring pitches are on concrete hardstandings with grass and a picnic table. All have 10A electricity connections, water and a drain.

There is a huge separate area for tents, and 70 chalet-style bungalows are for rent. Central Lisbon is easily reached by bus with a regular service from near the gate. There are shops, bars and restaurants in the immediate vicinity, but most people probably prefer to hop on a bus and go into Lisbon.

Eight solar-powered toilet blocks are well equipped and kept clean, although in need of some refurbishment. Controllable showers and hot water to open-style washbasins. Accessible Facilities. Launderette. Motorhome services. Shop, bar and self-service restaurant with takeaway (all year). Swimming and paddling pools (lifeguard June-Sept). Tennis. Minigolf. Sports field. Playgrounds. Entertainment in high season. Games and TV rooms. Booking service for excursions. WiFi in the restaurant area (free).

Key Features

📅 All Year

🐾 Pets allowed

♿ Accessible Facilities

⛱ Seaside Beach Nearby

🏊 Outdoor Pool on Site

🧒 Childrens Play Area

🍸 Bar on Site

Find Out More
Visit **ar.camp/po8140**
or scan the QR code.

Campo Maior, Portalegre

Alan Rogers Ref: PO8356
Accommodations: 1
Pitches: 30
GPS: 39.00833, -7.04838
Post Code: P-7371-909

what3words:
swelling.lighter.ribs

Contact:
info@campingosanjos.com
Tel: +351 268 688 138
www.campingosanjos.com

Open Dates:
All year.

Camping Rural Os Anjos

This really is rural Portugal. Set in rolling countryside in a working olive grove, Os Anjos (The Angels) is an ideal spot from which to explore this lesser-known corner of the Alentejo. The white fortified town of Campo Maior is within walking distance, and the historic city of Elvas, now a UNESCO World Heritage Site, is a short drive away.

Solange and Joris will provide a warm welcome and as much advice as you need on where to go on foot, by bike or by car, with appropriate route sheets. The site has 30 terraced pitches accessed by a circular track, with twelve electrical connections (6A) available.

The central toilet block has preset showers, some washbasins in cubicles with hot and cold water, and an accessible unit(which is heated and available to all in winter). Note: the terrain generally might cause problems for wheelchair users. Small bar with seating on the terrace and in the reception lounge. Pleasant little swimming pool with an attractively equipped terrace. Boules. Bicycle hire. Barbecue evening on Fridays (BYO meat). WiFi throughout (charged).

Key Features

- All Year
- Pets allowed
- Accessible Facilities
- Outdoor Pool on Site
- Bar on Site
- Bicycle Hire on Site

Find Out More
Visit **ar.camp/po8356**
or scan the QR code.

Porto Covo, Setúbal

Alan Rogers Ref: PO8159
Accommodations: 28
Pitches: 100
GPS: 37.85649, -8.78720
Post Code: P-7520-437

what3words:
undertaken.cleverer.rationality

Contact:
info@costadovizir.com
Tel: +351 269 959 100
www.costadovizir.com

Open Dates:
All year.

Camping Costa do Vizir

Picture beautiful beaches, warm sunshine and the Atlantic stretching away into the distance. It really is appealing, and Costa Do Vizir is the perfect spot for a family-friendly holiday. Located in Porto Covo on the west coast of Portugal, this site has an aquatic area, a beach a few metres away, varied activities, top-end accommodation and high-quality facilities. There is an exceptional fine dining restaurant on-site, and you will find the site's other restaurant on the beach, where you can watch the sunset.

There are over 100 hardstanding or grass touring pitches, each with a 6 amp electric hook-up point, as well as several chalets and apartments available to hire.

Three toilet blocks provide showers, wash basins and WCs. Laundry. Accessible facilities. Chemical toilet point. Motor home service point. An aquatic area with a swimming pool, children's pool and solarium. Varied activities on-site for people of all ages. Kids' Club. Outdoor fitness, health trail. Children's play area. Shop. Restaurant serving traditional and authentic dishes. Snack bar and takeaway. Bar. Bread. TV room. Tennis court. Cycle hire. Library. Communal BBQ area. Multi-sport pitch. Fitness equipment. WiFi free.

Key Features

- Book Online
- All Year
- Pets allowed
- Accessible Facilities
- Seaside Beach Nearby
- Indoor Pool on Site
- Childrens Play Area
- Bicycle Hire on Site

Find Out More
Visit **ar.camp/po8159**
or scan the QR code.

Albufeira, Faro

Camping Albufeira

Here's a charming, well-run site, close to bustling Faro and with a bus service to the resort of Albufeira from the gate. There's space for 1400 touring units on generally flat ground with some terracing on the upper area and trees and shrubs giving reasonable shade in most parts. Pitches are not marked or numbered; you can take as much space as you wish. Electrical connections (10A) are available throughout. Winter stays are encouraged, including a pool and the main facilities remaining open.

An attractively designed complex of traditional Portuguese-style buildings on the hill houses an impressive range of restaurants and bars with the popular pool complex adjacent. It has large sunbathing terraces with pleasant views and is surrounded by a variety of flowers, shrubs and well-watered lawns, complete with a fountain.

Very clean and spacious toilet blocks include hot showers and open-style washbasins (hot water to some). Accessible facilities, Launderette. Motorhome services. Very large supermarket. Kiosk (English papers). Waiter and self-service restaurants. Pizzeria. Bars. The main facilities are open all year. Swimming pools. Satellite TV. Soundproofed disco. Tennis. Playground. Bicycle hire. WiFi over part of the site (charged). First aid post with a doctor nearby. Car wash. ATM. Car hire.

Alan Rogers Ref: PO8210
Accommodations: 28
Pitches: 1400
GPS: 37.10639, -8.25361
Post Code: P-8200-555

what3words:
limped.dishing.variety

Contact:
geral@campingalbufeira.net
Tel: +351 289 587 629
www.campingalbufeira.pt/en

Open Dates:
All year.

Key Features

- All Year
- Pets allowed
- Accessible Facilities
- Seaside Beach Nearby
- Outdoor Pool on Site
- Childrens Play Area
- Bar on Site
- Bicycle Hire on Site

Find Out More
Visit ar.camp/po8210
or scan the QR code.

📍 Lagos, Faro

Alan Rogers Ref: PO8202
Accommodations: 139
Pitches: 240
GPS: 37.10111, -8.73278
Post Code: P-8600-109

what3words:
discuss.blogged.reintroduce

Contact:
info@turiscampo.com
Tel: +351 282 789 265
www.turiscampo.com

Open Dates:
All year.

Alan Rogers Awards Won
2022, 2019, 2016

Turiscampo Algarve

Yelloh! Village Turiscampo is an outstanding site run by the friendly Coll family. The site provides 240 pitches for touring units, mainly in rows of terraces, 216 of which have 6/10A electricity, some with shade. There are 75 deluxe pitches with water and drainage. One hundred thirty-eight bungalows for rent occupy the upper terraces.

Turiscampo boasts an impressive array of swimming pools. The centrepiece is the expansive California swimming pool complex, surrounded by a sun-kissed terrace and a lively bar, where refreshing drinks are served. The indoor heated pool offers warmth and relaxation, while the children's pool ensures endless fun for the little ones. Turiscampo pampers its guests with a host of wellness amenities. There is a modern gym, sauna and hammam. There is also a range of beauty treatments available.

Two excellent heated toilet blocks with a third facility beneath the pool. Spacious, controllable showers, hot water throughout. Children & baby room. Accessible Facilities. Dog shower. Laundry facilities. Shop. Gas supplies. Modern restaurant/bar with buffet & some theme party dinners. Pizza bar & takeaway. Swimming pools (All year) with extensive terrace and jacuzzi. Aquagym. Wellness facility. Bicycle hire. Entertainment on the bar terrace. Miniclub. Two playgrounds. Boules. Archery. Multisports court, WiFi (Partial coverage) on payment.

Key Features

- Book Online
- All Year
- Pets allowed
- Accessible Facilities
- Seaside Beach Nearby
- Indoor Pool on Site
- Childrens Play Area
- Bar on Site

Find Out More
Visit **ar.camp/po8202**
or scan the QR code.

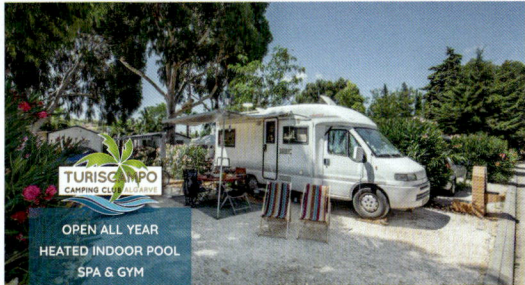

Lagos - Algarve | yelloh! VILLAGE | LeadingCampings | www.turiscampo.com

TURISCAMPO
CAMPING CLUB ALGARVE
OPEN ALL YEAR
HEATED INDOOR POOL
SPA & GYM

alan rogers

ABTA
Travel with confidence

Need a campsite for tonight?

Need inspiration at short notice?
Been let down or disappointed by your
original choice of campsite?

Find out more at
ar.camp/near-me

We can help you find campsites near you
and get you on your way. In most corners of
Europe, there are campsites situated close by.

We'll show you the campsites closest to your
current location based on the shortest distance
as the crow flies. Use the filters to narrow your
campsite choice further.

Capital Ljubljana
Currency Euro (€)
Language Slovene
Time Zone CET (GMT+1)
Telephone Code +386
Emergency Number 112
Tourist Website slovenia.info

Shops Hours vary throughout the year, with many shops operating shorter hours in low and shoulder seasons. In high season 8am to 7pm Mon to Fri, and until 1pm Sat.

Money ATMs are widespread and accessible 24hrs a day. Major cards widely accepted. If you're paying in cash, many businesses won't accept large denominations (over €50) for smaller purchases.

Travelling with children Great during the summer months. Most regions have castles that children will love exploring. Some attractions offer free entry for minors. Most restaurants cater for children.

Public Holidays 1 Jan New Year's Day; 8 Feb Prešeren Day; Mar/Apr Easter Sunday; Mar/Apr Easter Monday; 27 Apr Resistence Day; 1 May May Day; May/Jun Whit Sunday; 25 Jun National Day; 15 Aug Assumption; 31 Oct Reformation Day; 1 Nov All Saints; 25 Dec Christmas Day; 26 Dec Independence & Unity Day.

Accessible Travel Score

Very well-equipped. Public transport and buildings are fully accessible and car parks have reserved spaces.

Driving in Slovenia You must display a vignette as proof of payment to use motorways. You shouldn't indicate when entering a roundabout but must do so when leaving one. Winter driving equipment is mandatory between November and March. Headlights must be on at all times. Drink-driving and using a mobile whilst driving are illegal. There are no Low Emission Zones in place. The use of dashcams and speed camera detectors is legal, however use of the latter is advised against, so you may want to consider disabling the feature on sat navs and mobile devices before entering the country.

Slovenia

View all campsites in Slovenia
ar.camp/slovenia

See campsite map page 474

Climate Warm summers with occassional rain and cold, sometimes snowy winters.

☀
Avg. summer temp
22°C

🌧
Wettest month
September

What Slovenia lacks in size, it makes up for in exceptional beauty. Situated between Italy, Austria, Hungary and Croatia, it has a diverse landscape; mountains, rivers, forests and the warm Adriatic coast.

Mount Triglav is at the heart of the snow-capped Julian Alps, a paradise for lovers of the great outdoors, with hiking, rafting, and mountaineering opportunities. From the Alps down to the Adriatic coast, the Karst region is home to the famous Lipizzaner horses, vineyards and myriad underground caves, including the Postojna and Skocjan Caves.

The tiny Adriatic coast has several bustling beach towns, including Koper, Slovenia's only commercial port, whose 500 years of Venetian rule is evident in its Italianate style. Ljubljana, one of Europe's smallest capitals with beautiful baroque buildings, lies on the Ljubljanica river, spanned by numerous bridges, including Jože Plečnik's triple bridge.

Heading eastwards, the hilly landscape is dotted with monasteries, churches and castles, including the 13th-century Zuzemberk castle, one of Slovenia's most picturesque. The old city and castle sit alongside a thriving commercial centre. The Posavje region produces cviček, a famous blend of white and red wines.

Scan QR code to browse more campsites on our website

Ptuj, Slovenia

Alan Rogers Ref: SV4440
Accommodations: 23
Pitches: 120
GPS: 46.42268, 15.85495
Post Code: SLO-2251

what3words:
untruth.fixate.rulers

Contact:
info@terme-ptuj.si
Tel: +386 2749 4100
www.sava-camping.com

Open Dates:
All year.

Camping Terme Ptuj

Camping Terme Ptuj is close to the river, just outside the interesting town of Ptuj. It is a small site with around 120 level pitches, all for tourers and all with 10A electricity. The pitches to the left are part grass and gravel hardstanding in two areas and are mainly used for motorhomes. The pitches on the right-hand side are on grass under mature trees, off a circular, gravel access road. The main attraction of this site is the adjacent thermal spa and fun pool complex, attracting many local visitors.

The swimming complex consists of indoor and outdoor pools, giant slides, a wave pool, a slow-flow river pool, a children's pool and two whirlpools. The swimming pools and saunas are free for campsite guests. For children, activities are organised throughout the day: sports tournaments, swimming lessons, creative workshops and educational discovery courses. A mini golf course, multisport pitch and tennis courts are also at the complex next door. The restaurant at the Thermal Park serves local and international dishes; you can also grab an ice cream and pizza here.

Modern toilet block with British-style toilets, open washbasins and controllable, hot showers (free). En-suite accessible facilities with toilet and basin. Two washing machines. Resturant, Bar, Football field, Multsisport pitch, Tennis, Entertainment, Torch useful.

Key Features

Book Online

All Year

Pets allowed

Accessible Facilities

Childrens Play Area

Find Out More
Visit **ar.camp/sv4440**
or scan the QR code.

Dolenjske Toplice, Slovenia

Kamp Polje

Kamp Polje is a small modern campsite nestled amidst the picturesque landscape of Meniška Vas, Slovenia. It's situated at the junction of the Krka River and Sušica Stream, just 1.5 km from the renowned Dolenjske Toplice spa town. This is an ideal destination for campers seeking a relaxing retreat in the heart of Slovenia. Established in 2018, Kamp Polje boasts a well-maintained campground with 16 spacious pitches equipped with electricity and water connections.

Kamp Polje's commitment to sustainability is evident in its eco-friendly practices. The campsite utilises solar energy to power its facilities and encourages recycling among guests. Nearby is a public outdoor swimming pool perfect for cooling off in the summer. Visitors can embark on scenic hikes through the nearby forests, explore the picturesque village of Meniška Vas, or delve into the rich history of Dolenjske Toplice.

Modern sanitary facilities featuring separate male and female toilet blocks with ample showers, sinks, and mirrors. Accessible facilities, Motorhome services. A dedicated washing-up area, Communal seating area, Recycling, Fishing Kayaking, WiFi, Pets allowed.

Alan Rogers Ref: SV4435
Pitches: 16
GPS: 45.76800, 15.05132
Post Code: SLO-8350

what3words:
brawn.squashes.contest

Contact:
info@kamp-polje.si
Tel: +386 4046 6589
www.kamp-polje.si

Open Dates:
Mid April - Start November.

Key Features

🐾 Pets allowed

♿ Accessible Facilities

🚲 Bicycle Hire on Site

🐟 Fishing on Site

Find Out More
Visit **ar.camp/sv4435**
or scan the QR code.

📍 Postojna, Slovenia

Alan Rogers Ref: SV4330
Accommodations: 24
Pitches: 300
GPS: 45.79068, 14.19092
Post Code: SLO-6230

what3words:
grilled.purifies.accredited

Contact:
avtokamp.pivka.jama@siol.net
Tel: +386 5720 3993
www.camping-postojna.com

Open Dates:
Mid April - Late October.

Camping Pivka Jama

Camping Pivka Jama is a tranquil campsite nestled amidst a picturesque spruce forest in the heart of Slovenia's Notranjska region. Just a stone's throw from the captivating entrance of Pivka Cave, one of the country's prime tourist attractions. Staff at reception can arrange day trip excursions to the Postojna Caves for a fascinating insight into their formation. The campsite's 300 pitches are well dispersed amongst the trees and in small clearings, all connected by a neat network of paths and slip roads. Some level, gravel hard standings are provided.

The Pivka Cave is adjacent to the campsite restaurant, which serves traditional Slovenian cuisine, offering a taste of the region's culinary heritage. There are several activities to engage in at Camping Pivka Jama. A refreshing outdoor swimming pool provides a welcome respite on hot summer days, while a separate children's pool ensures fun-filled splashes for little ones. A multi-purpose sports field caters to sports enthusiasts, while bicycles are available for rent, allowing visitors to explore the countryside at their own pace.

Two toilet blocks with very good facilities. Washing machines. Motorhome services. Campers' kitchen with hobs. Supermarket (High season). Bar/restaurant. Swimming and paddling pools (High season). Tennis. Table tennis. Volleyball. Bicycle hire. Fishing. Riding. Bird watching. Day trips to Postojna Caves and other excursions can be organised. WiFi.

Key Features

🗓 Book Online

🐾 Pets allowed

🏊 Outdoor Pool on Site

🛝 Childrens Play Area

🍸 Bar on Site

🚲 Bicycle Hire on Site

Find Out More
Visit **ar.camp/sv4330**
or scan the QR code.

Kobarid, Slovenia

Kamp Koren

Kamp Koren is situated in the picturesque valley by the Soča River, 500 m from the historical town Kobarid. A unique campsite and sole holder of the eco certificates: EU Ecolabel and Ecocamping. Its policy is to keep the environment clean and have minimum effect on nature. Slovenia's first ecological site is in a quiet location above the emerald-coloured river, within easy walking distance of Kobarid.

The site has slightly sloping pitches, all with 6/16A electricity and ample tree shade. It is deservedly popular with those interested in outdoor sports, whether on the water, in the mountains or in the air. At the same time, its peaceful location makes it an ideal choice for those seeking a relaxing break. At the top of the site, there are also several well-equipped chalets and a shady area, mainly for tents and glamping.

Three attractive and well-maintained log-built toilet blocks, two recently renovated. Accessible Facilities. Laundry facilities. Motorhome services. Shop (March-Nov). Café/Bar serves light meals, snacks and drinks (flexible closing hours). TV. Multi-purpose hall. Play area. Volleyball. Table tennis. Boules. Gym. Fishing. Bicycle hire. Canoe hire. Climbing walls. Adventure park. Communal barbecue. Sauna. Grocery shop with eco products and electric vehicle charging station. WiFi.

Alan Rogers Ref: SV4270
Accommodations: 8
Pitches: 100
GPS: 46.25100, 13.58680
Post Code: SLO-5222

what3words:
humankind.crashing.beanbag

Contact:
info@kamp-koren.si
Tel: +386 5389 1311
www.campingslovenia.com

Open Dates:
All year.

Alan Rogers Awards Won
2013

Key Features

- Book Online
- All Year
- Pets allowed
- Accessible Facilities
- Childrens Play Area
- Bar on Site
- Bicycle Hire on Site
- Fishing on Site

Find Out More
Visit ar.camp/sv4270
or scan the QR code.

Bled, Slovenia

Camping Bled

Camping Bled is situated on the western tip of Lake Bled and is an excellent example of how a site should be run. Check-in is quick and efficient, and English is spoken. The site is large but well-spaced, with 244 touring pitches, all with electricity, 40 fully serviced pitches, and six with private sanitary facilities; most pitches benefit from shade. Pitches at the front are used mainly for overnighters. There are lovely views across the lake toward its famous island. This site is well-organised, and the facilities are modern and spotless.

You have direct access to Lake Bled, which does not disappoint if you wish to enjoy the view. The waterfront here has a small public beach immediately behind, which runs a gently sloping narrow wooded valley. A bar/Restaurant/Coffee and cake shop on site overlooks the lake. If you are feeling more active, walking or cycling around the lake is a good option, or you can rent a picnic basket, hire a rowing boat and enjoy a relaxing afternoon.

Toilet facilities in five blocks are of a high standard (with free hot showers). Three blocks are heated. Private bathrooms for rent. Accessible facilities. Solar energy used. Washing machines and dryers. Motorhome services. Gas supplies. Fridge hire. Supermarket. Restaurant. Play area and children's zoo. Games area. Trampolines. Organised activities in July/Aug, including children's club, excursions and sporting activities. Mountain bike tours. Live entertainment. Fishing. Bicycle hire. Free WiFi.

Alan Rogers Ref: SV4200
Accommodations: 8
Pitches: 244
GPS: 46.36155, 14.08075
Post Code: SLO-4260

what3words:
insulated.hothouse.retraces

Contact:
info@camping-bled.com
Tel: +386 4575 2000
www.camping-bled.com

Open Dates:
Start April - Mid October.

**Alan Rogers
Awards Won**
2022, 2017, 2011

Key Features

- Book Online
- Pets allowed
- Accessible Facilities
- Childrens Play Area
- Bar on Site
- Bicycle Hire on Site
- Fishing on Site

Find Out More
Visit **ar.camp/sv4200**
or scan the QR code.

Recica ob Savinji, Slovenia

Alan Rogers Ref: SV4405
Accommodations: 25
Pitches: 200
GPS: 46.31168, 14.90913
Post Code: SLO-3332

what3words:
undertones.alternative.
glimmers

Contact:
info@campingmenina.com
Tel: +386 3583 5027
www.campingmenina.com

Open Dates:
All year.

Camping Menina

Camping Menina is in the heart of the 35 km. long Upper Savinja Valley, surrounded by 2,500 m. high mountains and unspoilt nature. It is being improved every year by the young, enthusiastic owner, Jurij Kolenc, and has 200 pitches, all for touring units, on grassy fields under mature trees and with access from gravel roads. All have 10A electricity.

The Savinja River runs along one side of the site, but if the water is too cold, the site also has a lake which can be used for swimming. This site is a perfect base for walking or mountain biking in the mountains. A wealth of maps and routes are available from reception. Rafting, canyoning, and kayaking opportunities in the area encourage many groups to visit the site.

Four sanitary blocks have modern fittings with toilets, open-plan washbasins and controllable hot showers. Washing machine. Motorhome services. Bar/restaurant with open-air terrace (Seasonal) and open-air kitchen. Sauna. Playing field. Play area. Tree-top zip wire. Archery, Fishing. Russian bowling. Excursions. Live music and gatherings around the campfire. Hostel. Skiing in winter. Climbing wall. Rafting. Kayaking. Mountain bike hire. Mobile homes to rent. WiFi (free).

Key Features

📅 Book Online

📅 All Year

🐾 Pets allowed

🍸 Bar on Site

⛷ Skiing on Site

🚲 Bicycle Hire on Site

🐟 Fishing on Site

⛵ Sailing on Site

Find Out More
Visit **ar.camp/sv4405**
or scan the QR code.

Capital Madrid
Currency Euro (€)
Language Spanish (plus regional variants)
Time Zone CET (GMT+1)
Telephone Code +34
Emergency Number 112
Tourist Website spain.info

Shops Hours vary throughout the year with many shops operating shorter hours in low season. In high season 10am to 2pm and 5pm to 9pm Mon to Fri, 10am to 2pm Sat. Supermarkets operate longer hours.

Money ATMs are widespread, accessible 24hrs a day and most have multilingual instructions. Major cards widely accepted. When paying using card, you may be asked to show ID.

Travelling with children Spain is family-friendly and has a good range of attractions. Many restaurants cater well for kids and beaches are safe. Extremely hot during the summer, weather remains warm well into October.

Public Holidays 1 Jan New Year's Day; 6 Jan Epiphany; Mar/Apr Maundy Thursday; Mar/Apr Good Friday; Mar/Apr Easter Sunday; 1 May Labour Day; 16 Jun Corpus Christi; 15 Aug Assumption; 12 Oct Fiesta Nacional de España; 1 Nov All Saints; 6 Dec Constitution Day; 8 Dec Immaculate Conception; 25 Dec Christmas Day.

Accessible Travel Score

A push to improve, with Barcelona leading the way. Public buildings and transport in other major cities are adapting.

Driving in Spain Main roads are generally well-maintained. Some roads use tolls. You can buy an electronic tag called Via T for repeat trips. If your caravan or motorhome exceeds 12m, you must display one long or two short reflectors at the rear. Drink-driving, using a mobile whilst driving and using the horn in urban areas are illegal. Low Emission Zones are in place in all cities with a population above 50,000. All vehicles are affected (excl EVs), and foreign vehicles must register before entering. The use of dashcams and speed camera detectors is legal.

400

Spain

View all campsites in Spain
ar.camp/spain

See campsite map pages 478, 484, 485

Climate Temperate in the north, dry and hot in the centre, hot along the coast.

☀️
Avg. summer temp
22°C (N), 28°C (S)

🌧️
Wettest month
Nov (N), Oct (S)

One of the largest countries in Europe with glorious beaches, a fantastic sunshine record, vibrant towns and laid-back sleepy villages, plus a diversity of landscape, culture and artistic traditions, Spain has all the ingredients for a great holiday.

Spain's vast and diverse coastline is a magnet for visitors; glitzy, hedonistic resorts packed with bars and clubs are a foil to secluded coves backed by wooded cliffs.

Yet Spain has much more to offer – the verdant north with its ancient pilgrimage routes where the Picos de Europa sweep down to the Atlantic gems of Santander and Bilbao. Vibrant Madrid in the heart of the country boasts the Prado with works by Velázquez and Goya, the beautiful cobbled Plaza Major, plus all the attractions of a capital city.

Passionate Andalucía in the sun-soaked south dazzles with the symbolic art of flamenco. It offers the cosmopolitan cities of Córdoba, Cádiz and Málaga, alongside magnificent examples of the past, such as the Alhambra at Granada and the awe-inspiring Alcázar, a magical Moorish palace with scents of orange and Jasmine wafting through the air, a must-see in dreamy Seville. On the Mediterranean east coast, Valencia has a wealth of monuments and cultural sites, including the magnificent City of Arts and Science.

Scan QR code to browse more campsites on our website

401

📍 **Girona, Cataluña-Catalunya**

Camping Vell Empordà

Camping Vell Empordà is a friendly, family site close to the resort of Roses on the northern Costa Brava and the outskirts of the small town of Garriguella. There are 210 touring pitches, all with 6A or 10A (extra) electricity connections. Smaller pitches are available for campers with tents. Additionally, a range of fully equipped wooden chalets are to rent. The site is terraced and well-shaded.

On-site amenities include a good restaurant and a well-stocked supermarket. There is a pleasant bar with a large terrace on site, a prominent attractive swimming pool and a separate children's pool adjacent. The site has a strong Spanish presence and a loyal European clientèle, including some British tourists who have been visiting for many years.

Two large, clean, sanitary blocks have facilities for children and accessible facilities. Laundry. Motorhome services. Supermarket and bar (Seasonal), restaurant and takeaway (High season). Large outdoor swimming pool (Seasonal). Children's pool. Play area. Multisports area. Fronton court. Entertainment, Bicycle hire. Free WiFi over site. Chalets to rent.

Alan Rogers Ref: ES80140
Accommodations: 21
Pitches: 210
GPS: 42.33888, 3.06726
Post Code: E-17780

what3words:
names.undermining.envoy

Contact:
vellemporda@vellemporda.com
Tel: +34 972 53 02 00
www.vellemporda.com

Open Dates:
Start February -
Mid December.

Key Features

📅 Book Online

🐾 Pets allowed

♿ Accessible Facilities

🏖 Seaside Beach Nearby

🌊 Outdoor Pool on Site

🛝 Childrens Play Area

🍸 Bar on Site

🚲 Bicycle Hire on Site

Find Out More
Visit **ar.camp/es80140**
or scan the QR code.

Girona, Cataluña-Catalunya

Camping Las Palmeras

A very welcoming, open site that is attractive and well-maintained. The 230 grass pitches are flat and well maintained, with some shade and 10A electricity. Ten pitches also have water and drainage. Thirty smart mobile homes are placed unobtrusively at one end of the site. A pleasant pool complex, fringed by attractive palm trees, has a lifeguard, and the brightly coloured play areas are clean and safe.

It's just a 200-metre walk from a great beach, noted for watersports, which is part of the arc of magnificent sand known as the Platja Sant Pere Pescador, which runs along this sunny coastline. The area is generally flat, which makes it ideal for gentle cycling and walking excursions through the surrounding countryside of the adjacent Natural Park of Aiguamolls de l'Empordà and the sleepy little villages.

Two excellent, spotless, solar-powered toilet blocks include first-class accessible facilities. Baby rooms. Facilities may become a little busy at peak periods. Washing machines. Motorhome services. Supermarket, restaurant/bar/takeaway open all season (children's menu). Swimming pools (heated). Play areas. Tennis. Five-a-side. Fronton. Boules. Gym. Barbecue. Bicycle hire. Miniclub. Entertainment. Satellite TV. Internet. WiFi over site (charged). ATM. Torches useful.

Alan Rogers Ref: ES80330
Accommodations: 30
Pitches: 230
GPS: 42.18805, 3.10270
Post Code: E-17470

what3words:
citizenship.loveliness.cello

Contact:
info@campinglaspalmeras.com
Tel: +34 972 52 05 06
www.campinglaspalmeras.com

Open Dates:
Mid April - Late October.

Key Features

- Book Online
- Pets allowed
- Accessible Facilities
- Seaside Beach Nearby
- Outdoor Pool on Site
- Childrens Play Area
- Bar on Site
- Bicycle Hire on Site

Find Out More
Visit ar.camp/es80330
or scan the QR code.

📍 **Girona, Cataluña-Catalunya**

Alan Rogers Ref: ES80350
Accommodations: 152
Pitches: 872
GPS: 42.18147, 3.10405
Post Code: E-17470

what3words:
problematic.same.cockle

Contact:
info@campingamfora.com
Tel: +34 972 52 05 40
www.en.campingamfora.com

Open Dates:
Mid April - Late September.

📍 **Alan Rogers
Awards Won**
2017

Camping l'Amfora

Michelle, Josep and their daughter run this spacious, friendly site, which is always a popular destination. It is spotlessly clean and well-maintained, and the owners operate the site in an environmentally friendly way. Eight hundred seventy-two level grass pitches (720 for touring units) are laid out in a grid system, all with 10A electricity.

Attractive trees and shrubs have been planted around each pitch. There is good shade in the more mature areas, which include 64 large pitches (180 sq.m), each with an individual sanitary unit (toilet, shower and washbasin). The newer area is more open and has less shade; you can choose your preference.

Three excellent sanitary blocks, one heated, provide washbasins in cabins and roomy, free showers. Baby rooms. Accessible facilities, Laundry facilities and service. Motorhome services. Supermarket. Terraced bar, self-service and waiter-service restaurants. Pizzeria/takeaway. Restaurant and bar on the beach with a limited menu (high season). Disco bar. Swimming pools with two long waterslides (seasonal) Spa area. Pétanque. Tennis. Minigolf. Play area. Miniclub. Entertainment and activities. Windsurfing. Kite surfing (low season). Sailing, kayaking, fishing. Games rooms. Bicycle hire. Internet room and WiFi over site (charged). Car wash. Torches are required in most areas.

Key Features

📅 Book Online

🐾 Pets allowed

♿ Accessible Facilities

🏖 Seaside Beach on Site

🏊 Outdoor Pool on Site

🛝 Childrens Play Area

🍸 Bar on Site

🚲 Bicycle Hire on Site

Find Out More
Visit **ar.camp/es80350**
or scan the QR code.

📍 **Girona, Cataluña-Catalunya**

Alan Rogers Ref: ES80400
Accommodations: 175
Pitches: 1500
GPS: 42.16098, 3.10777
Post Code: E-17470

what3words:
delivering.rhythm.gratitude

Contact:
info@campinglasdunas.com
Tel: +34 972 52 17 17
www.campinglasdunas.com

Open Dates:
Mid May - Mid September.

⊙ **Alan Rogers Awards Won**
2018, 2015

Camping Las Dunas

Las Dunas is an extensive, impressive and well-organised resort-style site with many on-site activities and an ongoing programme of improvements. The site has direct access to a superb sandy beach stretching for nearly a kilometre, with a windsurfing school and beach bar. There is also a much-used, huge swimming pool, plus a large double pool for children.

Las Dunas has around 1,700 individual hedged pitches (1,500 for touring units) of about 100 sq.m. laid out on flat ground in long, regular parallel rows. All have electricity (6/10A), and 400 have water and drainage.

Five excellent large toilet blocks with electronic sliding glass doors. Toilets without seats, controllable hot showers and washbasins in cabins. Excellent facilities for children and babies. Accessible facilities. Laundry facilities. Motorhome services. Supermarket, boutique and other shops. Large bar with terrace. Large restaurant & takeaway. Ice cream parlour. Beach bar (seasonal). Disco club. Swimming pools. Adventure crazy golf. Playgrounds. Tennis. Minigolf. Sailing/windsurfing school and other watersports. Programme of sports, games, excursions and entertainment, partly in English. Exchange facilities. ATM. Safety deposit. Internet café. WiFi over site (charged). Dogs accepted in one section. Torches are required in some areas.

Key Features

🐾 Pets allowed

♿ Accessible Facilities

⛱ Seaside Beach on Site

🏊 Outdoor Pool on Site

🛝 Childrens Play Area

🍸 Bar on Site

🚲 Bicycle Hire on Site

🐟 Fishing on Site

Find Out More
Visit **ar.camp/es80400**
or scan the QR code.

CAMPING LAS DUNAS

CAMPING BUNGALOWPARK

www.campinglasdunas.com

COSTA BRAVA
SPAIN

SEASIDE HOLIDAY PARADISE FOR THE WHOLE FAMILY!

Camping & Bungalow Park located right at one of the most beautiful beaches in the Bay of Rosas. Offers a large variety of entertainment and activities for all ages, state-of-the-art sanitary facilities and a large shopping centre. AQUAPARK with slides guarantees fun and relax for the whole family.

Dunas
LAS
CAMPING BUNGALOW PARK

Camping Las Dunas
17130 L'Escala (Girona)
Tel. +34 972 521 717
info@campinglasdunas.com
www.campinglasdunas.com

📍 **Girona, Cataluña-Catalunya**

Camping Treumal

This beautiful terraced site has been developed on a hillside around the beautiful gardens of a large, spectacular estate house close to the sea. The floral displays in summer are quite something. The house is the focus of the site's excellent facilities, including a superb restaurant with terraces overlooking two tranquil beaches protected in pretty coves. Several excellent walking and cycling trails lead from the campsite entrance and invite guests to explore this rural hinterland.

The site has 536 pitches on well-shaded terraces. Of these, 371 are accessible to touring units, and there are some 50 pitches on flat ground alongside the sea – the views are stunning, and you wake to the sound of the waves. Electricity (6/10/16A) is available in all parts. Cars must be left in car parks or the site's roads.

Four well-maintained sanitary blocks have free hot water in the washbasins (with some private cabins), controllable showers, and a tap to draw from for the sinks. Beachside sanitary block. Washing machines. Motorhome services. Gas supplies. Supermarket, bar and takeaway (all season). Restaurant (seasonal). Beach bar. Fishing. Play area. Sports area. Games room. Bicycle hire. Satellite TV. Internet access and WiFi (charged). ATM. Safes. Dogs are not accepted.

Alan Rogers Ref: ES81400
Accommodations: 165
Pitches: 536
GPS: 41.83631, 3.08711
Post Code: E-17250

what3words:
honesty.slouched.implicit

Contact:
info@campingtreumal.com
Tel: +34 972 65 10 95
www.campingtreumal.com

Open Dates:
Mid March - End September.

Key Features

🏖 Seaside Beach on Site

🏊 Outdoor Pool on Site

🛝 Childrens Play Area

🍸 Bar on Site

🚲 Bicycle Hire on Site

🐟 Fishing on Site

⛵ Sailing on Site

Find Out More
Visit **ar.camp/es81400**
or scan the QR code.

📍 **Girona, Cataluña-Catalunya**

Alan Rogers Ref: ES80220
Accommodations: 280
Pitches: 200
GPS: 41.66202, 2.78043
Post Code: E-17300

what3words:
winter.trench.consultancy

Contact:
campingsolmar@
campingsolmar.com
Tel: +34 972 34 80 34
www.campingsolmar.com

Open Dates:
Mid March - Mid October.

Camping Solmar

The Ribas family has run Camping Solmar for over 40 years, and a warm welcome awaits you. The well-equipped site is located 150 metres from a sandy beach in the busy resort of Blanes and is sprinkled with palm trees. The accessible, shaded pitches are 65-85 sq.m., and all have 6A electricity connections. On-site amenities include an attractive restaurant, bar, terrace, and a central swimming pool complex with islands and bridges.

A children's club operates in the peak season (4-12 years), and an outdoor sports complex is available. A range of fully equipped mobile homes and wooden chalets are available for rent. Regular excursions are available in the town to all the area's main attractions, including Barcelona (65 km) and the Dalí Museum in Figueres. The town has a wide range of attractions, including some memorable fireworks displays.

Four toilet blocks are clean and have open-style washbasins, controllable showers in cabins and baby baths. Accessible Facilities. Washing machines. Motorhome services. Supermarket. Restaurant. Bar. Swimming pool and terrace complex. Outdoor sports complex. Play areas. Miniclub (June onwards). Evening entertainment (high season). Tourist information and excursions. WiFi over site (charged). Mobile homes and chalets for rent.

Key Features

🐾 Pets allowed

⛱ Seaside Beach Nearby

🏊 Outdoor Pool on Site

🛝 Childrens Play Area

🍸 Bar on Site

Find Out More
Visit **ar.camp/es80220**
or scan the QR code.

📍 **Barcelona, Cataluña-Catalunya**

Alan Rogers Ref: ES83120
Accommodations: 65
Pitches: 250
GPS: 41.27257, 2.04254
Post Code: E-08850

what3words:
smashes.supreme.lanes

Contact:
info@camping3estrellas.com
Tel: +34 936 33 06 37
www.camping3estrellas.com

Open Dates:
Mid January - Mid December.

Camping 3 Estrellas

Camping 3 Estrellas is a beach site with 200 pitches for touring, generally flat with 5A electricity, informally placed under trees. Many pitches are along the beachfront, those closer to the beach having little shade, but they are enjoyable with great views – beach access is through a security fence. There are three levels of pitches: standard, beach & premium. Beach pitches on the front are premium, so advanced booking is advised.

Amenities, including a large pool, are in a separate area of the site, nearer to but shielded from the road, keeping noise away from the pitches. Although busy, the site has a pleasant open feel, and there are 65 units for hire. The bar and restaurant are close to the beach, enjoying cool breezes in the evening. The bar is lively at times, with everyone having great fun, and it is located where there is little or no noise impact on the pitches, ideal in a site popular with all age groups. English is spoken, and the staff are efficient and friendly. A modest entertainment programme is provided in the high season.

Clean, spacious, modern facilities include accessible facilities and a well-equipped nursery room (key at reception). Washing machines and dryers. Dishwashing by EasyBe, Motorhome services. Supermarket, restaurant, bar, snack bar and takeaway. Outdoor swimming pools (seasonal). Play areas. Boules. Bicycle hire. Entertainment programme. ATM. Security boxes. Torches useful. WiFi throughout (free).

Key Features

📅 Book Online

🐾 Pets allowed

♿ Accessible Facilities

⛱ Seaside Beach on Site

🏊 Outdoor Pool on Site

🛝 Childrens Play Area

🍸 Bar on Site

Find Out More
Visit **ar.camp/es83120**
or scan the QR code.

📍 Barcelona, Cataluña-Catalunya

Alan Rogers Ref: ES83900
Accommodations: 940
Pitches: 343
GPS: 41.23237, 1.69092
Post Code: E-08800

what3words:
persuade.noted.boosted

Contact:
info@vilanovapark.com
Tel: +34 938 93 34 02
www.vilanovapark.com

Open Dates:
All year.

📍 **Alan Rogers Awards Won**
2023, 2019

Vilanova Park

Sitting on the terrace in front of the restaurant – a beautifully converted Catalan farmhouse dating from 1908 – it isn't easy to believe that in 1982, this was still a farm with few trees and known as Mas Roque (literally, Rock Farm). Since then, the imaginative planting of thousands of trees and gloriously colourful shrubs have made this large campsite most attractive. It has an impressive range of high-quality amenities and facilities open all year.

There are 343 marked pitches for touring units in separate areas, all with 6/10A electricity, while 168 larger pitches also have water and, in some cases, drainage. They are on hard surfaces, gently sloping ground and with plenty of shade. Chalets mostly occupy a further 1,000 or so pitches to rent and by tour operators.

Excellent, heated toilet blocks with controllable showers and many washbasins in cabins. Baby rooms. Accessible facilities. Serviced and self-service laundry. Motorhome services. Supermarket. Souvenir shop. Restaurants. Bar with simple meals and tapas. Outdoor pools (seasonal), indoor pool (all year, charged). Wellness centre including sauna, jacuzzi and gym. Play areas. Sports field. Games room. Excursions. Activity and entertainment programme for all ages. Bicycle hire. Tennis. ATM and exchange facilities. WiFi throughout (charged). Caravan storage.

Key Features

📅 Book Online

📆 All Year

🐾 Pets allowed

♿ Accessible Facilities

⛱ Seaside Beach Nearby

🏊 Indoor Pool on Site

🧗 Childrens Play Area

🍸 Bar on Site

Find Out More
Visit ar.camp/es83900
or scan the QR code.

📍 **Tarragona, Cataluña-Catalunya**

Alan Rogers Ref: ES84100
Accommodations: 177
Pitches: 800
GPS: 41.16945, 1.47075
Post Code: E-43883

what3words:
dean.wreckage.habitat

Contact:
info@barapark.es
Tel: +34 977 80 27 01
www.barapark.es

Open Dates:
Late March - End September.

Camping Park Playa Barà

Camping Park Playa Barà is a family-friendly campsite in Roda de Barà, approximately 20 km from Tarragona. The beach is just a short walk away and is a long stretch of fine golden sand with various water sports on offer. This is a well-equipped site with high-quality facilities, well-demarcated and well-shaded pitches and loads of activities for children, such as volleyball tournaments, handball, basketball, tennis, paddle tennis, mini-golf and table tennis. The pool complex is superb, and you can also relax in the hot tub or go to the solarium to top up your tan. The campsite's restaurant is ideal for sharing time with the family and enjoying local culinary specialities.

Roda de Barà, the main tourist centre of the Costa Daurada, is endlessly appealing for its successful blend of wonderful beaches and rich cultural heritage. It's a town rich in history, with numerous ancient monuments, notably the Arc de Barà, a 2,000-year-old Roman arch and something of a local icon.

Four sanitary blocks have showers, private washing cubicles and baby facilities. Accessible facilities, Washing machines and dryers. Supermarket & souvenir shop. Bar, Pool Bar, Restaurant, Beach Restaurant and takeaway. Outdoor pools. Spa Area. Daily entertainment program with nightly shows. Tennis & paddle courts. Minigolf. Bicycle hire.

Key Features

🐾 Pets allowed

♿ Accessible Facilities

⛱ Seaside Beach on Site

♨ Indoor Pool on Site

🛝 Childrens Play Area

🍸 Bar on Site

🚲 Bicycle Hire on Site

🐟 Fishing on Site

Find Out More
Visit **ar.camp/es84100**
or scan the QR code.

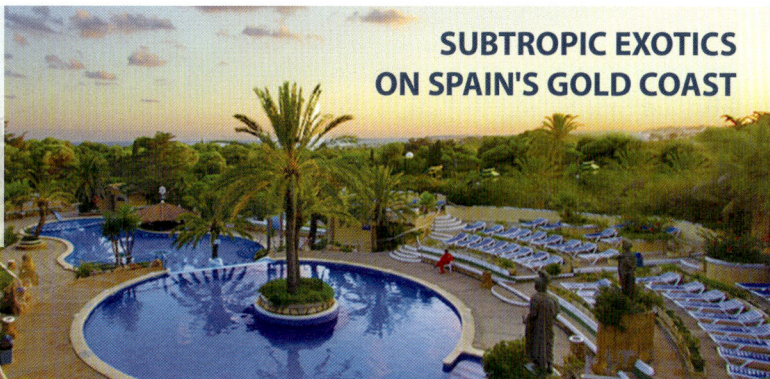

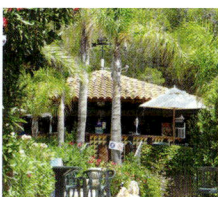

Tarragona, Cataluña-Catalunya

Alan Rogers Ref: ES85300
Accommodations: 263
Pitches: 990
GPS: 41.03345, 0.96921
Post Code: E-43300

what3words:
viscose.puppy.bins

Contact:
info@playamontroig.com
Tel: +34 977 81 06 37
www.playamontroig.com

Open Dates:
Late March - Mid October.

Camping Playa Montroig

Playa Montroig Camping Resort is about 30 kilometres from Tarragona, set in its own tropical gardens with direct access to a very long, narrow, soft sand beach. The central part of the site lies between the sea, road and railway (as at other sites on this coast, with occasional train noise on some pitches) with a huge underpass. Aside from a wide range of excellent facilities, notably an impressive aqua park and dining options, Port Aventura theme park is 20 km away, making this a highly desirable location for many families.

The site is divided into spacious, marked pitches with excellent shade provided by a variety of lush vegetation, including impressive palms set in wide avenues. There are 990 pitches with electricity (10A) and 661 with water and drainage. Some 47 pitches are directly alongside the beach. A member of the Leading Campings group.

Sanitary buildings with washbasins in private cabins and separate WCs. Accessible facilities. Several launderettes. Motorhome services. Gas. Good shopping centre. Restaurants and bars. Pool complex. Fitness suite. Hairdresser. TV lounges. Beach bar. Playground. Jogging track. Sports area. Tennis. Minigolf. Organised activities, including pottery. Open-air theatre. Pedalo hire. Boat mooring. Bicycle hire. WiFi over site. Dogs are not accepted.

Key Features

- Book Online
- Accessible Facilities
- Seaside Beach on Site
- Outdoor Pool on Site
- Childrens Play Area
- Bar on Site
- Bicycle Hire on Site
- Fishing on Site

Find Out More
Visit **ar.camp/es85300**
or scan the QR code.

PLAYA MONTROIG
CAMPING RESORT ★★★★★
CAMPING IN STYLE

tel. +34 977 810 637   www.playamontroig.com   info@playamontroig.com

ACSI

LeadingCampings

ADAC Superplatz 2024
★★★★★
ADAC

Erlebnis
camping
★★★★★

alan rogers

Book directly with over 1,500 campsites throughout Europe

Why book direct?

- Book your holiday direct with the campsite owner

- Pay the campsite's own 'at-the-gate' prices and standard booking fees*

- Make your payment direct to the campsite in the local currency by credit card

- If you prefer to 'deal direct' this is the option for you

Discover more at
alanrogers.com/book-direct

Book directly in:

Austria, Belgium, Croatia, Czech Republic, Denmark, France, Germany, Hungary, Italy, Luxembourg, Netherlands, Portugal, Slovenia, Spain & Switzerland.

*separate fee payable on each campsite booked

Castellón, Comunidad Valenciana

Camping Bravoplaya

Camping Bravoplaya is a vast site divided into two by a quiet road, with a reception on each side with friendly, helpful staff. There are three pool complexes (one can be covered in cooler weather and is heated), all of which are on the west side, whilst the beach (of shingle and sand) is on the east. Both sides have a restaurant – the one on the beach side has two air-conditioned wooden buildings and a terrace.

The flat pitches vary in size; some have their own sinks, and most have decent shade. All have 10A electricity, and a few have a partial view of the sea. This high-quality site offers a wide range of excellent facilities and is perennially popular with active families over the summer months. On the western side are a children's play park, a large disco and sporting facilities including a sports centre, tennis, squash, two football pitches, pétanque and an outdoor gym.

Toilet facilities in both sections, with British-style WCs, hot water to some sinks, and accessible facilities. Baby rooms. Washing machines (laundry service if required). Motorhome services. Shop, bars, restaurants and takeaway. Swimming pool complex with flumes (one pool has a bar in the centre). Jacuzzi and sauna (winter). Play park. Large disco. Sports centre. Tennis. Squash. Two football pitches. Pétanque. Outdoor gym. Games room. Bullring. Hairdresser. A varied programme of activities and entertainment. WiFi (charged). Torches are useful.

Alan Rogers Ref: ES85700
Accommodations: 512
Pitches: 517
GPS: 40.12781, 0.15894
Post Code: E-12595

what3words:
contributes.heeding.triads

Contact:
camping@bravoplaya.com
Tel: +34 964 31 97 44
www.bravoplaya.com

Open Dates:
All year.

Key Features

- Book Online
- All Year
- Pets allowed
- Accessible Facilities
- Seaside Beach on Site
- Indoor Pool on Site
- Childrens Play Area
- Bar on Site

Find Out More
Visit **ar.camp/es85700**
or scan the QR code.

A world of sensations

Bravoplaya
CAMPING - RESORT ★★★★★

Castellón, Comunidad Valenciana

Alan Rogers Ref: ES85850
Accommodations: 31
Pitches: 50
GPS: 39.87471, -0.51051
Post Code: E-12470

what3words:
thrilling.wanted.glared

Contact:
reservas@campingaltomira.com
Tel: +34 964 71 32 11
www.campingaltomira.com

Open Dates:
All year.

Camping Altomira

Camping Altomira is a terraced site in a rural hillside setting on the outskirts of a quiet village. It offers excellent views across the valleys and hills, an amiable welcome, and a Spanish and international clientèle.

There are 50 touring pitches on the higher levels of the site with some shade (artificial awnings are allowed). Access roads to the gravel pitches are steep with some tight turns. All pitches have shared electricity (6A) and water points; some have individual sinks and water and wastewater disposal. There are three toilet blocks and two designated children's facilities. In recent years, efforts have been made to make the site accessible for campers with mobility problems. The swimming pool and reception building with a shop, bar, and restaurant are on the lowest level, along with a children's play area and communal meeting room.

Three heated toilet blocks have showers in cubicles and open-style washbasins. Accessible facilities, Two laundry areas. Shop. Bar/restaurant with a terrace next to the play area. Outdoor swimming pool (June-Sept). Entertainment (High season). TV room. Bicycle hire. Kayak hire. Pets allowed (Bungalows and Pitches) Communal barbecue areas. WiFi over site (charged).

Key Features

- Book Online
- All Year
- Pets allowed
- Accessible Facilities
- Seaside Beach Nearby
- Outdoor Pool on Site
- Childrens Play Area
- Bar on Site

Find Out More
Visit ar.camp/es85850
or scan the QR code.

Valencia, Comunidad Valenciana

Alan Rogers Ref: ES86250
Accommodations: 40
Pitches: 75
GPS: 39.55218, -1.47456
Post Code: E-46317

what3words:
presumes.articulate.
bookkeeping

Contact:
info@kikoparkrural.com
Tel: +34 962 13 90 82
www.kikoparkrural.com

Open Dates:
All year.

Alan Rogers Awards Won
2018, 2011

KikoPark Rural

At an altitude of 700 metres on open land adjacent to olive plantations and set amongst pine-laden mountain scenery overlooking the picturesque 27km 'Embalse de Contreras' (reservoir), is the all-year 4.5ha unique campsite Kiko Park Rural. Constructed and built to represent a small pueblo (village) utilising reclaimed materials, it allows for an authentic, effective yesteryear atmosphere.

The attractive single street includes small houses (accommodation), a bar/restaurant (good food, takeaway), chairs/tables outside for that typical Spanish atmosphere, and reception. To the rear of the restaurant is a covered terrace overlooking two swimming pools (one for children), flanked by grass and a small children's play area. (Pools open on 15 May and close on 30 September).

Three toilet blocks are well equipped (but have short timers for lighting and showers), including accessible facilities. Motorhome services. Gas supplies. Pleasant bar. Excellent restaurant (seasonal, also supplies basics, eggs, bread etc). Takeaway (Easter-Oct). Swimming and paddling pools. Very good playground. Bicycle hire. Entertainment in high season. Many adventure activities can be arranged, including white-water rafting, gorging, orienteering, trekking, bungee jumping, paddle boarding, zip lines and riding. Large families and groups are catered for. Pets allowed.

Key Features

All Year

Pets allowed

Accessible Facilities

Outdoor Pool on Site

Childrens Play Area

Bar on Site

Bicycle Hire on Site

Find Out More
Visit ar.camp/es86250
or scan the QR code.

Valencia, Comunidad Valenciana

KikoPark Oliva

KikoPark Oliva is a smart site nestling behind protective dunes alongside a Blue Flag beach. There are sets of attractively tiled steps over the dunes or a long boardwalk near the beach bar (suitable for prams and wheelchairs) to take you to the fine white sandy beach and the sea. From the central reception point (where good English is spoken), flat, fine gravel pitches and access roads are divided to the left and right.

Backing onto one another, the 170 large pitches all have electricity, and the aim is to upgrade all these with full services progressively. Plenty of flowers, hedging and trees, adding shade, privacy and colour. A pleasant outdoor swimming pool with an adjacent children's pool has a paved area with a bar in summer. The restaurant (lunchtimes only out of season) overlooks the marina, beautiful beach and sea. A wide variety of entertainment is provided all year, and Spanish lessons are taught along with dance classes and aerobics during the winter.

Four heated shower and toilet blocks, including accessible facilities (who will find this site flat and convenient). Outdoor swimming pools. ATM. Laundry. Dishwashing by EasyBe, Restaurant, bar and beach-side bar. Supermarket. Motorhome services. Gas supplies. Playground. Watersports facilities. Diving school in high season. Paddle SUP. Entertainment for children. Pétanque. WiFi. Car rental. Bicycle hire. Pets are allowed on the pitch.

Alan Rogers Ref: ES86150
Accommodations: 31
Pitches: 170
GPS: 38.93160, -0.09680
Post Code: E-46780

what3words:
league.inwards.defiance

Contact:
info@kikopark.com
Tel: +34 962 85 09 05
www.kikopark.com

Open Dates:
All year.

Alan Rogers Awards Won
2022

Key Features

- Book Online
- All Year
- Pets allowed
- Accessible Facilities
- Seaside Beach on Site
- Outdoor Pool on Site
- Childrens Play Area
- Bar on Site

Find Out More
Visit ar.camp/es86150
or scan the QR code.

📍 **Alicante, Comunidad Valenciana**

Alannia Costa Blanca

Alannia Costa Blanca (formerly Marjal) is a fully equipped site situated 15 km. inland on the southern Alicante coast, close to the towns of Crevillente and Catral and the Parque Natural de El Hondo. Around 1,200 hardstanding pitches range in size from 90-95 sq.m, and all have electricity (16A), water, drainage, TV and high-speed internet connections (charged).

On-site amenities include a tropical-themed swimming pool complex and a state-of-the-art wellness centre. There is full accessible facilities including at the swimming pool and staffed gym. There is accommodation to rent, including 46 Balinese-style bungalows adapted for visitors with accessibility requirements. The site is ideal for family holidays in summer and winter sun-seekers.

Six modern, spotlessly clean toilet blocks have washbasins and free showers in cabins. Facilities for children and babies. Accessible facilities. Well-equipped shop. Bar, restaurant and takeaway (all year). Swimming pool complex with outdoor pool (Mar-Sept), heated indoor pool (all year), sauna and Hammam. Fully equipped gym. Wellness centre. Hairdresser. Play areas. Games rooms. Library. Multisports courts. Minigolf. Tennis. Football. Entertainment and activity programme (inc Spanish lessons). Kids club. Bicycle hire. Car hire service. Doctor and vet. Free WiFi areas. Mobile homes and chalets to rent.

Alan Rogers Ref: ES87435
Accommodations: 270
Pitches: 1200
GPS: 38.17790, -0.80950
Post Code: E-03330

what3words:
tins.objective.dazzle

Contact:
reservas@alannia.com
Tel: +34 965 48 49 45
www.alanniaresorts.com

Open Dates:
All year.

🎯 **Alan Rogers Awards Won**
2022, 2013

Key Features

📅 Book Online

📆 All Year

🐾 Pets allowed

♿ Accessible Facilities

⛱ Seaside Beach Nearby

🌊 Indoor Pool on Site

🛝 Childrens Play Area

🍸 Bar on Site

Find Out More
Visit ar.camp/es87435
or scan the QR code.

Alicante, Comunidad Valenciana

Alan Rogers Ref: ES87420
Accommodations: 91
Pitches: 450
GPS: 38.12965, -0.64958
Post Code: E-03194

what3words:
bluntest.sniff.anxiety

Contact:
info@lamarinaresort.com
Tel: +34 965 41 92 00
www.lamarinaresort.com

Open Dates:
All year.

Camping La Marina

Very efficiently run by a friendly family, Camping Internacional La Marina has 450 touring pitches of three different types and sizes ranging from 50 sq.m. to 150 sq.m. with electricity (10/16A), TV, water and drainage. Artificial shade is provided, and the pitches are well maintained on level, well-drained ground, with a particular area allocated for tents in a small orchard.

A walk through the pines and dunes takes you to the long sandy beach. Back on site, the vast lagoon swimming pool complex is fabulous and has something for everyone (with lifeguards). William Le Metayer, the owner, is passionate about La Marina and is constantly innovating. A magnificent, modern building which uses the latest architectural technology houses many superb extra amenities. A member of the Leading Campings group.

Sanitary blocks with private cabins and accessible facilities. Laundry facilities. Motorhome services. Gas. Supermarket. Bars. Restaurant and café. Ice cream kiosk. Swimming pools (seasonal). Indoor pool. Superb fitness centre. Sauna. Solarium. Jacuzzi. Playrooms. Extensive activity and entertainment programme including barbecues, soundproof disco and swimming nights. Sports area. Tennis. Huge playgrounds. Hairdresser. Bicycle hire. Road train to the beach. Exclusive area for dogs. Internet café (charged) and free WiFi.

Key Features

- All Year
- Pets allowed
- Accessible Facilities
- Seaside Beach Nearby
- Indoor Pool on Site
- Childrens Play Area
- Bar on Site
- Bicycle Hire on Site

Find Out More
Visit **ar.camp/es87420**
or scan the QR code.

www.samayresorts.com
Information and Bookings
Avda. de la Alegría s/n · E03194 LA MARINA
Playas de Elche (Alicante) · Spain
T. +34 96 541 92 00
reservas@samayresorts.com

Do as the sun does, spend your holidays at...

Do as the sun, spend your holiday at... You will find La Marina Resort located in a privileged area at Elche's coastline, surrounded by a wild pine-forest environment, dunes, and white sand beaches (EEC blue flag awarded). Its facilities comply different-size pitches, a wide variety of fully equipped 2-bedroom bungalows, as well as a luxury NEW Balinese area and Infinity pool for those who like to enjoy nature without missing all the luxuries. We offer the best leisure, health, and wellness experience at our more 3,000 m2 Marina Senses area and 2500m2 themed pool Water Park. Entertainment of the highest-level for adults and children. Price according to season and stay length.

Need a campsite for tonight?

Need inspiration at short notice?

Been let down or disappointed by your original choice of campsite?

We can help you find campsites near you and get you on your way. In most corners of Europe, there are campsites situated close by.

We'll show you the campsites closest to your current location based on the shortest distance as the crow flies. Use the filters to narrow your campsite choice further.

Find out more at
ar.camp/near-me

📍 **Alicante, Comunidad Valenciana**

Alan Rogers Ref: ES87400
Accommodations: 52
Pitches: 127
GPS: 37.86964, -0.77248
Post Code: E-03191

what3words:
just.staffing.spikes

Contact:
info@campinglomonte.com
Tel: +34 966 76 67 82
www.campinglomonte.com

Open Dates:
All year.

Camping Lo Monte

Lo Monte is an all-year site located at Pilar de la Horadada, the most southerly town on the Costa Blanca. It is just 1 km from Blue Flag beaches. There are 127 pitches, most of which are for touring units. All have 16A electricity (Europlug), water and drainage. Leisure facilities include an indoor pool (open all year), an outdoor pool (open May to September), and a wellness centre. This is a popular holiday destination with a good range of facilities.

For nature lovers, the areas around the town are rich in flora and fauna, and the tidal sections support an incredible variety of creatures, with species such as pipefish, seahorses and wrasse.

Three sanitary blocks with facilities for babies and accessible facilities. Dog shower. Shop (High season). Bar/restaurant with terrace (self-service, table service and takeaway). Three outdoor swimming pools (Seasonal, lifeguard). Wellness centre. Massage (charged). Play area. Entertainment includes yoga, crafts, aerobics, line dancing and Spanish courses (all July/Aug). Football, Paddle tennis. Mobile homes to rent. Fridge hire. Bicycle hire. Free shuttle bus to the beach. WiFi (free in restaurant and reception).

Key Features

🗓️ All Year

🐾 Pets allowed

♿ Accessible Facilities

⛱️ Seaside Beach Nearby

🏊 Outdoor Pool on Site

🛝 Childrens Play Area

🚴 Bicycle Hire on Site

Find Out More
Visit ar.camp/es87400
or scan the QR code.

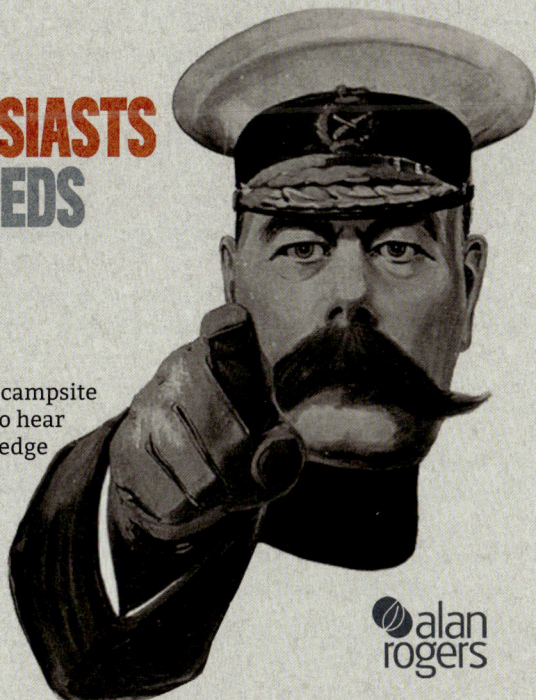

Jaén, Andalucia

Alan Rogers Ref: ES90895
Accommodations: 42
Pitches: 360
GPS: 37.90614, -2.93622
Post Code: E-23470

what3words:
disjointed.pixie.table

Contact:
info@puentedelasherrerias.com
Tel: +34 953 72 70 90
www.puentedelasherrerias.com

Open Dates:
Start April - Mid October.

Camping Puente de Las Herrerías

Camping Puente de Las Herrerías is a campsite in the heart of the Sierra de Cazorla National Park in Jaén, Spain. It is situated on the banks of the Guadalquivir River at an altitude of 1,000 meters above sea level. The camping pitches are spacious and well-maintained. There are touring 120 pitches equipped with electricity and water connections. The bungalows are an excellent option for those who want more comfort and privacy. They are fully equipped with kitchens, bathrooms, and living areas.

On-site facilities include a swimming pool open from June to September. The restaurant serves a variety of Spanish and international dishes. The bar also offers a large selection of beverages. The campsite also provides a range of other activities, including a children's club twice a week during the high season, which gives you a chance to try out the on-site tree adventure course with zip lines and treetop walkways. There are also archery and creative workshops. Live shows are held at the on-site restaurant during the summer, too.

Five sanitary blocks with showers and toilets, Laundry facilities, Restaurant, Bar, Takeaway food, Shop (limited) Children's playground, Outdoor swimming pool, River swimming, Kayaking, Fishing, Entertainment during high season, Kids club, Aerial walkways, Zip lines, Creative workshops, Rock climbing, Communal bbq area, Live shows, WiFi, Pets allowed.

Key Features

- Book Online
- Pets allowed
- Outdoor Pool on Site
- Childrens Play Area
- Bar on Site
- Fishing on Site

Find Out More
Visit **ar.camp/es90895**
or scan the QR code.

Almería, Andalucia

Alan Rogers Ref: ES87510
Accommodations: 2
Pitches: 179
GPS: 37.23700, -1.79800
Post Code: E-04617

what3words:
partnering.unafraid.payee

Contact:
reservas@cuevasmar.com
Tel: +34 950 46 73 82
www.campingcuevasmar.com

Open Dates:
All year.

Camping Cuevas Mar

A well-established campsite which proves popular and busy during the warm winter months. The 179 flat pitches on a stone chip are generally 80-100 sq.m. each with a 6/10amp electric supply. Shrubs and trees (some shade) act as pitch dividers, and those near the road are not overly affected as traffic volume is relatively low. Some areas have shade canopies erected during the hot summer months. Overall, throughout, there is a peaceful atmosphere.

The oval, tiled pool is in an attractive setting with sunbathing lawns. Close by a large building operating as a bar/restaurant in July/August and as an activity centre during the winter months to possibly include whist, line dancing, socials, painting and crafts. The nearby towns of Garrucha, Vera and Villaricos all have good street markets on Fridays, Saturdays and Sundays, respectively. The hilltop town of Mojacar dates back to 2000 BC. (good views) is geared toward the tourist.

The well-designed sanitary blocks provide sufficient showers and toilets for all. Accessible facilities, Washing machines and dryer. Water to the taps is European standard; however, a single tap near reception provides high-quality water from a nearby mountain spring source. Daily fresh bread, emergency provisions and gas from reception. Open-air unheated swimming pool (May-Sept). Caravan storage. WiFi throughout (weekly charge).

Key Features

- All Year
- Pets allowed
- Accessible Facilities
- Seaside Beach Nearby
- Outdoor Pool on Site
- Bar on Site

Find Out More
Visit ar.camp/es87510
or scan the QR code.

📍 **Granada, Andalucia**

Alan Rogers Ref: ES92850
Accommodations: 35
Pitches: 100
GPS: 37.16073, -3.45388
Post Code: E-18160

what3words:
stuffy.programmers.slowed

Contact:
info@campinglaslomas.com
Tel: +34 958 48 47 42
www.campinglaslomas.com

Open Dates:
All year.

Camping Las Lomas

This site is high in the Sierra Nevada Natural Park and looks down on the Pantano de Canales reservoir. After a scenic drive to Güéjar-Sierra, you are rewarded with a site boasting excellent facilities. It is set on a slope, but the pitches have been levelled and are pretty private, with high separating hedges and many mature trees giving good shade. Some pitches are fully serviced, with sinks and all but four have electricity.

The large bar/restaurant complex and pools have lovely views over the lake, and a grassy sunbathing area runs down to the fence, looking over the long drop below. A recent feature is private bathrooms for rent, including one with a spa tub, which is for hire by the hour. Some visitors may need a car to get around the site as some inclines are relatively steep.

Adequate sanitary blocks (heated in winter) provide clean facilities. First-class accessible facilities and well-equipped baby room (key at reception). Motorhome services. Good supermarket. Restaurant/bar. Swimming pool. Play area. Minigolf. Barbecue. WiFi (charged). Torches useful. A no noise policy (including cars) is strictly enforced from midnight to 07.00.

Key Features

- 📅 Book Online
- 📅 All Year
- 🐾 Pets allowed
- ♿ Accessible Facilities
- 🏖️ Seaside Beach Nearby
- 🌊 Outdoor Pool on Site
- 🛝 Childrens Play Area
- 🍸 Bar on Site

Find Out More
Visit ar.camp/es92850
or scan the QR code.

Granada, Andalucia

Alan Rogers Ref: ES87090
Accommodations: 19
Pitches: 203
GPS: 36.71837, -3.54628
Post Code: E-18613

what3words:
change.foamed.teaching

Contact:
info@campingplayadeponiente.com
Tel: +34 958 82 03 03
campingplayadeponiente.com

Open Dates:
All year.

Camping Playa Poniente

Camping Playa Poniente is in Motril, a coastal town in Granada, Spain. It is situated directly on the beach, with views of the Mediterranean Sea. The campsite is about 70 kilometres from Granada and 100 kilometres from Malaga. The campsite has 203 touring pitches and 19 bungalows to rent. The pitches are spacious and well-maintained, with eclectic hook-up points available, and most have shade. The bungalows are fully equipped and have air conditioning, heating, and a private bathroom.

It is a family-friendly campsite with various facilities and activities, including an outdoor swimming pool, a bar, a restaurant, and a supermarket. It also has a children's playground, a multisport pitch, table tennis, and various entertainment activities for children and adults alike. If this isn't enough to keep you occupied, you can rent bicycles to explore the surrounding area, and the beach also offers various water sports, such as kayaking.

Two excellent sanitary blocks provide WCs, wash basins and showers. Accessible facilities, newly built children's sanitary facilities, Laundry. Motorhome service point. Bar. Play area. Restaurant. Entertainment for all ages (High season) Kids club, Multisports Pitch. Swimming pool. Shop. Bike and canoe hire. WiFi. Pets allowed. Accessible accommodation to rent.

Key Features

- Book Online
- All Year
- Pets allowed
- Accessible Facilities
- Seaside Beach on Site
- Outdoor Pool on Site
- Childrens Play Area
- Bar on Site

Find Out More
Visit **ar.camp/es87090**
or scan the QR code.

📍 **Málaga, Andalucia**

Alan Rogers Ref: ES87920
Pitches: 234
GPS: 36.72444, -4.13472
Post Code: E-29749

what3words:
kindle.fidgeted.handshake

Contact:
info@campingalmayatecosta.com
Tel: +34 952 55 62 89
campingalmayatecosta.com

Open Dates:
All year.

Camping Playa Almayate

Situated between Málaga and Torre del Mar, this secluded campsite offers an idyllic escape in the less touristic area of the Costa del Sol. Located right on the beach camping, Camping Playa Almayate offers 234 touring pitches between 42 and 100 m2 with electric hookup points available and a television aerial. These are somewhat open and are close together with partial shade provided by trees but are mainly provided by a covering over each pitch. The best pitches are to be found on the site's perimeter and have sea views.

Paddle tennis, basketball, football, Ping Pong tables and a swimming pool are there. A varied entertainment programme for all ages is provided during the high season and Christmas, including group activities and friendly sports games. WiFi is free all over the site. The Restaurant, which offers a daily menu, specialises in Paella and other Mediterranian food.

One sanitary block equipped with showers and private washing cubicles. One facility near the swimming pool has a baby bathroom and an accessible bathroom. Well-stocked shop. Bar with daily fresh bread and breakfast. Restaurant with a daily changing menu and takeaway. Ecological outdoor swimming pool. Direct access to the beach. Football, Basketball and Paddle courts. Ping Pong Tables. Activity and entertainment programmes in Summer Holidays and festive season. Fishing. Free WiFi. Tea room. Library. Barbecue area. Washing Machines and Dryer (charged)

Key Features

- 📅 Book Online
- 📅 All Year
- 🐾 Pets allowed
- ♿ Accessible Facilities
- ⛱️ Seaside Beach on Site
- 🌊 Outdoor Pool on Site
- 🛝 Childrens Play Area
- 🍸 Bar on Site

Find Out More
Visit **ar.camp/es87920**
or scan the QR code.

Córdoba, Andalucia

Camping la Campiña

A charming site amongst the olive trees, set high on a hill to catch cool summer breezes. Matilde, the daughter of the Martin-Rodriguez family, and her husband run this site with enthusiasm and hard work, and visiting here is a delightful experience. Everything is immaculately kept with excellent amenities and standards.

The 35 pitches are level with a gravel surface, and most have shade. There is a large pool in a garden setting, and the restaurant, with its traditional rustic charm, has a delightful menu of homemade food. Breakfast is included in pitch prices. Fresh bread and croissants are cooked to order, or you can have an inclusive breakfast on the terrace with the piquant smell of olive trees drifting from the fields. The area is famous for its natural beauty, wine and olives (excursions can be arranged to see olive oil made and to a local 'bodega' for the winemaking). Reservation is essential for the high season and November-February.

Two small traditional sanitary blocks (heated in winter) have clean services, including separate accessible facilities (key at reception). Washing machines. Restaurant. Snack bar. Shop. Outdoor swimming pool (Apr-Oct). Bicycle hire. Play area. TV room. Yoga lessons. Torches useful. Walks and excursions arranged. WiFi throughout.

Alan Rogers Ref: ES90840
Accommodations: 5
Pitches: 35
GPS: 37.62300, -4.85870
Post Code: E-14547

what3words:
ordeals.disregards.fitness

Contact:
info@campinglacampina.es
Tel: +34 957 31 53 03
www.campinglacampina.es

Open Dates:
All year.

Alan Rogers Awards Won
2023, 2018

Key Features

- Book Online
- All Year
- Pets allowed
- Accessible Facilities
- Outdoor Pool on Site
- Childrens Play Area
- Bar on Site
- Bicycle Hire on Site

Find Out More
Visit **ar.camp/es90840**
or scan the QR code.

📍 **Cádiz, Andalucia**

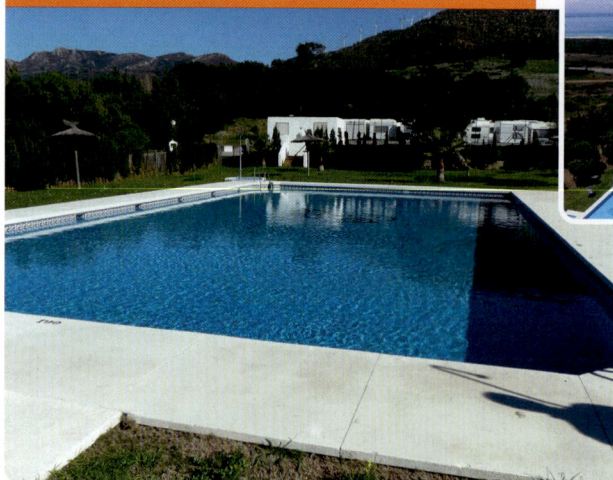

Camping Valdevaqueros

Camping Valdevaqueros is located at Tarifa on the Costa de la Luz. This is a friendly site with large pitches (60–80 sq.m), most of which have electrical connections. Several chalets and mobile homes are available to rent, as well as several apartments. Longer-term residents take up several pitches and can look slightly tired early in the season.

On-site amenities include a large swimming pool, surrounded by a grassy sunbathing area, and a tennis court. There is a friendly bar/restaurant and a takeaway food service. The toilet blocks, which are somewhat dated, are equipped with family rooms. Swallows nest around the site, including in the shower block.

Toilet blocks with facilities for babies and accessible facilities. Private bathrooms for hire. Motorhome services. Supermarket. Bar. Restaurant. Swimming pool. Children's pool. Tennis. Play area. Riding. Bicycle hire. Free limited WiFi over part of the site. Mobile homes, apartments and chalets to rent.

Alan Rogers Ref: ES88620
Pitches: 150
GPS: 36.06917, -5.68074
Post Code: E-11380

what3words:
grids.stoat.sweater

Contact:
info@campingvaldevaqueros.com
Tel: +34 956 68 41 74
campingvaldevaqueros.com/en

Open Dates:
All year.

Key Features

- Book Online
- All Year
- Pets allowed
- Accessible Facilities
- Seaside Beach Nearby
- Outdoor Pool on Site
- Childrens Play Area
- Bar on Site

Find Out More
Visit **ar.camp/es88620**
or scan the QR code.

📍 Huelva, Andalucia

Alan Rogers Ref: ES88720
Accommodations: 62
Pitches: 285
GPS: 37.20500, -7.26530
Post Code: E-21430

what3words:
texting.adopting.scour

Contact:
info@campingplayataray.es
Tel: +34 959 34 11 02
www.campingtaray.com

Open Dates:
All year.

Camping Playa Taray

Camping Playa Taray is close to the resort and fishing port of Isla Cristina, just 18 km. from the Portuguese border. A broad sandy blue flag beach is just 5 minutes on foot from the campsite. There are 285 pitches here, all with electrical connections. Pitches are generally well-shaded by pine trees. Several chalets and fully equipped tents are available to rent.

On-site amenities include a convivial bar/restaurant and a well-stocked shop. A wide range of activities are available on-site, including a tree-top adventure course with aerial walkways, zip lines, and a climbing wall. There are also plenty of water sports on the beach, including kite surfing and sailing, with discounts available to site residents.

Cleaning sanitary buildings with accessible facilities, Baby changing, Washing machines and dryers, Motor home service point, Outdoor swimming pool. Children's playground. Restaurant/bar. Snack bar, pizzeria, Shop, Chalets and fully equipped tents to rent. Entertainment programme, Tree top adventure course, Climbing wall, Water sports available at the beach, Pets allowed, TV, WiFi.

Key Features

📅 All Year

🐾 Pets allowed

♿ Accessible Facilities

🏊 Outdoor Pool on Site

🧗 Childrens Play Area

🍸 Bar on Site

Find Out More
Visit **ar.camp/es88720**
or scan the QR code.

Ciudad Real, Castilla-La-Mancha

Alan Rogers Ref: ES90960
Accommodations: 18
Pitches: 44
GPS: 39.32190, -4.64950
Post Code: E-13110

what3words:
dapper.subdivision.additionally

Contact:
info@campingcabaneros.com
Tel: +34 926 77 54 39
www.campingcabaneros.com

Open Dates:
All year.

Alan Rogers Awards Won
2013

Mirador de Cabañeros

With panoramic views all around the Sierra de Valdefuertes mountains, Camping El Mirador de Cabañeros is set in the Cabañeros National Park. This is a well-cared-for, landscaped site with 44 terraced pitches on gravel, all with 6A electricity. Although pitches are level once sited, the approach is steep, which may cause difficulties for larger units.

Run by an accommodating and friendly family, this site is in a very peaceful location where you can sit and relax or visit the many attractions the National Park offers. It is an ideal base for walking and birdwatching. The roads to the site have spectacular scenery but are narrow, twisting, and not well-surfaced in parts, so it is best to take it slowly and enjoy the journey.

One spotlessly clean central toilet block with solar heating includes open washbasins and cubicle showers. Accessible Facilities. Laundry. Motorhome services. No shop but basics from reception. Bar and restaurant (High season, w/ends in low season). Covered swimming pool (all year). Games room. Creative crafts during high season, Play areas. Multisport pitch, table tennis, Outside fitness area. WiFi. Pets allowed.

Key Features

- Book Online
- Pets allowed
- Accessible Facilities
- Indoor Pool on Site
- Childrens Play Area
- Bar on Site

Find Out More
Visit **ar.camp/es90960**
or scan the QR code.

Cáceres, Extremadura

Camping de Monfrague

Situated just 9 miles north of the Monfragüe National Park, this site is best located to engage with the abundant nature in this scenic area. The site is managed by the friendly Barrado family. You may be welcomed at the entrance by White Storks aloft on their nest or drift off to sleep listening to the Scops Owl.

Many of the 130 touring pitches are on slightly sloping terraced ground, with some having a degree of grass. Scattered trees offer some shade in the summer months, numerous water points, 10amp electricity, a refurbished large, clean toilet block, plus open all season: - a shop, bar and restaurant with the terrace providing stunning sunsets as you enjoy a quality meal.

Large modern toilet blocks, fully equipped, are very clean. Accessible facilities and baby baths. Laundry. Motorhome services. Supermarket/shop. Restaurant, bar with terrace and coffee shop. TV room with recreational facilities. Swimming and paddling pools (High season). Play area. Tennis court. Football field, Bicycle hire. Entertainment for children in season. Guided safaris into the park for birdwatching. Barbecue areas. WiFi near the bar (free).

Alan Rogers Ref: ES90270
Accommodations: 18
Pitches: 130
GPS: 39.94483, -6.08409
Post Code: E-10680

what3words:
froze.hawked.rainwater

Contact:
contacto@campingmonfrague.com
Tel: +34 927 45 92 33
campingmonfrague.es

Open Dates:
All year.

Key Features

- All Year
- Pets allowed
- Accessible Facilities
- Outdoor Pool on Site
- Childrens Play Area
- Bar on Site
- Bicycle Hire on Site

Find Out More
Visit ar.camp/es90270
or scan the QR code.

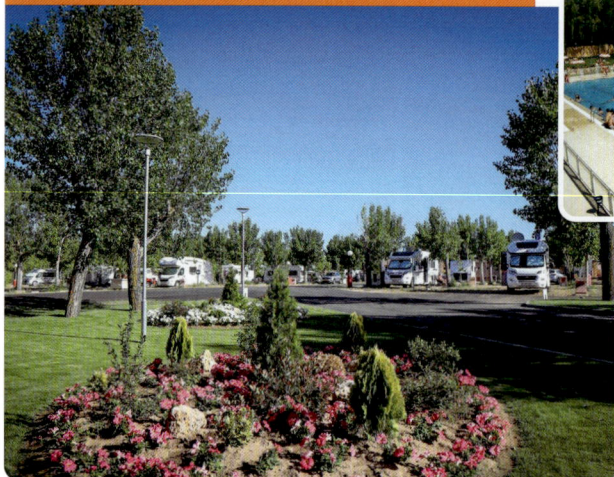

📍 **Salamanca, Castilla Y Leon**

Alan Rogers Ref: ES90250
Accommodations: 24
Pitches: 130
GPS: 40.94710, -5.61400
Post Code: E-37900

what3words:
supine.lengthening.dredged

Contact:
recepcion@campingregio.com
Tel: +34 923 13 88 88
www.campingregio.com

Open Dates:
All year.

Camping Regio

Salamanca is one of Europe's oldest university cities, and this beautiful ancient sandstone city has to be visited. This is also a helpful staging post en route to the south of Spain or central Portugal. The site is 7 km. outside the city on the old road to Madrid, behind the Hôtel Regio, and campers can take advantage of the hotel facilities.

The 130 pitches (with two large areas for tents without electricity) are clearly marked and almost flat throughout the site, with some shade in parts and 10A electricity. Access to those pitches not on the wide central road can be difficult for caravans. The hotel facilities include a quality restaurant, a cheaper cafeteria (discounts for campers), an excellent swimming pool and paddling pool (small charge) and a wellness centre (discounts available). There is a pool bar and a shaded patio.

A very large, fully equipped sanitary block with accessible facilities requires some updating. Washing machine and dryer. Gas supplies. Motorhome services. Bar. Cafeteria. Shop (High season). The hotel restaurant, cafeteria, pool and wellness centre may be used by campers (discounts available). Play area. Tennis. Multisport pitch, Car wash. Bicycle hire. Internet and WiFi within the hotel area. WiFi on site (free). EV Charging points. English is spoken.

Key Features

📅 Book Online

📅 All Year

🐾 Pets allowed

♿ Accessible Facilities

🏊 Outdoor Pool on Site

🧒 Childrens Play Area

🍸 Bar on Site

🚴 Bicycle Hire on Site

Find Out More
Visit **ar.camp/es90250**
or scan the QR code.

Leon, Castilla Y Leon

Camping Valle do Seo

Camping Valle do Seo is a small, peaceful, family-run site surrounded by mountains and woodland at the foot of the Barjas River. It is perfect to use as a stopover or to enjoy a holiday in the middle of nature, where you can enjoy peace and tranquillity. The site has 49 grass pitches, 44 for touring units, and a 10/6-amp hook-up point. It also has ten hikers' cabins, rooms and bungalows/chalets available to hire.

This small, authentic site has a play area for children, a climbing wall, a trampoline and a laser games field. If you didn't want to cook whilst staying here, you can relax, enjoy drinks and sample local tapas at the campsite's large bar with a terrace. The site also offers excursion programmes during peak season, and when the weather is warm enough, there are plenty of bathing and swimming opportunities in the Barjas River.

The toilet block has showers, washbasins, and WCs. Accessible facilities. Baby room. Dishwashing area. Laundry with washing machine and dryer. Motorhome service point. Chemical toilet point. Restaurant. Bar. Takeaway. Snack bar. Pizzeria. Bread to order. BBQs allowed, gas and electric only. Children's Play area has a climbing wall, trampoline, and laser games field. Late arrivals area without electric hook-up. WiFi partial site. Dogs allowed.

Alan Rogers Ref: ES90150
Accommodations: 10
Pitches: 49
GPS: 42.64769, -6.90155
Post Code: E-24523

what3words:
furnishes.roadie.smaller

Contact:
info@campingvalledoseo.com
Tel: +34 627 09 19 33
www.campingvalledoseo.com

Open Dates:
Start April - End September.

Key Features

Book Online

Pets allowed

Accessible Facilities

Childrens Play Area

Bar on Site

Fishing on Site

Find Out More
Visit **ar.camp/es90150**
or scan the QR code.

A Coruña, Galicia

Alan Rogers Ref: ES90240
Accommodations: 12
Pitches: 113
GPS: 42.88939, -8.52418
Post Code: E-15704

what3words:
slim.wades.hurt

Contact:
info@campingascancelas.com
Tel: +34 981 58 04 76
www.campingascancelas.com

Open Dates:
All year.

Camping As Cancelas

The beautiful city of Santiago has been the destination for European Christian pilgrims for centuries, and they now follow ancient routes to this unique city, the whole of which is a national monument. The As Cancelas campsite is excellent for sharing the experiences of these pilgrims in the city and around the magnificent cathedral.

It has 113 marked pitches (60-90 sq.m), arranged in terraces and divided by trees and shrubs. Electrical hook-ups (5A) are available; the site is lit at night, and a security guard patrols. The campsite is on a hillside overlooking the city; the views are delightful. The site has a steep approach road.

Two modern toilet blocks are fully equipped, with ramped access. The quality and cleanliness of the fittings and tiling is good. Laundry with service wash for a small fee. Small shop. Restaurant. Bar with TV. Well-kept, unsupervised swimming pool and children's pool. Small playground. Multi-sport court, Internet access. WiFi throughout. Pets allowed.

Key Features

- All Year
- Pets allowed
- Accessible Facilities
- Seaside Beach Nearby
- Outdoor Pool on Site
- Childrens Play Area
- Bar on Site
- Bicycle Hire on Site

Find Out More
Visit **ar.camp/es90240**
or scan the QR code.

A Coruña, Galicia

Camping A Lagoa

Camping A Lagoa is a small, family-run campsite located in the village of Valdoviño, on the north coast of Spain. The campsite is just a few steps from the beach and offers stunning views of the Atlantic Ocean. There are 73 touring pitches with electric hook-up points, which are non-delimited and mainly sunny. Almost all pitches are close to the campsite's restaurant and bar, with a terrace overlooking the beach.

There are few facilities on site, but it has the basic necessities to enjoy a comfortable stay here. There is a multisport court next to the campsite that can be used by guests when it isn't being used by the village and a small children's playground. This campsite is perfect for water sports enthusiasts as it has a more than 3,000m beach open to the immenseness of the Atlantic, making it excellent conditions for windsurfing, kite surfing and surfing.

Sanitary block with accessible facilities and baby change, Laundry facilities, Chemical disposal point, Bar, Restaurant, Snack bar, daily bread delivery service, Children's playground, Multisports pitch, Pets allowed, WiFi.

Alan Rogers Ref: ES89412
Accommodations: 8
Pitches: 73
GPS: 43.61303, -8.15314
Post Code: E-15552

what3words:
passing.unsaid.nursed

Contact:
reservas@campingalagoa.com
Tel: +34 881 06 26 56
campingalagoa.com

Open Dates:
All year.

Key Features

- Book Online
- All Year
- Pets allowed
- Accessible Facilities
- Seaside Beach on Site
- Childrens Play Area
- Bar on Site
- Fishing on Site

Find Out More
Visit **ar.camp/es89412**
or scan the QR code.

📍 **Ribadedeva, Asturias**

Camping Las Hortensias

Open for just four months, from June to September, Las Hortensias is a friendly site on the Cantabrian coast of northern Spain. The site enjoys a fine setting on a sheltered sandy beach adjacent to the Mirador Hotel. Well-lit tarmac roads connect 156 pitches. Each pitch has 6-10A electricity, and there are water points throughout. Many pitches are well-shaded by pine trees in pleasant, peaceful locations.

After a day on the beach or exploring the nearby rock pools, the campsites bar with terrace is a great spot to enjoy a bite to eat whilst watching the sunset overlooking the sea. In addition to the water-based activities, various leisure options are available, such as a football pitch, tennis court and Children's playground.

Two adequate and clean sanitary blocks, one with WCs only, the other with open plan washbasins and showers. Washing machine and dryer. Basic motorhome services. Small supermarket. Bar with terrace overlooking beach. Basic restaurant (campers can use the hotel restaurant with a discount), snack bar and takeaway. TV in the bar. Play area. Football pitch, Tennis court, Gas and charcoal barbecues only. WiFi.

Alan Rogers Ref: ES89570
Pitches: 156
GPS: 43.39161, -4.57571
Post Code: E-33590

what3words:
guessing.legions.embeds

Contact:
lashortensias@
campinglashortensias.com
Tel: +34 985 41 24 42
campinglashortensias.com

Open Dates:
Start June - End September.

Key Features

- 🗓 Book Online
- 🐾 Pets allowed
- ⛱ Seaside Beach on Site
- 🧒 Childrens Play Area
- 🍸 Bar on Site
- 🐟 Fishing on Site

Find Out More
Visit **ar.camp/es89570**
or scan the QR code.

📍 Cabuérniga, Cantabria

El Molino de Cabuérniga

Located in a peaceful valley with magnificent views of the mountains beside the Saja River and only a short walk from the picturesque and unspoiled village of Sopeña, this gem of a site is on an open, level, grassy meadow with trees. Wonderful stone buildings and artefacts are a feature of this unique site.

There are 102 marked pitches with 6A electricity, although long leads may be needed in places. This comfortable site is of excellent value and ideal for a few nights (or you may choose to stay longer once there) while exploring the Cabuérniga Valley, which forms part of the Reserva Nacional del Saja.

A superb, spotless sanitary block provides spacious, controllable showers and hot and cold water to washbasins. Washing machines and free ironing. Accessible Unit. Baby and toddler room. The bar serves breakfasts and 'bocadillos' (sandwiches) and includes a small shop section. Wonderful playground in a rustic setting – supervision recommended. Fishing. Bicycle hire. Attractive stone cottages and apartments to rent. No electric barbecues. WiFi throughout.

Alan Rogers Ref: ES89640
Accommodations: 12
Pitches: 102
GPS: 43.22594, -4.29034
Post Code: E-39510

what3words:
kooky.fellows.enlightening

Contact:
info@campingcabuerniga.com
Tel: +34 942 70 62 59
www.campingcabuerniga.com

Open Dates:
All year.

🎯 **Alan Rogers Awards Won**
2023, 2017

Key Features

📅 Book Online

📅 All Year

🐾 Pets allowed

♿ Accessible Facilities

🏖 Seaside Beach Nearby

🛝 Childrens Play Area

🍸 Bar on Site

🚲 Bicycle Hire on Site

Find Out More
Visit ar.camp/es89640
or scan the QR code.

📍 **Gipuzkoa, Pais Vasco-Euskadi**

Alan Rogers Ref: ES90390
Accommodations: 12
Pitches: 540
GPS: 43.28958, -2.14603
Post Code: E-20800

what3words:
meal.unspeakable.decorate

Contact:
info@grancampingzarautz.com
Tel: +34 943 83 12 38
www.grancampingzarautz.com

Open Dates:
All year.

Gran Camping Zarautz

This friendly site sits high in the hills east of the Basque town of Zarautz and has commanding views over the bay and the island of Getaria. Of the 540 pitches, 450 are for touring units, with 6A electricity; ten also have water and drainage. The remaining pitches are for tents and seasonal caravans. The grass pitches are of average size, shaded by mature trees, and those on the perimeter have superb sea views.

Gran Camping Zarautz offers a variety of facilities to enjoy a holiday here all year round; some services include table tennis, a football field, an indoor playground, and wellness facilities with a gym and sauna. For food options, the campsite has a restaurant designed for all audiences, serving traditional Spanish dishes and international cuisine. There is a communal BBQ area for those who like to cook, and you can purchase any food needed at the on-site shop.

Three well-equipped toilet blocks, one of which is modern. A sauna, gym, and spa area are above this block. Separate facilities for children and four large accessible toilet/shower rooms. Laundry facilities. New motorhome service point. Well-stocked shop. Restaurant with 'menu del día' and à la carte meals. Bar/snack bar with TV plus terrace. Communal barbecue area with picnic tables. Play area. Table tennis, football, EV charging points, surfboard rental, and WiFi (80% coverage).

Key Features

📅 All Year

🐾 Pets allowed

♿ Accessible Facilities

⛱ Seaside Beach Nearby

🛝 Childrens Play Area

🍸 Bar on Site

🚲 Bicycle Hire on Site

Find Out More
Visit **ar.camp/es90390**
or scan the QR code.

Etxarri-Aranatz, Navarra

Alan Rogers Ref: ES90420
Accommodations: 32
Pitches: 108
GPS: 42.91303, -2.07992
Post Code: E-31820

what3words:
biotech.quilting.crooned

Contact:
info@campingetxarri.com
Tel: +34 948 46 05 37
www.campingetxarri.com

Open Dates:
Start March - Mid October.

Camping Etxarri

Situated in the Valle de la Burundi, this pleasant and improved site has superb views of the 1,300 m. high San-Donator Mountains. The approach is via a road lined by giant 300-year-old oak trees, a feature of the site. Reception is in the main building beside the pool with a restaurant above (access also by lift). There are 108 pitches of average size on flat ground (50 for touring units) with 6A electricity to all and water to 25.

The site is well placed for fascinating walks in unspoilt countryside and is close to three recognised nature walks. The site gets very crowded during the Fiestas de San Fermín (bull running) in Pamplona early in July. It is essential to make a reservation if you wish to stay.

Toilet facilities are good and include a baby bath and accessible facilities. Laundry. Motorhome services. Gas supplies. Essential supplies are kept in high season. Bar (Seasonal). Restaurant and takeaway (Seasonal). Swimming and paddling pools (High season) are also open to the public and can get crowded. Bicycle hire. Minigolf. Play area. Entertainment for children in high season. Tennis and squash courts. No charcoal barbecues. WiFi throughout (charged).

Key Features

- Pets allowed
- Accessible Facilities
- Outdoor Pool on Site
- Childrens Play Area
- Bar on Site
- Bicycle Hire on Site
- Fishing on Site

Find Out More
Visit **ar.camp/es90420**
or scan the QR code.

Mendigorria, Navarra

El Molino de Mendigorria

This is an extensive site set by an attractive weir near the town of Mendigorria alongside the River Arga. It takes its name from an old water mill close by. It features a sophisticated dock and boat launching facility and an ambitious watersports competition programme in the season with a safety boat present at all times. A Roman aqueduct (4km) is well worth a visit, perhaps by bike. July is very busy due to the bull running festival in Pamplona (28 km).

Run by the friendly owner, Anna Beriain, the site is split into separate permanent and touring sections. The touring area has 90 good-sized flat pitches with electricity and water for touring units and a particular area for tents. All are grassy, and though many trees have been planted around the site, shade can still be at a premium.

Clean, well-equipped toilet block with cold water to washbasins, Accessible facilities. Washing machine. A large restaurant with a pleasant bar. Supermarket. 2 swimming pools for adults and children (June-mid Sept), including an indoor pool with spa and another outside with slide. Bicycle hire. Canoe/pedalo hire. Riverside bar. Weekly entertainment programme (July/Aug) and many sporting activities. Squash courts. Mini golf, Riverwalk. Torches useful. Wine-tasting tours can be arranged. Gas barbecues only. WiFi on the part of the site (charged).

Alan Rogers Ref: ES90430
Accommodations: 125
Pitches: 90
GPS: 42.62423, -1.84259
Post Code: E-31150

what3words:
traffic.leads.operational

Contact:
info@campingelmolino.com
Tel: +34 948 34 06 04
www.campingelmolino.com

Open Dates:
Mid January - Mid December.

Key Features

- Book Online
- Pets allowed
- Accessible Facilities
- Outdoor Pool on Site
- Childrens Play Area
- Bar on Site
- Bicycle Hire on Site
- Fishing on Site

Find Out More
Visit **ar.camp/es90430**
or scan the QR code.

Villoslada de Cameros, La Rioja

Camping Los Cameros

Situated 3 km from the small town of Villoslada de Cameros, this site is in a quiet valley surrounded by tree-covered mountains and has direct access to the river. The area provides the opportunity for plenty of hill walking, and a footpath from the site takes you into the town. Of the 173 pitches, 146 are available for touring. They are open with some shade and have 5/10A electricity. This is a simple site with limited facilities available, but it is well-kept and has character, ideal for relaxation.

A well-maintained amenities block with toilets, free hot showers, a washing machine, and a tumble dryer is available on-site. The well-stocked site shop has everything you need for your camping trip, and the café bar serves basic meals and drinks. There's a football table to keep you entertained. A large playing field allows children to play ball games, and bicycles can be hired from reception.

One heated sanitary block provides WCs, washbasins with cold water only (one with hot water) and cubicle showers. Cold water only for a washing machine and dishwashing. Shop, bar with games and restaurant with comprehensive menu and takeaway to order (all season). Playing field and play area. Picnic area. Only gas barbecues are permitted. WiFi in some areas (free).

Alan Rogers Ref: ES92260
Accommodations: 9
Pitches: 173
GPS: 42.08068, -2.67723
Post Code: E-26125

what3words:
rifts.vacancy.ranking

Contact:
info@camping-loscameros.com
Tel: +34 941 74 70 21
www.campingloscameros.com

Open Dates:
Mid January - Mid December.

Key Features

- Pets allowed
- Childrens Play Area
- Bar on Site
- Fishing on Site

Find Out More
Visit ar.camp/es92260
or scan the QR code.

📍 **Zaragoza, Aragon**

Alan Rogers Ref: ES91050
Accommodations: 35
Pitches: 100
GPS: 41.21800, -1.79200
Post Code: E-50210

what3words:
eyedrops.nachos.stereotype

Contact:
lagoresort@gmail.com
Tel: +34 976 84 90 38
www.lagoresort.com

Open Dates:
Start March - End October.

Camping Lago Resort

Lago Resort is situated in an attractive area that receives many visitors for the Monasterio de Piedra, just 3 km away. distant. It also enjoys pleasant views of the surrounding mountains. This site is suitable for transit stops or visiting the Monasterio or the surrounding unusual Aragon countryside, as it is the only one in the area. It is not recommended for extended stays.

The 100 touring pitches are on terraces, including a large tent area are set on a steep hillside. Only the lower rows are suitable for large units. These pitches are numbered and marked by trees and have 6A electricity. Most of the site is occupied by wooden cabins, mobile homes and apartments. The area is very popular with Spanish visitors at weekends and public holidays, when the site can be jam-packed with sightseers from the Spanish cities of Barcelona, Valencia, Madrid and Zaragoza.

The single, clean, sanitary block has WCs, washbasins with hot water on one side and controllable hot showers (no dividers). Accessible facilities. Restaurant/bar and shop (June-Sept). Shop (all season). Swimming pool (late June-Sept). Play area on gravel. Large club room with indoor barbecue. Bicycle hire. Gas supplies. Torches are needed in some areas. WiFi in some areas (free).

Key Features

🗓 Book Online

🐾 Pets allowed

♿ Accessible Facilities

🏊 Outdoor Pool on Site

🧒 Childrens Play Area

🍸 Bar on Site

🚲 Bicycle Hire on Site

Find Out More
Visit **ar.camp/es91050**
or scan the QR code.

📍 **Huesca, Aragon**

Camping Isabena

Alan Rogers Ref: ES90615
GPS: 42.30687, 0.54540
Post Code: E-22482

what3words:
pillowcases.iced.vivacious

Contact:
info@isabena.eu
Tel: +34 974 54 45 30
www.isabena.eu

Open Dates:
Mid March - Mid December.

Camping Bungalowpark Isábena is a family-run site in the small village of La Puebla de Roda at the southern range of the central Pyrenees within the Spanish region of Aragon and has set itself up to welcome guests of all ages: the large modern pool (open in high season) has a shallow area, there's a playground, and the team organises games in the illuminated pool at night for younger guests.

The Adults can enjoy Bungalowpark Isábena's wellness area after a long day hiking in the mountains, recharge in the sauna, whirlpool and steam bath. There is also an onsite bar and restaurant, which serves three-course traditional Spanish meals and individual dishes. Breakfast is available here, too, to set you up for a day of exploring the local area. Other facilities include a large field for ball activities, a playground for young kids, an outdoor chess game, ping-pong tables and a games room with billiards and table football.

The spacious shower and toilet block have hot running water and accessible facilities, Restaurant, Bar, Snack bar, Breakfast available, sauna, whirlpool and steam bath, Outdoor swimming pool, Children's playground, outdoor chess game, ping-pong tables, games room with billiards and table football, WiFi, Pets allowed.

Key Features

- Book Online
- Pets allowed
- Accessible Facilities
- Outdoor Pool on Site
- Childrens Play Area
- Bar on Site

Find Out More
Visit ar.camp/es90615
or scan the QR code.

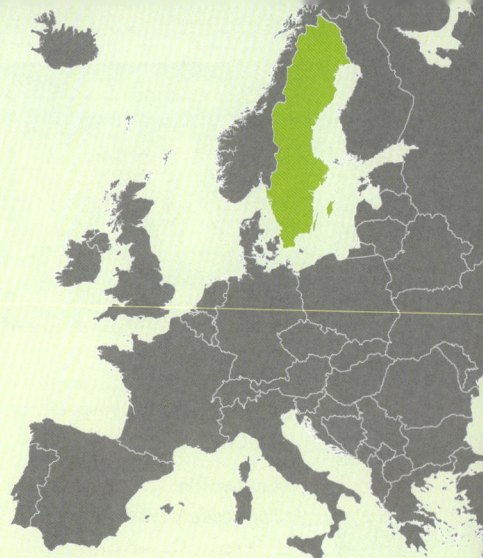

Capital Stockholm
Currency Swedish Krona (SEK)
Language Swedish
Time Zone CET (GMT+1)
Telephone Code +46
Emergency Number 112
Tourist Website visitsweden.com

Shops Hours vary throughout the year, with many shops operating shorter hours in low and shoulder seasons. In high season 9am to 6pm Mon to Fri, and until 1pm Sat.

Money ATMs are widespread, accessible 24hrs a day and have multilingual instructions. Major cards are widely accepted. There is a shift towards a cashless society though cash is still accepted in most places.

Travelling with children Sweden is great for all ages with good transport links and accommodating, friendly locals. Most museums are free for minors. Restaurants often offer a kids menu.

Public Holidays 1 Jan New Year's Day; 6 Jan Epiphany; Mar/Apr Good Friday; Mar/Apr Easter Sunday; Mar/Apr Easter Monday; 1 May Labour Day; May Ascension; May/Jun Whit Sunday; 6 Jun National Day; Jun Midsummer Day; 5 Nov All Saints; 25 Dec Christmas Day; 26 Dec Boxing Day.

Accessible Travel Score

Excellently equipped. Most transport, public buildings and outdoor spaces are accessible or offer adapted facilities.

Driving in Sweden Dipped headlights are obligatory year-round. Away from large towns, petrol stations are rarely open 24hrs, but most have self-serve pumps. There are no services or emergency phones on motorways. Come prepared if driving in winter months. Beware of large animals on the road. Drink-driving and using a mobile whilst driving are illegal. Low Emission Zones are in place in all major cities but only affect cars (pre-2016) in Stockholm. The use of dashcams is legal, however, speed camera detectors are not, so make sure to disable this feature on sat navs and mobile devices before entering the country.

Sweden

View all campsites in Sweden
ar.camp/sweden

See campsite map page 486

Climate Extremely cold in the north, mild across the rest of the country.

☀ **Avg. summer temp**
13°C (N), 17°C (S)

🌧 **Wettest month**
July (N), Aug (S)

With giant lakes and waterways, rich forests, majestic mountains and glaciers, and vast, wide-open countryside, Sweden is almost twice the size of the UK but with a fraction of the population.

With their beautiful sandy beaches, Southern Sweden's unspoiled islands offer endless boating and island hopping opportunities. The coastal cities of Gothenburg and Malmö, once centres of industry, now have an abundance of restaurants, cultural venues and attractions.

With the Oresund Bridge, Malmö is just a short ride from Copenhagen. Stockholm, the capital, is a delightful place built on fourteen small islands on the eastern coast. It is a vibrant city with magnificent architecture, fine museums and historic squares.

Sparsely populated northern Sweden is a land of forests, rivers and wilderness inhabited by moose and reindeer.

Östersund, located at the shores of a lake in the heart of the country, is well known for winter sports, while Frösö Zoo is a popular attraction. Today Sweden is one of the world's most developed societies and enjoys an enviable standard of living.

Scan QR code to browse more campsites on our website

Kiruna, Lappland

Camp Ripan

Nestled amidst the breathtaking scenery of Swedish Lapland, Camp Ripan is an oasis of comfort and adventure. This family-owned establishment, just a short drive from Kiruna city centre, invites travellers to immerse themselves in the region's natural splendour while enjoying many amenities and activities. On-site, you will find 92 touring pitches with electric hook-up points available from Easter to September, and there are a variety of cosy accommodation options to suit every traveller's needs available all year. Choose from modern cabins, each equipped with its own ski shed, or opt for one of the hotel's comfortable rooms.

The service building is next to the caravan area and has a communal kitchen, dining area, laundry room, showers, sauna and bathrooms. The site also features a restaurant and bar which serves delicious meals featuring traditional Swedish and Sami specialities prepared with fresh, locally sourced ingredients. Relax at the spa, which offers a range of massage and beauty treatments. There is also a sauna, steam room and indoor swimming pool.

Sanitary building with accessible facilities, Laundry services, Motorhome services, drying room for wet clothes, Ski storage, Restaurant and bar, communal kitchen, Dining area, Children's play area, mini golf, Padel court and gym, Spa facilities including sauna, steam room and indoor swimming pool (charges apply), WiFi, Pets allowed.

Alan Rogers Ref: SW2868
Accommodations: 96
Pitches: 92
GPS: 67.86090, 20.24039
Post Code: S-981 35

what3words:
voter.football.themes

Contact:
info@ripan.se
Tel: +46 980 630 00
www.ripan.se

Open Dates:
Easter - End September.

Key Features

- Pets allowed
- Indoor Pool on Site
- Childrens Play Area
- Bar on Site
- Skiing on Site

Find Out More
Visit ar.camp/sw2868
or scan the QR code.

Camping Saiva

Saiva Camping is situated by Lake Baksjön at the edge of Vilhelmina, about 1 kilometre from the town centre. The campsite has 55 touring pitches, 40 of which have electric hook-up points, and there are also 21 cabins available to hire. For those who want to take full advantage of Lake Baksjön, the campsite has a sandy beach where you can take a dip and go swimming. You will also find a diving board with hours of fun jumping into the water. The campsite also offers rentals of kayaks and pedal boats for those who want to explore the surrounding area by water. There is also plenty of fishing here and in the surrounding area of the campsite for avid anglers.

Children can enjoy a large playground right on the beach. There is also a mini golf course, football pitch, table tennis and tennis court. An on-site sauna is available for those who want to relax after a long day of exploring. The reception houses a café serving various food and beverages; it has a lounge area with a TV, fireplace and sofas. The site also has a shop where you can get your essentials to cook at your pitch.

Clean sanitary building with separate shower cubicles, accessible facilities, Baby changing, Laundry facilities, Motorhome services, Café, Communal kitchen, Shop with fresh bread daily, Children's playground, volleyball, Mini golf, Football pitch, Tennis, Table tennis, Trampoline, Sauna, Outdoor gym, Lake swimming, Fishing, Kayak and pedal boat hire, Bicycle hire, TV, BBQs allowed. WiFi available. Pets are allowed.

Alan Rogers Ref: SW2864
Accommodations: 21
Pitches: 55
GPS: 64.62165, 16.67917
Post Code: S-912 31

what3words:
igniting.smothered.banner

Contact:
info@saiva.se
Tel: +46 940 107 60
www.saiva.se

Open Dates:
Start May - End September.

Key Features

- Pets allowed
- Accessible Facilities
- Childrens Play Area
- Bar on Site
- Bicycle Hire on Site
- Fishing on Site

Find Out More
Visit **ar.camp/sw2864**
or scan the QR code.

📍 **Umeå, Västerbottens**

Alan Rogers Ref: SW2860
Accommodations: 122
Pitches: 450
GPS: 63.84333, 20.34056
Post Code: S-906 54

what3words:
quilts.realm.dude

Contact:
umea@firstcamp.se
Tel: +46 907 026 00
www.en.firstcamp.se/
destinations/nydala-umea

Open Dates:
All year (full services Mid May -
End August)

Camp Nydala-Umeå

An ideal stopover for those travelling the E4 coastal route and a good base from which to explore the area, this campsite is 6 km. from the centre of this university city. It is almost adjacent to the Nydalsjön lake, ideal for fishing, windsurfing, bathing and canoeing. There are 450 grassy pitches arranged in bays of 10-20 units, 320 with electricity (10/16A), and some are fully serviced.

This is a popular destination, with many returning guests in both the summer and winter. The campsite offers a wide range of fun activities during the summer, including workout sessions, a popular kids' club, evening entertainment, and the rental of bicycles and pedal cars. You can also play a round of mini golf or play a game of paddle tennis. The on-site bistro is the perfect place to enjoy a meal after a busy day of fun-filled activities. The menu includes international dishes; you can eat indoors or on the terrace when it's sunny.

The large, heated, central sanitary unit includes controllable hot showers with communal changing areas. Accessible facilities. Facilities may be stretched in high season. Laundry facilities. Kitchen. Large dining room. Motorhome services. TV. Shop (Seasonal). Fully licensed restaurant, bar and takeaway (High season). Giant chess. Playgrounds. Bicycle hire. Rowing boat hire. Fishing in the lake. Canoes and pedal cars for hire. Sauna, Adventure golf. Kids club and entertainment in summer, WiFi throughout (charged).

Key Features

📅 All Year

🐾 Pets allowed

♿ Accessible Facilities

🛝 Childrens Play Area

🍸 Bar on Site

🚲 Bicycle Hire on Site

🐟 Fishing on Site

⛵ Sailing on Site

Find Out More
Visit **ar.camp/sw2860**
or scan the QR code.

Kramfors, Västernorrlands Län

Flogsta Camping

Kramfors lies just west of the E4, and travellers may pass by over the Höga Kusten bridge and miss this friendly little site. This area of Ådalen and the High Coast reaches as far as Örnsköldsvik. The attractive garden-like campsite has 32 pitches, 21 with electricity connections (10A), arranged on level grassy terraces, separated by shrubs and trees into bays of two to four units. The non-electric pitches are on an open terrace nearer to the reception. All pitches overlook the heated outdoor public swimming pool complex and an attractive minigolf course.

The surrounding area of Flogsta Camping offers a wealth of activities. Fishing enthusiasts can enjoy their days casting their line along the Kramfors River, while nature lovers can embark on scenic hiking trails through the picturesque landscape.

Sanitary facilities comprise nine bathrooms, each with British-style WCs, a basin with a hand dryer, and a shower. Laundry facilities. More WCs and showers are in the reception building, along with a free sauna. A further sanitary block with a sauna and outside hot tub. Separate building housing a kitchen, with hot plates, fridge/freezer and TV/dining room (all free). The reception building has a small shop and snack bar. Heated outdoor swimming pools. Playground. Snowmobile hire.

Alan Rogers Ref: SW2855
Accommodations: 16
Pitches: 32
GPS: 62.92562, 17.75642
Post Code: S-872 80

what3words:
mailing.reveal.bunkers

Contact:
flogstacamping@telia.com
Tel: +46 612 100 05
www.flogstacamping.n.nu

Open Dates:
Mid May - End September.

Key Features

- Pets allowed
- Outdoor Pool on Site
- Childrens Play Area
- Bicycle Hire on Site

Find Out More
Visit ar.camp/sw2855
or scan the QR code.

📍 **Skärholmen, Stockholms Län**

Bredäng Stockholm

Bredäng Camping is a busy city site with easy access to Stockholm's city centre. Large and fairly level, with very little shade, there are 380 pitches, of which 204 have electricity (10A) and 115 have hardstanding. A separate area has been provided for tents. Reception is open from 08.00-22.00 in the high season (June-August), with reduced hours in the low season, and English is spoken. The campsite offers a selection of facilities to enjoy whilst staying on-site, including a restaurant with local and international dishes, a mini-golf course, and a children's playground.

The campsite is conveniently situated a 2-minute walk through the woods to Mälarhöjdsbadet, a famous sandy beach on the shores of Lake Mälaren. Here, you can relax by the water and take a refreshing swim during the summer months.

Four high-standard heated sanitary units provide British-style WCs, controllable hot showers and some washbasins in cubicles. One has a baby room, accessible facilities and a first aid room. Cooking facilities are in three units around the site. Laundry facilities. Motorhome services and car wash. Well-stocked shop, bar, takeaway and fully licensed restaurant (Open May - mid-Sept). Hostel. Cabins. Sauna. Playground. Minigolf. Frisbee Golf. Outdoor Gym. WiFi throughout (free).

Alan Rogers Ref: SW2842
Accommodations: 20
Pitches: 380
GPS: 59.29560, 17.92315
Post Code: S-127 31

what3words:
leaflet.musician.curiosity

Contact:
bredangcamping@gmail.com
Tel: +46 89 770 71
www.bredangcamping.se

Open Dates:
Mid May - Mid September.

Key Features

🐾 Pets allowed

♿ Accessible Facilities

🏖 Seaside Beach Nearby

🛝 Childrens Play Area

🍸 Bar on Site

Find Out More
Visit ar.camp/sw2842
or scan the QR code.

Lidköping, Västra Götalands Län

Camping Lidköping

KronoCamping Lidköping is located on the shores of Lake Vänern, just a 15-minute walk from the centre of Lidköping. This high-quality, attractive site provides 410 touring pitches on flat, well-kept grass plus 53 excellent hardstanding pitches for motorhomes. All the pitches have electricity (10A/16A) and TV connections, and many are fully serviced. There are 30 cabins to rent and 125 seasonal units. It is surrounded by some mature trees, with the lake shore as one boundary and some tall pines providing shade and shelter.

A small shop (a shopping centre is very close) and a pleasant, fully licensed restaurant with a conservatory seating area in the reception complex. The lake is available for watersports, kayaking and fishing, with swimming opportunities from the sandy beach, and there is a swimming pool complex (free for campers) adjacent to the campsite.

Four excellent, modern sanitary facilities with underfloor heating. Hot water is free. Make-up and hairdressing areas, baby room and accessible facilities. Private cabins. Good kitchen with seats, cookers, microwaves and dishwashers. Motorhome services. Small shop. Restaurant (closed Jan-March). Minigolf. Playgrounds. TV room. Games and amusements room. Bicycle hire. Play field. Small gym. Paddle tennis, table tennis, kids' club, creative crafts, lake swimming, fishing, and watersports. Sauna and jacuzzi (charged). Free WiFi.

Alan Rogers Ref: SW2710
Accommodations: 155
Pitches: 410
GPS: 58.51306, 13.13853
Post Code: S-531 54

what3words:
busters.reflect.legislative

Contact:
info@kronocamping.com
Tel: +46 510 268 04
www.kronocamping.com

Open Dates:
All year (full services June - August)

Key Features

All Year

Pets allowed

Accessible Facilities

Childrens Play Area

Bar on Site

Bicycle Hire on Site

Fishing on Site

Find Out More
Visit ar.camp/sw2710
or scan the QR code.

📍 Färjestaden, Kalmar Län

Alan Rogers Ref: SW2680
Accommodations: 169
Pitches: 435
GPS: 56.68727, 16.48182
Post Code: S-386 95

what3words:
rivers.happen.transcribe

Contact:
info@kcsaxnas.se
Tel: +46 485 357 00
www.kcsaxnas.se

Open Dates:
Late April - Late September.

Camping Saxnäs

Well placed for touring Sweden's Riviera and the fascinating and beautiful island of Öland, this large, family-run site, part of the Krono group, has 540 marked and numbered pitches, of which around 400 are for touring. Arranged in rows on open, well-kept grassland dotted with a few trees, all have electricity (10/16A), and 112 also have water. An unmarked area without electricity can accommodate around 60 tents. The site has about 140 long-stay units and cabins to rent.

Reception is efficient and friendly, with good English spoken. Many activities keep the children entertained in the high season, with kids' clubs hosting sports games and mini-golf tournaments. There is a large children's playground with a bouncy cushion, too. Dance evenings and live shows are also held in the evenings.

Three heated sanitary blocks provide roomy shower cubicles, washbasins, some washbasin/WC suites and WCs (shower cards required). Accessible Facilities. Well-equipped laundry room. Good kitchen with cookers, microwaves, dishwasher (free), and sinks. Gas supplies. Motorhome services. Shop (May-Aug). Snack bar/takeaway, licensed restaurant and café (Seasonal). Pool bar. Outdoor heated swimming pool (June-Aug, charged). Pontoon with slides. Sauna. Playgrounds. Bouncy cushion. Boules. Football. Minigolf. Family entertainment and activities. Bicycle and pedal car hire. WiFi throughout (charged).

Key Features

🐾 Pets allowed

♿ Accessible Facilities

🏖 Seaside Beach on Site

🏊 Outdoor Pool on Site

🛝 Childrens Play Area

🍸 Bar on Site

🚲 Bicycle Hire on Site

🎣 Fishing on Site

Find Out More
Visit **ar.camp/sw2680**
or scan the QR code.

📍 Röstånga, Skåne Län

Röstånga Camping

Röstånga Camping is a family-friendly campsite located in the heart of the Söderåsen National Park in southern Sweden. The campsite is situated on the banks of the Röstångaån River, which offers opportunities for swimming, fishing, and canoeing. There are 200 large, level, grassy pitches with electricity (10A) and a quiet area for tents with views over the fishing lake. The tent area has its service building and several barbecue places. Some holiday homes and 24 pleasant cabins are available to rent all year round.

During the summer, various activities and entertainment are held on-site for all ages. There is a children's club with a program of creative crafts, treasure hunts and sporting games. There is a mini golf course where you can have a competitive game or two. The swimming pool has a children's pool and water slide, heated during the summer. Live shows and dance nights can be found at the on-site restaurant during the evening.

Six good, heated sanitary blocks with free hot water and facilities for babies and accessible facilities. Motorhome services. Laundry with washing machines and dryers. Kitchen with cooking rings, oven and microwave. Small shop at reception. Bar, restaurant and takeaway. Minigolf (charged). Tennis. Fitness trail. Two fishing lakes and lake swimming. Canoe hire. BMX track. Boules. Children's club (High season). Free WiFi throughout.

Alan Rogers Ref: SW2630
Accommodations: 24
Pitches: 200
GPS: 55.99658, 13.28005
Post Code: S-268 68

what3words:
fonts.fetch.soppy

Contact:
rostanga@firstcamp.se
Tel: +46 435 910 64
firstcamp.se/destinationer/
rostanga-soderasen

Open Dates:
Late April - Late September.

Alan Rogers Awards Won
2015

Key Features

🐾 Pets allowed

♿ Accessible Facilities

🍸 Bar on Site

🐟 Fishing on Site

Find Out More
Visit ar.camp/sw2630
or scan the QR code.

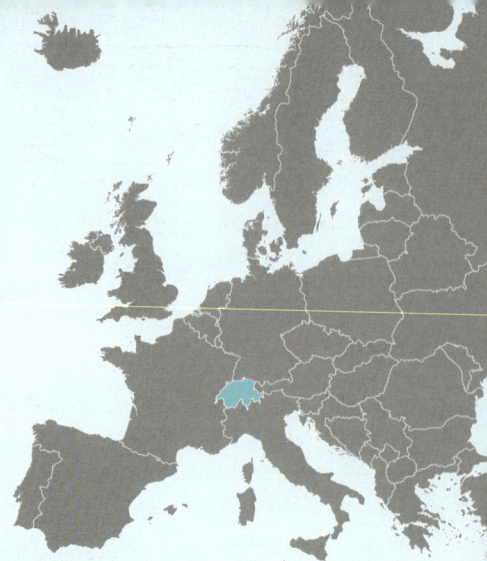

Capital Bern
Currency Swiss Franc (CHf)
Language German, French, Italian and regional variants
Time Zone CET (GMT+1)
Telephone Code +41
Emergency Number 112
Tourist Website myswitzerland.com

Shops Hours vary throughout the year, with many shops operating shorter hours in low and shoulder seasons. In high season 10am to 6pm Mon to Fri, and until 4pm Sat.

Money ATMs are widespread, accessible 24hrs a day and have multilingual instructions. Major cards are widely accepted. Payment in cash is still very common. Most restaurants and shops accept euros but will give change in CHf.

Travelling with children Switzerland is a great destination for families. Most restaurants offer a kids menu. Children aged 6 years or under travel free on trains.

Public Holidays 1 Jan New Year's Day; Mar/Apr Good Friday; Mar/Apr Easter Monday; May Ascension; May/Jun Whit Monday; May/Jun Corpus Christi; 1 Aug National Day; 1 Nov All Saints; 25 Dec Christmas Day; 26 Dec Boxing Day.

Accessible Travel Score

Public transport and outdoor spaces are accessible. Most walking trails are wheelchair-friendly.

Driving in Switzerland An annual road tax is levied on all cars using Swiss motorways, and the vignette windscreen sticker must be purchased at the border or in advance, plus a separate one for a towed caravan or trailer. Many mountain resorts are vehicle-free, instead use park-and-ride schemes and cable cars. Drink-driving and using a mobile whilst driving are illegal. There are no Low Emission Zones in place. The use of dashcams is legal but advised against as there are many rules regarding their use. Speed camera detectors are illegal, so make sure to disable this feature on sat navs and mobile devices before entering the country.

Switzerland
& Liechtenstein

View all campsites in Switzerland
ar.camp/switzerland

View all campsites in Liechtenstein
ar.camp/liechtenstein

See campsite map page 487

Climate Mild and refreshing in the north. South of the Alps it is warmer.

☀

Avg. summer temp
18°C

🌧

Wettest month
June

A small, wealthy country best known for its outstanding mountainous scenery, fine cheeses and delicious chocolates. Centrally situated in Europe, it shares its borders with France, Austria, Germany and Italy, each one having its own cultural influence on the country.

With its snowy peaks and rolling hills, the Bernese Oberland is the most popular area; Gstaad is a favourite haunt of wealthy skiers, while the mild climate and breezy conditions around Lake Thun are perfect for watersports.

German-speaking Zurich is a multicultural metropolis with museums, sophisticated shops and colourful festivals set against a breathtaking backdrop of lakes and mountains. The southeast of Switzerland has densely forested mountain slopes and the glamorous resort of Saint Moritz.

Geneva, Montreux and Lausanne make up the bulk of French Switzerland, with vineyards that border the lakes and medieval towns. The southernmost canton, Ticino, is home to the Italian-speaking Swiss, with the Mediterranean-style lakeside resorts of Lugano and Locarno.

Scan QR code to browse more campsites in Switzerland

Scan QR code to find out more about Liechtenstein

📍 Estavayer-le-Lac, Fribourg

Alan Rogers Ref: CH9032
Accommodations: 148
Pitches: 60
GPS: 46.85721, 6.84796
Post Code: CH-1470

what3words:
clays.crowbar.nametag

Contact:
info@nouvelle-plage.ch
Tel: + 41 26 663 16 93
www.nouvelle-plage.ch

Open Dates:
End March - Mid October.

La Nouvelle Plage

Situated right beside Lake Neuchâtel in Switzerland, Camping La Nouvelle Plage is the perfect site for active holidaymakers as it offers families a chance to enjoy all kinds of water-based activities. The campground is on an attractive sandy beach with direct access to the lake. You'll find plenty of water sports, including water skiing, paddle boarding and pedalos. Beach volleyball and ping pong are also available for active families.

The campsite has 60 touring pitches, with electric hookups available and the option to be positioned near the lake's beach or closer to the nature reserve. For those who aren't into water sports, there are many facilities to keep the whole family occupied, including volleyball, a multi-sport pitch, a water slide and a children's playground, or there are plenty of spaces to lounge around by the lake and watch the activities in comfort. Alternatively, visit the local vineyards or the region's dramatic castles and picturesque villages.

Accessible sanitary facilities. Fresh bread. Bar. Snack Bar. Restaurant. Shop. Pizzeria. Takeaway meals. Children's playground. Bicycle hire. Kayaking. Volleyball. Multisport field. Sailing. Pedal boats. Table tennis table. Multi-sports field. Fishing on-site. Open water swimming. Pets allowed. WiFi.

Key Features

🐾 Pets allowed

♿ Accessible Facilities

🛝 Childrens Play Area

🍸 Bar on Site

🐟 Fishing on Site

⛵ Sailing on Site

Find Out More
Visit **ar.camp/ch9032**
or scan the QR code.

Le Landeron, Neuchâtel

Camping des Pêches

This relatively recently constructed touring campsite is on the side of Lake Biel and the river Thielle, close to the old town of Le Landeron. The site is divided into two sections: on the lake side of the road are residential seasonal caravans, and on the other is the modern campsite for tourists. The 160 touring pitches are all on level grass, numbered but not separated; a few have shade, all have 13A electricity and many conveniently placed water points.

All the facilities are well maintained and in good condition. There is a specially designed outdoor area for children: A water play area with a specially designed shock-absorbing floor with fountains and sprinklers. There is also a play area with climbing ropes, a trampoline, swings and a slide. There is also an outdoor community swimming pool located 5 minutes by foot from the campsite.

The spacious, modern sanitary block contains all the usual facilities, including a food preparation area with six cooking rings, a large freezer and a refrigerator. Payment for showers is by card. Baby room. Accessible Facilities. Laundry. Motorhome services. Community room and small café in the reception building. Shop, restaurant and takeaway (all season). Playground. Bicycle hire and Electric bicycle hire. TV and general room. WiFi throughout. Pets allowed, Dog walking field.

Alan Rogers Ref: CH9040
Accommodations: 10
Pitches: 160
GPS: 47.05253, 7.07001
Post Code: CH-2525

what3words:
enjoys.harmonica.waxing

Contact:
info@camping-lelanderon.ch
Tel: +41 32 751 29 00
www.camping-lelanderon.ch

Open Dates:
Start April - Mid October.

Key Features

- Pets allowed
- Accessible Facilities
- Outdoor Pool on Site
- Childrens Play Area
- Bicycle Hire on Site

Find Out More
Visit ar.camp/ch9040
or scan the QR code.

📍 **Interlaken-Thunersee, Bern**

Alan Rogers Ref: CH9425
Accommodations: 83
Pitches: 92
GPS: 46.67999, 7.81728
Post Code: CH-3800

what3words:
ordeals.funds.backdrop

Contact:
info@camping-alpenblick.ch
Tel: +41 33 822 77 57
www.camping-alpenblick.ch

Open Dates:
All year.

Camping Alpenblick

Alpenblick is an all-year site in a stunning setting, located at the heart of the Bernese Oberland just 100 metres from the beautiful Lake Thun. A Swiss chalet-style building houses the reception, shop and bar/restaurant that is very popular with campers and locals alike (try the 'schnitzelbrot' and dine on the terrace in good weather). There are around 100 touring pitches and a further 80 residential pitches. The touring pitches are mostly grassy and level, with moderate shade, and all have 10/16A electrical connections. Some good hardstanding pitches are available for motorhomes.

Campers can use a special tourist card with many benefits, including free local bus transport. This is a superb area for cycling and walking, with trails taking you through magnificent scenery all around the lake. The lake is popular for all manner of watersports, and cruisers depart from a point very close to Alpenblick. The views everywhere are majestic.

Sanitary block with hot showers, some washbasins in cubicles and a family shower room. Accessible Facilities. Laundry facilities. Shop (Seasonal) with daily delivery of bread. Bar, restaurant and takeaway (all year). Bar and barbecue for socialising and events. Playground. Boules. Basketball. WiFi throughout (charged).

Key Features

📅 Book Online

📆 All Year

🐾 Pets allowed

♿ Accessible Facilities

🛝 Childrens Play Area

🍸 Bar on Site

Find Out More
Visit **ar.camp/ch9425**
or scan the QR code.

Interlaken-Thunersee, Bern

Alan Rogers Ref: CH9420
Accommodations: 110
Pitches: 230
GPS: 46.68129, 7.81524
Post Code: CH-3800

what3words:
simmer.otter.mascot

Contact:
info@manorfarm.ch
Tel: +41 33 822 22 64
www.manorfarm.ch

Open Dates:
All year.

Camping Manor Farm 1

Manor Farm continues to be popular with British and Dutch visitors; located in one of the traditional touring areas of Switzerland. The flat terrain is divided into 230 individual, numbered pitches, varying considerably in size (40-100 sq.m) and price. There is shade in some places.

There are 120 pitches with 4/13A electricity, water and drainage, and 55 also have cable TV connections. Reservations can be made, although you should find space, except perhaps in late July/early August when the best places may be taken. Around 40 per cent of the pitches are taken by permanent or letting units and four tour operators.

Seven separate toilet blocks are practical, heated and fully equipped. They include free hot water for baths and showers. Accessible facilities. Twenty private toilet units are available to rent. Laundry facilities. Motorhome services. Gas supplies. Excellent shop (Seasonal). Site-owned restaurant adjacent (Seasonal). Snack bar with takeaway (High season). TV room. Playground and paddling pool. Minigolf. Bicycle hire. Sailing school. Lake swimming. Boat hire (slipway for campers' own boats). Fishing. Daily activity and entertainment programme in high season. Excursions. Max. 1 dog. WiFi in some parts (charged).

Key Features

- Book Online
- All Year
- Pets allowed
- Accessible Facilities
- Childrens Play Area
- Bar on Site
- Bicycle Hire on Site
- Fishing on Site

Find Out More
Visit **ar.camp/ch9420**
or scan the QR code.

📍 **Lauterbrunnen, Bern**

Alan Rogers Ref: CH9460
Pitches: 391
GPS: 46.58807, 7.91077
Post Code: CH-3822

what3words:
fearfully.rebel.shortage

Contact:
info@campingjungfrau.swiss
Tel: +41 33 856 20 10
www.campingjungfrau.swiss

Open Dates:
All year.

🏅 **Alan Rogers Awards Won**
2023

Camping Jungfrau

This friendly and ever-popular site has a very imposing and dramatic situation in a steep valley with a fine view of the Jungfrau at the end. Mountain meltwater cascades hundreds of feet down the sheer rock walls of the valley. Many active pursuits are available in the area, as well as trips on the Jungfrau railway and mountain lifts. In winter, the site runs a free shuttle bus to the local ski lifts, and large community lounges are available for après-ski enjoyment.

A large area is made up of grass pitches and hardcore access roads. All 391 pitches (250 for touring) have shade in parts and electrical connections (13A), and 50 have water and drainage too. This family-owned, friendly site offers a warm welcome, and English is spoken. It is a perfect spot for relaxing amid epic scenery.

Three fully equipped modern sanitary blocks (heated in winter), one providing accessible facilities. Baby baths. Laundry facilities. Motorhome services. Well-equipped campers' kitchen. Excellent shop. Self-service restaurant with takeaway (all year). General room with tables and chairs, TV, drinks machines, and amusements. Playgrounds and covered play area. Excursions and some entertainment in high season. Mountain bike hire. ATM. Drying room. Ski store. Free shuttle bus in winter. Internet point. WiFi throughout (free).

Key Features

📅 Book Online

📅 All Year

🐾 Pets allowed

♿ Accessible Facilities

🛝 Childrens Play Area

🍸 Bar on Site

⛷️ Skiing on Site

🚴 Bicycle Hire on Site

Find Out More
Visit **ar.camp/ch9460**
or scan the QR code.

Tenero, Ticino

Alan Rogers Ref: CH9890
Accommodations: 91
Pitches: 712
GPS: 46.16895, 8.85592
Post Code: CH-6598

what3words:
workloads.cover.agenda

Contact:
camping@campofelice.ch
Tel: +41 91 745 14 17
www.campofelice.ch

Open Dates:
Late March - End October.

Alan Rogers Awards Won
2014

Campofelice Camping

Considered by many to be the best family campsite in Switzerland, Campofelice Camping Village borders Lake Maggiore and the Verzasca estuary, where the site has its own marina. There are 712 generously sized touring pitches on flat grass on either side of hard access roads. Mostly well-shaded, all pitches have electricity connections (13A, 360 Europlug), and 376 also have water, drainage and TV connections. A particular area is reserved for small tents. Pitches near the lake cost more (these are not available for motorhomes until September).

It's a little more expensive than other sites in the area, but excellent value for the range and quality of the facilities. The surrounding scenery is sublime, with sensational views from the gently shelving beach and the cycle trails into Locarno.

Modern heated sanitary facilities. Accessible facilities, Laundry. Sandy beach (400m). Pool and Wellness Area. Aquapark. Charging station for Tesla and electric cars. Two playgrounds. Tennis courts. Minigolf. Bike track. Beach volleyball. Bicycle hire. Canoe. SUP and pedalo hire. Car hire. Car wash. Free WiFi. Boat launch. Football field. Pizzeria. Restaurant. Snack bar. Camping accessories and various shops. Lifeguards. Pavilion with an LED wall. Doctor on call. Entertainment program with shows. Games and sports competitions. Pets are not accepted. Accommodation is available.

Key Features

- Book Online
- Accessible Facilities
- Outdoor Pool on Site
- Childrens Play Area
- Bar on Site
- Bicycle Hire on Site

Find Out More
Visit **ar.camp/ch9890**
or scan the QR code.

📍 Brienz am See, Bern

Camping Aaregg

Alan Rogers Ref: CH9510
Accommodations: 69
Pitches: 227
GPS: 46.74830, 8.04871
Post Code: CH-3855

what3words:
media.cross.initiates

Contact:
mail@aaregg.ch
Tel: +41 33 951 18 43
www.aaregg.ch

Open Dates:
Start April - End October.

Brienz, in the Bernese Oberland, is a delightful little town on the lake of the same name and the centre of the Swiss wood carving industry. Camping Aaregg is an excellent site of the highest quality, situated at the eastern end of the lake with breathtaking views across the water to the surrounding mountains.

 Cabins to rent and seasonal pitches occupy part of the site, with over 200 pitches available for touring, all with electricity (10/16A). Of these, eight lakeside pitches have been upgraded with full services, and 18 have hardstandings, water and drainage. The trees, flowers and well-tended grass make an attractive and peaceful environment.

Very attractive sanitary facilities, built and maintained to a high standard. Showers with washbasins. Washbasins (open style and in cubicles). Children's section. Family shower rooms. Baby room. Accessible Facilities. Laundry facilities. Motorhome services. Pleasant restaurant with a café/bar and shop. Guest lounge with TV. Play area. Fishing. Bicycle hire. Boat launching. Lake swimming in clear water (unsupervised). English is spoken. WiFi in the reception area. New camping pods and mini chalets for hire.

Key Features

🐾 Pets allowed

♿ Accessible Facilities

🛝 Childrens Play Area

🍸 Bar on Site

🚲 Bicycle Hire on Site

🐟 Fishing on Site

⛵ Sailing on Site

Find Out More
Visit **ar.camp/ch9510**
or scan the QR code.

Triesen, Liechtenstein

Camping Mittagsspitze

Camping Mittagsspitze is attractively and quietly situated for visiting Liechtenstein. Set on a hillside, it has all the scenic mountain views one could wish for. Extensive grassy terraces on a steep slope provide unmarked but level pitches, and electricity connections (6A) are available. Trees provide some shade, mainly along the terrace edges. About 80 touring pitches are available, with the remainder of the site given over to seasonal pitches.

The on-site restaurant "Zur Alten Eiche" (The Old Oak) serves high-quality, seasonal, local dishes and has an extensive wine menu. The terrace and beer garden can be enjoyed in the summer. The surrounding mountain scenery of the local area is well worth exploring - pick up one of the marked trails, some passing the campsite entrance. The Liechtenstein capital, Vaduz, is around 10 minutes drive away, with the Swiss border less than 5km away. It's worth noting that the campsite has Swiss-style power sockets, so an adaptor will be required if you have a CEE or Euro connector.

Two good quality sanitary blocks provide all the usual facilities. Washing machine, dryer and ironing. Shop, bar and takeaway (seasonal; bread to order). Restaurant (March - December). Small swimming pool and paddling pool (seasonal), not heated but very popular in summer. Playground. TV room. Wifi.

Alan Rogers Ref: FL7580
Accommodations: 10
Pitches: 80
GPS: 47.08570, 9.52590
Post Code: FL-9495

what3words:
rinses.crimson.public

Contact:
info@campingtriesen.li
Tel: +423 392 26 88
www.campingtriesen.li

Open Dates:
All year.

Key Features

- All Year
- Pets allowed
- Outdoor Pool on Site
- Childrens Play Area
- Bar on Site
- Fishing on Site

Find Out More
Visit ar.camp/fl7580
or scan the QR code.

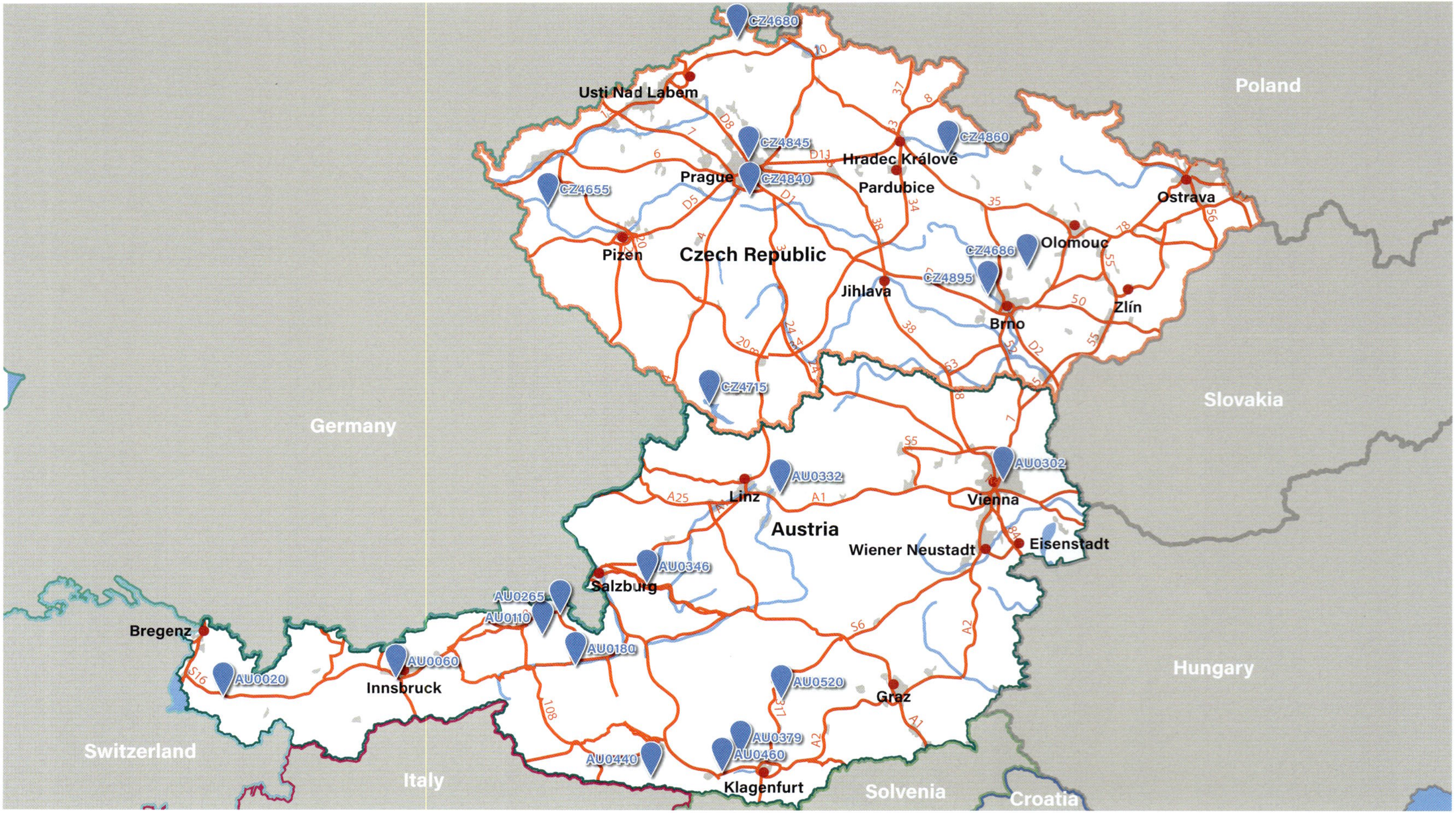

Poland

Slovakia

Hungary

Croatia

Ostrava

56

Zlín

78

55

Olomouc

50

55

CZ4860

35

Brno

D2

52

CZ4686

37

8

Hradec Králové

34

CZ4895

38

3

Pardubice

38

Jihlava

CZ4680

10

CZ4845

D13

CZ4840

D1

D11

24

20

CZ4715

Czech Republic

Prague

D8

7

Usti Nad Labem

6

20

CZ4655

Pizen

4

Germany

AU0302

7

Vienna

84

Eisenstadt

Wiener Neustadt

A2

Austria

A1

Graz

55

S6

AU0332

A1

Linz

A25

A14

AU0520

317

AU0379

AU0460

Klagenfurt

A2

Solvenia

AU0346

Salzburg

AU0180

A10

AU0440

108

AU0265

AU0110

Italy

AU0060

Innsbruck

AU0020

S16

Bregenz

Switzerland

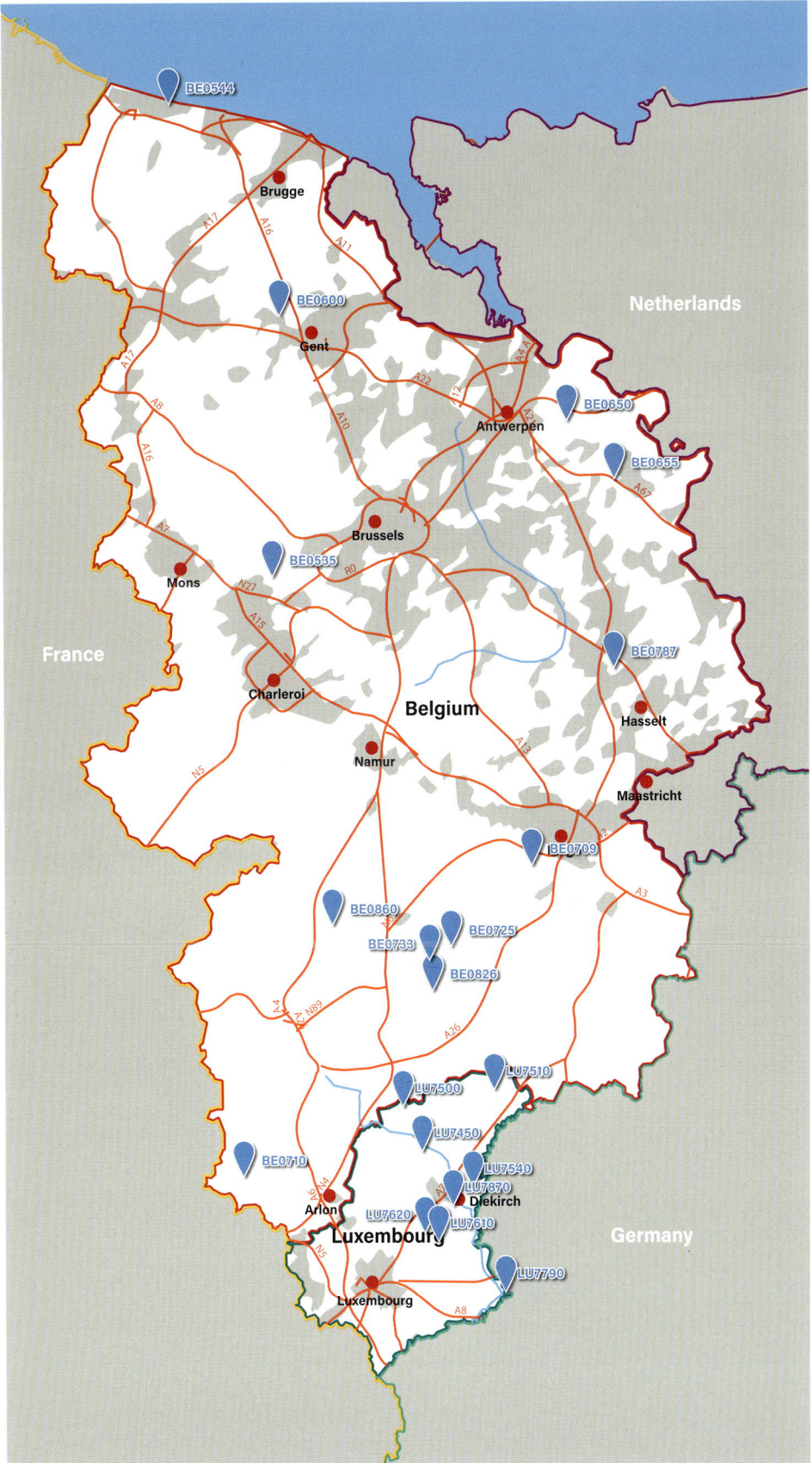

BE0544

Brugge

BE0600

Gent

Netherlands

BE0650

BE0655

Antwerpen

BE0787

Brussels

BE0535

Mons

France

Charleroi

Belgium

Hasselt

Namur

Maastricht

BE0709

BE0860

BE0725

BE0733

BE0826

LU7510

LU7500

BE0710

LU7450

LU7540

LU7870

Arlon

Diekirch

LU7620

LU7790

Luxembourg

LU7610

Germany

Luxembourg

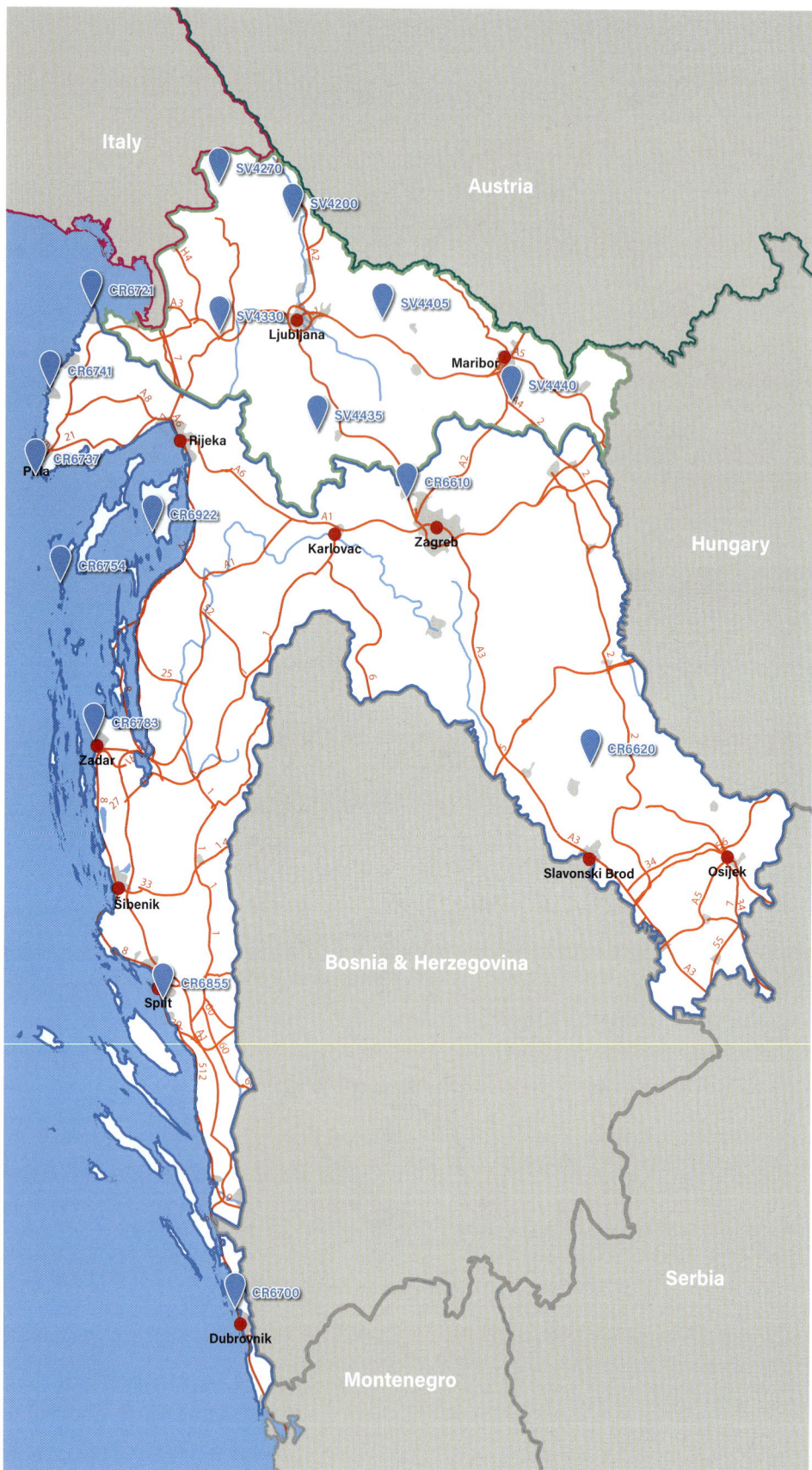

Italy

Austria

SV4270

SV4200

CR6721

SV4330

SV4405

Ljubljana

Maribor

CR6741

SV4440

SV4435

CR6737

Pula

Rijeka

CR6922

CR6610

Zagreb

CR6754

Karlovac

Hungary

CR6620

CR6783

Zadar

Slavonski Brod

Osijek

Šibenik

Bosnia & Herzegovina

CR6855

Split

Serbia

CR6700

Dubrovnik

Montenegro

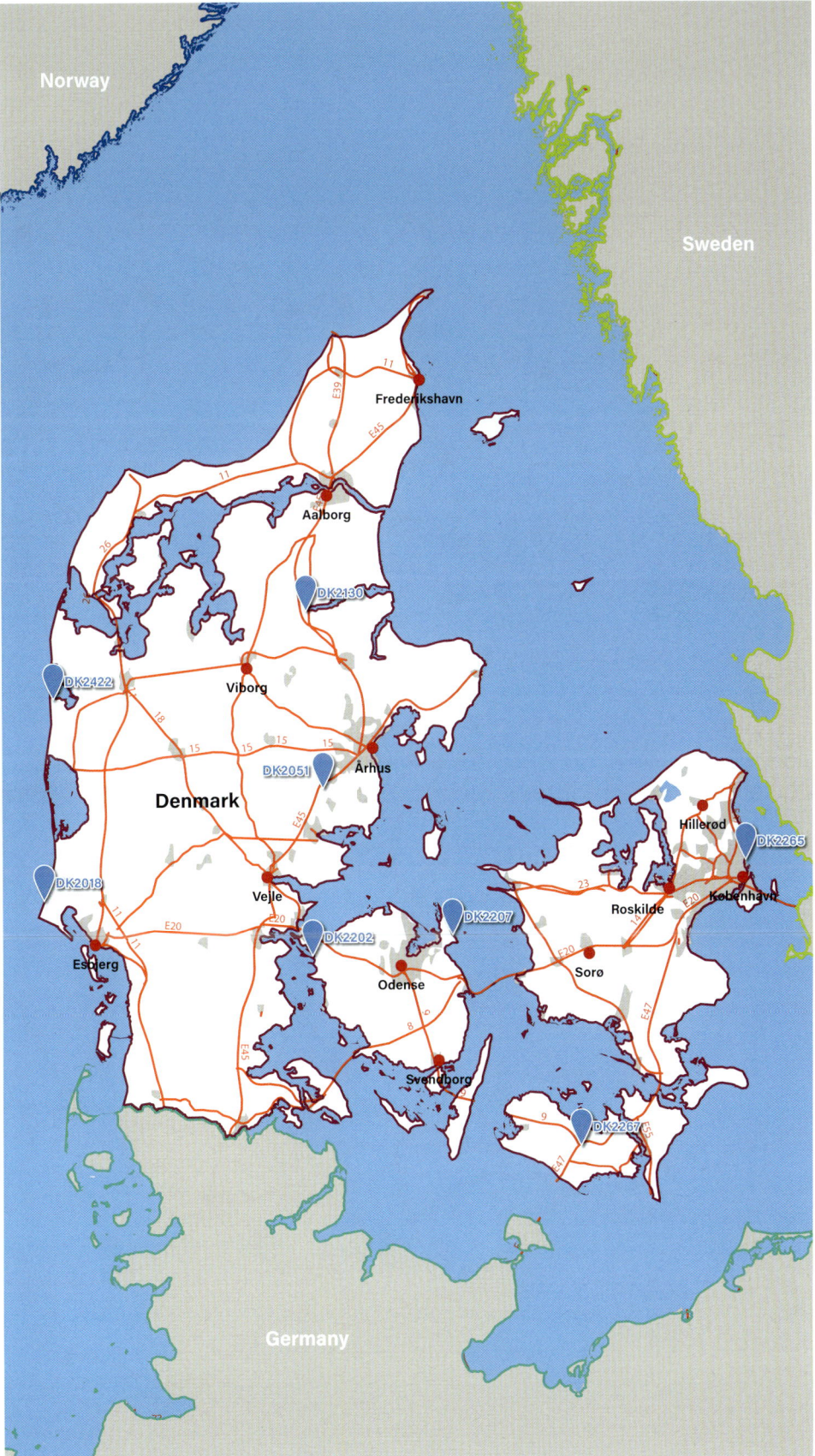

Norway

Sweden

Frederikshavn

E39
E45
11

11

Aalborg

26

DK2130

DK2422

Viborg

18

15   15   15   15

DK2051   Århus

Denmark

E45

DK2018

Vejle

E20

E20

DK2202

Odense

DK2207

Roskilde

Hillerød

DK2265

København

E20

23

Sorø

E20

E47

Esbjerg

E20

E45

11   11

8   9

Svendborg

DK2267

9

E47   E55

Germany

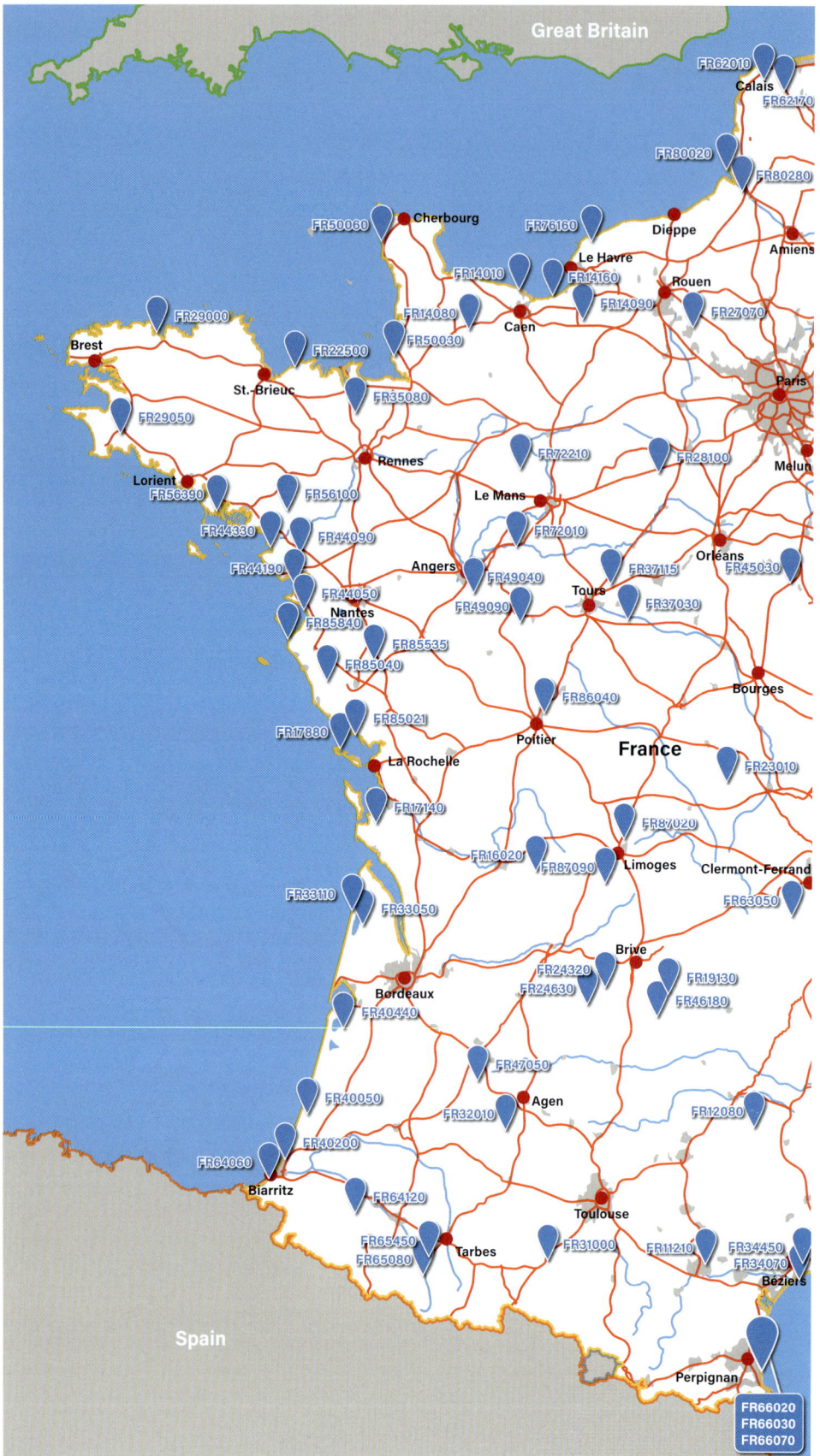

Great Britain

FR62010
Calais
FR62470

FR80020
FR80280

FR50060
Cherbourg
FR76160
Dieppe
Amiens

FR14010
Le Havre
FR14160
Rouen
FR14090
FR27070
Paris

Brest
FR29000

FR22500
Caen
FR14080
FR50030

St.-Brieuc
FR35080

FR29050

Rennes
FR72210
FR28100
Melun

Lorient
FR56390
FR56100
Le Mans
FR72010

FR44330
FR44090
Angers
FR49040
FR37115
Orléans
FR45030

FR44190
FR49090
Tours
FR37030

FR44050
Nantes
FR85840
FR85535
FR86040
Bourges

FR85040

FR85021
Poitier
France

FR17880
FR23010
La Rochelle
FR17140

FR16020
FR87020
Limoges
Clermont-Ferrand
FR33110
FR87090
FR63050

FR33050
Brive
FR24320
FR19130
FR24630
FR46180
Bordeaux
FR40440

FR47050
FR40050
FR12080
FR32010
Agen

FR40200
FR64060
Biarritz
Toulouse
FR64120
FR31000
FR11210
FR34450
FR65450
Tarbes
FR34070
FR65080
Béziers

Spain

Perpignan
FR66020
FR66030
FR66070

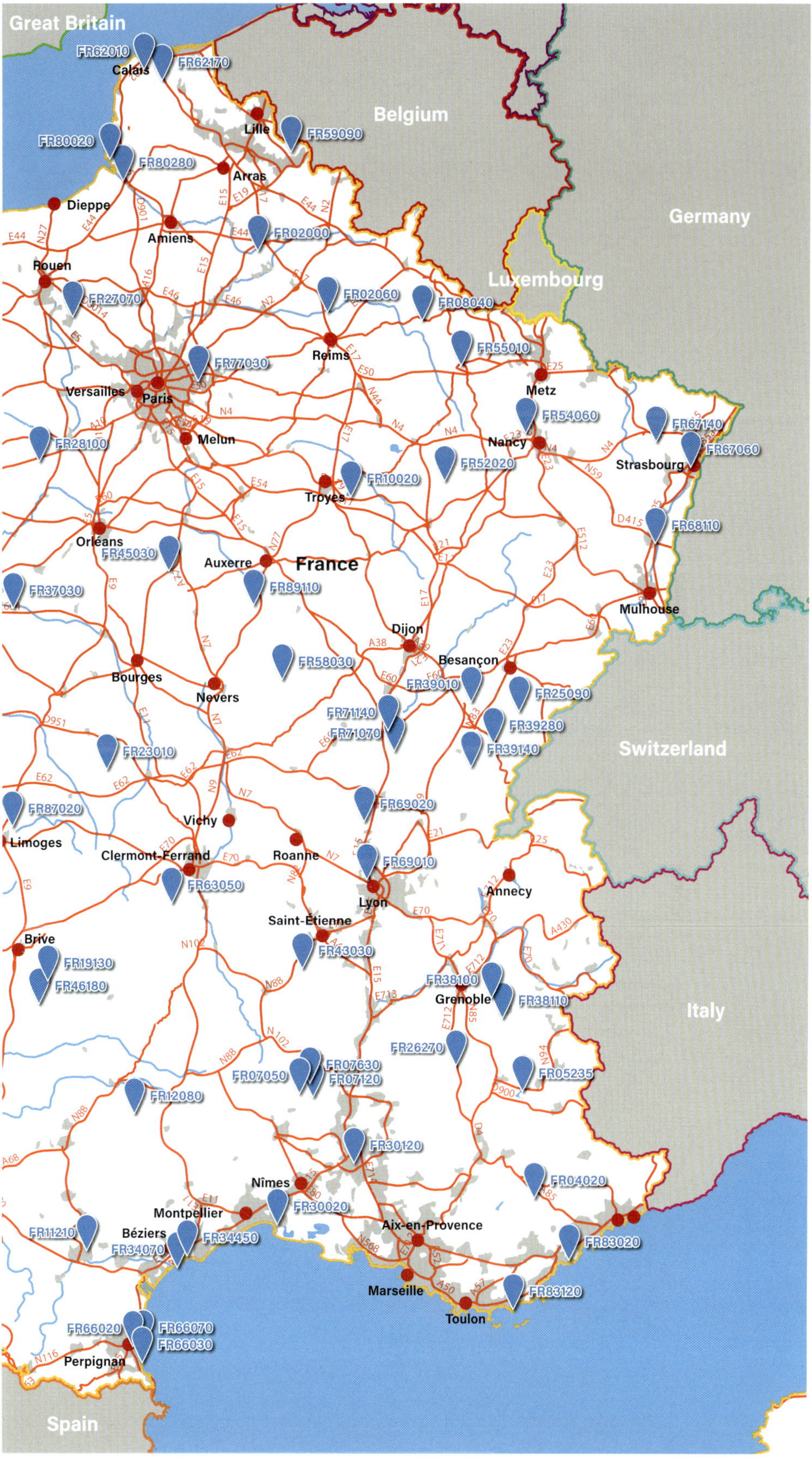

Great Britain

FR62010
FR62170
Calais

Belgium

Lille
FR59090

FR80020
FR80280
Arras

Dieppe

Amiens
FR02000

Germany

Rouen
FR27070

Luxembourg

FR02060
FR08040

FR77030
Reims
FR55010

Versailles
Paris
Metz

FR28100
Melun
FR54060
Nancy
FR67140
FR67060

FR52020
Strasbourg

Troyes
FR10020
FR68110

Orléans
France
Auxerre
FR45030
FR89110
Mulhouse

FR37030

Dijon
Besançon
FR25090

Bourges
FR58030
FR39010
FR39280

Nevers
FR71140
FR71070
FR39140

FR23010

Switzerland

FR87020
FR69020

Limoges
Vichy
FR69010

Clermont-Ferrand
Roanne
Annecy

Brive
FR63050
Lyon

FR19130
Saint-Étienne

FR46180
FR43030
FR38100
FR38110
Grenoble

FR26270
FR05235

FR07630
FR07050
FR07120

FR12080

Italy

FR30120

FR04020

Nîmes
FR30020

Montpellier
FR34450
Aix-en-Provence
FR83020

FR11210
Béziers
FR34070
Marseille
FR83120

FR66020
FR66070
FR66030
Toulon

Perpignan

Spain

FR07630
FR07050
FR07120

FR30120

Aix-en-Provence

Toulon

Marseille

Nîmes

FR30020

Montpellier

FR34450
FR34070

Béziers

FR11210

FR66070
FR66020
FR66030

Perpignan

ES80140

ES81400

ES80220

Mataró

Barcelona

ES83120

ES83900

ES84100

Denmark

Sweden

Poland

Netherlands

Czech Republic

France

Austria

Switzerland

Italy

Solvenia

Germany

Flensburg DE25700

Kiel

DE30080

Lübeck

Rostock

Stralsund DE37900

DE30050

Hamburg

Schwerin

Bremerhaven DE29380

Bremen

DE29220

Berlin DE38270

Osnabrück DE31850

Hannover

Braunschweig

Magdeburg

DE39120

Cottbus

Münster

Bielefeld

DE33420

Leipzig DE38330

Dortmund DE32100

Kassel

DE40720

Dresden

Düsseldorf

Chemnitz

Cologne

Erfurt

Bonn DE31970

Gießen

Koblenz

DE37350

Coburg

Hof

Frankfurt

Würzburg

DE36100

Nürnberg

Heidelberg DE35070

Regensburg

Karlsruhe

DE36160

DE37050

DE34060

Ingolstadt

Passau

Stuttgart

DE36420

DE34070

Ulm

Augsburg

DE34450

Munich

DE40890

Freiburg

Rosenheim

Saarbrücken

Great Britain & Ireland Map

Lerwick
UK7975

Kirkwall

UK7725
Wick

UK7930
UK7666

UK7751
Inverness
UK7639
UK7530

Fort William

UK7276
Aberdeen

UK7320
Perth

Greenock
Glasgow
Edinburgh

Ayr
UK6910
UK5755

IR8635
Donegal
Londonderry
UK8395
Carlisle
UK5810
Newcastle
Sunderland

IR8730
Sligo
IR8690
UK8550
Omagh
Lisburn Belfast
UK8320
UK5625
UK5520
Middlesbrough
UK4596
UK4576
Scarborough

Muineachán
UK8415

IR8860
Ros Comain
IR8870
Galway
Dundalk
Douglas
UK5272
Blackpool
UK4787
York
UK4497

IR8965
Drogheda
Dublin
UK6637
UK5360
Bradford
Leeds
Ireland
Liverpool
Manchester
Kingston upon Hull

IR9100
UK6662
IR9155
IR9150
Chester
Sheffield
UK3925
UK3639

Limerick
UK6337
UK5220
UK3800
UK6385
Stoke

IR9400
IR9410
IR9600
IR9620
IR9380
UK6243
UK6305
Nottingham
Birmingham
Leicester
UK3586
Peterborough
Norwich
UK3387

Killarney
IR9480
IR9345
Waterford
IR9305
UK6019
UK4340
Coventry
UK3357

Cork
IR9505
UK4351
UK4065
Cambridge
Ipswich

UK5993
UK3260
UK3055
UK5937
UK4105
UK2620
Luton
UK3305

Swansea
Cardiff
Bristol
Oxford
London
UK2690
Reading
UK2940
UK3040
Dover

UK0681
UK1390
Bath
UK2510
Brighton

Exeter
UK1000
Southampton
Portsmouth

UK0007
UK0170
UK0802
UK2060
Bournemouth

Penzance
UK0180
UK0819
Plymouth

UK9790

UK9710

France

480

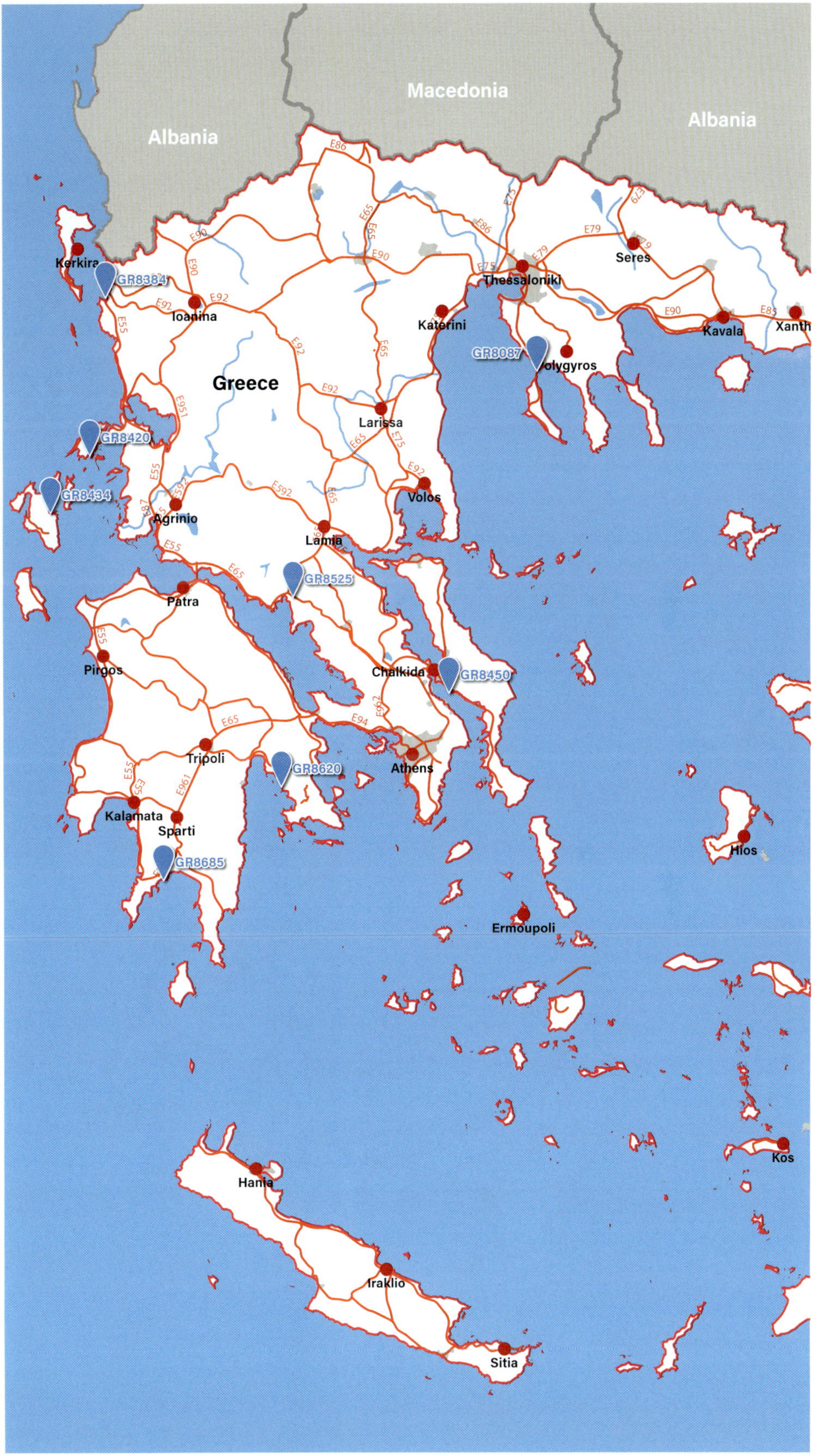
Macedonia
Albania
Albania
Greece
Kerkira
GR8384
Ioanina
Thessaloniki
Seres
Katerini
Kavala
Xanth
GR8087
olygyros
Larissa
GR8420
GR8434
Agrinio
Volos
Lamia
GR8525
Patra
Pirgos
Chalkida
GR8450
Tripoli
GR8620
Athens
Kalamata
Sparti
GR8685
Hios
Ermoupoli
Kos
Hania
Iraklio
Sitia
E86
E90
E92
E55
E65
E75
E79
E85
E951
E592
E87
E94
E961
E962

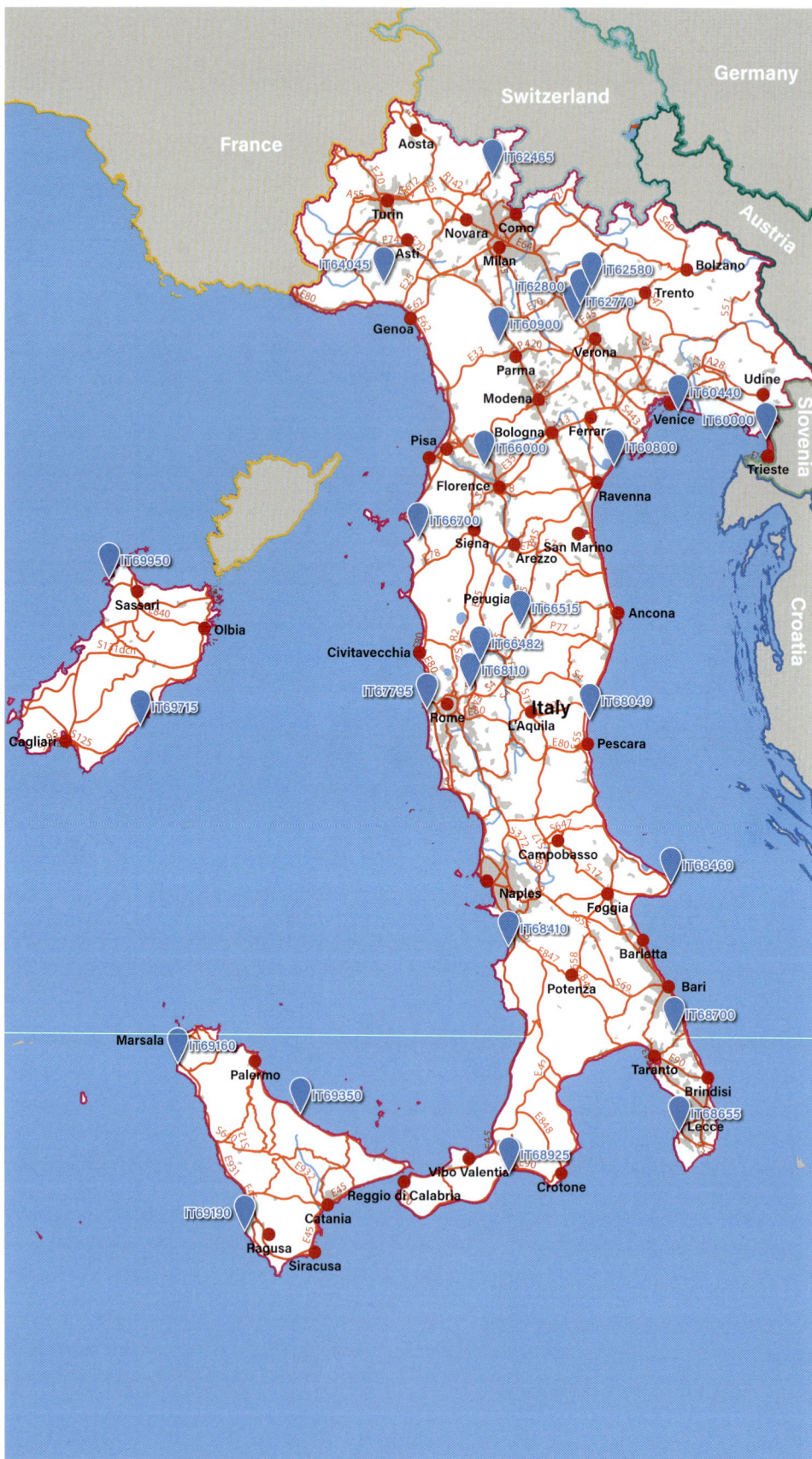

Germany

Switzerland

France

Austria

Aosta
IT62465

Turin
Novara   Como
Asti   Milan   Bolzano
IT64045   IT62800 IT62580 Trento
                        IT62770
Genoa   IT60900

                    Verona   Udine
          Parma   IT60440
          Modena   Venice IT60000
Pisa   Bologna Ferrar   Slovenia
          IT66000 IT60800   Trieste
Florence   Ravenna

IT66700
          Siena San Marino   Croatia
                  Arezzo
IT69950
          Perugia
Sassari   IT66515 Ancona
Olbia   IT66482
          Civitavecchia IT68110
IT69715   IT67795   IT68040
Cagliari   Rome Italy
                  L'Aquila Pescara

                  Campobasso IT68460
                  Naples Foggia
                  IT68410
                        Barletta
                  Potenza Bari
                        IT68700
Marsala   Taranto
IT69160   Brindisi
Palermo IT69350   IT68655
                        Lecce
          Vibo Valentia IT68925
          Reggio di Calabria Crotone
IT69190   Catania
Ragusa
      Siracusa

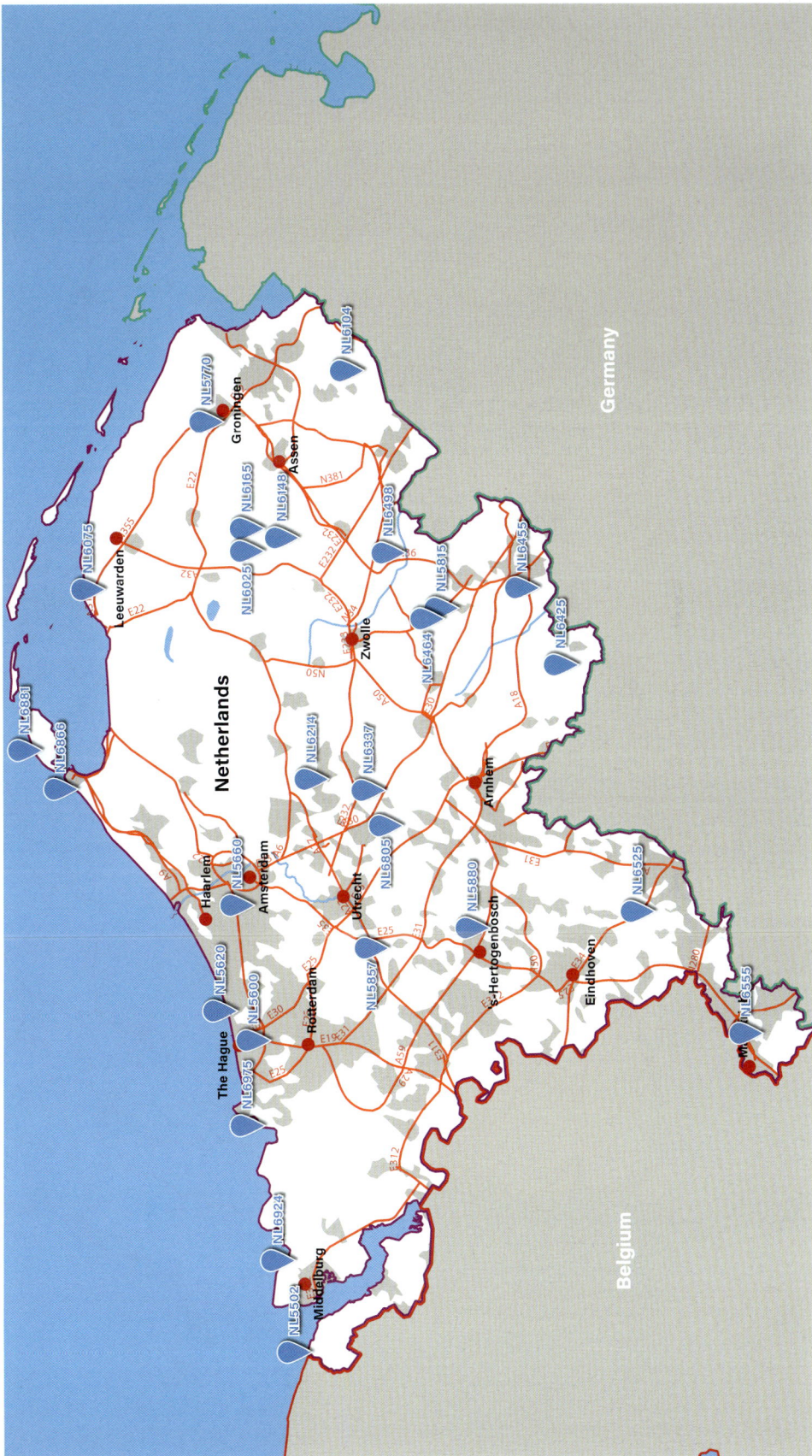

East Spain Map

France

ES80330
ES80350
ES80400

ES80140

ES90390
San Sebastián
Bilbao
ES90420
Pamplona
Vitoria
ES90430
Logroño
ES92260

ES81400

ES80220

Mataró
Barcelona
ES83120
ES83900
ES84100

Zaragoza

ES90615

ES85300
Tarragona

ES91050

Spain

ES85700

Guadalajara

Madrid

Palma

ES85850
Castello

Toledo

ES86250
Valencia

ES86150

Albacete

Alicante

ES87435
ES87420

ES87400

Murcia

ES90895
Linares
Lorca
Cartagena

Córdoba
Jaén
ES87510

ES92850
Granada
Almería

ES87920
ES87090

Málaga

Marbella

620

Ceuta

Russia

Finland

Vadsø
Kirkenes

Hammerfest

Alta

NO2443

Tromsø

Finnsnes

SW2868

Harstad

Narvik

Kiruna

NO2465

Svolvær

Bodø

Mo i Rana

Luleå

E12

Skellefteå

SW2864

Rørvik

NO2499

Sweden

SW2860

Umeå

Namsos

Örnsköldsvik

Steinkjer

SW2855

Östersund

Härnösand

Trondheim

Sundsvall

NO2451

Molde

Ålesund

Bollnäs

Gävle

Norway

NO2375

Lillehammer

Borlänge

Leikanger

Uppsala

Västerås

SW2842

Stockholm

NO2581

Vossavangen

Karlstad

Örebro

Nyköping

Bergen

Moss

Mariestad

SW2710

Skien

Linköping

NO2656

Visby

Haugesund

Vannersborg

Jönköping

NO2599

Borås

SW2680

Sandnes

Arendal

Göteborg

Växjö

Kalmar

Kristiansand

Halmstad

Karlskrona

SW2630

Kristianstad

Helsingborg

Denmark

Malmö

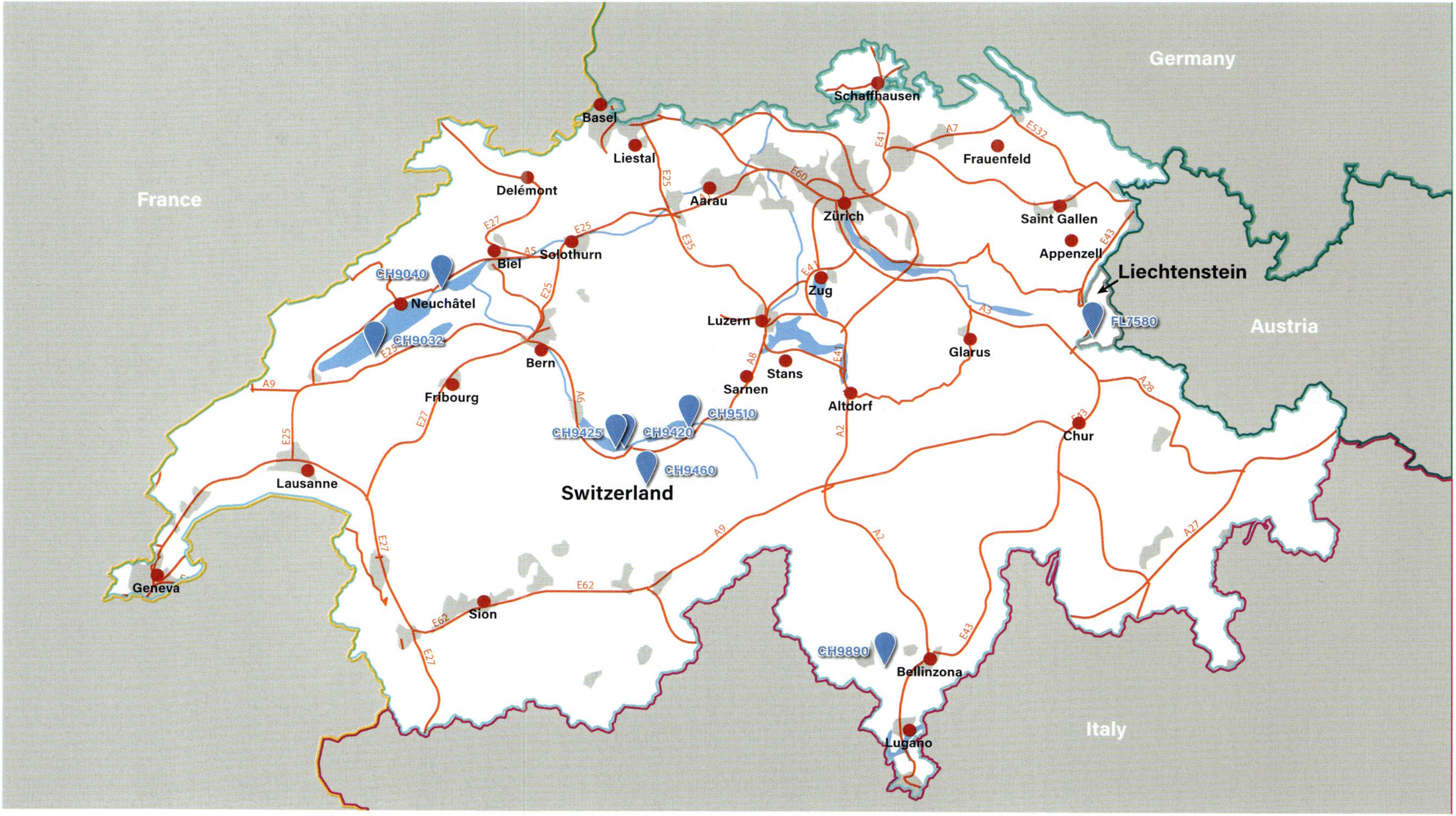

Switzerland & Liechtenstein Map

Index By Location

Index By Alan Rogers Code & Name